Artificial Intelligence and Cybersecurity

Tuomo Sipola • Tero Kokkonen • Mika Karjalainen
Editors

Artificial Intelligence and Cybersecurity

Theory and Applications

 Springer

Editors
Tuomo Sipola
JAMK University of Applied Sciences
Jyväskylä, Finland

Tero Kokkonen
JAMK University of Applied Sciences
Jyväskylä, Finland

Mika Karjalainen
JAMK University of Applied Sciences
Jyväskylä, Finland

ISBN 978-3-031-15032-6   ISBN 978-3-031-15030-2   (eBook)
https://doi.org/10.1007/978-3-031-15030-2

This Springer imprint is published by the registered company Springer Nature Switzerland AG
The registered company address is: Gewerbestrasse 11, 6330 Cham, Switzerland

Preface

The rapid development of technology is evident in our everyday lives. However, underneath it all lies the concern about cybersecurity. We have also witnessed the rise of artificial intelligence (AI) applications that surpass human intellect in specific tasks. The interplay of AI and cybersecurity is becoming increasingly relevant, as AI needs to be assessed from the cybersecurity point of view, and correspondingly, cybersecurity can benefit immensely from the advances in AI. This path will hopefully lead to less human work and more automated detection and classification in the world of cybersecurity.

Our idea was to bring together a group of international experts, whose research is connected to cybersecurity, artificial intelligence, and their interconnections. The first part of this book reflects on these cybersecurity topics from several points of view. Vähäkainu and Lehto introduce the use of AI in cybersecurity by reviewing several cybersecurity solutions. Lundgren and Padyab review how these topics are relevant in security management. Van Bossuyt et al. discuss critical systems and what can be done when AI components are introduced. Varga et al. present their analysis of automation of cybersecurity work. Moreover, Beuran et al. take us into the world of education and training. Finally, the cyber kill chain and defense are also discussed in depth in two chapters by Turtiainen et al.

In the second part, concerning privacy and ethics, the reader will get a glimpse of differential privacy and learn about ethical and legal considerations. These topics are often overlooked among the more technologically minded people but become more important as technology itself becomes more capable. Kilpala et al. introduce differential privacy and review literature related to it. Furthermore, Helkala et al. discuss AI in cyber operations and its ethical and legal considerations for end-users.

The third part of the book is dedicated to applications in the areas of malware analysis, radio signal intelligence, quantile regression, and medical imaging. Millar et al. show how to use deep learning to detect malware in smartphones. Zhu and Nandi discuss the use of AI in radio signal intelligence. Ben Or et al. demonstrate the use of deep learning quantile regression. Finally, the editors survey model fooling threats in the medical domain. As can be seen from all these applications, research in this area covers a wide range of both cybersecurity and AI.

This book is intended for professionals and researchers who want to dive deeper into the world of AI and cybersecurity. Their interests might include fusion of these topics in different contexts, efficient use of AI, latest ideas covering the topics, and innovative AI applications. The book is also useful for those who want to get an idea of the potential of AI or the latest trends in cybersecurity in general.

We are grateful to the chapter authors, who timely delivered the initial manuscripts and revised the chapters according to feedback. This book could not have been done without the insightful and diverse chapters the authors produced. Thank you! We would like to extend our gratitude to our team of peer reviewers from multiple universities and research institutes. They dutifully undertook the task of scrutinizing each contributed chapter.

Jyväskylä, Finland   Tuomo Sipola
December 2021   Tero Kokkonen
                                                                           Mika Karjalainen

Contents

Part III   Applications

Contributors

Dvir Ben Or Playtika, Tel Aviv, Israel

Razvan Beuran Japan Advanced Institute of Science and Technology, Nomi, Ishikawa, Japan

Joel Brynielsson KTH Royal Institute of Technology, Stockholm, Sweden
FOI Swedish Defence Research Agency, Stockholm, Sweden

James Cook United State Air Force Academy, Colorado Springs, CO, USA

Andrei Costin University of Jyväskylä, Jyväskylä, Finland

Britta Hale Naval Postgraduate School, Monterey, CA, USA

Timo Hämäläinen University of Jyväskylä, Jyväskylä, Finland

Kirsi Helkala Norwegian Defence University College/Cyber Academy, Lillehammer, Norway
Peace Research Institute Oslo, Oslo, Norway

Zhenguo Hu Japan Advanced Institute of Science and Technology, Nomi, Ishikawa, Japan

Mika Karjalainen JAMK University of Applied Sciences, Jyväskylä, Finland

Tommi Kärkkäinen University of Jyväskylä, Jyväskylä, Finland

Minna Kilpala University of Jyväskylä, Jyväskylä, Finland

Tero Kokkonen JAMK University of Applied Sciences, Jyväskylä, Finland

Michael Kolomenkin Playtika, Tel Aviv, Israel

Martti Lehto University of Jyväskylä, Jyväskylä, Finland

George Lucas United State Naval Academy, Annapolis, MD, USA

Martin Lundgren Luleå University of Technology, Luleå, Sweden

Jesus Martinez del Rincon CSIT, Queen's University Belfast, Belfast, UK

Niall McLaughlin CSIT, Queen's University Belfast, Belfast, UK

Stuart Millar Rapid 7 LLC, Boston, MA, USA

Paul Miller CSIT, Queen's University Belfast, Belfast, UK

Asoke K. Nandi Brunel University London, London, UK

Bryan O'Halloran Naval Postgraduate School, Monterey, USA

Tanya Osokin Playtika, Tel Aviv, Israel

Ali Padyab School of Informatics, University of Skövde, Skövde, Sweden

Nikolaos Papakonstantinou VTT Technical Research Centre of Finland, Espoo, Finland

Frank Pasquale Brooklyn Law School, Brooklyn, NY, USA

Alex Polyakov Adversa.AI, Tel Aviv, Israel

Gregory Reichberg Peace Research Institute Oslo, Oslo, Norway

Jarno Salonen VTT Technical Research Centre of Finland, Tampere, Finland

Gil Shabat Playtika, Tel Aviv, Israel

Hanan Shteingart Playtika, Tel Aviv, Israel

Tuomo Sipola JAMK University of Applied Sciences, Jyväskylä, Finland

Teodor Sommestad FOI Swedish Defence Research Agency, Stockholm, Sweden

Henrik Syse Peace Research Institute Oslo, Oslo, Norway

Yasuo Tan Japan Advanced Institute of Science and Technology, Nomi, Ishikawa, Japan

Hannu Turtiainen University of Jyväskylä, Jyväskylä, Finland

Petri Vähäkainu University of Jyväskylä, Jyväskylä, Finland

Douglas L. Van Bossuyt Naval Postgraduate School, Monterey, CA, USA

Stefan Varga KTH Royal Institute of Technology, Stockholm, Sweden
Swedish Armed Forces Headquarters, Stockholm, Sweden

Youmeizi Zeng Japan Advanced Institute of Science and Technology, Nomi, Ishikawa, Japan

Zhechen Zhu Soochow University, Suzhou, China

Part I
Cybersecurity Concerns

Use of Artificial Intelligence in a Cybersecurity Environment

Petri Vähäkainu and Martti Lehto

1 Introduction

Originally, Artificial Intelligence (AI) was introduced as a concept to mimic the human brain, and to investigate the real-world problems with a holistic human approach. It can be considered as a combination of information technology and physiological intelligence, which can be computationally used to reach goals. AI makes it possible to utilize and process large amount of stored data intelligently enabling the creation of functional tools. AI has been used to provide intelligent applications in various areas, such as defense, healthcare, and space exploration. In healthcare [34]. New areas of application for AI include structural health management (SHM), where AI can provide forecasts, and eventually save in repair costs.

Organizations are starting to utilize AI in cybersecurity to provide better information security against increasingly skilled attackers. AI assists in automating complex and complicated processes to identify attacks, and to react to information systems breaches. These kinds of applications are developing and becoming more advanced and comprehensive by taking an advantage of AI. Machine learning is a core area of artificial intelligence. It refers to technologies that provide a means to teach computers to learn and adapt through experience. This technological component stimulates human cognition, such as learning from experience and patterns instead of reasoning (i.e., cause and effect).

The following cybersecurity areas discussed are:

1. Infrastructure security,
2. Endpoint security,

P. Vähäkainu (✉) · M. Lehto
University of Jyväskylä, Jyväskylä, Finland
e-mail: petri.vahakainu@jyu.fi; martti.j.lehto@jyu.fi

3

3. Application security,
4. IoT-security,
5. Web-security,
6. Security operations and incident response,
7. Threat intelligence,
8. Mobile security,
9. Cloud security,
10. Identity and access management,
11. Network security,
12. Human security.

This study discusses applications that utilize artificial intelligence from different manufacturers. Applications studied make use of artificial intelligence to predict, recognize and prevent information security threats and anomalies. The discussion of applications is intended to give an overview of what kind of cybersecurity solutions utilizing artificial intelligence exist, and what they can offer in problem solving. We present 10 AI -based cybersecurity solutions covering various areas of cybersecurity. Solutions presented in this study were gathered when conducting the previous research paper: "Artificial Intelligence in the Cyber Security Environment", re-examined and researched further. A classification principle used in this study can be understood as taxonomy. It describes the most crucial areas of cybersecurity discussed in this study.

2   Artificial Intelligence and Machine Learning

Artificial intelligence can be thought of as an umbrella term. It can be used to simulate human activities and to solve problems faster and more efficiently than humans. Various tasks can be performed by utilizing methods, such natural language processing (NLP), predictive and prescriptive analytics or machine and deep learning. These methods may also be used to solve problems in cybersecurity [6].

Machine Learning can be divided into two main types, which are supervised machine learning and unsupervised machine learning. Supervised ML uses algorithms that can learn from the data entered by a user; hence human intervention is required to label, classify and enter the data in the algorithm [23]. An advantage of using supervised ML is to collect data and produce data output from previous experiences, performance optimization based on criteria with the help of experience, and a possibility to solve real -world computational problems. In turn, classifying big data can be challenging and training may require remarkable amount of computation time [26].

Supervised machine learning can be further grouped into regression and classification problems. Classification problems utilize specific algorithm to allocate test data into categories, and then classify an object within different classes, e.g., determine if an email is spam and separate spam emails from inbox. Regression method predicts a numerical value, e.g., when checking demand of occupation of a hotel [22]. Well known classification methods are, for example, Support Vector Machines (SVM), Naïve Bayes and K-Nearest neighbor methods. Typically utilized regression methods are Linear Regression, SVR, Ensemble Methods, Decision Trees and popular Neural Networks [48].

Unsupervised machine learning is training of a machine using information that is neither classified nor labeled. Unsupervised method utilizes specific machine learning algorithms in order to analyze and cluster unlabeled datasets without need of human intervention. ML algorithm groups unsorted information according to differences, patterns and similarities without prior training of data by finding hidden structure in unlabeled data [26].

Unsupervised models can be grouped to two main types as follows: clustering and association. Clustering is a data mining technique, which can be used to classify unlabeled data into groups based on their similarities or differences. Clustering can be used, for example, to perform customer segmentation according to what they have purchased by using e.g., K-means clustering to assign similar data points into groups. Association can discover rules and find relationships between variables within the specific dataset. The method has been utilized, for example, for market basket analysis and recommendation engines [22].

Machine learning has a subfield, Deep Learning, where the learning is done with models that have multiple layers within their structure. DL can be supervised, semi-supervised or unsupervised. The additional depth can help the models to learn more complex associations within the given data than regular AI models [36]; hence DL models are called deep. AI is a very enticing choice for many different use cases, where the function to be estimated is either unknown or difficult to implement in practice, such as machine translations. In practice, the quality and quantity of data, the structure of the model, and training time, as well as the training method, affect how any AI learns to make its choices.

Neural network (NN) is a popular base model and the backbone of DL algorithms, used in the development of artificial intelligence solutions. The model has three layers: an input layer, hidden layer, and output layer, where data flows from the input layer through the hidden layer consisting of multiple layers, and the result is produced to the output layer. Neural networks are a collection of structured, interjoined nodes whose values are comprised of all the weights of the connections coming to each node. Every value of a node is inputted to an activation function, such as a rectified linear unit (ReLu). The activation function is typically the same for all the nodes in the same layer.

3 Cybersecurity

Cybersecurity measures are associated with managing risks, patching vulnerabilities, and improving system resilience. Key research subjects include techniques associated with detecting different network behavior anomalies and malware, and

IT questions related to IT security. In short, cybersecurity can be defined as a range of actions taken in defense against cyber-attacks and their consequences and includes implementing the required countermeasures. Cybersecurity is built on the threat analysis of an organization or institution. The structure and elements of an organization's cybersecurity strategy and its implementation program is based on the estimated threats and risk analyses. In many cases it becomes necessary to prepare several targeted cybersecurity strategies and guidelines for an organization [37].

Threat, vulnerability, and risk form an intertwined entity in the cyber world. The underlying system is a valuable physical object, competence or some other immaterial right, which needs protection and safeguarding. A threat is a harmful cyber event, which may occur. The numeric value of the threat represents its degree of probability. Vulnerability is the inherent weakness in the system, which increases the probability of an occurrence or exacerbates its consequences. Vulnerabilities can be divided into those that exist in human action, processes, or technologies. Risk is the value of the expected damage. Risk equals probability times the loss. It can be assessed from the viewpoint of its economic consequences or loss of loss at face value. Risk management consists of the following factors: risk assumption, risk alleviation, risk avoidance, risk limitation, risk planning and risk transference. Countermeasures can be grouped into the three following categories: regulation, organizational solutions (i.e., management, security processes, methods, procedures, and security culture) and security technology solutions [37].

4 Artificial Intelligence and Cybersecurity Solutions

Cyber-attacks directed against organizations can be conducted in many forms, which may consist of a single act, or a combination of discrete steps threaded together. Such acts may be a Complicated exploitation of coding or the simple use of social engineering to reveal or to gain access to confidential information [3].

Artificial intelligence not only includes threats and risk factors, but it can also act as a problem solver. Artificial intelligence and cognitive data processing are used to detect, defend against and examine cyber-attacks. Modern information security solutions are either man- or machine-made. So-called analytical solutions are based on the rules created by IT security experts, which ignore attacks that do not match the established rules. Machine-learning-based approaches rely on identifying anomalies that can identify false positive results, creating a sense of mistrust toward the system and thus require human-effort to investigate cases ([11], 6).

Effective artificial intelligence solutions are needed to manage the cybersecurity of large amounts of data. They can be used to improve situational awareness and implement effective protection measures. The industry has developed a variety of artificial intelligence-based cybersecurity solutions, which are presented in the next section.

4.1 AI2

MIT Computer Science and Artificial Intelligence Laboratory (CSAIL) and Pat-ternEx have developed an artificial intelligence AI2 platform to predict cyber-attacks by incorporating input from human experts. Typical cyber-attack has a behavioral signature requiring various steps involved in committing it. The relevant information to quantify these signatures is stored in the raw data and is provided as logs. In general, anomaly detection systems trigger plenty of false positive alarms taking significant amount of time and efforts to investigate. Combining artificial intelligence with human intelligence provide much better results compared to traditional systems and systems that uses only unsupervised machine learning [9].

According to Conner-Simons [9], the AI2 platform was able to reach 86% accuracy in detecting cyber-attacks, which is approximately three times better than results of previous studies. Tests were conducted with 3.6 billion data components (log lines), which were generated by millions of users in a three-month research period. To prevent attacks, AI2 identifies suspicious activity by applying clustering algorithms to the input data by utilizing unsupervised machine learning algorithms. AI2 combines three various unsupervised-learning methods and provides the results to analysts for labeling. Hence, the results will be presented to analysts, who use intuition to confirm which incidents are real attacks. Analysts also incorporate the outcome into platform models (supervised learning) for the next set of data, which enables further learning and forms a continuous active learning system. The system is also capable of continuously generating new models within hours, which can significantly improve the speed of its detection ability of cyber-attacks.

In AI2, features are extracted from log entries and on day one AI2 pics the 200 most abnormal events and provides them to the expert. As learning process of AI progresses over time, it can identify more and more of the events as real attacks, which means experts could only focus on studying 30–40 events per day. An ensemble of unsupervised learning models generates a set of k events to be analyzed per day, where the daily budget k of events that can be analyzed is a configurable parameter. To train a supervised model, human judgement is required. The results of supervised and ensemble of unsupervised methods to refine the k events are to be presented to the experts, who can then retrain the supervised model. The process continues as iterative manner.

Researchers gathered 3 months of data with awareness of attacks, which were used to evaluate whether the solution can improve attack detection rates (recall), while reducing the number of alerts shown to the analyst ("daily investigation budget" K). Attack detection rates of at most 86% can be reached with AI2, even with an extremely low daily investigative budget ($K = 200$), compared to 9% by using an ordinary unsupervised machine learning algorithm. When daily investigation budget is at 200, false positive rate is only 4.4%. By utilizing unsupervised machine learning, a detection rate of approximately 73.5% can be achieved, while the false positive rate is more than 22% of suspicious events. The

AI2 platform functions with considerably smaller investments than a system using and an ordinary, unsupervised machine learning algorithm ([55], 49).

4.2   CylanceProtect

CylanceProtect [10] an enterprise-class threat prevention tool designed for all sizes of businesses and capable to stop known and unknown attacks. The tool combines the benefits of artificial intelligence with additional information security controls to safeguard against prevent malware infections and script-based, fileless, memory and external device-based attacks. Unlike traditional security tools based on the analysis of signatures and user behavior in identifying security threats in the environment, CylanceProtect:

- Detects and prevents memory exploitation: capability to identify and stop fileless attacks with immediate, automated prevention responses,
- Detects and prevents unknown and zero-day attacks,
- Detects employees from running unauthorized and potentially malicious scripts,
- Prevents malicious email attachments from detonating their payloads,
- Prevents ransomware attacks, such as NotPetya, WannaCry, Goldeneye, and Satan from executing and hijacking important data,
- Provides application control for Fixed-Function Devices,
- Supports script management to determine when and where scripts are allowed to run and by whom,
- Utilizes device usage policy enforcement: assign access rules on external devices that can be potential attack vectors,
- Utilizes sophisticated machine learning models, which are capable to analyze 2.7 million file properties in order to detect whether it's benign or malicious.

CylanceProtect also works as mobile threat defense (MTD) solution, and it can be utilized to protect all endpoints and mobile devices against advanced malicious threats without disrupting end-users. The MTD solution is capable of monitoring threats as both the application and device levels. At device level the solution has capabilities to identify vulnerabilities and potential malicious activities by monitoring OS updates, system parameters, device configurations, and system libraries. At application level, the solution utilizes application sandboxing and code analysis, and application-level security testing in order to identify malware and grayware. Additionally, the solution concerned uses artificial intelligence and machine learning-based detection in identifying malware threat from sideloaded applications, providing an additional layer of protection. The solution also provides advanced containerization solution for mobile applications [5].

4.3 Darktrace

Darktrace is an intrusion detection system (IDS) and intrusion prevention system (IPS), which can help in detecting and recognizing emerging cyber threats that are able to circumvent traditional information security protections. Darktrace Immune System provides means for security teams to move away from legacy siloed solutions offering limited visibility, to the direction of a single AI 'brain' solution, which can take an advantage of enterprise-wide context leaving adversaries less opportunities to hide. Darktrace's Immune System operates similar way than the immune system of human body, which is natural defense mechanism against infection and disease, including cancer. For example, the immune system has unique capability to identify what is part of us and what is not. The immune system can quickly detect and contain bacteria, viruses and other pathogens daily, and even those our bodies have never encountered before. Darktrace's Immune System has taken steps towards completely new approach to cyber defense following the same principles than human immune system does.

4.3.1 Darktrace Enterprise Immune System (EIS)

The solution consists of Enterprise Immune System (EIS) technology, which represents a core capability of a broader self-learning platform and detects threats in real time. EIS interfaces with Cyber AI Analyst to enable autonomous investigations into security incidents and feeds an adaptive Autonomous Response framework via Darktrace Antigena to contain the threat in seconds, without relying on rules or signatures. The EIS system identifies the full range of cyber-threats, which differ from an ordinary known pattern, wherever they may appear in business. EIS is capable to protect the dynamic workforce in countering zero-days, ransomware, and insider threats. EIS covers the full digital DNA of an organization across cloud, endpoints, IoT, and network tackling even the most subtle and persistent attacks [16].

Enterprise Immune System technology (EIS) utilizes machine learning algorithms and mathematical principles in order to detect anomalies within an organization's information network. EIS operates automatically, learning continuously without human input or intervention. Self-learning AI enables the system to identify full range of cyber threats that deviate from normal patterns. EIS relies on this kind of AI technology to understand the dynamic behaviors and relationships in an enterprise by learning 'normal' from scratch without any prior assumptions and adapting continuously as the business and workforce evolve. The system illuminates the earliest signs of a threat as it deviates from the multidimensional norm. Incoming attack can be known or unknown, internal or external, subtle or fast moving.

EIS uses mathematical approaches, which implies it does not need to take an advantage of signatures or rules, and it can identify unknown cybersecurity attacks that have not been experienced before. EIS has capabilities to identify a respond to most of the proficiently implemented cyber threats, including the insider's threats hidden in the information networks. By utilizing machine learning and mathematics, the EIS can adapt and automatically learn how each user, device and information network behave, in order to identify behaviors that reflect real cyber threats. Darktrace's self-learning technology provides companies with a visibility of the information network and allows them to respond proactively to threats and reduce risk [12].

4.3.2 Darktrace Cyber AI Analyst

Darktrace R&D Center's research initiative, Cyber AI Analyst, was designed to augment security teams and optimize threat investigation. Cyber AI Analyst examines incipient cyber events in real time and emulates human professional analyst thinking and decision-making process for autonomous triaging and reporting. The technology unites professional analyst intuition with consistency, speed and scalability of AI, enlightens the highest priority threats and composes all the context around the attack into a natural language report to be utilized by cyber professionals and augmenting human cybersecurity teams. In addition, Cyber AI Analyst's analytical capability decreases triaging time up to 92% [15].

Cyber AI Analyst utilizes several artificial intelligence technologies, such as deep learning, unsupervised and supervised machine learning. The purpose of utilizing AI technologies is to combat novel cyber-attacks that can bypass traditional rule-based security defenses, such as firewalls and signature-based gateways, and in addition can penetrate defenses to access file shares and accounts. Threat landscape is evolving rapidly and when present adversary is recognized, it may already be transformed into unidentifiable threat. Situations like this highlighted the need to utilize artificial intelligence technologies to identify novel and unrecognizable sophisticated threats, which are not possible to detect by using conventional systems [17].

Unsupervised machine learning does not require labeled training data, but it can identify patterns and trends in the data without human intervention. Darktrace utilizes unsupervised machine learning algorithms in order to analyze the data concerned and carries out probability-based calculations based on the visible evidence. The algorithm classifies data and detects an essential key pattern in order to construct a behavioral model concerning to cloud containers, devices, sensors and users. The algorithm also identifies deviations, which may develop to a relevant and malicious threat in the future. Machine learning methods can significantly improve the threat detection due to its capability to utilize ample amount of computational analysis [17].

Darktrace utilizes Bayesian probability as a part of unsupervised machine learning to discover previously unknown relationships, independently classify data, detect key patterns, and operate without anterior assumptions. Darktrace does not require knowledge about previous attacks, but instead is capable to learn continuously. It constantly reviews assumptions about behavior by using probabilistic mathematics. Darktrace's unsupervised machine learning algorithm can detect up to now undetected cyber-attacks, threats and vulnerabilities, such as advanced spear phishing, cloud- and SaaS -based attacks, insider threats, latent vulnerabilities, machine-speed attacks, stealthy attacks, and zero-day attacks [17].

Darktrace can produce outputs marked with differing degrees of potential threats, providing tool to rank alerts and prioritize them according to the need of immediate action. Darktrace also uses unsupervised machine learning to recognize significant groupings. In order to gather information concerning relationships within the network, various clustering methods, such as matrix-based clustering, density -based clustering and hierarchical clustering methods are utilized. Clusters are then used to inform the modeling of the normative behaviors. Potential predictor variables result in a significant challenge to modeling the behaviors of a dynamically evolving infrastructure. For example, observation of packet traffic and host activity within LAN or WAN networks, both input and output may contain inter-related features (protocols, source, and destination machines, log changes, and rule triggers). Therefore, it is important to learn a sparse and consistent structured predictive function. Darktrace strives to understand sparse structure in models of network connectivity by utilizing L1 -regularization techniques (e.g., Lasso method) in order to find true associations between different elements of a network [17].

Sophisticated deep and machine learning technologies provide Cyber AI Analyst a capability to cover threats that are most vital for investigation, to deal with connected incident events, and handle the process how attack should be managed. Cyber AI Analyst starts to analyze after Enterprise Immune System (or equivalent) detects unusual behavior. Cyber AI Analyst then acts like a human analyst by asking questions in order to generate a credible hypothesis concerning the nature of the potential threat and the ultimate cause. Then it queries the data through the organization to confirm, deny or refine the hypothesis. The process is iterated until the Cyber AI Analyst receives the high-level description of the nature and root cause of the wider security incident [15].

The Cyber AI Analyst also utilizes supervised machine learning in a capability that mimics the way human professional performs the threat investigation process. Cyber AI Analyst does not use historical attack data, but instead of that, it learns on the data set of human analyst behaviors that has been gathering during the past years. The AI monitors Darktrace expert's behavior and how they investigate threats and triage threatening and suspicious activity. The results of investigation can then be classified by using supervised machine learning in order to determine incidents of interest, and to provide details that human professional could miss, or might not have time to identify. The technology also classifies and stores the results of the investigations, presenting solely a small number of priority incidents at one time [15].

4.3.3 Darktrace Antigena

Darktrace Antigena Network is autonomous response technology, which utilizes self-learning Cyber AI. Antigena Network interrupts and neutralizes novel and undetected threats within cloud services, corporate network, and Internet of Things (IoT). Antigena Network's decisions is not based on simplistic pattern matching and static logic than pre-programmed response tools, but instead are informed by evolving understanding and awareness of normal and benign behavior. Self-learning AI provide categorically different response utilizing how, when, and where to neutralize an emerging threat making Autonomous Response to be effective across a diverse variety of threats, also novel and unexpected. The technology scales up to defend ample and complex organizations without requiring considerable amount of human work and intervention. Core use cases are of the solution are machine-speed ransomware containing novel strains of malware and ransomware before they can escalate, insider threat and account takeover functionality prevents malicious insiders and unexpected data loss, IoT compromise prevents attacks from spreading or exfiltrating critical data via IoT devices and compliance, which can be configured to respond to non-compliant behavior and connections. Antigena can autonomously and precisely contain in-progress attacks faster than human analyst is able to do [13].

Darktrace Antigena Email is a self-learning technology, which purpose is to neutralize targeted email campaigns and impersonation attacks that can evade the email gateway. Antigena Email is passively waiting the data, which is passed to it. Antigena neutralizes the emails containing links associated with threats detected and prevented by Antigena Network. When Antigena Email receives an email message, it extracts its raw metadata, processes it various times and multiple times in the future as new evidence is introduced. The solution examines the contents and verifies if what is discovers has previously been normal throughout an organization environment [24]. According to Cambridge [7], Darktrace's Antigena Email is: "A very novel context-based approach that asks not whether an incoming email is malicious but crucially whether it belongs – clearly valuable for organizations.".

Antigena Email utilizes artificial intelligence to determine whether an email provided differs from normal interactions between a sender, recipient, and wider organization unveiling signs of a novel threats. Antigena Email threats recipients as dynamic individuals and peers when it analyses inbound, outbound, and lateral email traffic. If Antigena Email's AI model detects an incoming threat, it processes it and makes distinctive decision for each email in order to ascertain justified email flow is enabled and permitted. Antigena Email can accurately distinguish between benign and malicious, and efficiently neutralize malicious emails before they can make an impact. The solution neutralizes, for example, spear phishing and impersonation attacks in Exchange, Office 365, Gmail, Google Workspace, etc. [13].

Darktrace Antigena Email can determine, which links shared by people and domains they visit are rare in the context of an organization. Antigena Email can detect if an attacker sends multiple emails to several recipients in the organization and estimate likelihood that the group concerned could be receiving an email from the same source. Fascinating feature of Antigena Email is the capability to learn how different senders construct their emails by analyzing hidden email metadata and patterns in the body content. In addition, Antigena Email utilizes artificial intelligence to every inbound email in order to identify delicate changes indicating that the email has most likely been sent by a possible adversary instead of the legitimate account holder [14].

Darktrace Antigena SaaS is an autonomous response and self-learning technology, which is capable of neutralizing unpredictable attacks in cloud and collaboration tools. The solution is used alongside Antigena Email extending the protection of an organization's Microsoft 365 environment. Antigena SaaS provide organizations the scope of the technology to enable autonomous detection, investigation, and response across additional data sources and types of behavior at scale. The solution protects from subtle attacks that can evade traditional static and siloed defenses. Antigena SaaS can be utilized to neutralize admin abuse and insider data theft, interrupt account takeover and brute-force attacks or stop accidental data loss, manipulation, or destruction. Darktrace Antigena SaaS has a user interface (UI), which is designed to highlight malicious or risky behavior occurs in cloud footprint. The UI provides security teams tools to visualize and monitor security incidents and Antigena SaaS actions in one centralized location [18].

4.4 Amazon Macie

Amazon Macie is an information security service launched in the summer of 2017 that utilizes machine learning pattern matching capabilities. Artificial intelligence provides tools for Macie to find, classify and protect sensitive data on Amazon Web Services (AWS) [2]. The automated service provides an inventory of end-user's S3 buckets by utilizing machine learning and pattern matching to alert if the service detects potential security problems. An end-user can view Amazon Macie's results in the AWS Management Console and filter the results to examine the details needed. The service is particularly valuable for organizations, which subject to rules and regulations, such as EU's General Data Privacy Regulation (GDPR) or U.S. Health Insurance Portability and Accountability ACT (HIPAA) [35].

Amazon Macie also utilizes natural language processing (NLP) methods in order to help interpret and classify various kinds of data types and content. NLP bases on utilizing principles from computational linguistics and computer science to look at the interactions between computers and the human language. In short, how computers should be programmed to make them to understand and decipher language data. Amazon Macie orders findings on a priority basis by automatically assigning business values to data that is assessed in the form of a risk score. This procedure provides means for end-users to focus on the most critical alerts first. The service is also capable of monitor and discover security changes governing the data concerned, and to identify security-centric data, e.g., access keys stored within S3 bucket [43].

Protective and proactive security monitoring provides Amazon Macie tools to identify critical, sensitive, and security focused data such as API keys and secret keys. Macie also runs an engine specifically to detect common sources of personally identifiable information (PII) and protected health information (PHI) data. The service takes an advantage of AWS CloudTrail and continuously checks CloudTrail events for PUT requests in S3 buckets and automatically classify new objects near to real time. In addition to that, the service can detect alterations and changes in being security policies and access control lists effecting to data within end-user's S3 buckets. Macie will also initiate alerts, when anomalous user behavior is detected and maintain compliance requirements needed [56].

Macie recognizes sensitive data such as personal information or copyrights. In addition, it can monitor how copyrighted material, such as documents, are copied, moved or viewed. Macie has a dashboard view, which helps to conclude how the data has been used or where it has been moved. The service continuously monitors data usage and anomalies and provides detailed alerts if the data is subject to unauthorized usage or unintentional data leakage. Macie can also automatically detect the risk to business data, if the data has been distributed outside the organization without an authorization, or if the data has otherwise been unintentionally accessed [1].

Amazon Macie explores data and searches for keyword file formats such as Microsoft Word, Excel, .txt files. Macie compares file format extensions to evaluate data security levels. For example, Macie places .pem files in a higher risk category than an ordinary txt-files. In addition, Macie examines information related to files and S3 objects when issuing security classification. Macie also utilizes the Amazon CloudTrail service, which logs almost all API requests, and uses these log files when exploring object level S3 API activities. It also gathers data on users and their roles [47].

4.5 Deep Instinct

Deep Instinct has been one of the first company to apply end-to-end deep learning to cybersecurity. Deep Instinct's Developers utilized deep learning algorithms in their implementation of the solution, which made it possible to identify structures used in malicious software. Deep Instinct can detect and preventing the execution of malicious software at all levels of the organization [44]. Neural network technology has been utilized in countering cyberattacks, such as Spora, Wannacry, NotPetya, and BadRabbit, without the help of a specific center focusing on cybersecurity issues, and before malware has had any impact on the customer's IT solutions. The Deep Instinct's technology works side-by-side with traditional systems by expanding existing infrastructure and investments, so customers do not have to make any compensatory measures for their operations [4].

Deep Instinct's solution is designed to protect organization's cross device support for endpoints, mobile devices, and servers against known and unknown and even the most sophisticated malicious attacks in real- and zero-time. The software is based on the exploitation of artificial neural network brain, which has a capability to identify incoming attacks pre-emptively with the highest rate of detections and minimal false positives. The brain itself is lightweight and less than 30 MB of memory footprint. The ANN brain technology can classify between seven malware family types, which are the following: Backdoor, Dropper, Potential Unwanted Applications (PUAs), Ransomware, Spyware, Virus, and Worms. Using appropriate deep learning algorithms, the software can anticipate yet unrecognized cyber-attacks. The solution can present classification results, for example, for a malware sample that is mostly a ransomware, but also contains characteristic of a Spyware [19].

Benefit of utilizing Deep Learning in analyzing files and vectors before execution is zero-time protection, which means that Deep Instinct can scan the file/process in less than 20 milliseconds preventing malicious items from running. In addition, instant file reputation, blacklists, and dynamic script control can be used to mitigate number of false positives and improve output across the entire security team. Zero-time protection is implemented in Deep Instinct by Run-Time Detect and Defend layer utilizing dynamic behavior analysis to quickly uncover suspicious behavior. Deep Instinct uses native anti-ransomware, remote code injection, known shellcodes and PowerShell command or script execution in order to provide a solution, which has a capability to detect and prevent advanced attacks prior to execution [20].

Deep Instinct has an On-Time Review and Remediate layer functionality, which provides visibility into the adversaries threating the organization concerned. Security information teams are provided information they need by Auto-threat classification and advanced threat analysis in order to be able to comprehend how an attack has taken place and what kind of endeavors adversaries had. Deep Instinct combine security capabilities, for example, in Microsoft Windows and let the existing AV suite to handle other tasks such as personal firewalls and encryption. Deep Instinct demands no regular updates or additional trained model, but as part of initial deployment, comprehensive scan of the asset will be conducted. Deep Instinct's Static Analysis scans changes made to files by a user and determine if the file is malicious and therefore needs to be blocked and sent to quarantine. If a malicious file passes the static analysis phase, behavior analysis capability to root out the activity commonly associated with malicious intent is utilized and process is terminated [20].

In 2016, the University of Göttingen conducted a malicious software identifi-cation test, which explored up to 16,000 malicious software samples gathered by Siemens CERT, Bit-Defender, McAfee, AVG, Kaspersky, Sophos, among others.". The above-mentioned companies have their own antivirus software, which can reach up to a 61% average malicious software detection rate, compared with Deep Instinct's average detection rate of 98.86%. Some of the malicious software samples were already mutated, but in a way that did not permanently affect the behavior of those malicious software. Deep Instinct could identify up to 99.7% of harmful PDF files and 99.2% of harmful executable files.". Deep Instinct's application was taught with 8000 malicious samples." [44]

A US -based software & hardware provider operating in more than 50 countries, was looking for a novel protection solution to augment existing Symantec Endpoint protection. In the case study, the client company invested a lot on performance, monitoring and administrative capabilities concerning the solution. DeepInstinct was the last company of six company's evaluated as an option to provide better protection to and meet the increasing requirements of endpoint security to counter, for example, unknown malware and APT threats. Evaluation results indicated that the DeepInstinct's security solution reached the detection and prevention rate of over 99%. In addition, the footprint of DeepInstinct's agent was relatively small [21].

Results in the case study also indicated that even the protection was implemented by using next-generation endpoint solution, more than 10% of devices were still found as infected. In the first week of deployment, up to 12 endpoints were detected to be infected with malicious campaigns, such as coin miners, worms, spyware and other PUA. After the deployment had been conducted for up to 1500 endpoints, 147 devices were discovered to be infected, which corresponds 10% of the Symantec Endpoint protected devices. In total 462 malicious campaigns were found including PUA and dual-use tools, and a total of 140 pure malicious campaigns, which includes dormant WannaCry ransomware, various Spyware and info stealer families including Nymaim, Loki, Fareit, and Agent Tesla, banking trojans (Emotet), and other worms and viruses. Malicious campaigns also included trojans and other hacking tools, such as tools to scan and map the network [21].

4.6   SparkCognition DeepArmor

SparkCognition DeepArmor can detect and prevent the threat of malware, viruses, worms, trojans and ransomware programs, using mathematical methods such as machine learning and natural language processing. The DeepArmor architecture consists of a small endpoint agent integrated into a cloud-based cognitive engine, as well as a platform exploring threats. The low-profile endpoint agent identifies and prevents malicious programs and other more advanced threats, regardless of signatures. The agent is designed to protect the client, server, mobile and IoT devices, and to protect integrated information security for an organization. An agent can also be configured to operate autonomously in headless mode without a user interface, providing a security solution for IoT devices [45].

The cloud-based cognitive engine of the DeepArmor solution uses a multi-layer filtering process to identify threats. The first layer of protection performs file analysis, as well as application and risk control to quickly identify known malicious or abnormal files. DeepArmor is capable to apply machine learning to the pre-execution detection of weaponized documents like PDFs, legacy Office (e.g., .doc, .xls), and modern Office (e.g., .docx, .xlsx) without using signatures, heuristics, or rudimentary control features. After filtering the detected files, DeepArmor uses cognitive algorithms to scan unknown files and forms threat scores for each file.

At the next step and after identifying the threat, the cloud-based management console provides a natural language processing (NLP) tool. Deep NLP not only looks for evidence on the Internet, but also understands the context around threats. DeepArmor can distinguish precisely what is harmful based on abnormal cases [45].

SparkCognition's Deep NLP technology functions in a way that thousands of pages of relevant information concerning various threats are taken as the base input for SparkCognition's Deep NLP technology. This data is also used to contextualize the threats themselves. NLP technology also explores the Internet for possible evidence of threats, from which an evidentiary summary will be produced. Risk assessment scoring will also be computed based on the know risks. Finally, a threat analysis summary can be produced from the generated information that can be used to for policy strategies and tackle the most relevant issues [45].

DeepArmor also has autonomous alert handling capability on its cloud-based management console, which mitigates workload of the security analyst by autonomously initiating actions concerning alerts and in addition, diminishes false positives. Security operations teams can then make more informed decisions based on system information at the time of the event and key data points extracted during static file analysis [8]. DeepArmor continue to improve features and the latest technical features for Windows are personal firewall and exploit protection. Personal firewall prevents hackers and malware from threatening end-user's computer(s) by tracking connections performed by applications and in addition, by providing advanced control of network activity. Exploit protection protects the device from exploitation by utilizing a collection of host intrusion protection features [46].

4.7   *Vectra Cognito Threat Detection and Response Platform*

The Vectra Cognito Threat Detection and Response Platform utilizes AI-based machine learning algorithms in prioritizing and stopping incoming cyber-attacks. The platform ranges from hybrid and cloud-native AWS and Azure environments, including Software-as-a-Service (SaaS) applications, e.g., Microsoft Office 365 using identity on Azure AD to data center workloads, IoT, and enterprise networks. The platform consists of Cognito Detect for Network for detecting and prioritizing hidden threats in data centers and enterprise networks, Cognito Detect for Microsoft Office 365 for detecting and prioritizing hidden threats in Microsoft Azure AD and Office 365, Cognito Recall for performing threat-hunting and investigations in the cloud and Cognito Stream services for delivering security-enriched metadata to SIEMs for custom detection [54].

Vectra Cognito platform utilizes supervised and unsupervised machine learning technologies in combating malicious cyber-attackers. Traditional information security systems attempt to identify cyber-attacks by searching already known signatures and exploits. A cyber-attacker can use this information against the system. Cognito learns from the network activity for a long time, such as days, weeks, or months. Cognito identifies attacker's online behavior at every step of the cyber-attack chain.

The attacker's identified behavior is categorized and compared to ordinary user behavior, using servers that are already risk-assessed. Those who are part of an individual coordinated cyber-attack campaign are identified as exhibiting attacker's behavior. In this case, the administrators can concentrate on directing their resources to the attacks that pose the greatest business risk ([41], 1).

Cognito Detect uses artificial intelligence to generate a detailed real time image of current cyber-attacks to react to them. Cognito combines sophisticated machine learning technologies, such as deep learning and neural networks, with continuous learning conceptual models, in order to quickly and efficiently locate hidden and unknown attackers before they cause damage. Cognito detect instantly triages highest-risk threats and correlates and prioritizes them to hosts to provide means for security teams to be able to initiate action faster and stop in-progress attacks and prevent loss of data. Cognito also eliminates so-called "blind spots" by analyzing all the information security and authentication systems and SaaS 'applications' network traffic and log files. This provides a comprehensive snapshot of the situation for users and IoT devices concerning running processes on cloud and data centers, preventing attackers from hiding ([41], 1).

Cognito Detect also extracts network metadata instead of performing deep packet inspection and provides real-time visibility into cloud and enterprise traffic. Metadata analysis can be applied to all internal traffic, internet-bound traffic, virtual infrastructure, and cloud environments. Cognito can identify, track, and score all IP-enabled devices and software, such as laptops, servers, printers BOYD and IoT devices, operating systems and applications and even SaaS applications from the cloud to the enterprise. The collected metadata is then analyzed by behavioral detection algorithms, which can reveal hidden and unknown adversaries. Common behaviors performed by adversaries, such as remote access tools, hidden tunnels, backdoors, credential abuse, internal reconnaissance and lateral movement, etc. are exposed [51].

Cognito detect can be integrated with other services, such as firewalls, endpoint security solutions, NACs, SIEM solutions, such as ArcSight, Splunk or QRadar and other enforcement points to automatically prevent yet obscure incoming cyber-attacks. Cognito REST API enables automated response and enforcement with basically every security solution providing more comprehensive security solution [51].

Cognito Detect for Office 365 expands Cognito platform, which has capabilities to safeguard public clouds, private data centers, and enterprise environments to cover Microsoft Office 365. Due to deficiencies in traditional preventative security, Cognito Detect for Office 365 is capable of detect and stop known and unknown cyberattacks prior to causing security breaches. The tool autonomously detects and prioritizes adversary behaviors, speeds up investigations, and applies proactive cyber threat discovery. Cognito Detect for Office 365 has a feature to read activity logs from various services, such as O365, Azure AD, SharePoint/OneDrive, Teams, and Exchange. Vectra Cognito AI has an extensive understanding of O365 application semantics, and it utilizes unsupervised and supervised machine learning models. The tool is capable to perceive behavior patterns of an adversary through the structure (kill chain) of the whole attack by analyzing e.g., logins, file creation/manipulation, DLP configuration, and mailbox routing configuration and automation changes resulting high precision actionable detections instead of anomaly alerts. These detections can detect are able to detect novel and never seen adversaries with high success rate [52].

Cognito Detect automates the real-time detection of hidden adversaries in cloud and data center workloads, and in addition, user and IoT devices providing Cognito Recall a starting point to perform AI-assisted threat hunting. Cognito Recall is a cloud service from Vectra that can store historical network metadata to support forensic security investigation and AI -assisted threat hunting in cloud and data center workloads and user and IoT devices. Cognito Recall stores the metadata that is extracted by the network sensors and makes it available to analysts in order to assist them in threat hunting. Cognito Recall processes information (e.g., IP-address, account and devices names, HTTP Cookies, Keyboard layout, etc.) to search malicious activity in the network [53]. Capabilities of Vectra Recall as summarized are empowering threat hunters, enabling intelligent investigation of device activity, providing enterprise-wide visibility and deliver cloud-powered limitless scale [49].

Cognito Stream application provides visibility into network traffic by transferring security-enriched searchable metadata from native cloud, hybrid cloud, internet-bound, internal and virtual infrastructure traffic in compact and easy-to-understand Zeek format that leverages existing tooling to data lakes and SIEMs for correction, search and analysis purposes. Data lakes concerned may possess Kafka, syslog and Elastic support. Every device that utilizes IP-address on the network is identified and tracked. Machine learning has been utilized to generate security insights embedded in the metadata for threat hunters to rapidly obtain notable results in order to reach correct conclusions. The application also provides visibility to servers, laptops, printers, BOYD and IoT devices, operating systems and applications, and in addition, traffic between virtual workloads in data centers and the cloud [50].

4.8   IBM Maas360

IBM Maas360 provides cloud -based Unified Endpoint Management (UEM) solution designed to assist organizations to manage and secure wide variety of endpoints, end users, including applications, content and data. Various kinds of threats target users and devices UEM is designed to defend. The MaaS360 provides a secure environment that keeps prospective organization's apps and content separate allowing for easy removal and access revocation [40]. Native built identity management provides legitimate users access only to the data and resources approved, while integrated threat defense proactively guards corporate data. MaaS360 can keep prospective organizations files consisting of commercial secrets distinct from applications installed on a mobile device. This enables employees on organizations to work without endangering both data and device information security. The solution simplifies IT management, as it only needs to monitor the environment controlling an application and not the entire device [25].

MaaS360 can be utilized on all major computing platforms, such as iOS, MacOS, Android and Windows devices. The solution also provide support for legacy Windows platforms, Windows XP SP3, Windows Vista, Microsoft Windows 7, 8 and 10 and Microsoft Windows 10 mobile. MaaS360 UEM allows IT administrators to consolidate management of all kinds of devices, despite of the platforms or operating systems devices operate on. Traditional solutions, such as a combination of mobile device management (MDM) and client management tools generally doesn't provide means to integrate with each other, hence consolidated view of device security status and user activity is not possible to be presented [28].

MaaS360 includes a certain kind of data container built for data management and storage. When container is utilized, the UEM app becomes a productivity suite, delivering mail, calendar, contacts, and other enterprise applications and resources to an encrypted sandbox designed and implemented to restrain copying, exporting, or downloading of sensitive data. Applications within the container mimics the look and user usability of the device OS's correspondents, which makes transitioning straightforward. The containment is also possible to be extended to external applications of the container by utilizing mobile app management (MAM), which provide a way to configure certain enterprise applications to demand authentication or to restrict the means of a user to migrate data outside of the application concerned [32]. Despite of restrictive functionality, the solution allows administrators to add and distribute documents to enrolled devices and provide an access to distributed content and cloud repositories, such as Microsoft Sharepoint, Box, OneDrive and google Drive.

The container also helps to ensure that data is stored on a mobile device rather than on servers, which makes it accessible for service provider personnel. In addition, the container provides tools to ensure that the rights to data processing are regulated on-demand-based basis. The data is encrypted using the AES-256 CTR encryption algorithm, CommonCrypto FIPS 140-2 compliant algorithm (Apple devices) or the SQLCipher + OpenSSL (AES-256) encryption algorithm on Android devices. The software is compliant with General Data Protection Regulation (GDPR) requirements [29].

A crucial feature of the MaaS360 is the cognitive analytics provided by IBM Watson, which is a cognitive technology that can be analyze and interpret all types of data. Its natural language, machine learning, and data mining capabilities have been utilized to solve wide variety of problems, from cancer treatment decisions to weather forecasting [27]. MaaS360 with cognitive analytics enables historical data, current information, future predictions and forecasting to be utilized in improving the decision-making process. In turn, this helps IT and information security officers to account for GDPR requirements [29].

IBM MaaS360 takes an advantage of IBM Watson's machine learning through Advisor tool. The core of MaaS360 Advisor lays an effective cognitive engine that provides contextual information on relevant alerts regarding emerging security threats. This actionable intelligence information is based on both structured and unstructured data and is specific to the organization's industry, size and mobile environment, including the type of devices, platforms and applications used within the organization. The Advisor helps organizations to find best practices for employee productivity, recommendations for optimizing IT services and information concerning potential information security risks. MaaS360 Advisor has built-in feedback mechanism, learning models and automation functionality in order to enhance productivity, improve IT efficacy and mitigate risks, which may arise with time. In addition, it provides recommendations to facilitate end-user notification and education, bringing the value of the insight to the organization [27].

4.9   IBM QRadar Advisor with Watson

IBM QRadar Advisor with Watson applies IBM Watson's cognitive abilities (i.e., artificial intelligence) QRadar Security Platform, a platform designed for information security analysis, to reveal hidden threats and automate the authentication process of threats. Advisor provides prioritized alert research and correlated data and in order to assists analysts focus on more impactful, strategic analysis and threat hunting [33]. The system automatically examines hazardous indicators, applies its cognitive abilities for gaining critical insights and ultimately accelerates the reaction cycle to security threats. QRadar Advisor with Watson also uses the features of Watson for Cyber Security to investigate and respond to information security threats [38].

QRadar groups and prioritizes all related events under a single offense and provides analysts with a full view of potentially evolving attack scenario. QRadar's cross-investigation analysis automatically links investigations through connected incidents in order to provide comprehensive context on alerts that mitigate duplication of efforts and extend the investigation further concerning the current probable alert and incident. Additionally, Advisor with Watson provides a combination of cognitive insights and data mining, which can be utilized to unveil related indicators of compromise (IOCs). QRadar can graphically illustrate relationships within an investigation to provide visualization to enriched investigation data and explore connections to other IOCs, users, or investigations [33].

QRadar Advisor with Watson works through the following steps:

1. When the QRadar Security Intelligence platform detects an information security threat, an information security analyst can transfer it to QRadar Advisor with Watson for more precise investigation. The Advisor initiates a wider scanning of information security threats by mining data from local QRadar software. The software will then use Watson for Cyber Security to perform a more thorough analysis of the threat.
2. Watson for Cyber Security compiles data from various sources, such as web sites, information security forums and news bulletins, into a human-readable format.

On completion, the software searches for additional information-security-related information concerning harmful files and suspicious IP addresses.

3. Finally, QRadar Advisor with Watson processes the information it receives from Watson for Cyber Security, seeking for key factors related to information security threats.

Key features of IBM QRadar with Watson [30] among others are automated threat investigations and usage of Artificial Intelligence in detecting high-level risks. The solution can be used to prioritize list of investigations in order to recognize investigations with the greatest risk, to run multiple investigations at the same time and to sort and filter through the data to reveal focus areas. Proactive tuning of the environment feature provides better security to determine the necessity to do additional tuning of the environment. Performing cross-investigation analysis to mitigate duplication of efforts automatically links investigations through connected incidents and mitigates duplication of efforts and extends the investigation further. The solution provides means to apply attack alignments to the MITRE ATT&CK chain and use the confidence level for each attack progression in order to validate the threat, visualize attack occurrence, progression of the attack and possible tactics to be used. In addition, analyst learning loop for more decisive escalation process can be utilized to analyze the local environment to get recommendations concerning the new investigations to be escalated [38].

QRadar implements local data mining of information security attacks by collecting relevant network data. The application investigates whether one or some of the information security threats have passed layered defenses, or if they blocked. By taking and advantage of lists and certain suitable indicators, the inspection can be automated. Cognitive reasoning can identify the most liable threats and connect threats to original events such as malicious files and suspicious IP addresses, to draw connections between them. QRadar automatically uses Watson for Cyber Security to exploit external unstructured data such as web pages, forums, and threat intelligence. IBM QRadar also reveals the criticality of events, like whether a malware code has been executed or not, enabling more efficient time management, in order to examine higher priority risks [38].

4.10   IBM QRadar UBA

User Behavior Analytics (UBA) has been receiving widespread attention in the domain of information security. While developing an organization's protection against external threats, organizations must also protect themselves against threats that may arise from inside an organization. Threats can be caused, for instance, by an employee or an external actor, capable of causing damage in some capacity due to negligent behavior. Such threats are challenging to identity, and may cause significant damage to an organization's property, weakening its intangible assets and consumer confidence and harming an organization's brand or reputation [42].

Machine learning algorithms augments the UBA application, and it can be applied to understand accustomed end-user behavior, detect relevant deviations, identify early warning signs of irregular user actions, categorize risky user behavior, and provide security analysts with the necessary tools to prevent possibly expensive damages in the future [39]. In addition, ML augments the existing UBA app by supplementing it with visualization features that illustrate learned behavior (models), current behavior and alerts. The models can use more than 4 weeks of historical data in QRadar in order to make predictive models and baselines of what is normal behavior for a user [31].

Such algorithms have been included in IBM's QRadar UBA application for detecting suspicious and anomalous end-user behavior. These machine learning algorithms can identify consecutive and time series anomalies. To identify deviations, user's activities are monitored. Based on monitoring results, the norms of behavior, resources and networking utilization operating models are created. These models can be used to determine when the end-user will begin acting abnormally and trigger the UBA application, whose user's risk scores are increased on demand [42].

By monitoring end-user activity of each organization's information system, the tool can identify roles users have in the organization. This implies users can be allocated to role-based peer groups, users can be allocated to role-based peer groups. Unique behavior deviating from these roles can also be identified. Such behavior can be an early indicator of harmful intent. The tool's algorithms function independently and monitor user activity from a variety of points of view, so that the number of false positive results may decrease [42].

The UBA application runs along with the QRadar system, collecting data from users on the organization's network. The graphical user interface of the UBA application presents data from the Docker container (with an SQLite database). Collectible data include user aliases, latest risk scores, system points, alerts, and trends. The user interface also presents information from the QRadar system. The data provided by the QRadar system is information, status and sources related to the attack. In addition, the QRadar system's ARIEL database provides generic data and user activity records, for instance. The latter corresponds to activities performed with aliases. The UBA application sends information to the QRadar system concerning ongoing attacks for more detailed investigation.

Using a predefined ruleset, the application looks for issues that would cause end-users a "sense event", which UBAapplication would then register. The application policies require that events have performed username, and other, tests. At the next phase, UBA reads the senseValue and user ID values from the "sense event", and then increases the user's risk score by senseValue. When the user risk scores exceed the threshold set in the UBAapplication settings, the application sends an event triggering the "UBA: Create Offence" rule in the UBAapplication, creating a policy violation for the specified user.

5   Conclusion

The study was conducted by using a classification principle (taxonomy) to classify the 12 most crucial areas of cybersecurity presented in this study. When conducting the study, information on 10 security solutions utilizing artificial intelligence were gathered, and other crucial areas classified were left for further studies. These solutions selected were divided into following areas: endpoint security, application security, IoT-security, web-security, security operations and incident response, threat Intelligence, mobile security, cloud security, network security and human security. The solutions studied have extensive coverage of cybersecurity threats.

At present, comprehensive, and ever-increasing number of AI -based cyber-security solutions and tools are available for organization's needs. In relatively conventional scenario, an adversary could take an advantage of siloed organizational solutions that have been compromised, but which have an impact on the organi-zation's entire ICT system. One of the major challenges is the fragmentation of solutions and tools, as well as the problems of the implementation and maintenance of new systems, which cause management difficulties and increase complexity within the whole system. The complexity of systems requires the development of integrated systems that identify both external and internal threats, and which have comprehensive, built-in cybersecurity systems. Integrated and holistic system solutions provide the required visibility for all levels of the ICT system, which means identification and preventing of cyber-attacks can be implemented as a whole rather than as individual procedures. Within an integrated security system, a strong network information security protection, terminal management and security, active monitoring of data streams, creation of detection capability and preventing attack vectors is created.

The system requires the ability to understand the ever-changing field of attacks and novel attack vectors. The system under development must include intelligent analytic solutions within the entire organization's IT infrastructure. The system must be able to perceive both the organization's internal processes, as well as external ones. The IT infrastructure must contain necessary information security capabilities. The system should detect and quickly react to symptoms of a network attack, such as an abnormal login to a server containing valuable data, or suspicious usage of cloud services. Novel ways to detect threats are required as an organization may face up to 200,000 information security events per day. Investigating all the suspicious events by using human information security specialists is expensive and is time-consuming.

Artificial intelligence provides significant means in conducting early-stage anal-ysis and observations and detecting anomalies. The benefit of using artificial intel-ligence -based technologies is to tackle novel cyber-attacks, which can circumvent traditional rule-based security defenses like firewalls and signature-based gateways or bypass the defenses to access file shares and accounts. Threat environment is variating swiftly and when an adversary is identified, it may already be evolved into unidentifiable threat. This kind of situations emphasize the need to use artificial intelligence in order to detect novel and yet unrecognizable threats that are not possible to be detected by using possibly old-fashioned traditional information security solutions, not being able to respond to today's sophisticated threats.

An intelligent cybersecurity can be utilized to form a platform that provides a broad ecosystem of integrated information security solutions. The platform solution enables an effective co-operation between cybersecurity specialists and an artificial-intelligence-based solution in which the artificial intelligence component acts as an expert assistant by executing necessary operations, and at the same time produces processed information as a basis for decision-making.

References

1. Amazon: Amazon Macie FAQs. Amazon Web Services (AWS). Retrieved 17 October 2018. https://aws.amazon.com/macie/faq (2018)
2. Amazon: Amazon Macie. Amazon Web Services (AWS). Retrieved 24 May 2021. https://aws.amazon.com/macie (2021)
3. APTA: Cybersecurity considerations for public transit. Report APTA SS-ECS-RP-001-14, American Public Transportation Association, Washington, DC. https://www.apta.com/wp-content/uploads/Standards_Documents/APTA-SS-ECS-RP-001-14-RP.pdf (2014)
4. Arboleda, N.: Deep learning cybersecurity provider Deep Insinct launches Australian operations. Nextmedia Pty Ltd. https://www.crn.com.au/news/deep-learning-cybersecurity-provider-deep-instinct-launches-australian-operations-478594 (2017)
5. BlackBerry: AI-driven security for a mobile world. Whitepaper, BlackBerry. https://www.blackberry.com/content/dam/blackberry-com/asset/enterprise/pdf/direct/wp-mobile-threat-defense.pdf (2020)
6. Buczkowski, A.: What's the difference between Artificial Intelligence, Machine Learning and Deep Learning? Geoawesomeness. http://geoawesomeness.com/whats-difference-artificial-intelligence-machine-learning-deep-learning (2018)
7. Cambridge: Antigena email and Enterprise immune system designated march cyber catalysts 2020. Cambridge Network. Retrieved 2 July 2021 https://www.cambridgenetwork.co.uk/news/antigena-email-and-enterprise-immune-system-designated-marsh-cyber-catalysts-2020 (2021)
8. ChannelPro: SparkCognition adds new AI-built cyber defence capabilities to major DeepArmor v2.0 release. ChannelPro Network. Retrieved 25 May 2021. https://www.channelpronetwork.com/news/sparkcognition-adds-new-ai-built-cyber-defense-capabilities-major-deeparmor-v20-release (2021)
9. Conner-Simons, A.: System predicts 85 percent of cyber-attacks using input from human experts. Phys.org. https://phys.org/news/2016–04-percent-cyber-attacks-human-experts.html (2016)
10. Cylance: Comparing CylancePROTECT with Cylance Smart Antivirus. BlackBerry Cylance. Retrieved 28 May 2021. https://blackberry.com/content/dam/bbcomv4/blackberry-com/en/products/blackberry-protect-vs-blackberry-smart-antivirus/CylancePROTECTvsCylanceSmartAntivirus.pdf (2020)
11. Dale, R.: An introduction to natural language generation. European Summer School in Logic, Language and Information (ESSLLI) (1995)
12. Darktrace: Darktrace Enterprise: detects and classifies cyber-threats across your entire enterprise. Darktrace. Retrieved 17 October 2018. https://www.darktrace.com/en/products/ (2018)
13. Darktrace: Darktrace Antigena. Product overview, Darktrace. Retrieved 2 July 2021. https://www.darktrace.com/en/resources/ds-antigena.pdf (2021)

14. Darktrace: Antigena Email: building immunity for your inbox. Product brief, Darktrace. Retrieved 5 July 2021. https://www.darktrace.com/en/resources/ds-cyber-ai-for-email.pdf (2021)
15. Darktrace: Darktrace cyber AI analyst: autonomous investigations. White Paper, Darktrace. Retrieved 30 May 2021. https://darktrace.com/en/resources/wp-cyber-ai-analyst.pdf (2021)
16. Darktrace: Enterprise Immune System. Product overview, Darktrace. Retrieved 30 May 2021. https://www.darktrace.com/en/resources/ds-enterprise.pdf (2021)
17. Darktrace: Darktrace AI: combining unsupervised and supervised machine learning. Technical White Paper, Darktrace. Retrieved 2 July 2021. https://www.darktrace.com/en/resources/wp-machine-learning.pdf (2021)
18. Darktrace: Darktrace for SaaS. Darktrace. Retrieved 5 July 2021. https://www.darktrace.com/en/saas (2021)
19. DeepInstinct: Malware classification using deep learning. Whitepaper, Deep Instinct. https://bit.ly/2UxwAiw (2020)
21. DeepInstinct: Deep Instinct security buyer's guide: Transforming security: prevention first. Deep Instinct. Retrieved 7 July 2021. https://www.ciosummits.com/Deep_Instinct_-_Security_Buyers_Guide.pdf (2021)
21. DeepInstinct: Tier-1 technology software & hardware provider chose Deep Instinct's Deep Learning cybersecurity solution for threat prevention, operational efficacy and connection-less security. Deep Instinct. Retrieved 8 JuDly 2021. shorturl.at/rzBN3 (2021)
22. Delua, J.: Supervised vs. unsupervised learning: what's the difference? IBM. https://ibm.co/2TfUNJX (2021)
23. Estapé, N. E.: The differences between supervised and unsupervised machine learning. Bismart. Retrieved 22 May 2021. https://blog.bismart.com/en/difference-between-machine-learning-deep-learning (2021)
24. Fein, D.: How Antigena Email caught a fearware attack that bypassed the gateway. Darktrace. https://www.darktrace.com/en/blog/how-antigena-email-caught-a-fearware-attack-that-bypassed-the-gateway (2021)
25. FinancesOnline: IBM MaaS360 review. FinancesOnline. Retrieved 22 October 2018. https://reviews.financesonline.com/p/ibm-maas360 (2018)
26. GeeksforGeeks: Supervised and unsupervised learning. GeeksforGeeks. Retrieved 22 May 2021. https://geeksforgeeks.org/supervised-unsupervised-learning (2021)
27. IBM: Mobility insights and analytics with IBM Watson. White Paper, IBM Security. https://www.ibm.com/downloads/cas/KNJN6JWO (2017)
28. IBM: IBM MaaS with Watson: a cognitive approach with unified endpoint management. IBM. Retrieved 9 July 2021. https://www.ibm.com/downloads/cas/YD73W7GA (2017)
29. IBM: IBM MaaS with Watson: preparing for GDPR Compliance with Endpoint and Mobile. Retrieved 8.11.2021. https://ibm.co/3EQBedy (2018)
30. IBM: Key features. IBM QRadar Advisor with Watson. Retrieved 12 July 2021. https://ibm.com/products/cognitive-security-analytics/details (2021)
31. IBM: QRadar user behavior analytics. IBM QRadar common. Retrieved 12 July 2021. https://www.ibm.com/docs/en/qradar-common?topic=app-qradar-user-behavior-analytics (2021)
32. IBM: IBM Security MaaS360 with Watson: a guide to how MaaS360 establishes effective device and end user security. IBM Security. Retrieved 9 July 2021. https://www.ibm.com/downloads/cas/XWL4B1AE (2021)
33. IBM: IBM Security QRadar: visibility, detection, investigation, and response. IBM Corporation. https://www.ibm.com/downloads/cas/OP62GKAR (2021)
34. Kannan, P.V.: Artificial intelligence: applications in healthcare. Asian Hospital & Healthcare Management. **19**. https://www.asianhhm.com/technology-equipment/artificial-intelligence (2009)
35. King, P.: Amazon Macie: new enhanced version with lower pricing available. TechGenix. https://techgenix.com/amazon-macie-enhanced-version (2020)
37. LeCun, Y., Bengio, Y., Hinton, G.: Deep learning. Nature. **521**(7553), 436–444 (2015)

37. Lehto, M.: Phenomena in the cyber world. In: Lehto, M., Neittaanmäki, P. (eds.) Cyber Security: Analytics, Technology and Automation, pp. 3–29. Springer, Berlin (2015)
38. MetroConnect: What can artificial intelligence do for security analysis? IBM QRadar Advisor with Watson. Retrieved 20 October 2018. https://www.metroconnect.co.th/products/ibm-software/ibm-qradar (2018)
39. Midland: AI security SIEM QRadar machine learning user behavior analytics. Midland Information Systems. Retrieved 12 July 2021. https://www.midlandinfosys.com/ibm-power/all-categories/ai-security-siem-qradar-uba.html (2021)
40. OrbData: IBM Maas360 with Watson. Org Cata. Retrieved 9 July 2021. https://www.orb-data.com/what-we-do/software-products/mobile-device-management (2021)
41. Palmer, T.: Vectra Cognito – automating security operations with AI. ESG Lab Review. Retrieved 8 November 2021. https://bit.ly/3nZZ5k0 (2017)
42. Patel, M.: QRadar UBA app adds machine learning and peer group analyses to detect anomalies in user's activities. Security Intelligence. https://securityintelligence.com/qradar-uba-app-adds-machine-learning-and-peer-group-analyses-to-detect-anomalies-in-users-activities (2017)
43. Scott, S.: What is Amazon Macie? Cloud Academy. Retrieved 24 May 2021. https://cloudacademy.com/course/enforcing-compliance-security-controls-amazon-macie/what-is-amazon-macie (2021)
44. Selden, H.: Deep Instinct: a new way to prevent malware, with deep learning. Tom's Hardware. Retrieved 18 October 2018. https://www.tomshardware.com/news/deep-instinct-deep-learning-malware-detection,31079.html (2016)
45. SparkCognition: A cognitive approach to system protection. SparkCognition. Retrieved 18 October 2018. https://www.sparkcognition.com/wp-content/uploads/2021/04/deeparmor-a-cognitive-approach-to-system-protection.pdf (2018)
46. SparkCognition: Next-generation endpoint protection built from AI. SparkCognition. Retrieved 25 May 2021. https://www.sparkcognition.com/deeparmor-small-business (2021)
47. StoneFly: Amazon Macie: artificial intelligence for efficient data security. StoneFly. https://stonefly.com/blog/amazon-macie-artificial-intelligence-efficient-data-security (2017)
48. Tsymbal, O.: 5 essential machine learning techniques for business applications. MobiDev. Retrieved 22 May 2021. https://mobidev.biz/blog/5-essential-machine-learning-techniques (2021)
49. Vectra: Vectra introduces Cognito Recall to deliver AI-assisted threat hunting and enable conclusive incident investigations. News release, Vectra AI. https://bit.ly/3oQiWlW (2018)
50. Vectra: Cognito Stream: network metadata with an option. Vectra AI. https://threatscape.com/wp-content/uploads/2019/07/Vectra-Cognito-Stream-Datasheet.pdf (2019)
51. Vectra: Cognito Detect is the most powerful way to find and stop cyberattacks in real time. Data sheet, Vectra AI. https://content.vectra.ai/rs/748-MCE-447/images/Datasheet_CognitoDetect.pdf (2020)
52. Vectra: Cognito Detect for Office 365. Data sheet, Vectra AI. https://content.vectra.ai/rs/748-MCE-447/images/Datasheet_CognitoDetecto365.pdf (2020)
53. Vectra: Cognito Recall – security and privacy statement. Data sheet, Vectra AI. https://content.vectra.ai/rs/748-MCE-447/images/Datasheet-Recall-SecurityPrivacy.pdf (2020)
54. Vectra: The Cognito Threat Detection and Response platform. Data sheet, Vectra AI. Retrieved 26 May 2021. https://content.vectra.ai/rs/748-MCE-447/images/Datasheet_CognitoNDRPlatform.pdf (2021)
55. Veeramachaneni, K., Arnaldo, I., Korrapati, V., Bassias, C., Li, K.: AI^2: training a big data machine to defend. In: 2016 IEEE 2nd International Conference on Big Data Security on Cloud (BigDataSecurity), IEEE International Conference on High Performance and Smart Computing (HPSC), and IEEE International Conference on Intelligent Data and Security (IDS), pp. 49–54. IEEE (2016)
56. Walker, T.: Launch – Hello Amazon Macie: automatically discover, classify, and secure content at scale. Amazon Web Services (AWS). https://aws.amazon.com/blogs/aws/launch-amazon-macie-securing-your-s3-buckets (2017)

A Review of Cyber Threat (Artificial) Intelligence in Security Management

Martin Lundgren and Ali Padyab

1 Introduction

Managing cybersecurity within organizations typically relies on careful consideration and management of its risks. By following an iterative—often sequential—risk
management process, an organization's exposure to risks can be assessed by
weighing organizational digital asset values against the probability of being harmed
by a threat [29]. However, this approach has been criticized for reflecting only a
snapshot of the organization's assets and threats. Furthermore, identifying threats
and the ability to remain updated on current threats and vulnerabilities are often
dependent on skilled and experienced experts, causing risks to be primarily determined based on subjective judgment [46]. Nevertheless, this also poses a challenge
to organizations that cannot stay up-to-date with what assets are vulnerable or
attain personnel with the necessary experience and know-how to obtain relevant
information on cybersecurity threats towards those assets [8, 30, 37].

To this end, numerous tools have been proposed that can aid the extensive and
automated gathering of cybersecurity threats, e.g., platforms to share information
about the latest vulnerabilities and what threats might exploit them [4]. During
the past few years, a trend has evolved where organizations have demonstrated
increased willingness to collect, share, and exchange information on vulnerabilities,
threats, incidents, and mitigation strategies [42, 52, 57]. Effective cybersecurity
management requires up-to-date information on relevant threats from various

M. Lundgren (✉)
Department of Computer Science, Electrical and Space Engineering, Luleå University of
Technology, Luleå, Sweden
e-mail: martin.lundgren@ltu.se

A. Padyab
School of Informatics, University of Skövde, Skövde, Sweden
e-mail: ali.padyab@his.se

sources to establish a base of reliable knowledge that can enable immediate reaction. Based on cybersecurity sharing platforms, monitoring solutions, and other relevant sources (e.g., forums, blogs, and white-papers) data on past (e.g., trends in tactics, techniques, and procedures) and current (e.g., active threat actors, intrusion alerts, malicious IPs or URLs) cyber threats can be identified [11]. Although this type of data collection can be automated and provides valuable insights, it does not constitute actionable information on its own. It must first be analyzed. That is to say, data on cyber threats must first be interpreted and put into context in order to extract that which is relevant before actionable threat information can be generated, i.e., cyber threat intelligence (henceforth 'CTI').

However, along with this emerging trend of collecting and sharing cyber threat data, several new challenges arose regarding how such information should be interoperable. For example, in what shape and format the shared information should conform to be intelligible, and how it should be sanitized so as not to reveal any sensitive legal, ethical, or business details—yet at the same time give enough details to be actionable? Furthermore, security managers have previously indicated that a stream of up-to-date threat information would not necessarily result in more effective risk management [9]. Instead, research has indicated several managerial challenges [11, 16], adding an extra layer of complexity [37, 57]. As noted by Cortex [12], because of lacking external threat context and cyber-related skills in general, security managers often find it challenging to work efficiently, especially when faced with a high volume of low-fidelity threat alerts [12].

To address the challenges of achieving 'actionability' [57] from cyber threat data, artificial intelligence (henceforth 'AI'), through the use of, e.g., machine learning and data mining, has been applied to help interpret and generate relevant, helpful threat intelligence for security managers—without overwhelming them [37]. Indeed, some have even argued that generating such actionable threat intelligence is not possible without the aid of artificial intelligence [11]. However, as much of these efforts have been driven by cybersecurity vendors, little is still known on the actual value provided to security managers by obtaining threat intelligence aided by artificial intelligence [52]. Therefore, to further this research stream, the following chapter looks into how cyber threat intelligence, aided by artificial intelligence, can support managing cybersecurity within organizations.

The remainder of the chapter is structured as follows. First, we present security management, CTI, and AI and draw a red thread between the three fields. Next, we review the literature on how previous literature has contributed to these three fields. Finally, future directions, along with the conclusion, are presented.

2   Security Management

The primary purpose of security management is to protect valuable digital assets through a systematic approach based on managerial practices and protective mea-sures (or 'security controls') enacted on the organization's strategic, operational, and tactical levels [1]. While the managerial practices are many, they typically revolve around risk management to help identify and prioritize what to protect, to what extent, and from what. For example, for a security expert to allocate resources and decide what network security controls to implement (or not), he/she should weigh the value of the assets to be protected on the network against the probability of an incident and the potential impact thereof. Indeed, this type of coordination of activities to identify and implement relevant security controls to treat unacceptable risks is often referred to as elements of security management.

Management practices—the security decisions and activities enacted to protect the organization's digital assets—thus require continuous monitoring of current threats as well as the level of effectiveness of existing security controls to interrelate and coordinate such security activities since circumstances, dependencies, and efficiency often change over time in relation to the organization's security objective [22]. A security objective can be categorized into three different levels within the organization: strategic, operational, and tactical [21, 39].

At the *strategic* level—or the organizational layer—decisions and actions focus on enabling the organizational mission, direction, and objectives [39]. From a security management aspect, questions circle around protecting anything unique, valuable, and thereby critical to the organization/business's function. In other words, try to establish what assets malicious actors might be interested in and to what extent [33]. Each answer to these questions must be prioritized according to how valuable they concern each other to determine what level of protection to put in place to not over-or under-protect the assets. Decisions can then be made about what risk treatment strategies to formalize or if the threat can be ignored altogether [59].

At the *operational* level—or business/mission layer—decisions and actions are focused on sustaining day-to-day operation, aligned with the direction set out at the strategic level [39]. From a security management perspective, questions revolve around how various threats may materialize, e.g., how malicious actors operate, plan, and prepare their attacks [33]. That is to say, having, on a strategic level, established the level of protection needed for various assets, the threat landscape should be assessed on an operational level in order to understand what threat actors aim to achieve and by what means they are likely to achieve those aims [33]. Understanding the motive and capability of malicious actors behind a previous, current, and—possibly—future attacks could help security managers decide on and prepare for a more robust security posture by, e.g., introducing new or refining existing security controls either preventative (e.g., firewall or authentication systems) or responsive (e.g., incident response or business recovery plans) in nature [6].

The *tactical* level—or the information systems layer—is perhaps where most attention has been placed in cybersecurity [33, 38]. Decisions and actions on this level focus on the defensive measures to directly thwart threats that have already become incidents or are about to. From a security manager's perspective, security surveillance and monitoring feedback is essential to gain insight into what is currently happening within the organization and thwart cyber-attacks before they cause any damage [38]. Therefore, this type of information enables security managers to make apt and timely decisions about how to act in a specific situation at a given time to minimize the harm of a particular threat best.

The activities and decisions taken at each level often overlap and affect each other [28, 29, 33]. For example, the decisions taken on the strategic level prioritizes what risks to address and the level of protection, thereby directing, e.g., funding for the development of the organization's security posture on an operational level, which in turn influences what security controls are implemented on a tactical level [39]. Likewise, learning from incidents on a tactical level can provide new insights into how, e.g., a threat actor operates and what they were trying to achieve, such as theft of intellectual property, which could have led to the loss of competitive advantage. Drawing new operational insights can help security managers to prioritize the recent threat on a strategic level and adapt responsive and defensive security controls accordingly [1].

As such, security managers need knowledge about the state of the world in terms of cyber threats and actors to make relevant and effective operational, tactical, and strategic decisions [36]. One such source of knowledge is cyber threat intelligence.

3   Overview of Cyber Threat Intelligence

Cyber threat intelligence (or simply 'CTI') has no widely accepted definition [4]. Nevertheless, several descriptions of the concept [31, 43] circle the explanation of CTI as data that is collected and assessed regarding cyber security threats, vulnerabilities, actors, exploits, and malware but also indications of compromises [54]. CTI is a collective term for knowledge gained from analyzing trends in tactics, techniques, and procedures (often referred to as 'TTP') of past, current, and—possibly—future cyber-attacks. As such, CTI typically follows an automated process, as outlined in Fig. 1 above (adapted from [13, 25, 49, 56]): (1) collecting streams of raw, unstructured, and uncontextualized cyber threat data from various sources (see section 'Cyber Threat Sources: Gathering the Haystacks' below); (2) the collected data is then prepared by being processed and converted into a readable, normalized format that can be further analyzed; (3) the normalized data is then sorted and enriched, i.e., contextualized with prior incidents or similar threat activities and analyzed using various quantitative and qualitative techniques to assess patterns and event correlations; and, finally, (4) the result can then automatically be disseminated as cyber threat intelligence through reporting or visual tools to help an organization defend and ultimately improve their cyber security posture. Having robust CTI within the organization can thus help develop timely, contextualized, and actionable information on the security threats that pose real risks to the organization's assets [37]. The objective of CTI is to provide decision-makers with a stream of continuously updated information, thus enabling security managers not only to stay alert and take proactive measures before threats

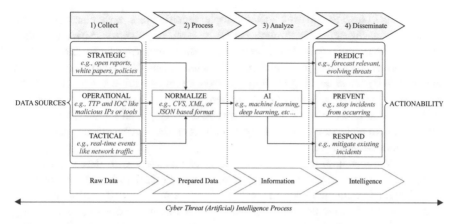

Fig. 1 Cyber Threat (Artificial) Intelligence Process: From raw data to intelligence

become incidents but also insights on how to act after they have occurred [11]. As such, CTI can provide 'actionability,' i.e., valuable insights that can aid security managers in making decisions on the strategic, operational, and tactical level [16, 33].

Strategic threat intelligence, for example, provides security managers priority metrics for strategic decisions to be made based on business concerns and likely attacks [18]. Threat intelligence on a strategic level enables decision-makers to make informed decisions on what and how much resources to allocate to achieve the organization's strategic objectives [33]. For example, information on threats that are endangering business goals, such as compromising or leaking customer data, can be seen as intelligence regarding strategic threats to the organization's corporate image [18]. Therefore, required is threat intelligence (typically in the form of reports, white papers, or policy documents) that provide high-level information on cyber threat trends, patterns, and evolution. As such, threat intelligence on a strategic level must be presented to high-level executives, such as Chief Information Security Officers (or 'CISO' for short) and other decision-makers, to help establish an overall picture of the intent and capabilities of different threats, as well as a briefing on what threats to focus organizational resources on [37]. A challenge with this type of threat intelligence is that security managers often become flooded with alerts on potential threats but are seldom provided with information on what threats can be ignored, thereby making any prioritization a challenge in itself [16]. Obtaining too much threat information can thus be just as bad as obtaining too little [57].

Operational threat intelligence provides security managers context on previous cyber-attacks to understand them better and identify and prepare for similar future attacks [18]. Threat intelligence on an operational level can be said to bridge the non-technical, often broader, nature of strategic cyber threat intelligence and the technical, often narrower, nature of tactical cyber threat intelligence [33]. For example, operational threat intelligence could be information on a particular threat actor that is known to exploit a specific implementation of a particular technology, such as cross-site scripting through HTTP headers, to extract sensitive user data [18]. Therefore, it is required that threat intelligence provides insights into the TTPs used by adversaries. If appropriately implemented, it can give security managers an upper hand by understanding malicious behavior that can guide and assist with the response to specific incidents [37]. A challenge with this type of threat intelligence is that it often takes a lot of time and resources to digest and gather the relevant information to understand threats fully, re-construct prior cyber-attacks, and prevent similar future attacks [16].

Tactical threat intelligence provides security managers with details on prioritizing alerts of ongoing cyber-attacks and focuses in particular on threat patterns [18]. Threat intelligence on a tactical level thus aims to aid the effort to detect and respond to threats already happening, e.g., malicious actors that have already penetrated and are currently operating within the organization's network [33]. For example, a specific business asset (e.g., an industrial control system that controls the business production line) is currently being targeted in a denial of service attack is intelligence regarding a tactical threat to the organization [18]. Therefore, (near) real-time evaluation of events and activities within the organization to oversee the day-to-day operations is required. One way of achieving such evaluation is by feeding various security-related events from diverse sources into a central security information and event management (or 'SIEM' for short) system to provide a bird's eye view of the IT infrastructure [7]. As such, threat intelligence in the form of indications of compromise (or 'IOC' for short), like known malicious domain names, IP addresses, URLs, file hashes, network traffic anomalies, etc., can be integrated and combined in a SIEM system to be normalized and correlated in order to form a critical overview for the security manager [37]. A challenge with this type of threat intelligence is that it often creates a flood of alerts and false positives, in other words, noise that could end up hiding incidents as they happen, i.e., actual threats causing real harm to the organization [16].

3.1   Cyber Threat Sources: Gathering the Haystacks

In order to produce actionable threat intelligence, there must first be a source of information to harness, i.e., threat-related data that can be analyzed and put into context to inform decision-makers on relevance and action. In other words, information is not intelligent on its own, but the building blocks out of which intelligence can be constructed through analysis [16]. There are numerous sources to scour for cyber threat related data, which can be publicly available, overt sources (typically referred to as Open Source Intelligence, or 'OSINT' for short), or restricted to a particular crowd behind a user registration, paywalls, or subscriptions. Threat-related data sources can be categorized as either formal or informal [36].

Two examples of formal OSINT are NIST and MITRE, which have formulated enumerations for different types of malware, exploits, and vulnerabilities [42].

MITRE, for example, provides lists of known vulnerabilities in various products and systems, called Common Vulnerabilities and Exposures (or 'CVE' for short) and libraries of known software weaknesses (or 'CWE' for short) [50]. In comparison, NIST provides the National Vulnerability Database (or 'NVD' for short), a repository of standards-based vulnerability management data. In the case of NVD, it builds upon CVE and enhances the information by adding, e.g., severity scores and impact ratings to help security managers estimate the extent of a particular threat. Both CVE and NVD are available to the public and free to use [34].

Informal OSINT can be everything from forums, blogs, newspapers, social media, websites, video sharing sites, magazines, wikis, and similar. The term 'informal' is used since there is no standardized format of the threat information. For example, vulnerabilities and threats reported via informal OSINT, such as Twitter [35] or security forums found on the Darknet (Kadoguchi et al. 2020), do not usually follow any predetermined structure—although providing rich insights into new security matters. Hence, some human-like processing is required before the information can be turned into intelligence.

CTI itself can take many forms. It can be through some structured data feed, like standards such as the Structure Threat Information Expression (or 'STIX' for short), maintained by OASIS, which provides an XML/JSON-structured language for sharing CTI in a structured way. Alternatively, it can be unstructured data reports, such as PDF or Word documents [47]. From an automated perspective, standards such as STIX enable a shared, standardized form of describing CTI, thereby allowing consistency in how it can be shared, stored, and analyzed.

3.2 Artificial Intelligence and Cyber Threats: Finding the Needles

CTI often faces challenges of creating threat data overload and quality [47]. While there are several sources from where CTI can be collected, many of these feeds provide an overwhelming amount of data to analyze and act upon [17, 57]. Indeed, an annual study by the Ponemon Institute in 2019 showed that 40% of the respondents said they could not keep up with the volume of threat intelligence [45]. What is more, the provided CTI is difficult to understand and not dependable in terms of its quality over time [47]. Considering this situation from a security manager's perspective, not being able to analyze the CTI content in time or understand its vital details is not far off from not having any CTI in the first place. It is not necessarily that the security manager is lazy or slow, but simply unable [36]. As such, there is a need to automate the analysis of the CTI to sift through the haystack of vast cyber threat information to find the needles that can aid security managers to make timely and informed decisions. One such approach is using artificial intelligence, or 'AI' for short [36].

AI is a broad discipline but is limited to simply enabling computers to perform human-like tasks [5, 19]. For example, one branch of AI is machine learning which refers to algorithms capable of adapting, or learning, through simulations [5]. Machine learning falls into two categories based on supervised or unsupervised learning [19]. Supervised learning means that the algorithm is provided with solving problems to learn from, while in unsupervised learning, the algorithm is not explicitly instructed on what type of answer to produce; however, it is programmed to find patterns in the data [19].

There have been several proposed approaches to ease the threat analysis for security managers using AI. For example, Alves et al. [3] proposed supervised machine learning to build an automated classification that can streamline threat identification taken from Twitter feeds and cluster it to avoid unnecessary information while keeping the information relevant for a particular infrastructure. Mittal et al. [35] have also proposed using Twitter to obtain threat intelligence and proposed an approach to automatically generate linked vulnerability descriptions with other data sets and map relevant information based on custom infrastructure profiles. Like Alves et al. [3], Ghazi et al. [17] proposed a technique to tackle duplicate threat information using a supervised machine learning-based natural language processing approach to extract threat feeds from unstructured cyber threat information sources. One challenge of this type of automation from unstructured cyber threat information, as noted by Li et al. [27], is the semantics and contextual information analysis. In their work, Li et al. [27] proposed an automized way for analyzing unstructured text to obtain relevant cyber threat intelligence using natural language processes, machine learning, and data mining. Others, such as Nunes et al. [41], have similarly addressed this challenge by text classification performance of hacker forums using various data mining and machine learning techniques. In contrast, Deliu et al. [41] analyzed threat information collected from hacker forums one step further and compared using convolutional neural network and machine learning to see which performed better. Compared to the convolutional neural network, the authors found that machine learning can yield high-performance levels aiding security managers for better threat intelligence.

Although there are various branches within AI, such as an algorithm for machine learning of various kinds, specific approaches are out of scope in this chapter. Hence the focus lies with the AI-produced intelligence and how that intelligence can be helpful for security managers.

4   Security Management with AI-Driven CTI

We opted for a literature review as a natural starting point to summarize the research trends. The literature search was performed on recent publications between 2018 and 2021, limited to articles in English only. The reason for selecting this period was that AI-driven CTI is a relatively new research area. The starting point of any review is to retrieve small sets of highly relevant publications in high-ranked journals, typically indexed in the Web of Science, followed into conference proceeding databases. ACM Digital library, IEEE, and AIS proceeding databases were selected for this purpose since they cover a fair amount of proceeding publications. We used the search engines of digital databases and a combination of terms "AI OR Artificial Intelligence" + "CTI OR Cyber Threat Intelligence," "Information security," and "Management." Our strategy was to consider the most relevant hits returned from this search for inclusion. We, therefore, examined the titles and abstracts of each article to verify for inclusion, and after initial screening, the articles then acceded into a more detailed investigation. The authors excluded articles that focused only on technical upshots (e.g., algorithms, mathematical sophistication, or software code) from the review. The papers that we identified to be relevant were concentrated on AI, CTI, and information security management. The final part of the review was to analyze the studies using a concept-centric approach [58]. In this regard, we organized and compared the studies based on the security objectives explored in the articles, based on the tactical, operational, and strategic aspects of information security management [21, 39].

In the following section, an analysis of AI-aided CTI is presented. In particular, we have looked at: what type of threat intelligence was gathered on a strategic, operational, and tactical level, if there was more focus on one or more levels, and how security managers' use of the CTI was addressed.

4.1 Strategic

In Sun et al. [55], the authors propose collecting CTI from open-source threat intelligence publishing platforms. An experiment was conducted using a combined natural language processing, machine learning method, and multiple cybersecurity threat intelligence sources. The study shows how CTI can, using the proposed atomization approach and based on multiple threat information sources, be visualized and build a database that can be queried to understand relevant threats intelligence better. The authors argue that their approach can help security managers better sort CTI for future analysis, thereby making their initial overview of CTI on a strategic level less overwhelming. For example, security managers could use the proposed approach to better grasp public opinion on specific threats, get insights into what emergency events could become relevant for their own organization, and get an overview of current advanced persistent threats [55].

Ghazi et al. [17], Kadoguchi et al. [23], and Kadoguchi et al. [24] similarly propose a natural language processing approach to extract cyber threat data from unstructured sources. In Ghazi et al.'s [17] study, the authors set out to find a more efficient way of generating strategic cyber threat intelligence. By training a supervised model over threat data collected from cybersecurity blogs, the authors demonstrated how the approach described in the study was capable of making inferences and drawing relations between otherwise seemingly disconnected cyber attacks. Consequently, a security manager gets an overview of the threat landscape, what threats are currently active, and what targets are currently under attack. Kadoguchi et al. [23], Ebrahimi et al. [15], and Kadoguchi et al. [24] similarly used natural language processing to identify current threats from forum posts on the Darknet to stay ahead of current and evolving cyber threats and be an active part of security managers' strategic defense. However, in the future, the proposed approach could be extended to include TTPs of cyber threats and thereby give more detailed insights on an operational level, such as hacking techniques, among other variables [24]. In similar research, Schäfer et al. [53] presented BlackWidow, an automated modular system that monitors Dark Web services and extracts data for interactive visual exploration. Using BlackWidow, decision-makers can understand the relationships between authors and forums and detect trends for cybersecurity-related topics.

4.2   Operational

Like Ghazi et al. [17], some researchers propose a natural language processing approach to obtain insight into specific threats (e.g., actors, what industries are affected, tools and techniques). Others, such as Li et al. [27], have taken similar approaches and suggested how past or current cybersecurity events can be studied to analyze the chain of events on a particular cyber threat which makes it easier for security managers to understand past or ongoing cyber threats and take actions to prevent similar, future attacks. A cyber security open-source threat intelligence framework was proposed for the event-based CTI discovery and analysis to achieve this threat intelligence. The threat data is based on unstructured, natural language text (e.g., CVE-descriptions, white papers, reports, etc.). Previous research has proposed techniques on how data from unstructured sources can be collected and filtered using natural language processing, machine learning, and data mining to extract cybersecurity event-related information. Such techniques can finally generate a report based on a structured, predefined CTI template from the extracted threat information [27, 40].

Dealing with false positives is one of the challenges of CTI that researchers have attempted to resolve via AI. In a study to automate the process of data triage, Zhong et al. [60] showcased a system based on a graph-based trace mining method that examines the various data sources (such as IDS alerts and firewall logs) and eliminates the false positives to facilitate the separation of different attack campaigns (i.e., attack plots) from each other. The proposed system helps reduce the workload of security analysts to analyze a large number of logs from network devices and systems with a satisfactory false positive rate within a short amount of time. Other research has focused on reducing the number of falsely identified cyber threats hosted by the Darknet marketplaces via semi-supervised data labeling [15].

4.3 Tactical

Several proposed approaches to detect and alert security managers on ongoing cyber-attacks are built on machine learning [20]; Kumar and Sinha [26]. One such example is presented in Sari [51]. In his study, a firewall system based on an artificial neural network radial basis function approach is outlined. The system outlined in the study can detect different types of attacks through numerous different network services, traffic, and protocols. The system can classify different attacks based on an intrusion dataset, like current probing techniques (e.g., port scanning) and denial of service, thus, aiding security managers to thwart ongoing cyber attacks. As the author discusses, the system can be extended in the future to include automated, artificial intelligence-driven mitigation techniques to better handle successful or otherwise disruptive cyber attacks [51]. However, while detection of ongoing attacks provides valuable intelligence for security managers, they are often based upon known vulnerabilities or attack patterns. Detecting zero-day attacks—i.e., vulnerabilities and patterns unknown to vendors or the security industry—poses new challenges.

Intrusion detection systems (or 'IDS' for short) can be used to alert security managers about current threats targeting or already inside the organization's defensive borders. However, as with firewalls, they often rely on previously known attack patterns and vulnerabilities. To overcome this limitation, Hindy et al. [20] propose an IDS model built on an 'autoencoder' that can detect zero-day attacks while keeping the miss rate (false-negatives) to an acceptable minimum. Others have tackled the challenge with zero-days with different approaches. In their work on automating the detection of zero-day attacks, Kumar and Sinha [26] propose a concept based on 'heavy-hitter' and 'graph technique' to detect zero-day attacks through the signature generation and evaluation. The authors experimented with their proposed approach and, by using raw hexadecimal byte format, could capture unknown attacks and detect anomalies, thereby notifying security managers of the detection [26]. Sameera and Shashi [48] propose a deep transductive transfer learning framework to detect zero-day attacks. The authors suggest that future research could include predefined and target specific types of new zero-day attacks.

Heterogeneous open sources (e.g., the cyber threat intelligence feeds and reports) are valuable sources for the CTI. Research has enabled machine-readable data structures for the automatic process usable for further CTI operations. Bo et al. [10] proposed Threat Operating Model (TOM) model for automatically clustering the threat intelligence reports using a semi-supervised matrix decomposition-based method and an unsupervised term frequency-based method. Their model ultimately helps the security experts facilitate the automated risk assessment and achieve the early warning of likely cyber-attacks.

5 Future Directions

The use of AI in CTI is still in its infancy. Articles reviewed in this chapter (Table 1) show that the proposed solutions are inclined towards one or two layers of cybersecurity management. One of the challenges caused by such solutions is integrating the AI-based CTI across the overall cybersecurity management plan. It implies that the future of AI should facilitate the CTI to harmonize the balance between strategic, operational, and tactical levels. Previous research has shown that security analysts are often confronted with a plethora of intelligent reports that make it challenging to take a timely decision [2], negatively affecting the organization's overall security posture. In this regard, it would be fruitful for CTI to integrate AI approaches that could translate in-between layers of cybersecurity management in the future. Such an approach could be, for example, to use neural networks to analyze and weed out false positives of threats collected by the firewall logs (tactical), correlate them with the external threat intelligence reports (operational) to find whether such threats are a trend. It could finally generate reports that give management the necessary food for thoughts in orienting the organization's security posture (strategic).

To this end, an additional social aspect is ripe for further studies. For example, researchers have previously noted that having a steady stream of updated and relevant threats will not necessarily improve security management [9, 16]. Some of these concerns can be solved using the AI-based solutions presented in our review concerning sorting and prioritization. Nevertheless, the question remains to what extent security managers would (prefer to) use such AI-based tools. While there is much research towards new and efficient ways of gathering CTI, little is still

Table 1 An overview of the AI-based CTI with respect to three layers of cybersecurity management

Authors (↓), Levels (→)	Strategic	Operational	Tactical
Bo et al. [10]		×	×
Ebrahimi et al. [15]		×	×
Ghazi et al. [17]	×	×	
Hindy et al. [20]			×
Kadoguchi et al. [23]	×		
Kadoguchi et al. [24]	×		
Kumar and Sinha [26]			×
Li et al. [27]		×	
Noor et al. [40]		×	
Sameera and Shashi [48]			×
Sari [51]			×
Schäfer et al. [53]	×		
Sun et al. [55]	×		
Zhong et al. [60]		×	

known how the CTI is actually used and applied in practice by security managers. We, therefore, recommended this area for further research, e.g., by the use of case studies and in-depth interviews with security managers and practitioners alike, to get a better understanding of CTIs possibilities and challenges in practice.

There are several indicators that such research is needed. For example, the review revealed that AI-based solutions rely on the analysts' expertise who utilizes the system more explicitly. Different systems require input and interpretation from the analyst who might not possess the necessary knowledge to interact and harvest the presented intelligence. Moreover, the AI facilitated CTI seems to present technical details that are hard to grasp by top management. The same criticism faced by AI also applies to the AI-enabled CTI, i.e., deviations from datasets can cause problems, and all statistical techniques suffer from deviation from their assumptions, and the problem of generalization outside of the training set still exists [32]. Moreover, the incorporation of collaboration (e.g., interacting with non-data-scientists) and translation (e.g., effective communication of results) [44] enables trust in the outcome of CTI. The remaining challenge is for the cybersecurity managers to regulate diverse experts to translate different forms of knowledge (ibid). In this regard, future research should focus on interpretational and narrative affordances of CTI outcomes focused on different cybersecurity management levels.

6 Conclusion

In this chapter, we provided an overview of the application of AI within CTI. Many organizations are integrating threat intelligence data into their cybersecurity management, and due to the extensiveness of the available data, a stream of research has proposed various AI techniques to help organizations sharpen their cybersecurity posture. The AI approaches in cybersecurity are often discussed as tools to protect and prevent cyber threats, while their application in cybersecurity management is less frequently discussed. Therefore, in this chapter, we took the recommendation from the NIST framework [39] to map AI-driven CTI into three different levels within the organization: strategic, operational, and tactical.

Our review showed that the solutions are either focused on one or two levels of cybersecurity activities. Future research could strive for approaches that help organizations translate opportunities in-between all levels of the organization. Moreover, the review showed that different solutions require AI-related knowledge that might be missing in the organization. Therefore, security analysts must be equipped with the necessary knowledge to operate with such systems and reflect on how automated CTI reports are helpful. Lastly, there is a danger that AI-facilitation in the CTI becomes counter-intuitive, meaning that organizations become over-reliant on such systems. The danger, however, is that organizational resources are spent finding a needle in the haystack, which neglects the cyber threat landscape.

References

1. Ahmad, A., Desouza, K.C., Maynard, S.B., Naseer, H., Baskerville, R.L.: How integration of cyber security management and incident response enables organizational learning. J. Assoc. Inf. Sci. Technol. **71**(8), 939–953 (2020). https://doi.org/10.1002/asi.24311
2. Agyepong, E., Cherdantseva, Y., Reinecke, P., Burnap, P.: Challenges and performance metrics for security operations center analysts: a systematic review. J. Cybersecur. Technol. **4**(3), 125–152 (2020)
3. Alves, F., Ferreira, P.M., Bessani, A.: Design of a classification model for a twitter-based streaming threat monitor. In: 2019 49th Annual IEEE/IFIP International Conference on Dependable Systems and Networks Workshops (DSN-W), pp. 9–14. IEEE, Portland (2019). https://doi.org/10.1109/DSN-W.2019.00010
4. Amthor, P., Fischer, D., Kühnhauser, W.E., Stelzer, D.: Automated cyber threat sensing and responding: integrating threat intelligence into security-policy-controlled systems. In: Proceedings of the 14th International Conference on Availability, Reliability and Security, pp. 1–10. ACM, Canterbury (2019). https://doi.org/10.1145/3339252.3340509
5. Armstrong, G.W., Lorch, A.C.: A(eye): a review of current applications of artificial intelligence and machine learning in ophthalmology. Int. Ophthalmol. Clin. **60**(1), 57–71 (2020). https://doi.org/10.1097/IIO.0000000000000298
6. Baskerville, R., Spagnoletti, P., Kim, J.: Incident-centered information security: managing a strategic balance between prevention and response. Inf. Manag. **51**(1), 138–151 (2014). https://doi.org/10.1016/j.im.2013.11.004
7. Bhatt, S., Manadhata, P.K., Zomlot, L.: The operational role of security information and event management systems. IEEE Secur. Priv. **12**(5), 35–41 (2014)
8. Bergström, E., Lundgren, M.: Stress amongst novice information security risk management practitioners. Int. J. Cyber Situat. Aware. **4**(1), 128–154 (2019)
9. Bergström, E., Lundgren, M., Ericson, Å.: Revisiting information security risk management challenges: a practice perspective. Inf. Comput. Secur. **x**(x), xx–xx (2019)
10. Bo, T., Chen, Y., Wang, C., Zhao, Y., Lam, K.Y., Chi, C.H., Tian, H.: Tom: a threat operating model for early warning of cyber security threats. In: International Conference on Advanced Data Mining and Applications, pp. 696–711. Springer, Cham (2019)
11. Conti, M., Dargahi, T., Dehghantanha, A.: Cyber threat intelligence: challenges and opportunities. In: Dehghantanha, A., Conti, M., Dargahi, T. (eds.) Cyber Threat Intelligence, vol. 70, pp. 1–6. Springer International Publishing, Cham (2018). https://doi.org/10.1007/978-3-319-73951-9_1
12. Cortex: How SOAR Is Transforming Threat Intelligence. Palo Alto Networks (2020)
13. CREST: What is cyber threat intelligence and how is it used? *CREST*, Level 2, The Porter Building, 1 Brunel Wy., Slough SL1 1FQ, United Kingdom (2019)
14. Deliu, I., Leichter, C., Franke, K.: Extracting cyber threat intelligence from hacker forums: support vector machines versus convolutional neural networks. In: 2017 IEEE International Conference on Big Data (Big Data), pp. 3648–3656. IEEE, Boston (2017). https://doi.org/10.1109/BigData.2017.8258359
15. Ebrahimi, M., Nunamaker Jr., J.F., Chen, H.: Semi-supervised cyber threat identification in dark net markets: a transductive and deep learning approach. J. Manag. Inf. Syst. **37**(3), 694–722 (2020)
16. Friedman, J., Bouchard, M.: Definitive Guide to Cyber Threat Intelligence: Using Knowledge About Adversaries to Win the War against Targeted Attacks. CyberEdge Group (2015)
17. Ghazi, Y., Anwar, Z., Mumtaz, R., Saleem, S., Tahir, A.: A supervised machine learning based approach for automatically extracting high-level threat intelligence from unstructured sources. In: 2018 International Conference on Frontiers of Information Technology (FIT), pp. 129–134. IEEE, Islamabad (2018). https://doi.org/10.1109/FIT.2018.00030
18. Gschwandtner, M., Demetz, L., Gander, M., Maier, R.: Integrating threat intelligence to enhance an organization's information security management. In: Proceedings of the 13th

International Conference on Availability, Reliability and Security, pp. 1–8. ACM, Hamburg (2018). https://doi.org/10.1145/3230833.3232797

19. Handelman, G.S., Kok, H.K., Chandra, R.V., Razavi, A.H., Huang, S., Brooks, M., Lee, M.J., Asadi, H.: Peering into the black box of artificial intelligence: evaluation metrics of machine learning methods. Am. J. Roentgenol. **212**(1), 38–43 (2019). https://doi.org/10.2214/AJR.18.20224

20. Hindy, H., Atkinson, R., Tachtatzis, C., Colin, J.-N., Bayne, E., Bellekens, X.: Utilising deep learning techniques for effective zero-day attack detection. Electronics. **9**, 1684 (2020). https://doi.org/10.3390/electronics9101684

21. ISO/IEC, 27000: ISO/IEC 27000: information technology — Security techniques — Information security management systems - Overview and vocabulary, *ISO* (2014)

22. ISO/IEC 27001: SS-EN ISO/IEC 27001:2017: information technology-security techniques - information security management systems – requirements, ISO, (2017)

23. Kadoguchi, M., Hayashi, S., Hashimoto, M., Otsuka, A.: Exploring the dark web for cyber threat intelligence using machine leaning. In: 2019 IEEE International Conference on Intelligence and Security Informatics (ISI), pp. 200–202. IEEE (2019). https://doi.org/10.1109/ISI.2019.8823360

24. Kadoguchi, M., Kobayashi, H., Hayashi, S., Otsuka, A., Hashimoto, M.: Deep self-supervised clustering of the dark web for cyber threat intelligence. Deep self-supervised clustering of the dark web for cyber threat intelligence. In: 2020 IEEE International Conference on Intelligence and Security Informatics (ISI), pp. 1–6. IEEE (2020). https://doi.org/10.1109/ISI49825.2020.9280485

25. Kim, D., Kim, H.K.: Automated dataset generation system for collaborative research of cyber threat analysis. Secur. Commun. Netw. **2019**, 1–10 (2019). https://doi.org/10.1155/2019/6268476

26. Kumar, V., Sinha, D.: A robust intelligent zero-day cyber-attack detection technique. Complex & Intelligent Systems. (2021). https://doi.org/10.1007/s40747-021-00396-9

27. Li, K., Wen, H., Li, H., Zhu, H., Sun, L.: Security OSIF: toward automatic discovery and analysis of event based cyber threat intelligence. In: 2018 IEEE SmartWorld, Ubiquitous Intelligence & Computing, Advanced & Trusted Computing, Scalable Computing & Communications, Cloud & Big Data Computing, Internet of People and Smart City Innovation (SmartWorld/SCALCOM/UIC/ATC/CBDCom/IOP/SCI), pp. 741–747. IEEE, Guangzhou (2018). https://doi.org/10.1109/SmartWorld.2018.00142

28. Lundgren, M.: Making the dead alive: dynamic routines in risk management (2020)

29. Lundgren, M., Bergström, E.: Dynamic interplay in the information security risk management process. Int. J. Risk Assess. Manage. **22**(2), 212 (2019a). https://doi.org/10.1504/IJRAM.2019.101287

30. Lundgren, M., Bergström, E.: Security-related stress: a perspective on information security risk management. In: 2019 International Conference on Cyber Security and Protection of Digital Services (Cyber Security). IEEE, Oxford (2019b)

31. McMillan, R.: Definition: threat intelligence. Retrieved August 13, 2021, from https://www.gartner.com/doc/2487216/definition-threat-intelligence (2013)

32. Marcus, G.: Deep learning: a critical appraisal. *arXiv preprint arXiv:1801.00631* (2018)

33. Mattern, T., Felker, J., Borum, R., Bamford, G.: Operational levels of cyber intelligence. Int. J. Intell. CounterIntell. **27**(4), 702–719 (2014). https://doi.org/10.1080/08850607.2014.924811

34. MITRE: CVE - CVE and NVD Relationship. December 11 (2020). https://cve.mitre.org/about/cve_and_nvd_relationship.html. Accessed 31 July 2021

35. Mittal, S., Das, P.K., Mulwad, V., Joshi, A., Finin, T.: CyberTwitter: using twitter to generate alerts for cybersecurity threats and vulnerabilities. In: 2016 IEEE/ACM International Conference on Advances in Social Networks Analysis and Mining (ASONAM), pp. 860–867. IEEE, San Francisco (2016). https://doi.org/10.1109/ASONAM.2016.7752338

36. Mittal, S., Joshi, A., Finin, T.: Cyber-all-Intel: An AI for security related threat intelligence. *ArXiv:1905.02895 [Cs]* (2019). http://arxiv.org/abs/1905.02895

37. Montasari, R., Carroll, F., Macdonald, S., Jahankhani, H., Hosseinian-Far, A., Daneshkhah, A.: Application of artificial intelligence and machine learning in producing actionable cyber threat intelligence. In: Montasari, R., Jahankhani, H., Hill, R., Parkinson, S. (eds.) Digital Forensic Investigation of Internet of Things (IoT) Devices, pp. 47–64. Springer International Publishing, Cham (2021). https://doi.org/10.1007/978-3-030-60425-7_3

38. Naseer, A., Naseer, H., Ahmad, A., Maynard, S.B., Masood Siddiqui, A.: Real-time analytics, incident response process agility and enterprise cybersecurity performance: a contingent resource-based analysis. Int. J. Inf. Manag. **59**, 102334 (2021). https://doi.org/10.1016/j.ijinfomgt.2021.102334

39. NIST SP 800-39: Managing Information Security Risk: Organization, Mission, and Information System View," No. NIST SP 800-39. National Institute of Standards and Technology, Gaithersburg, MD (2011). https://doi.org/10.6028/NIST.SP.800-39

40. Noor, U., Anwar, Z., Amjad, T., Choo, K.K.R.: A machine learning-based FinTech cyber threat attribution framework using high-level indicators of compromise. Futur. Gener. Comput. Syst. **96**, 227–242 (2019)

41. Nunes, E., Diab, A., Gunn, A., Marin, E., Mishra, V., Paliath, V., Robertson, J., Shakarian, J., Thart, A., Shakarian, P.: Darknet and Deepnet mining for proactive cybersecurity threat intelligence. In: 2016 IEEE Conference on Intelligence and Security Informatics (ISI), pp. 7–12. IEEE, Tucson (2016). https://doi.org/10.1109/ISI.2016.7745435

42. Osliak, O., Saracino, A., Martinelli, F., Dimitrakos, T.: Towards collaborative cyber threat intelligence for security management. In: Proceedings of the 7th International Conference on Information Systems Security and Privacy, pp. 339–346. Online Streaming, — Select a Country —: SCITEPRESS - Science and Technology Publications (2021). https://doi.org/10.5220/0010191403390346

43. Pace, C.: The threat intelligence handbook a practical guide for security teams to unlocking the power of intelligence (2018). Retrieved from https://go.recordedfuture.com/hubfs/ebooks/threat-intelligence-handbook.pdf

44. Passi, S., Jackson, S.J.: Trust in data science: collaboration, translation, and accountability in corporate data science projects. In: Proceedings of the ACM on Human-Computer Interaction, 2(CSCW), pp. 1–28 (2018)

45. Ponemon Institute: The Value of Threat Intelligence: Annual Study of North American & United Kingdom Companies. Ponemon Institute LLC (2019)

46. Riesco, R., Villagrá, V.A.: Leveraging cyber threat intelligence for a dynamic risk framework: automation by using a semantic reasoner and a new combination of standards (STIX™, SWRL and OWL). Int. J. Inf. Secur. **18**(6), 715–739 (2019). https://doi.org/10.1007/s10207-019-00433-2

47. Sahrom Abu, M., Rahayu Selamat, S., Ariffin, A., Yusof, R.: Cyber threat intelligence – issue and challenges. Indones. J. Electr. Eng. Comput. Sci. **10**(1), 371 (2018). https://doi.org/10.11591/ijeecs.v10.i1.pp371-379

48. Sameera, N., Shashi, M.: Deep transductive transfer learning framework for zero-day attack detection. ICT Express. **6**(4), 361–367 (2020). https://doi.org/10.1016/j.icte.2020.03.003

49. Samtani, S., Abate, M., Benjamin, V., Li, W.: Cybersecurity as an industry: a cyber threat intelligence perspective. In: Holt, T.J., Bossler, A.M. (eds.) The Palgrave Handbook of International Cybercrime and Cyberdeviance, pp. 135–154. Springer International Publishing, Cham (2020). https://doi.org/10.1007/978-3-319-78440-3_8

50. Sanguino, L.A.B., Uetz, R.: Software vulnerability analysis using CPE and CVE. *ArXiv:1705.05347 [Cs]*. http://arxiv.org/abs/1705.05347 (2017)

51. Sari, A.: Turkish national cyber-firewall to mitigate countrywide cyber-attacks. Comput. Electr. Eng. **73**, 128–144 (2019)

52. Sauerwein, C., Sillaber, C., Mussmann, A., Breu, R.: Threat intelligence sharing platforms: an exploratory study of software vendors and research perspectives. *Wirtschaftsinformatik Und Angewandte Informatik* (2017)

53. Schäfer, M., Fuchs, M., Strohmeier, M., Engel, M., Liechti, M., Lenders, V.: BlackWidow: monitoring the dark web for cyber security information. In: 2019 11th International Conference on Cyber Conflict (CyCon), vol. 900, pp. 1–21. IEEE (2019)

54. Shackleford, D.: Who's Using Cyberthreat Intelligence and How? SANS Institute (2015)
55. Sun, T., Yang, P., Li, M., Liao, S.: An automatic generation approach of the cyber threat intelligence records based on multi-source information fusion. Future Internet. **13**(2), 40 (2021). https://doi.org/10.3390/fi13020040
56. Voutilainen, J., Kari, M.: Strategic cyber threat intelligence: building the situational picture with emerging technologies. In: Proceedings of the 19th European Conference on Cyber Warfare. Presented at the The 19th European Conference on Cyber Warfare. ACPI (2020). https://doi.org/10.34190/EWS.20.030
57. Wagner, T.D., Mahbub, K., Palomar, E., Abdallah, A.E.: Cyber threat intelligence sharing: survey and research directions. Comput. Secur. **87**, 101589 (2019). https://doi.org/10.1016/j.cose.2019.101589
58. Webster, J., Watson, R.T.: Analyzing the past to prepare for the future: writing a literature review. MIS Q. **26**(2), 13–23 (2002)
59. Whitman, M.E., Mattord, H.J.: Management of Information Security, Fourth edn. Cengage Learning, Stamford (2014)
60. Zhong, C., Yen, J., Liu, P., Erbacher, R.F.: Learning from experts' experience: toward automated cyber security data triage. IEEE Syst. J. **13**(1), 603–614 (2018)

Model Based Resilience Engineering for Design and Assessment of Mission Critical Systems Containing Artificial Intelligence Components

Douglas L. Van Bossuyt, Nikolaos Papakonstantinou, Britta Hale, Jarno Salonen, and Bryan O'Halloran

1 Introduction

The rapidly evolving field of cyber-physical systems where Artificial Intelligence (AI) components are integrated into physical systems is presenting new challenges to the resilience of systems to a variety of threats. Systems that perform mission-critical tasks such as controlling cooling water for nuclear power plants, operating jet engines on airliners, collecting intelligence, surveillance, and reconnaissance (ISR) data on adversary activity, operating safety and protection devices on the power grid, discerning friend from foe on air defence systems, operating radiation therapy machines, and many others are vulnerable to attack not only from the physical side but also from the embedded cyber components containing AI. Threats can come from malicious insiders, the supply chain, compromised personnel, external hacks, etc. during the design and manufacturing process, and also during operations, maintenance and retrofits—in other words, throughout the system life cycle. Traditional physical threats such as intentionally designing a mechanical component to prematurely fail or introducing counterfeit parts in a supply chain are well understood.

AI is probably most familiar to us through search engines where it is used for generating responses to queries. The term "artificial intelligence" was first introduced as an academic discipline in 1956 at a conference in Dartmouth [23] and even though it first seemed to gain interest only in programming related to checkers strategies in the 1960s and other similar topics [24, 25], it eventually

D. L. Van Bossuyt (✉) · B. Hale · B. O'Halloran
Naval Postgraduate School, Monterey, CA, USA
e-mail: douglas.vanbossuyt@nps.edu; britta.hale@nps.edu; bmohallo@nps.edu

N. Papakonstantinou · J. Salonen
VTT Technical Research Centre of Finland, Espoo, Finland
e-mail: nikolaos.papakonstantinou@vtt.fi; jarno.salonen@vtt.fi

© The Author(s), under exclusive license to Springer Nature Switzerland AG 2023
T. Sipola et al. (eds.), *Artificial Intelligence and Cybersecurity*,
https://doi.org/10.1007/978-3-031-15030-2_3

gained the interest of the US Department of Defense (DoD) that invested in the technology [4] and slowly machine learning and artificial intelligence evolved into a viable technology for problem solving and many other things. At the moment, AI has already gained a strong foothold in large industrial sectors such as healthcare and automotive, and a similar invasion is also being seen in the manufacturing sector such as Robotic Process Automation (RPA) and other automation companies. According to MarketsandMarkets, the artificial intelligence market size is valued at USD $58.3B in 2021 and it is estimated to expand at an annual growth rate of almost 40% until 2026 with data-based AI, deep learning and the need to achieve robotic autonomy are expected to lead the path [15].

There are not many publicly known cyber attacks against AI, but the increasing use of the technology in both industry and society will most likely showcase them in the near future. The apparent first known AI attack was the Lockheed Martin RQ-170 Sentinel crash landing in Iran in 2011. It was claimed to be the result of Global Positioning System (GPS) spoofing, which fooled the onboard AI into descending the drone into enemy territory [26, 22]. Yamin et al. [33] discuss about the weaponization of AI in cyberspace, listing two other examples such as the Microsoft bot "Tay" which was fed malicious data in March 2016, causing it to exhibit sexist and racial tendencies, and social media manipulation during the 2016 US Election. Even though these latter cases differ from the first one by the attacks not focusing on AI specifically in mission critical systems, the objective is still somewhat the same: using the weaknesses in AI to achieve the ultimate objective of the cyber attack. Based on the previous examples, we can estimate that the cyber attack potential against AI in mission critical systems is definitely increasing, but the nature of future attacks will depend on the level of AI adoption within the systems as well as their vulnerabilities, but also countermeasure and mitigation capabilities. Since this aforementioned information is still quite unknown, forecasting the potential based on real attacks is difficult.

Recent publicized attacks and proof of concepts such as the TBONE zero-click exploit of several Tesla models that likely could be employed on any device using ConnMan in embedded systems to takeover said systems [13] illustrate the potential for attacks during operation. Supply chain attacks pose a similar threat to a whole host of industries. Recent attacks via third party software vendors have impacted wide swaths of industry [7]. Indeed, the entire digital tool chain across many industries can be at risk of many types of cyber attacks [1]. As a result of the myriad of types, times, and places in a system's design life cycle where it can be attacked either externally or from within, it is vitally important that systems be designed, manufactured, and operated to improve resilience to said threats.

Special focus is put on emerging threats to AI components, including data poisoning, trojans and backdoors, model interference attacks, hijacking, and others. The potential impact of such vulnerabilities triggers the need for new resilience assessment and design methodologies that are able to protect the systems in a holistic way and even when the vulnerabilities are not known during design.

This chapter presents a method to improve the resilience of mission-critical cyber-physical systems that contain AI components to threats and attacks throughout the system life cycle. A Model-Based Systems Engineering (MBSE)-driven approach is developed to identify vulnerabilities in a system throughout its life cycle to allow for resilience measures such as redundancy and diversity to be implemented. The method is demonstrated on a case study of a heterogeneous System of Systems (SoS) Unmanned System (UxS) fleet of Unmanned Aerial Systems (UASs) and Unmanned Surface Vessels (USVs) conducting patrol of a littoral zone performing a national security mission.

In addition to cyber-physical systems that contain AI components, the proposed method can be applicable to complex systems in general. The proposed methodology can handle black box components, subsystems, and etc. including AI-based components. We believe the proposed method is needed and is directly applicable to systems containing significant AI components because there currently does not exist a unified assessment tool that bridges between AI and physical hardware. Most existing assessment methods focus on specific components (i.e.: only AI, only mechanical components, only electro-mechanical components, etc.) and are challenging to integrate together into a unified analysis.

Many highly complex systems that have mission critical functions (i.e.: nuclear reactors, defense systems, flood control dams, etc.) contain black box components and subsystems that systems engineers in charge of the systems may not be able to see into. This, for instance, is common in defense systems where subcontractors provide proprietary subsystems built to interface control diagrams and other specifications but with explicit clauses in contracting language to prohibit sharing details of the inner workings of the subsystems. The systems engineers must trust the subcontractor that everything inside the black box works as intended and without unintended consequences. Such a black box can be and almost always is rigorously tested via the inputs/outputs before system integration occurs. However, that is often the extent of testing outside of what the subcontractor performs. This is very similar to AI in the sense that much of AI being deployed today is not readily explainable (e.g.: complex neural networks, deep networks). An AI is built, and then the systems engineers must trust the AI developer that the AI is applicable to the system and situations, etc.

Thus we believe it is important to have a method such as the one we present here to be able to analyze an entire complex system, especially including the AI components, in an integrated manner.

2   Defining the Threat

System security is based on a triad balance: adversarial capabilities, adversarial goals, and security goals. In defining this triad, we follow a similar set of design principles as [5]. A further basis for this taxonomy can be found in [17, 12]. Inside the zero trust environment, where any component or entity could be malicious or corrupted, defining adversarial capabilities and goals becomes particularly challenging—especially with the inclusion of AI where the AI component is based on external data and training as is therefore reliant on several layers of protection. Yet these adversarial capabilities and goals must be juxtaposed against the security requirements in order to determine whether or not a system is *secure*. Namely, security is defined in the context of requirements and adversarial capabilities vs. as a stand-alone assessment. With the continuing development of AI use and associated adversarial attack vectors, it is essential to continually develop out the security requirements and system assessment accordingly.

2.1 Security Modeling Considerations

In this section we consider each aspect of the triad in the context of AI and provide example considerations to factor into system modeling. There are further aspects of security modeling that are separate from the AI considerations and will appear in the case study including e.g. kinetic actions against a device (an adversarial ability) with an intent to destroy it (an adversarial goal).

2.1.1 Adversarial Capabilities

Adversarial capabilities cover the range of actions that an adversary may perform, including how it may interact with the system. This includes access to training data, e.g. with a malicious insider, allowing the adversary to perform data poisoning attacks. Through partial access or ability to contribute to the training data, an adversary may also be able to produce AI trojans [14]. If a model is updated through renewed training, an adversary may also be able to affect training inputs, e.g. simply by providing data collection samples that are disturbed or modified [32]. For example, if a UAS collects image data over a region that is later used to update the AI model, an adversary has the ability to simply place objects on the ground or in the air that will disturb the later training and AI accuracy, e.g. through objects that appear similar to humans, UASs, or underwater abnormalities. Notably, AI model accuracy and actionability is also contingent on the security of the Command and Control (C2) communication link. Adversaries that can compromise the channel between e.g. a UAS and controller can trivially modify an AI model's reported observance. This capability greatly enhances an adversary's effectiveness under the following adversarial goals.

2.1.2 Adversarial Goals

Classic AI testing methods assess whether or not a model does what it is intended to do, i.e. they assess a model against positive expected behavior. What is not regularly assessed is negative, unexpected behavior; indeed, an outcome that is unexpected is by definition difficult to plan for. This leads to many potential adversarial goals, including ways to circumvent training, abuse the model, or cause the model to be misinterpreted.

A notable adversarial goal against AI is information misclassification. If data is misclassified or is classified with a low confidence score [3], an operator may not correctly act on the intelligence provided or even be unaware of it entirely. For example, a successful attack against the AI of an ISR UAS could result in the operator being unaware of the adversary's presence or action in a region. Data poisoning [9, 32] and trojans both support this adversarial goal. AI evasion techniques that do not require access to the training data set can also support this adversarial goal, e.g. through irregular objects adversarially placed on the ground that are collected in ISR imagery and fed back into the Machine Learning (ML) training update set.

Destruction of a device or its usability is another adversarial goal. Although this appears kinetic, these goals could potentially be realized through attacks on the AI model. For example, if a UAS determines location or elevation through application of AI, or makes AI-influenced gyroscopic assessments, then device destruction could be realized through attacks on the AI classification and/or confidence level.

2.1.3 Security Goals

Security goals are dependent on the use case. Putting a generalized "secure" solution into practice can lead to unexpected vulnerabilities and security failures if not tailored to the specific goals of the system. For example, suppose that a control component on a UAS uses AI to detect significant gyroscopic aberrations and, if detected, signals the UAS to land immediately. In the case of a hobbyist UAS, this may be an excellent system response that places a potentially malfunctioning device within the control of the operator on the ground below and thereby potentially preventing more significant damage from a UAS crash. However, for a military operational case, such a response would be a vulnerability, as it could place the UAS in control of adversaries on the ground while the operator is remote.

Consequently, security goals are highlighted here as part of the triad of security considerations, but the discussion of these goals is placed within the context of the use-case scenario. This action is underscored as critical to the assessment of any system—the security of the system cannot be considered orthogonally to the intended use.

Particular security goals for AI may include data protection from adversarial tainting; secure channels resistant to manipulation for transmission of data, AI decisions and confidence levels, and operator instructions based on the same; AI model robustness to adversarial inputs (or accidentally sub-optimal inputs) in the original data training set; AI model robustness to malicious environment data input for re-training; and AI sensitivity to valid outliers. The last point is a necessary security goal due to potential bias in a model that is normalized against outlier inputs. While such models may work well on "normal" inputs, their lack of sensitivity to valid irregularities opens the door for malicious exploitation as the model is not adaptable to the full range of valid inputs.

2.2 Adversarial Destabilization of Military AI Systems

Naturally, adversarial interest in military and national security systems is anticipated, both from strategic near-peer competitors and from more minor actors looking to bypass standard protections (such as with smuggling). As high-value targets, attacks on AI that may seem otherwise unlikely in day-to-day applications become viable against military systems. There is financial backing among state actors for the time investment needed to prepare for and realize such attacks. Thus, while clear cases of at-scale data poisoning or trojan development are not readily apparent among e.g. industry marketing uses of AI, it should not be considered outside the realm of possibility—and even probability—that such attacks are currently under development or deployment.

Not only are attacks against AI in military systems likely, the effects of such attacks can be severe. These effects cross pollinate over national security, weapons systems, and human protection. For this it is essential to recognize not only first order effects, but also second and third order.

The differentiation between human-based and AI-based systems is notable. Under a non AI-based system, system redundancies and often human intervention is used, creating defense-in-depth. In contrast AI, by design, replaces some of the decision making steps of the system via "educated guesses" signified by a confidence level associated with each AI decision. Both the human and AI decision making processes are fallible, but with personal familiarity it is often relatively clear what types of mistakes a given individual is susceptible to. It is not always clear what mistakes the AI is susceptible to. Some efforts are addressing this through a research vector known as Explainable AI [8]; however, much work and field development is required before such analysis is scalable for use in the military systems already employing AI.

2.3 Model Driven Engineering for Safety and Security

Model Driven Engineering (MDE) or MBSE is an established paradigm for engineering complex systems [29] that has been extended in the Industry 4.0 "revolution" [6] towards the concept of digital twin [30, 2]. The basic idea is that models are generated and updated during the life cycle of the system (specification, design, testing, operation, maintenance, decommission, etc.) to answer engineering questions and document the system. These models can describe different aspects of the environment or the system itself. The models can have various levels of detail, from first principles to high level dependency models, and can aim to capture topology, behavior, communication and other perspectives [21]. Different notations and modelling languages are used for different domains and applications. Metamodels contain the domain specific concepts that can be used to create customized models for that domain. The Unified Modeling Language (UML) is a generic but highly customizable modelling language that can be used for high level system modelling [18]. UML uses profiles as a metamodelling mechanism, i.e. as a way to ease the creation of domain specific models. Systems Modeling Language (SysML) is a UML profile for more detailed system engineering models [28]. MBSE has been used for risk assessment in safety [10] and security applications [16].

3 A Model Driven Methodology for Resilience

The methodology presented in this section is a refinement of past work [11, 19] and our focus in this research is to explain and demonstrate its application to a case study of a complex System of Systems with multiple AI-based components in key data acquisition and decision making roles. The basic overview of the methodology and supporting modelling techniques are presented in this section for readability and completeness reasons.

The objective of this methodology is the systematic assessment and design for resilience, covering static configuration/topology/architecture as well as dynamic procedures (see Fig. 1). The method combines traditional Probabilistic Risk Assessment (PRA) techniques (aiming to minimize risk of undesirable outcomes), Defence in Depth principles like redundancy and diversity as well as Zero Trust principles (no human or machine is completely trusted at any given time). The final goal is

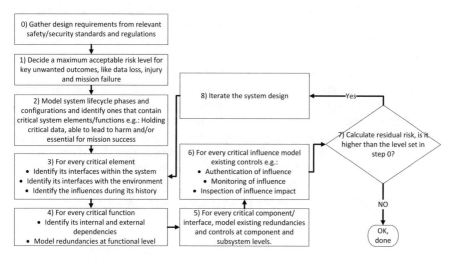

Fig. 1 An overview of the workflow of the proposed methodology

to ensure that no event, reliability or security related, can lead to an undesirable outcome (e.g. injury, mission failure, information leak). This is an extension and refinement of previous work [11, 20].

At a high level the methodology calls for proper preparation before the design even starts, by using the relevant standards and regulations to establish the basic set or safety and security requirements (Step 0). The stakeholders (depending on the domain) need to define the possible unwanted scenarios relevant to the system and then the maximum risk levels (Step 1). Defining these resilience targets helps to allocate engineering/material/financial resources.

The next phase of the methodology calls for system modelling and more specifically dependency models for the different life cycle phases where undesirable outcomes can happen (e.g. mission execution) (Step 2). The functional model of the system as well as a basic component model should be developed and the critical functions and components should be identified. These are functions/components that are directly linked to the undesirable outcomes (e.g. components that can actively cause harm or contain sensitive data, functions essential for mission success). Additional models capturing past influences on critical components help to identify resilience weaknesses during historical operation or due to the supply chain (Step 3). Redundancy and controls needs to be deployed for critical functions (Step 4) and critical components (Step 5). Controls need to be added for the influences on the critical components (Step 6).

After the initial high level design is completed, a risk assessment step (Step 7) calculates the residual risk for each of the undesirable outcomes and compares it to the maximum set in Step 1. If the residual risk levels are lower than the acceptance thresholds, the method ends. If the remaining risk is higher, then more redundancies and controls need to be added, depending on the results of the risk assessment (Step 8).

In comparison to traditional approaches like PRA, the proposed methodology doesn't rely on a knowledge base of root causes, but on establishing mitigation measures and resilient architecture regardless the basic events (failure modes or specific attacks). This approach complements the traditional resilience assessment approaches and it is motivated by the fact that AI-based components are too new and diverse to establish a usable enumeration of their vulnerabilities and failure modes. In a similar way, heavily software-based components, black box components and humans in the system can be untrustworthy and not verifiable. So, the question "How a system component can get compromised?" should be handled separately from the question "if this system component is compromised (for whatever reason), what happens next?" Additionally the proposed methodology supports a holistic approach and highlights risks emerging from the supply chain, humans indirectly affecting components as well as humans who get compromised.

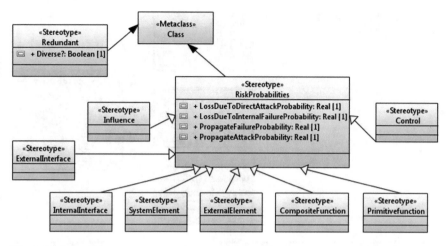

Fig. 2 UML Profile

3.1 A Metamodel for Basic Resilience Modelling

A "metamodel" can be described as a collection of domain specific concepts that allow modelling for specific purposes (e.g. to answer specific engineering design questions). UML uses "Profile" diagrams to capture such metamodels, the profiles contain "Stereotypes" linked to the special concepts to support the simple resilience models needed to apply the proposed methodology. These profiles can then be applied to generic UML diagram types for the creation of custom models.

A UML profile was designed to support the modelling needed for the application of the proposed methodology (see Fig. 2). The stereotypes of this profile extend the UML Class element of class diagram models and define the concepts of internal/external system elements, internal/external interfaces, functions (with hierarchy), past influences, and controls. It also includes the properties needed to hold risk probabilities as well as sterotypes allowing the definition of a system element/function/interface as "redundant" and "diverse".

This profile is expected to be extended/modified to cover the resilience concepts of different domains. When the profile is ready, then it is straight forward to create UML models with the domain specific concepts.

3.2 Simple Example

The modelling aspect of proposed resilience methodology can be demonstrated over a small generic example.

We can assume that during the operation phase there is risk of causing harm, thus we investigate further the system in that configuration. The functional model is

Fig. 3 Functional model of
the simple example

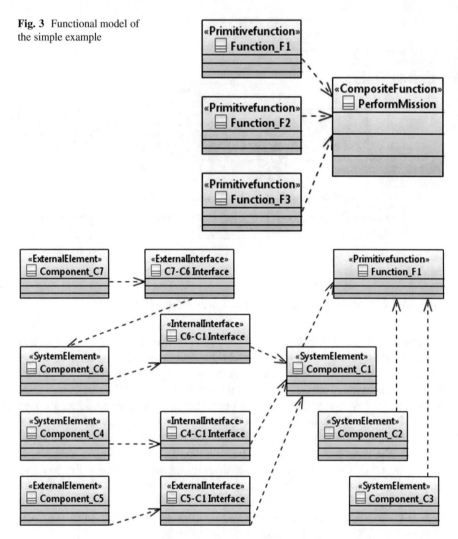

Fig. 4 Simple components model for Function F1 of the example generic system

presented in Fig. 3. The top level function is the basic system purpose, to perform
its mission, and it breaks down to three lower level functions—Functions F1-3.

If we assume that Function F1 is interesting, because it is related to potential risk,
we can continue to create a component model with the system elements relevant to
that function, as shown in Fig. 4. This is a dependency model with the internal and
external interfaces of the system elements.

If the component, Component C1, is identified as a critical component (can
cause harm, in our case) the modelling can go deeper into the past influences
on the Component C1 as shown in Fig. 5. There we can model who has access

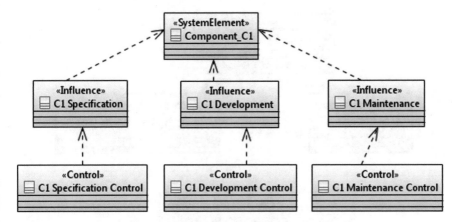

Fig. 5 Example model of past influences on the critical component C1

to this component during its design, development, manufacturing, supply chain, assembly, testing, deployment, maintenance, decommission, etc. and also include any deployed controls in place to secure these influences (supervision, team work, quality control, independent inspections, etc.). In this simple example we model the influences during specification, development and maintenance with relevant supervision.

Redundancy and diversity can be modelled as in Fig. 6. Redundant elements are ideally also diverse (they do not use the same technology/vendors or are not affected by the same influences). The redundancy can be at a functional level (a whole function is replicated and is available to take over if needed) or at a component/interface level. Controls are added to determine when to reroute the process flow from the original function/component/interface to the redundant one.

4 Case Study

We now introduce a case study to demonstrate the methodology, as well as modeling used.

4.1 Case Study Definition

Let us consider a heterogeneous SoS comprised of UASs and USVs that is tasked with performing both routine and ad-hoc freedom of navigation exercises in a busy littoral zone comprised of a continental coastline and many outlying islands as part of a broader national security mission performed by allied naval forces. The

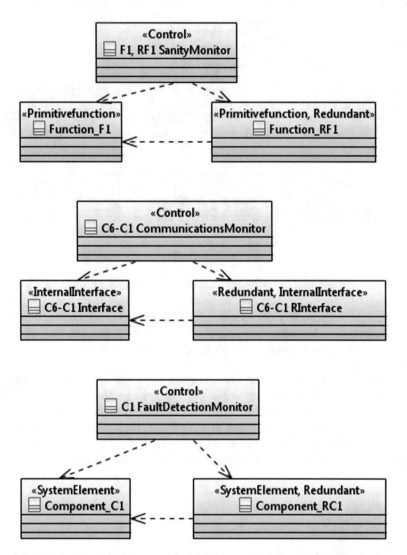

Fig. 6 Example model of functional, interface, and component redundancies

UASs and USVs work in concert to detect, identify, track, report on, and potentially target and engage or defend against aggression by adversaries including belligerent countries, syndicates, private militias, and break-away provinces of surrounding countries. The adversaries attempt to restrict lawful freedom of movement of ships and aircraft through the area for a variety of complex reasons. Restriction of movement can range from blocking shipping channels so that vessels cannot pass to hijacking of vessels to interdicting aircraft and forcing landings at adversary-controlled airports to sinking of ships and shoot-downs of planes. Adversary attacks can range from small fast Inshore Attack Crafts (FIACs) equipped with nets and

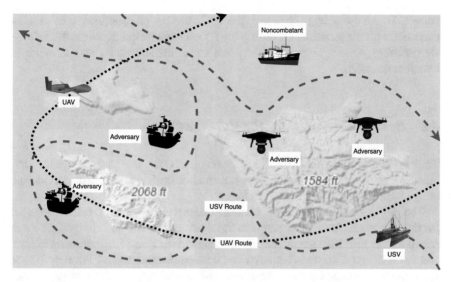

Fig. 7 Concept of operations. UxS conducting patrols are shown moving through contested areas with adversaries present

spear guns to major warships and fighter aircraft equipped with sophisticated electronic countermeasures and offensive capabilities, and even UxSs with offensive capabilities both in the physical and the cyber domains. In the case of the syndicates and state actors, it is possible that penetration/compromise of some portions of the design, manufacturing, and supply chain may have occurred where engineers, technicians, logistics workers, and others may be compromised or acting in the interest of the syndicates or state actors. A concept of operations of the case study is presented in Fig. 7.

The UASs are a standardized fixed-wing design that is able to loiter for several days between landing and resupply. The USVs are a standardized mono-hull vessel that has multi-day endurance between resupply. Both UxSs contain on-board AI components that can autonomously operate, navigate, communicate, and make tactical decisions based upon available on-board sensor data and data being fed to the UxSs from other nearby UxS, a command center, nearby naval vessels, etc. The UxSs can be configured with a variety of mission packs such as ISR, defensive systems, weapons systems, and etc. The AI components aboard the UxS are a mix of pre-trained and federated learning AI.

Both UxS platforms are designed and assembled by major defense contractors. Manufacture and design of many subsystems are performed by subcontractors. Some subcontractors produce multiple subsystems within one UxS platform and/or across both UxS platforms. The UxS platforms are interoperable via the C2 function that is embedded in the navigation, communications, and autopilot subsystems. Each UxS serves as a node in a communications mesh network to ensure that C2 functionality is preserved back to the command center and/or nearby naval vessels. In the event that C2 is lost, the UxSs are pre-programmed with mission parameters for the particular sortie they are undertaking including automatic defense subsystem responses, way-point navigation and collision avoidance, and return to base functionality.

4.2 Resilience Models for the Case Study

The methodology asks for establishing the required safety and security specification based on standards, regulations, or contractual obligations. This will provide the design basis for the system under study.

The risks of interest should be identified next and maximum thresholds are set for the risk levels. This corresponds to the threat model and security goals. In this case the risks identified are the risk for causing unintentional harm, mission failure, and the risk that a drone is captured and data and/or Intellectual Property (IP) is compromised. The maximum acceptable risk probability is an arbitrary number decided by the stakeholders, e.g. 1 incident of causing unintended harm every 10k operation days.

The life cycle phases in which the risk can manifest are identified next. In this case we use the mission operation phase as an example. Then the system is modelled as configured in this life cycle phase. Functions of the SoS (including the UASs and USVs), whose loss due to fault or attack at least affects mission success are (see Fig. 8):

1. Structure, armor, and buoyancy: loss can also cause other vulnerabilities to the UASs/USVs leading to possible information/IP leak (e.g. the drones are disabled and captured).
2. Propulsion and power: loss can also cause other vulnerabilities to the UASs/USVs leading to possible information/IP leak (e.g. the drones are disabled and captured).
3. Navigation: failure can mislead the drones to enter prohibited zones which can cause provocation and/or the drones being captured causing information/IP leak. This function contains AI components.

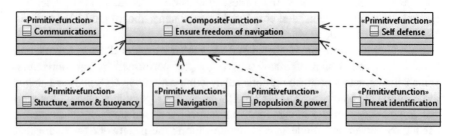

Fig. 8 Partial functional model for the case study

4. Threat identification: Loss can lead to causing unintended harm as well as provocation. This function has AI-based components.
5. Self defense: Loss can lead to causing unintended harm as well as provocation. This function has AI-based components.
6. Communications: Loss can cause hijacking of the UxSs and if an adversarial remote operator takes control of the drones, the is risk of harming civilians, provocation, disabling the drones leading to information/IP leak.

The functional model gives a good overview of the system under study and helps to identify which functions are the most critical for the risks of interest. These functions are mapped to the components implementing them. In this example, Fig. 9 shows the system elements related to the Threat Identification function. This function is implemented both by USVs and the UASs of the SoS. This model includes the internal/external system elements/interfaces and the dependency to the environment related to the USVs.

The component model helps to identify critical components whose past influences need to be studied further. In this example the "Object recognition AI" and the "Threat identification AI" are elements of special interest since they contain AI data processing and decision functionality that is vulnerable to adversarial AI attacks (during operation as well as during development/training). In Fig. 10 there are example influences to these system elements during design and testing. This is a simple model; in real systems there are teams of engineers and other stakeholders involved in the specification/design/development/testing/operation/maintenance of these subsystems. Thus, the model of the influences is much more complicated.

A PRA method [27, 31] can be applied to get a early estimation of the residual risk present in the system if basic risk probabilities can be estimated. If this risk is higher that the maximum levels set for the system, there needs to be an iteration to the design. Additional supervision and controls can be added to the influences acting upon the key system elements (see Fig. 10) and redundancies can be added.

A simple and partial model of the redundancies for this case study is shown in Fig. 11. the redundancies can be at functional level (e.g. there can be a redundant function for threat identification, physically separated from the main function), at an interface level, and at a component level. Ideally the redundant functions/interfaces/components are diverse, i.e. they are based on different technology solutions, from different vendors and influenced by different people.

5   Conclusion and Discussion

This chapter focused on the security and safety challenges emerging from the presence of AI and black box components in safety critical systems. These components often implement key functions of the system like data processing and decision making, and thus contribute to the risks related to the operation of the system like

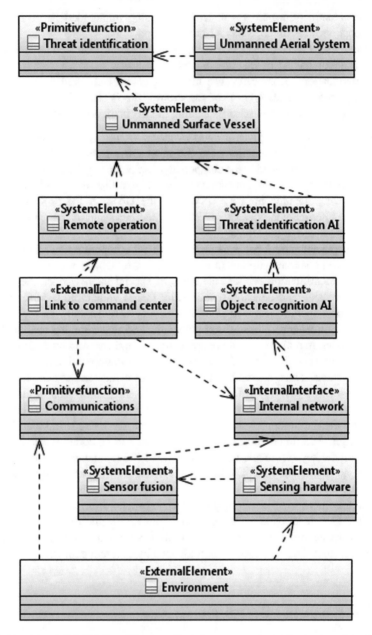

Fig. 9 Zero-Trust USV CM Class Diagram—Partial component model for the threat identification function

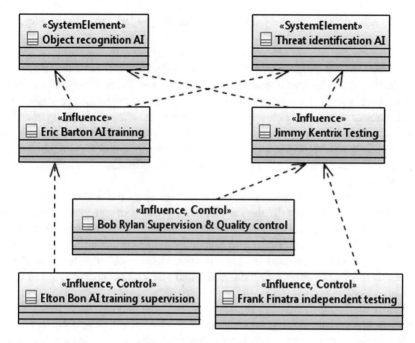

Fig. 10 Partial model of the past influences on the Object recognition AI and Threat identification AI system elements of the USVs

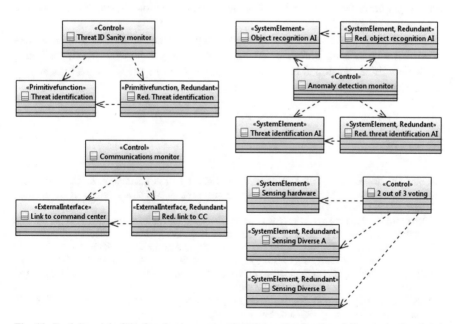

Fig. 11 Partial model of the function/component/interface redundancies of the case study related to the threat identification function

injuries, mission failure, compromised intellectual property and information, and etc.

The approach taken in the proposed methodology was to not focus on specific vulnerabilities and propose specific controls/mitigation technologies, but rather assume that every system element (artificial or human) can be a potential threat and the goal is to design a system architecture so that no single system element can lead to unacceptable risk. This approach is common in safety engineering of critical systems, like nuclear power plants. The proposed methodology complements the design basis based on the particular standards and regulations of the domain and can be one more tool alongside other domain specific established design and assessment methodologies.

The proof of concept application of the methodology presented in this chapter can be modified to adapt to the development process of specific projects. The information needed to compile the resilience models (functional representation of the system, connection with system components, interface modelling, supply chain and development process modelling) can be often found (unfortunately many times scattered) in existing engineering databases and various data sources related to the system.

Ideally resilience assessment should be an essential part of system development for all design phases and the application of the assessment would be build-in to computer aided engineering tools. Knowledge bases can also support the designer to identify solutions to architecture design challenges based on past designs and other common engineering topologies addressing specific issues. The designer should be able to get early feedback and implement corrective actions during design and not after major milestones.

Overall it is expected that due to the dynamic nature of the vulnerabilities of systems containing software, AI and black box components, more resilience methods will be developed to cover the cyber aspect of systems as well the supply chain aspect.

References

1. Basu, K., Saeed, S.M., Pilato, C., Ashraf, M., Nabeel, M.T., Chakrabarty, K., Karri, R.: Cadbase: An attack vector into the electronics supply chain. ACM Trans. Design Autom. Electron Syst. **24**(4), 1–30 (2019)
2. Bickford, J., Van Bossuyt, D.L., Beery, P., Pollman, A.: Operationalizing digital twins through model-based systems engineering methods. Syst. Eng. **23**(6), 724–750 (2020)
3. Brown, T.B., Mané, D., Roy, A., Abadi, M., Gilmer, J.: Adversarial patch (2018)
4. Buchanan, B.G.: A (very) brief history of artificial intelligence. Ai Mag. **26**(4), 53–53 (2005)
5. Datta, A., Franklin, J., Garg, D., Jia, L., Kaynar, D.K.: On adversary models and compositional security. IEEE Secur. Privacy **9**, 26–32 (2011)
6. Davies, R.: Industry 4.0: Digitalisation for productivity and growth. Briefing PE 568.337, European Parliamentary Research Service (2015)
7. Fingas, J.: Hackers conduct one of the largest supply chain cyberattacks to date: a breach at Kaseya has affected over 200 companies. Engadget (2021). https://www.engadget.com/kaseya-ransomware-cyberattack-155719139.html

8. Goebel, R., Chander, A., Holzinger, K., Lecue, F., Akata, Z., Stumpf, S., Kieseberg, P., Holzinger, A.: Explainable ai: the new 42? In: International Cross-Domain Conference for Machine Learning and Knowledge Extraction, pp. 295–303. Springer, Berlin (2018)
9. Goodfellow, I., Shlens, J., Szegedy, C.: Explaining and harnessing adversarial examples (2015). CoRR abs/1412.6572
10. Gran, B.A., Fredriksen, R., Thunem, A.P.J.: An approach for model-based risk assessment. In: International Conference on Computer Safety, Reliability, and Security, pp. 311–324. Springer, Berlin (2004)
11. Hale, B., Van Bossuyt, D.L., Papakonstantinou, N., O'Halloran, B.: A zero-trust methodology for security of complex systems with machine learning components. In: International Design Engineering Technical Conferences and Computers and Information in Engineering Conference. American Society of Mechanical Engineers (2021)
12. Kavak, H., Padilla, J.J., Vernon-Bido, D., Diallo, S.Y., Gore, R., Shetty, S.: Simulation for cybersecurity: state of the art and future directions. J. Cybersecur. **7**, tyab005 (2021)
13. Kovacs, E.: Tesla car hacked remotely from drone via zero-click exploit. Security Week (2020). https://www.securityweek.com/tesla-car-hacked-remotely-drone-zero-click-exploit
14. Liu, Y., Mondal, A., Chakraborty, A., Zuzak, M., Jacobsen, N., Xing, D., Srivastava, A.: A survey on neural trojans. In: 2020 21st International Symposium on Quality Electronic Design (ISQED), pp. 33–39 (2020)
15. MarketsandMarkets Research Staff: Artificial intelligence market by offering (hardware, software, services), technology (machine learning, natural language processing), deployment mode, organization size, business function (law, security), vertical, and region—global forecast to 2026. Tech. rep., MarketsandMarkets (2021). https://www.marketsandmarkets.com/Market-Reports/artificial-intelligence-market-74851580.html
16. Mili, S., Nguyen, N., Chelouah, R.: Model-driven architecture based security analysis. Systems Engineering (2021)
17. Myagmar, S., Lee, A.J., Yurcik, W.: Threat modeling as a basis for security requirements. In: Symposium on Requirements Engineering for Information Security (SREIS) (2005). http://d-scholarship.pitt.edu/16516/
18. Object Management Group Inc.: Welcome to UML Web Site! Accessed 12 Aug 2021. https://www.uml.org/
19. Papakonstantinou, N., Hale, B., Linnosmaa, J., Salonen, J., Van Bossuyt, D.L.: Model driven engineering for resilience of systems with black box and ai-based components. In: Annual Reliability and Maintainability Symposium (RAMS). IEEE, Piscataway (2022)
20. Papakonstantinou, N., Van Bossuyt, D.L., Linnosmaa, J., Hale, B., O'Halloran, B.: A zero trust hybrid security and safety risk analysis method. J. Comput. Inform. Sci. Eng. **21**(5), 050907 (2021)
21. Pidd, M.: Systems Modelling: Theory and Practice. Wiley, New York (2004)
22. Ruegamer, A., Kowalewski, D., et al.: Jamming and spoofing of GNSS signals–an underestimated risk?! Proc. Wisdom Ages Challenges Modern World **3**, 17–21 (2015)
23. Russell, S.J., Stuart, J.: Norvig. Artificial Intelligence: A Modern Approach, pp. 111–114 (2003)
24. Samuel, A.L.: Some studies in machine learning using the game of checkers. IBM J. Res. Dev. **3**(3), 210–229 (1959)
25. Schaeffer, J.: Didn't Samuel solve that game? In: One Jump Ahead, pp. 1–11. Springer, Berlin (2009)
26. Shane, S., Sanger, D.E.: Drone Crash in Iran Reveals Secret Us Surveillance Effort. The New York Times, vol. 7 (2011)
27. Stamatelatos, M., Dezfuli, H., Apostolakis, G., Everline, C., Guarro, S., Mathias, D., Mosleh, A., Paulos, T., Riha, D., Smith, C., et al.: Probabilistic risk assessment procedures guide for NASA managers and practitioners. Tech. rep., National Air and Space Administration (2011)
28. SysML.Org: SysML Open Source Project—What is SysML? Who created SysML? Accessed 12 Aug 2021. https://sysml.org/

29. Systems Engineering Research Consortium: Model based systems engineering (mbse) (2020). https://www.nasa.gov/consortium/ModelBasedSystems
30. Tao, F., Zhang, H., Liu, A., Nee, A.Y.C.: Digital twin in industry: state-of-the-art. IEEE Trans. Ind. Inform. **15**(4), 2405–2415 (2019). https://doi.org/10.1109/TII.2018.2873186
31. US Nuclear Regulatory Commission: Probabilistic risk assessment (pra) (2020). https://www.nrc.gov/about-nrc/regulatory/risk-informed/pra.html
32. Xiang, Z., Miller, D.J., Kesidis, G.: A benchmark study of backdoor data poisoning defenses for deep neural network classifiers and A novel defense. In: 29th IEEE International Workshop on Machine Learning for Signal Processing, MLSP 2019, Pittsburgh, PA, USA, October 13–16, 2019, pp. 1–6. IEEE, Piscataway (2019)
33. Yamin, M.M., Ullah, M., Ullah, H., Katt, B.: Weaponized ai for cyber attacks. J. Inform. Secur. Appl. **57**, 102722 (2021). https://doi.org/10.1016/j.jisa.2020.102722

Automation of Cybersecurity Work

Stefan Varga ⓘ, Teodor Sommestad ⓘ, and Joel Brynielsson ⓘ

1 Introduction

Automated solutions have shown great potential within the cybersecurity field, and much of current research is directed towards automated solutions. By automation, we here mean the execution of some task by a machine agent (usually a computer) that was previously carried out by a human, according to Parasuraman and Riley's definition [33, p. 231]. Examples of machine agents in cybersecurity, are intrusion detection systems and vulnerability assessment tools. In a future scenario where high-quality cybersecurity automated solutions are widespread, a plausible reality may be that:

- complex cyber operations, both offensive and defensive, are easy to execute, even for actors who lack resources,
- the ones who possess the most powerful automated solutions have dominant positions within the cyber domain, and
- some current (human) work roles are obsolete, significantly changed, or simplified.

S. Varga (✉)
KTH Royal Institute of Technology, Stockholm, Sweden
Swedish Armed Forces Headquarters, Stockholm, Sweden
e-mail: svarga@kth.se

T. Sommestad
FOI Swedish Defence Research Agency, Stockholm, Sweden
e-mail: teodor.sommestad@foi.se

J. Brynielsson
KTH Royal Institute of Technology, Stockholm, Sweden
FOI Swedish Defence Research Agency, Stockholm, Sweden
e-mail: joel@kth.se

© The Author(s) 2023   67
T. Sipola et al. (eds.), *Artificial Intelligence and Cybersecurity*,
https://doi.org/10.1007/978-3-031-15030-2_4

This chapter seeks to examine the preconditions for further automation of cybersecurity tasks, especially in light of developments in the artificial intelligence, AI, field. The chapter mainly focuses on the third aspect listed above, namely: automation in relation to human work. Even if increased automation is desirable, there are several obstacles that have to be overcome first. For example, research on intrusion detection has not yet nullified the role of human system operators, and humans are still needed in the loop [22, 40]. Why have these efforts failed?

More precisely, we seek to shed light on the following research questions:

1. What variables affect how hard a cybersecurity role is to automate?
2. How likely is it that current cybersecurity roles will be automated?
3. What variables constrain the potential for automation of today's cybersecurity roles?

A keystone of the analysis is the *National Initiative for Cybersecurity Education*, NICE, framework for cybersecurity work roles, brought forward by the U.S. National Institute of Standards and Technology, NIST [31]. This document delineates cybersecurity roles by describing various tasks and the demands that the fulfillment of those tasks require in terms of knowledge, skills, and abilities.

2   Cybersecurity Automation Research

Progress is continuously being made within the fields of AI and automation. At the same time there is an urgency to cope with cybersecurity threats due to the increasingly severe implications that breaches may bring. There is, however, no comprehensive research that addresses the intersection of these perspectives: the full automation of cybersecurity work. This subject has, to our knowledge, only been treated as a cybersecurity issue synoptically. This chapter seeks to outline relevant theories and models that describe what is easy and what is hard to automate, both in general and specifically for cybersecurity. The characteristics of this topic is cross-disciplinary, and the research questions addressed in this chapter are neither fully answered, nor extensively treated in the cybersecurity literature. Relevant related work can instead be found within a variety of other (academic) fields. Work related to the two first research questions concerns economics, while references for the last research question, which mainly deals with technical issues, can be found in literature about technology development. The references in this chapter are therefore attributed mainly to fields other than cybersecurity.

2.1   *Variables That Influence Automation in General*

Even if automation largely can be seen as a cornerstone of human progress [26], empirical research that unequivocally states what circumstances that make a human task easy or hard to automate, is hard to find. For instance, comprehensive studies of successful or failed automation attempts are difficult to find. The earliest identified attempt to create comprehensive assessment criteria to this respect was, to our knowledge, made by Frey and Osborne [21]. They used variables from the U.S. Department of Labor's Occupational Information Network, known as O*NET, which is used to describe requirement levels for various professions. They then let a panel of computer science machine learning researchers judge whether 70 randomly chosen professions were possible to automate or not. Panel members read the job descriptions and answered the question: "Can the tasks of this job be sufficiently specified, conditional on the availability of big data, to be performed by state of the art computer-controlled equipment" [21, p. 30].

The resulting judgments were then used as a baseline for a regression model that calculated the importance of the different O*NET variables. These steps resulted in the following list of variables deemed as relevant for whether an occupation is technically feasible to automate (e.g., whether they were to be seen as potential bottleneck indicators for automation, given data availability): perception and manipulation, creative intelligence, and social intelligence. It should be noted that some of the correlations, like the requirement for originality (as part of creative intelligence), were nonlinear.

Besides Frey and Osborne, others have performed similar analyses with other sets of variables. McKinsey [30], for example, used 18 variables split into five groups [30, p. 4], the groups being: sensory perception, cognitive capabilities, natural language processing, social and emotional capabilities, and physical capabilities. These types of requirements were not chosen for tasks that were particularly easy or hard to automate. They were rather used to reason about the requirement levels for various professions, and if automation to this level was feasible with today's technology or not. One example of a capability level, is the requirement for *natural language*, where the requirement level ranges from no requirements to "...nuanced human interaction" [30, p. 120]. To calibrate the meaning of these requirements, they set the highest level to correspond to the skill-level of the best quarter (25%) of the workforce. Van der Zande et al. [47] fused the McKinsey model with a simpler model conceived by Autor et al. [2]. They characterized the various professions into two new dimensions. First, on an axis ranging from whether they consisted mainly of routine tasks or not, to if they involved encounters of many novel situations or not. Second, on an axis ranging from if they primarily required physical capabilities, to whether they instead required cognitive capabilities. When van der Zande et al. [47] coupled the McKinsey analysis to these two new dimensions they, perhaps unsurprisingly, found that routine work is easier to automate than varied work.

Arntz et al. [1] used Frey and Osborne's analysis [21] as a blueprint to determine to what extent jobs in the United States are prone to automation. They suggested that this susceptibility was related to several variables divided into four categories: the characteristics of the workers (3 variables), the skill of the workers (3), the general characteristics of the work (11), and the characteristics of the tasks (25). Most of these variables were related to the automation assessments made by Frey and Osborne.

Suta et al. [43] aggregated variables used in studies such as the ones mentioned above, into factors that hinder or promote automation. The aggregation of the variables show only minor differences compared to the variables used by Frey and Osborne [21].

In a survey, Deloitte [16] also found that a major obstacle when new technology is introduced, is the lack of qualified and competent personnel who can use it. In other words, a certain kind of skill-set is required for the use of automated solutions. The following competencies were identified as desirable:

- specialist skills within the field of automation and AI to be able to create and deploy solutions,
- general abilities and subject matter knowledge possessed by users and various types of specialists (for example, economists), to be able to understand and make use of automated solutions in their respective fields,
- skills that can be leveraged to supplement the proposed automated solutions, when they are perceived to have deficiencies, e.g., to assess situations and to utilize interpersonal communication.

In addition to these competencies there are several other variables that can be assumed to greatly influence whether a profession or some part of it can or should be automated:

- Tasks that are performed with a high frequency by an expensive personnel category, e.g., personnel with high salaries, ought to be more prone for automation than tasks that are carried out seldom by low-cost personnel. In a development and innovation perspective, profitability and cost efficiency increase the market potential for automation [32].
- Resistance from personnel categories that may be negatively affected by automation is another variable that can affect whether a profession or task is automated or not. In some jobs, especially those that can be characterized by the so-called 3Ds: *Dirty*, *Dangerous*, and *Demanding* [10], such resistance can be believed to be low. For other jobs, especially ones that are perceived to be stimulating and creative, resistance can be expected to be greater.
- Resistance from potential *users* is another imaginable obstacle. According to the *Technology Acceptance Model* [27], information systems that are perceived to be useful and easy to use, are often readily accepted by users. For the opposite case, acceptance can be lower.
- Ethical and legal questions may affect whether a task is allowed to, or should, be automated. The question of liability for self-driving cars, or laws about personal privacy, serve as pertinent examples.

The motive for listing other potential factors that affect automation, is to highlight the existence of factors besides the ones that are brought up in this chapter.

2.2 Variables That Influence Automation of Cybersecurity Work

The analyses described this far are generic and pertain to the labor market in general. They encompass a range of jobs where only a fraction is connected to cybersecurity. For cyber jobs, Frey and Osborne [21] found, for example, that "[c]omputer systems analyst" jobs are difficult to automate, while "[c]omputer operators" are relatively easy to automate. Table 1 shows some cybersecurity jobs' proneness for automation according to Frey and Osborne. The previously mentioned McKinsey analysis [30] judged that 51% of the total hours worked in "[t]echnology, media and telecom", can be automated.

Current and emerging technologies hint about the limits of future automation. Technologies that can handle vulnerabilities and logs, prevent data loss, perform authentication control (including to networks), and advanced antivirus software, are common today. Technologies that ensure safety-critical development processes and services that extract intelligence from data, are less common. It has been argued, however, that any part of a job description that can be reduced to an algorithm or computational process can be automated [34], even if today's technology does not permit it. When tasks have been automated, the human part of the work could be simplified, reduced or transformed to some extent. Antivirus software, for example, checks software—a task that system administrators otherwise would have to do manually. The use of new technologies can also bring changes to current work practices. When, e.g., the signing of legally binding contracts is substituted for digital signatures, new additional cybersecurity work is probably needed to fully ensure the integrity of the involved IT systems. Another driver for cybersecurity, is the need to defeat tools and technologies used by attackers (and vice versa). This means that there is a cyber "arms race" going on. An example is when automatically generated attack code [3] forces defenders to rethink or completely redesign their intrusion detection processes. Another example is when the AI automation itself is the target for adversarial AI examples specifically designed to defeat cybersecurity

Table 1 The probability for cybersecurity-related jobs being automated according to Frey and Osborne [21]

Rank	Profession	Probability of automation
32	Computer systems analysts	0.0065
69	Computer and information research scientists	0.015
110	Database administrators	0.03
118	Computer and information systems managers	0.035
208	Information security analysts, web developers, and computer network architects	0.21
212	Computer occupations, all other	0.22
405	Computer, automated teller, and office machine repairers	0.74
428	Computer operators	0.78

efforts [14]. We assert that one of the goals of cybersecurity research is to automate to the widest extent possible, all in line with the goal of engineering at large. There are, however, oftentimes technical obstacles that prevent successful outcomes of automation efforts.

As an example case we highlight efforts to automate intrusion detection; a central problem in cybersecurity. This is an active research field that has gained much attention, but results this far have unfortunately not led to full automation of surveillance work in practice. Most approaches for automating surveillance tasks rely heavily on rule-based solutions [50, 51]. Existing rules are adapted and developed to suit organizational needs. This strand of research ultimately aims to develop models that are able to correlate events to automate threat classification and threat mitigation processes with different kinds of machine learning techniques. Possible reasons for the mediocre performance of event correlation are erroneous simplifications of the attack process, or reliance on incorrect information about the state of the IT system [39, 41]. Sommer and Paxson [37] propose the following explanations to why research based on machine learning approaches has failed:

1. the high cost of classification errors (e.g., sensitivity for false positives is too high due to a large amount of traffic),
2. the variety of formats in input data (e.g., numerous protocols with varying frequency of occurrence and content),
3. the lack of training data (e.g., realistic network traffic, where both attack-related and normal traffic flows have been appropriately labeled),
4. ambiguous output data (e.g., questions about the exact meaning of an anomaly and how it should be further investigated),
5. difficulties in determining the value or feasibility of proposed solutions (largely as an effect of items 3 and 4).

A second central problem in cybersecurity is to detect and identify software vulnerabilities [29]. The lack of automated *test oracles* that determine whether a function or calculation is adequate or not, is a problem [4]. Humans are as a rule still needed to conclusively judge whether a piece of software performs correctly or not. There are, however, many suggestions on how code reviews could be performed by computers. One proposal is to use formal methods to prove that software has certain secure properties. Formal methods, in short, use a specification of what the software is supposed to do, and then typically try to check that the software does precisely that and nothing else. This approach requires a human to set up an appropriate testing environment for the problem [17, p. 1176]. Another route to solve the problem is through more lightweight (semiformal) methods. Such methods do not require massive efforts during the problem formulation phase. However, although state of the art methods are fairly effective, they tend to result in additional work to ensure the safety of software [36]. The extra work is presumed to reduce the need for security-related work in the long run. A third research area targets vulnerability assessments of larger interconnected systems, computer networks and organizations. In this respect, many approaches model vulnerabilities and conceivable attacks in the form of trees or graphs, in approximately the same way as fault trees are used to calculate risk or availability values.

The research community has produced several variants of modeling languages and associated software tools for the purpose of conducting vulnerability analyses using, e.g., graph-based models [28]. The actual use of such tools among practitioners is probably not widespread, neither in government, nor in the commercial sector. The sole test available that compares the data output produced by such a tool with the capabilities of actual attackers, show that the predictions provided are poor [41]. These kinds of disheartening results, however, are not only representative for cybersecurity research that models attacks in the form of graphs. In an extensive overview over research that seeks to quantify elements in security-related issues, Verendel [48] found that nearly no research had been validated with empirical data, and that the underlying research assumptions were not empirically validated either. In conclusion, it is difficult to assess whether any existing vulnerability assessment method actually works, if it has not been tested properly with realistic data. A commonly used excuse, or reason to waive this deficiency, is to refer to some need for secrecy. In general, one's cybersecurity stance appears to be a closely guarded and vigorous protection of the properties of so-called zero-day exploits [25], as suggested by the substantive underreporting of cybercrime [46].

In relation to the factors related to automation identified in other domains, the examples given above illustrate requirements on creativity (e.g., when possible ways of attacking a system shall be identified in vulnerability analyses), requirements on social interaction (e.g., ambiguous data from detection systems), and the need for data (e.g., to train or test solutions).

3 Method

This section describes the method that was employed to answer our three research questions. Section 3.1 describes the NIST NICE framework. Section 3.2 outlines the evaluation criteria for automation, while Sect. 3.3 describes the assessment process. Finally, in Sect. 3.4 the process of aggregating the assessments is described.

3.1 The Content of Cybersecurity Tasks

This study uses the U.S. National Institute of Standards and Technology (NIST) *National Initiative for Cybersecurity Education (NICE) Cybersecurity Workforce Framework* [31], henceforth the NICE framework, as a reference for the work that needs to be carried out to increase the level of cybersecurity. It should be noted that there exist other similar frameworks. Examples include *The Cyber Security Body of Knowledge* (CyBOK),[1] the British NCSC[2] *Certification for Cyber Security/IA Professionals* framework, and the U.S. military DoD Directive 8570, originally from 2005. This latter-mentioned directive was later replaced by DoD Directive 8140, which in turn drew heavily on NIST publications.

The NICE framework was chosen because it has several advantages compared to other alternatives. It was conceived and prepared by the U.S. government in cooperation with industrial partners, and is in our judgment very detailed and predominantly well-structured. It is also widely spread and used, not least as a basis for further work. Moreover, it is regularly updated.

A factor that speaks against the use of NICE is that it is adapted to U.S. circumstances that do not necessarily fully reflect realities in other countries. Chen et al. [9, p. 63] point out that the descriptions of knowledge, skills and abilities in the NICE framework omit mentioning many details about the work's cognitive and collaborative aspects. There are also, in our opinion, some less well-worked parts in the document (see Sect. 5.1.1).

The content of the NICE framework can be used in many different ways. The analyzed version contains a high-level classification that divides security work into seven categories; further, there are 33 specialty areas in which people can work, and there are 52 distinct roles. Every role is coupled to tasks, knowledge requirements, skills and abilities that a person who should master it, should have. In the framework version used for this chapter, a total of 1006 tasks, 589 knowledge requirements, 365 skills and 176 abilities were listed [31].

This chapter, like previous studies [21], focuses on skills and abilities for specific tasks. These skills and abilities are the factors that form the foundation from which assessments are made regarding how easy or hard it is to automate various roles and specialty areas. Some examples of how skills and abilities are listed in the NICE framework are given in Table 2.

Table 2 Examples of skills and abilities as listed in the NICE framework [31]

Skills	Abilities
Skill in reviewing and editing target materials	Ability to conduct vulnerability scans and recognize vulnerabilities in security systems
Skill in configuring and utilizing network protection components (e.g., Firewalls, VPNs, network intrusion detection systems)	Ability to operate common network tools (e.g., `ping`, `traceroute`, `nslookup`)
Skill to analyze strategic guidance for issues requiring clarification and/or additional guidance	Ability to monitor measures or indicators of system performance and availability
Skill in creating and utilizing mathematical or statistical models	Ability to identify the requirements of in-process accounting for communications security (COMSEC)

---

[1] https://www.cybok.org/.

[2] https://www.ncsc.gov.uk/.

The meaning of the term knowledge is ambiguous. What knowledge is, and how it should be defined, has been the subject for lively discussions through the years. The imprecise meaning of the term is duly noted in the NICE framework. For the sake of this chapter, neither further problematization, nor additional extensive discussions on this subject, is necessary. We simply assert that knowledge can be codified into the memory of computers with relative ease. This (our) standpoint diminishes or abolishes the knowledge requirement criterion in the assessment of whether a role is possible to automate or not. This assertion is consistent with how earlier similar analyses have handled this question.

3.2 Assessment Criteria

As described in Sect. 2.1, previous research largely agrees on what factors affect whether a task is easy or hard to automate. The four criteria used in this study (see Table 3) are in line with these. The first three mirror the barriers for automation used by Frey and Osborne, whilst the fourth is used to refine (quantify) their premise of data availability [21].

The motive for why the criterion "existing statistical data" has been included in the assessment, is the assumption that the availability of data is important for cybersecurity. It has been shown that data availability can be a problem. The reasons for the unavailability of data can be that it often is sensitive and difficult to use due to security (confidentiality) concerns, and because many tasks are performed in environments where the meaning of specific data points is unclear, e.g., if

Table 3 Criteria used to grade abilities and skills, and cases that correspond to simple and difficult automation prerequisites, respectively. These represent the extremes in our grading scheme 1–5

	The nature of the skill or ability	Easy to automate (1)	Difficult to automate (5)
1	Requirements for creativity	There is only one (natural) way to perform the task that does not vary over time	The task may require that action alternatives no one has previously thought of be identified and applied
2	Requirements for social interaction	Does not require any interaction with humans	Requires situation-adapted and/or dynamic interpersonal communication with nuances
3	Requirements for physical work	Can be solved completely within a computer. Requires no physical work	Requires varied fine motor work with little tolerance for errors
4	Existing statistical data	High-quality basic data in sufficient quantity is available. Data produced to describe or document the work is available	Data does not exist, or exists to a very limited extent. There are very few cases to learn from

certain traffic patterns are indeed part of an attack or not (see Sect. 2.2). These two factors contribute to the difficulties in extracting and making high-quality conclusive data available for training of machine learning models. Furthermore, these are also prohibiting factors for the automation of cybersecurity work, and therefore motivates the introduction of this assessment variable.

The characteristics of the skills and abilities were judged according to the four criteria (see Table 3) on a scale ranging from one (1) to five (5), where one (1) corresponds to that a task is easy to automate, and five (5) corresponds to that it is hard. The assessors also judged whether the NICE description of the skill or ability was at all understandable.

3.3   Assessment Process

The 541 descriptions (176 skills and 365 abilities) were extracted and assessed by four researchers. They were:

- a Ph.D. (computer science) and deputy research director within the cybersecurity field,
- an associate professor (computer science) and research director working with decision support systems,
- a Ph.D. student (computer science) and military officer with a background from intelligence and cybersecurity,
- a master of laws (LL.M.) graduate specializing in cyber operations.

The work started with a calibration round where 30 randomly chosen task descriptions were assessed independently. This initial work was carried out at different geographical locations, without any communication between the assessors. It was later found that the researchers in some cases had to acquire additional background material from the NICE framework to make fair assessments. The need for this arouse from the desire to get an understanding for the context of the various descriptions of skills and abilities. The correlation coefficients between the assessments in the calibration round were overall moderately positive (e.g., ranging between 0.3–0.6 for the "requirements for social interaction" criterion), but also highlighted some differences in how the four researchers interpreted and implemented the criteria. The largest difference was detected for the "requirements for creativity" criterion.

After the initial calibration round, a seminar was held. Detected differences as well as other results were discussed. The seminar resulted in a refined scale. The seminar also improved consensus as of how to interpret the NICE texts, and thus probably contributed to a higher quality in the assessments for the main body of the data. After the seminar, the assessment work was continued with the assessments of all 541 descriptions. It could be noted that some differences between the views of the assessors remained even after the seminar. The mean deviations were 0.7 for "existing statistical data", 0.6 for "requirements for creativity", 0.5 for "requirements for social interaction", and 0.1 for "requirements for physical work".

In Table 4, the correlation coefficients between the four researchers' assessments are listed. They varied between 0.24 and 0.76 with a mean value of 0.45. The differences were probably not a result of a faulty research design, but rather the fully natural variance of the competencies of the researchers due to their backgrounds. The mean value can thus be seen as an approximation of how a skill and an ability can be viewed from various perspectives. Overall mean values of the different criteria can also be seen in Table 4. A deeper data analysis (not shown here) indicates that the requirements for creativity and statistical data resemble normal distributions, with their mean values in the middle of the scale. The frequency of requirements for social interaction is linearly decreasing, which means that there are significantly more tasks with low requirements than high. Requirements for physical work are almost nonexistent.

3.4 Aggregation and Analysis

The assessments resulted in judgments about each and every skill and ability with regard to what requirements they have on (1) creativity, (2) social interaction, (3) physical work, and (4) how difficult it is to produce statistical data to be used for machine learning (or similar), in order to train a computer to perform a task. Mean values were used to obtain an aggregated answer from the panel. The examples displayed in Table 2 were used to obtain the assessments in Table 4.

The values indicate what is easy and hard to automate, given our method. The ability "to operate common network tools (e.g., `ping`, `traceroute`, `nslookup`)" receives lower values than the skill "to analyze strategic guidance for issues requiring clarification and/or additional guidance" on all four criteria, i.e., has fewer obstacles for being automated. The mean value of the different judgments can be seen as an indication on whether a skill or ability can be performed by a computer. A word of caution is in place here, because several additional factors not included in our model, can also come into play:

- As has been described in, e.g., Sect. 2.1, previous studies found nonlinear relations between the criteria and proneness for automation. It is imaginable that the highest level of creativity is next to impossible to achieve, when at the same time the preceding level is quite easily reached, e.g., the "distance" between the requirement levels vary in a nonlinear fashion. Similarly, it is also possible that the requirement for physical work at the highest level is unattainable. The obstacles for automation can in other words be an exponentially increasing function of the criteria. A way to remedy this problem, related to our method, can be to further "calibrate" the different assessors, that is, to make sure that they think about the problem in the same way through additional seminars or rules.

Table 4 Examples of skills and abilities together with the panel's assessments. Mean deviation between assessors can be seen within brackets

Skill or ability	Requirements for creativity	Requirements for social interaction	Requirements for physical work	Existing statistical data
Skill in reviewing and editing target materials	2.0 (0.5)	2.5 (1.5)	1.3 (0.4)	2.8 (0.4)
Skill in configuring and utilizing network protection components (e.g., Firewalls, VPNs, network intrusion detection systems)	2.5 (1.0)	1.0 (0.0)	1.0 (0.0)	2.0 (1.0)
Skill to analyze strategic guidance for issues requiring clarification and/or additional guidance	3.3 (0.4)	3.3 (0.4)	1.3 (0.4)	4.0 (0.5)
Skill in creating and utilizing mathematical or statistical models	3.0 (1.5)	1.0 (0.0)	1.0 (0.0)	2.8 (0.9)
Ability to conduct vulnerability scans and recognize vulnerabilities in security systems	2.0 (0.5)	1.0 (0.0)	1.0 (0.0)	2.5 (0.8)
Ability to operate common network tools (e.g., ping, traceroute, nslookup)	1.8 (0.4)	1.0 (0.0)	1.0 (0.0)	1.8 (0.8)
Ability to monitor measures or indicators of system performance and availability	1.5 (0.5)	1.0 (0.0)	1.0 (0.0)	2.3 (1.3)
Ability to identify the requirements of in-process accounting for communications security (COMSEC)	2.3 (0.9)	1.3 (0.4)	1.3 (0.4)	2.7 (0.9)

- It may be difficult to overcome several obstacles by combining different techniques. It could, for example, be more difficult to conceive a creative solution that is able to act in a social context, than it is to create separate solutions; where one is creative and the other one social, for the same problem. The difficulty to automate can in other words consist of the product of the criteria.
- There may exist interactions between the criteria that make it either easier or harder to automate them. A requirement for creativity may be easy to fulfil if there is an abundance of available statistical data to utilise. This problem would perhaps be very hard, or close to impossible, to solve without *any* statistical data. This serves to illustrate that the availability of statistical data affects/constrains the values of the *other* criteria.
- A single criterion can sometimes be decisive for whether a skill or an ability can be automated at all (even if all the other criteria suggest that it can). It may be the case that *any* task that requires a high or very high social competency, in principle is impossible to automate. This could be seen as a definite obstacle for automation, rather than the maximum value for the four criteria combined.

Due to the reasons given above, calculations were made with other models besides the mean value analysis. In total, we used five different models to compute the numerical values of the criteria (k_1–k_4). All models yield a value for each skill or ability, based on the scores from all four assessors. The five models are described in Table 5. Model one is the easiest and most straightforward. When nothing else is stated, the values from this model are used in discussions. The motive for our preference for model one, is that simple predictive models often outperform more complex ditto [20].

All the computed values (according to the mentioned models) provide information about whether a skill or ability is susceptible to automation in the form of a scalar (e.g., 3.3 or 47.2), where a low value relative to the other computed values according to the same model, suggest that automation is easy. The maximum values that can be obtained vary with the different models—from the value five (5) in model five, to 625 in model three. To achieve commensurability the values were normalized

Table 5 The five different models that were used to assess automability

Model	Explanation	Formal description
1	The effect is simple, additive, and linear. The sum of the four criteria is used	$\sum_{i=1}^{4} k_i$
2	The effect is exponential. The sum of exponential functions for the four criteria is used	$\sum_{i=1}^{4} 2^{k_i}$
3	Interactions make it much more difficult if several different obstacles need to be overcome. The product of the four criteria is used	$\prod_{i=1}^{4} k_i$
4	Access to statistical data (k_4) limits how much the other criteria affect	$\sum_{i=1}^{3} \min(k_i, k_4)$
5	The highest value for the various criteria is decisive/limiting	$\max_{i=1,\dots,4} k_i$

against an index by dividing every computed value with the overall lowest value given by that model. The computed values are thus comparable relative to each other, with value one (1) being the easiest skill or ability to automate within each model. Then, aggregation with the structure of the NICE framework was done, in order to derive to what extent roles, specialty areas and categories can be automated. The mean values of the normalized skills and abilities were used, to this respect.

In addition to what is mentioned above, it can be concluded that the technology level and the prerequisites to meet the demands for automation, are on different levels today. There is nothing to suggest that they will not diverge even more in the future. It is entirely possible to argue that it is possible to meet the demands of physical work with, e.g., autonomous lawn mowers, and to solve a range of tasks that require fine motor ability, e.g., the peeling of prawns, while at the same time computers still do not have the capability to adequately produce synopses of texts (level three for social interaction in our scale). The present technological level, and thereby the prerequisites to meet the demands for the various criteria, can be uneven and also vary unevenly. In what way such developments affect the evaluation scores is tested in a *what-if* analysis, in which all combinations of the five levels for all the four criteria, is set to be unattainable. For each such combination (a total of 625), binary values indicating whether a skill or an ability is possible to automate or not, were set. The proportion of skills and abilities that could be automated for 21 selected scenarios were then aggregated to the seven categories of the NICE framework.

4   Results

In the following, results describing to what extent roles, specialty areas and categories can be automated according to the five models in Table 5, are presented. The values in the tables can be used for comparisons, e.g., the meaning of the value 2.6 is that a role is twice as hard to automate than a role that has the value 1.3. The assessments are then contrasted to 21 selected scenarios that represent different contexts. The figures in this part (Sect. 4.1) shall be seen as a measure of to what extent, or proportion, it is possible to automate cybersecurity work in each scenario.

The most detailed result presented in this chapter is presented in Table 6, in which it is shown to what extent NICE roles can be automated according to the five models. The presented colors, which are based on a mean (average) of the results of the models, show how easy (green) and hard (red) the different roles are to automate. The role *Database Administrator* is easiest to automate in all five models. The value 1.00 was therefore set as a base (index) for this case. The possibilities to automate other roles are, hence, expressed by how easy or hard they are to automate relative to the *Database Administrator* role. The results should be interpreted as, for example, the role *Systems Developer* being 26 percent (index 1.26) harder to automate than the *Database Administrator* role according to model four, and at the same time 160 percent (index 2.60) harder to automate according to model three. The mean value indicates that the work of a *Systems Developer* is 65 percent harder (index 1.65) to automate than the work of a *Database Administrator*. Moreover, the table shows that the two roles *Cyber Legal Advisor* and *Executive Cyber Leadership*, are the ones that are hardest to automate according to all models.

The results aggregated into specialty areas are shown in Table 7. In this table some patterns emerge more clearly:

- Tasks that can be regarded as purely technical, such as database administration (e.g., *Data Administration*), network maintenance (e.g., *Cyber Defense Infrastructure Support*), and programming (e.g., *Software Development*), are relatively easy to automate.
- Tasks that require technical knowledge and are also of analytical nature (e.g., *Systems Development*), or that require coordination efforts with other functions (e.g., *Cybersecurity Management*), can be found in the middle of the scale.
- Intelligence work (e.g., *Collection Operations* and *Threat Analysis*) is relatively hard to automate.
- Areas associated with high levels of responsibility (e.g., *Executive Cyber Leadership*), and those that regularly require that a manifold of complex issues need to be weighed together (e.g., *Legal Advice and Advocacy*), are the hardest to automate.

The abovementioned tendencies can be discerned in all models.

At the highest level in the NICE framework, categories of cybersecurity work are listed. Table 8 shows to what extent these categories can be automated. There are less discrepancies at this level compared to the more detailed results presented in Tables 6 and 7. However, it can be noted that the categories *Operate and Maintain*, *Protect and Defend*, and *Investigate*, are generally easier to automate than the other categories.

4.1 Scenarios

There are a total of $5^4 = 625$ possible combinations of the four used criteria. Each and everyone can be regarded as a scenario—a hypothetical situation where the potential for automation has reached a certain level. In the scenarios, this level is expressed by the values of our evaluation criteria (1–5) according to Table 3. To clarify the meaning of this reasoning, we list some examples in Table 9. It could, for example, be imagined that technology has reached, or will reach, a level so that it becomes possible to satisfy the needs of:

- level three (3) on creativity, where multiple variables need to be weighed together and uncertainty has to be accounted for (which, for example, can be manifested by a capability to accurately target specific individuals with advertising),

Table 6 Roles in the NICE framework. The figures are to be read as a measure of how easy/hard it is to automate a role relative to other roles. The easiest role to automate in all models has index 1.0 (the *Database Administrator*)

Role	Mean	Model				
		1	2	3	4	5
Database Administrator (OM-DTA-001)	1.00	1.00	1.00	1.00	1.00	1.00
Data Analyst (OM-DTA-002)	1.13	1.07	1.16	1.27	1.04	1.13
Network Operations Specialist (OM-NET-001)	1.27	1.10	1.21	1.82	1.07	1.16
Cyber Operator (CO-OPS-001)	1.34	1.17	1.29	1.86	1.13	1.24
Software Developer (SP-DEV-001)	1.41	1.21	1.35	1.99	1.16	1.31
Cyber Defense Infrastructure Support Specialist (PR-INF-001)	1.42	1.20	1.34	2.14	1.18	1.23
Cyber Defense Analyst (PR-CDA-001)	1.45	1.22	1.39	2.18	1.19	1.27
Secure Software Assessor (SP-DEV-002)	1.47	1.24	1.41	2.18	1.18	1.34
Cyber Defense Incident Responder (PR-CIR-001)	1.49	1.25	1.41	2.21	1.22	1.33
Cyber Defense Forensics Analyst (IN-FOR-002)	1.53	1.23	1.40	2.51	1.18	1.34
Communications Security (COMSEC) Manager (OV-MGT-002)	1.56	1.26	1.52	2.46	1.22	1.33
Forensics Analyst (IN-FOR-001)	1.57	1.24	1.42	2.63	1.19	1.35
System Administrator (OM-ADM-001)	1.59	1.25	1.46	2.72	1.21	1.30
Systems Developer (SP-SYS-002)	1.65	1.33	1.57	2.60	1.26	1.47
System Test & Evaluation Specialist (SP-TST-001)	1.68	1.33	1.56	2.81	1.28	1.44
Systems Security Analyst (OM-ANA-001)	1.72	1.35	1.66	2.83	1.27	1.49
Cyber Crime Investigator (IN-INV-001)	1.75	1.36	1.62	3.02	1.29	1.48
Exploitation Analyst (AN-EXP-001)	1.76	1.34	1.67	3.04	1.28	1.46
Vulnerability Assessment Analyst (PR-VAM-001)	1.77	1.37	1.64	3.06	1.31	1.46
Research and Development Specialist (SP-TRD-001)	1.78	1.38	1.66	3.03	1.32	1.51
Security Architect (SP-ARC-002)	1.90	1.39	1.76	3.51	1.33	1.50
Knowledge Manager (OM-KMG-001)	1.90	1.37	1.72	3.66	1.35	1.41
Information Systems Security Developer (SP-SYS-001)	1.95	1.43	1.81	3.59	1.38	1.55
Systems Requirements Planner (SP-SRP-001)	1.96	1.45	1.74	3.69	1.43	1.49
Cyber Instructor (OV-TEA-002)	1.98	1.42	1.85	3.77	1.36	1.51
Enterprise Architect (SP-ARC-001)	2.01	1.46	1.84	3.80	1.40	1.57
Product Support Manager (OV-PMA-003)	2.03	1.48	1.83	3.83	1.43	1.58
Technical Support Specialist (OM-STS-001)	2.04	1.47	1.99	3.72	1.38	1.61
Security Control Assessor (SP-RSK-002)	2.04	1.45	1.90	3.89	1.38	1.57
Target Network Analyst (AN-TGT-002)	2.06	1.46	1.97	3.89	1.40	1.57
IT Program Auditor (OV-PMA-005)	2.06	1.50	1.85	3.90	1.47	1.57
Information Systems Security Manager (OV-MGT-001)	2.08	1.46	1.93	4.01	1.42	1.57
All Source-Collection Manager (CO-CLO-001)	2.08	1.46	1.89	4.07	1.41	1.57
All Source-Collection Requirements Manager (CO-CLO-002)	2.09	1.47	1.90	4.06	1.42	1.58

(continued)

Table 6 (continued)

Multi-Disciplined Language Analyst (AN-LNG-001)	2.10	1.45	1.92	4.14	1.39	1.58
Information Technology (IT) Project Manager (OV-PMA-002)	2.14	1.52	1.90	4.19	1.49	1.59
Program Manager (OV-PMA-001)	2.14	1.52	1.90	4.19	1.49	1.59
Cyber Workforce Developer and Manager (OV-SPP-001)	2.22	1.51	2.08	4.42	1.44	1.65
Target Developer (AN-TGT-001)	2.22	1.52	2.15	4.34	1.44	1.66
IT Investment/Portfolio Manager (OV-PMA-004)	2.32	1.58	2.02	4.82	1.56	1.63
Cyber Instructional Curriculum Developer (OV-TEA-001)	2.33	1.55	2.18	4.76	1.47	1.68
Authorizing Official (SP-RSK-001)	2.37	1.57	2.16	4.90	1.51	1.70
Threat/Warning Analyst (AN-TWA-001)	2.39	1.58	2.32	4.85	1.48	1.73
Mission Assessment Specialist (AN-ASA-002)	2.44	1.60	2.38	4.97	1.51	1.76
All-Source Analyst (AN-ASA-001)	2.47	1.60	2.40	5.05	1.51	1.77
Cyber Policy and Strategy Planner (OV-SPP-002)	2.64	1.65	2.36	5.84	1.61	1.72
Cyber Intel Planner (CO-OPL-001)	2.69	1.67	2.41	5.94	1.61	1.80
Privacy Officer/Privacy Compliance Manager (OV-LGA-002)	2.71	1.68	2.42	6.03	1.63	1.77
Cyber Ops Planner (CO-OPL-002)	2.77	1.70	2.53	6.13	1.62	1.84
Partner Integration Planner (CO-OPL-003)	2.90	1.73	2.64	6.62	1.65	1.86
Executive Cyber Leadership (OV-EXL-001)	3.06	1.78	3.03	6.82	1.69	1.96
Cyber Legal Advisor (OV-LGA-001)	3.16	1.84	2.93	7.25	1.75	2.02

- level three (3) on social interaction, where computers are capable of interpreting simple forms of communication (for example, produce a written synopsis of an oral conversation),
- level three (3) on physical work, where machines are able to maneuver in spaces where there are irregularities and obstacles (for example, warehouse robots that, in addition to the main task, are able to handle unforeseen obstacles),
- level three (3) on availability of statistical data, where structuring of existing data to be useful for machine learning can be performed easily within acceptable time frames (as, for example, when it comes to annotation of large amounts of images).

Table 9 describes the proportion of tasks within each category in the NICE framework that can be automated in 21 systematically chosen scenarios (out of the 625 theoretically possible). This reduced set was chosen to reflect a range of different cases that have plausible conditions. Scenario number three (3)—all 3s— is the one described above. Under these circumstances it can be seen that 61% of the skills and abilities can be automated on average, and a full 83% in the category *Operate and Maintain*.

The table also shows to what extent the four criteria affect the potential for automation:

Table 7 NICE framework specialty areas. The figures are indexed and should be read relative to other specialty areas. The easiest specialty area to automate (index 1.0) is *Data Administration*

Specialty area	Mean	Model 1	2	3	4	5
Data Administration (DTA)	1.00	1.00	1.00	1.00	1.00	1.00
Network Services (NET)	1.14	1.04	1.07	1.48	1.04	1.05
Cyber Operations (OPS)	1.20	1.11	1.14	1.51	1.10	1.12
Cyber Defense Infrastructure Support (INF)	1.26	1.13	1.19	1.74	1.15	1.11
Software Development (DEV)	1.28	1.16	1.22	1.68	1.14	1.20
Cyber Defense Analysis (CDA)	1.29	1.15	1.23	1.78	1.15	1.15
Incident Response (CIR)	1.32	1.19	1.25	1.80	1.18	1.20
Digital Forensics (FOR)	1.37	1.17	1.25	2.09	1.15	1.22
Systems Administration (ADM)	1.41	1.18	1.29	2.21	1.18	1.17
Test and Evaluation (TST)	1.49	1.26	1.38	2.28	1.24	1.30
Systems Analysis (ANA)	1.53	1.28	1.46	2.30	1.24	1.35
Cybersecurity Management (MGT)	1.55	1.27	1.48	2.47	1.26	1.28
Cyber Investigation (INV)	1.55	1.29	1.44	2.46	1.25	1.34
Exploitation Analysis (EXP)	1.56	1.27	1.48	2.48	1.24	1.32
Vulnerability Assessment and Management (VAM)	1.57	1.29	1.45	2.49	1.27	1.32
Technology R&D (TRD)	1.58	1.31	1.46	2.46	1.28	1.37
Systems Development (SYS)	1.63	1.32	1.52	2.62	1.29	1.38
Knowledge Management (KMG)	1.67	1.30	1.52	2.98	1.31	1.27
Systems Architecture (ARC)	1.71	1.34	1.58	2.94	1.32	1.38
Systems Requirements Planning (SRP)	1.73	1.38	1.54	3.00	1.38	1.34
Customer Service and Technical Support (STS)	1.80	1.40	1.76	3.03	1.34	1.46
Risk Management (RSK)	1.82	1.38	1.71	3.25	1.35	1.43
Collection Operations (CLO)	1.83	1.39	1.68	3.31	1.37	1.42
Training, Education, and Awareness (TEA)	1.84	1.38	1.73	3.33	1.35	1.42
Language Analysis (LNG)	1.84	1.38	1.70	3.37	1.35	1.43
Project Management/Acquisition and Program (PMA)	1.86	1.43	1.66	3.33	1.43	1.43
Targets (TGT)	1.88	1.41	1.81	3.33	1.38	1.46
Strategic Planning and Policy (SPP)	2.09	1.48	1.94	4.04	1.46	1.51
Threat Analysis (TWA)	2.10	1.49	2.05	3.95	1.44	1.56
All-Source Analysis (ASA)	2.15	1.51	2.11	4.07	1.46	1.59
Cyber Operational Planning (OPL)	2.41	1.60	2.21	5.01	1.57	1.65
Legal Advice and Advocacy (LGA)	2.41	1.61	2.19	5.02	1.59	1.63
Executive Cyber Leadership (EXL)	2.66	1.68	2.68	5.55	1.64	1.77

- The requirement for creativity appears to be of high importance. *All* roles can be. very hard to automate if the requirement for creativity is not fulfilled (Scenario 18).

Table 8 NICE framework categories. The figures are indexed and should be read relative to other categories. The easiest category to automate (index 1.0) is the *Operate and Maintain* category

Category	Mean	Model				
		1	2	3	4	5
Operate and Maintain (OM)	1.00	1.00	1.00	1.00	1.00	1.00
Protect and Defend (PR)	1.07	1.06	1.06	1.12	1.07	1.06
Investigate (IN)	1.09	1.05	1.05	1.22	1.04	1.08
Securely Provision (SP)	1.30	1.18	1.29	1.62	1.17	1.21
Analyze (AN)	1.48	1.27	1.55	2.01	1.25	1.31
Oversee and Govern (OV)	1.49	1.28	1.53	2.10	1.27	1.29
Collect and Operate (CO)	1.56	1.31	1.57	2.30	1.30	1.33

- The requirement for physical work is more or less insignificant. The possibilities for automation remain good even if physical work cannot be carried out at all (Scenario 20).

The table, hence, shows that creativity is more important than the ability to perform physical work. This makes intuitive sense, and should come as no surprise. Further, it can be seen that the requirements for creativity and access to statistical data are the two most important criteria. The requirement for social interaction is the third most important criterion.

5 Discussion

The quantitative measures produced by the panel as well as the different models can be interpreted in many ways. Some noteworthy results that can serve as a starting point for a discussion are listed below:

- The results obtained by the various models differ. The hardest role to automate is 1.75 times more difficult than the easiest role in model four, while it is 7.25 times harder in model three (see Table 6).
- Even if there are differences between the models they yield robust values. The ranking of the proneness for automation for various roles, is more or less equal in all models. That is, there are no major differences in the results depending on whether the criteria interact or not: some tasks are always difficult to automate, while others are always easy.
- Technical or more practically oriented roles, such as database administrators, data analysts, and network operators, seem to be the ones that are easiest to automate. Roles that require formal responsibility, such as legal advisors and executive directors, are more difficult to automate.
- Tasks that deal with systems development and system administration are easier to automate than roles dealing with intelligence issues.

Table 9 Scenarios where the automation criteria have been met to varying degrees. The figures indicate the proportion of skills and abilities that can be automated in each scenario

| Scenario | Technology and preconditions | | | | Automability | | | | | | | |
	Requirements for creativity	Requirements for social interaction	Requirements for physical work	Existing statistical data	Mean	Protect and Defend (PR)	Securely Provision (SP)	Operate and Maintain (OM)	Oversee and Govern (OV)	Investigate (IN)	Analyze (AN)	Collect and Operate (CO)
1	1	1	1	1	1%	2%	0%	2%	0%	0%	2%	1%
2	2	2	2	2	19%	29%	11%	39%	12%	24%	9%	8%
3	3	3	3	3	61%	82%	62%	83%	47%	67%	49%	37%
4	4	4	4	4	96%	100%	98%	97%	91%	100%	90%	93%
5	5	5	5	5	100%	100%	100%	100%	100%	100%	100%	100%
6	1	2	2	2	2%	2%	2%	4%	1%	4%	3%	1%
7	2	1	2	2	8%	11%	4%	21%	5%	12%	3%	3%
8	2	2	1	2	18%	29%	10%	36%	12%	20%	9%	7%
9	2	2	2	1	1%	2%	0%	3%	0%	0%	2%	2%
10	1	3	3	3	2%	2%	2%	4%	1%	4%	3%	1%
11	3	1	3	3	15%	16%	12%	32%	9%	22%	8%	5%
12	3	3	1	3	54%	77%	54%	72%	46%	47%	47%	35%
13	3	3	3	1	1%	2%	0%	3%	0%	0%	2%	2%
14	1	4	4	4	3%	2%	2%	4%	1%	8%	3%	1%
15	4	1	4	4	17%	16%	13%	36%	9%	33%	8%	5%
16	4	4	1	4	82%	95%	88%	82%	89%	59%	81%	84%
17	4	4	4	1	2%	2%	0%	3%	0%	4%	2%	2%
18	1	5	4	5	3%	2%	2%	4%	1%	8%	3%	1%
19	5	1	5	5	18%	16%	13%	36%	11%	33%	10%	5%
20	5	5	5	5	87%	95%	90%	84%	97%	59%	91%	92%
21	5	5	5	1	2%	2%	0%	3%	0%	4%	2%	2%

- Technological advances or other developments that can automate functions that require creativity, determine how much and how well the cybersecurity area can be automated. Developments of robotics that can meet requirements for physical work, is of comparably limited importance.
- The availability of statistical data is, in parallel with creativity, also decisive for whether, and how, automation within the cybersecurity area can be achieved.
- When the prerequisites for automation, according to our models, are at Levels 2–3, which it is reasonable to assume that they are today, 19–61% of the skills and abilities can in general be automated. Hence, many tasks still remain to automate.

In the remainder of this section we discuss how deficiencies in our methodology may have affected the validity of the results.

5.1   Limitations

The method used for this study can be summarized by the following steps where we:

1. obtained descriptions for various types of cybersecurity work,
2. determined sensible criteria for the purpose of assessing cybersecurity work,
3. carried out assessments by using the criteria developed in step 2, and
4. performed several analyses and syntheses of the results for different abstraction levels.

Every step has inherent weaknesses that affect the result. In the following an assortment of the potentially most serious ones are discussed.

5.1.1   Descriptions of Cybersecurity Work

To encompass the entire scope of cybersecurity work, the analysis was based on the NICE framework. NICE seeks to cover the whole range of tasks that can be related to the field. Here it can be noted that there probably exist discrepancies regarding how roles are described in NICE, and to what extent such roles are prevalent on, for example, the Swedish labor market. Furthermore, the roles in NICE are described with varying granularity. The role *Database Administrator* can probably be defined with a fairly narrow unambiguous process description, while a role such as *Cyber Policy and Strategy Planner* probably does not allow itself to be succinctly defined. But, even if roles were well-defined, which, for example, is the case for the *Software Development* specialty area in which [a developer] "[d]evelops and writes/codes new (or modifies existing) computer applications" [31, p. 12], they can still differ significantly in practice. In a Swedish study about software development it was found that the competence requirements for software developers in various industrial sectors were extremely heterogeneous. There were wildly varying requirements regarding knowledge in areas such as artificial intelligence, embedded software, app programming, and e-commerce [5].

The roles in NICE also appear to be heavily influenced by tasks that are common in the U.S. (federal) defense and intelligence sector. This sector, however, probably only constitutes a minor part of the commercial sector as a whole. As a consequence, there is a risk that government-specific roles are given too much relative weight, given that all roles in NICE are "treated equally". In other words, an exaggeration of the importance of government-only jobs risks to influence the overall validity of the results negatively.

A final remark concerning NICE is that it contains a number of skills and abilities that become obsolete when tasks are automated. One example is skills related to the use of man-machine interfaces. There is no need for such skills when machines solely communicate with other machines.

5.1.2 The Assessments

As has already been brought forward, the variance of the judgments of the panel does not necessarily have to be seen as something negative. The variations can to some part be explained by their different backgrounds and knowledge levels. It was a deliberate goal of the research design to allow for variance and the use of mean values, as described, in order to produce well-balanced assessments. The panel members' scoring on skills and abilities relative to the four criteria was positively correlated, i.e., the assessments generally pointed in the same direction: if one assessor judged a value to be high, the others typically also thought so. The mean deviations between the scores of the assessors were moderate (on average 0.4 on a five-point scale). There were also systematic differences where, for example, the average scores for creativity differed between the assessors. For creativity the difference was almost a whole point (0.8) with mean values of 2.1, 2.4, 2.8, and 2.9 for the four assessors.

None of the factors mentioned this far are judged to be problematic. There were, however, also skills and abilities that showed discrepancies in judgments, that were probably not only due to the different backgrounds and knowledge levels of the assessors. During the seminar it was discovered that the actual meaning of certain skills and abilities were interpreted differently, because they were described in vague terms. One such example was the skill to perform intelligence collection on the so-called *dark web*. This skill was the one that showed the largest assessor score deviance of all skills and abilities. When this was discussed, it turned out that the assessors had made different assumptions about the context. This, in turn, led to that the skill was assessed to require anything between no social skills at all, to excellent skills. The former would be reasonable if the task was primarily about sifting through large amounts of text in search for specific information. The latter would be more sensible if social interactions were thought to be part of tricking informants to give up information. This example illustrate, again, that there can be different interpretations of the NICE descriptions. We assert that it would be hard, not to mention *extremely* time-consuming, to completely unify the views of all assessors for all the descriptions of the 541 analyzed tasks. In light of these remarks, the mean values that we used can be seen as a good approximation.

5.1.3 The Aggregation

The aggregation, in our opinion, was made in a straightforward and transparent manner. However, it also involved some simplifications. Two major ones are that:

1. all skills and abilities had the same weight, even if some probably are more important for successfully carrying out work in a role, than others,
2. all roles and specialties also had the same weight, even though there is a larger number of people working with, e.g., *System Administration* than with, e.g., *Executive Cyber Leadership* in the labor market.

Consequently, the analysis would be improved if the *portions* of the requirements of skills and abilities were judged for each role. Further, the assignment of weights to the various roles and specialties would, likewise, be helpful for improving analyses of market potential and addressing questions involving automation of multiple roles. This remains as future work.

Another deficiency in the aggregation process was that it relied on the underlying assumption that all tasks within a role can be fully automated, and not that only certain parts of it can. Further, some specific skills and abilities are more determinate than others for whether a role can be successfully automated. A survey filled out by participants at the large cybersecurity conferences DEF CON and Black Hat, can serve to illustrate this point. Respondents judged how important certain skills and abilities were for the specialty *Vulnerability Assessment and Management* [20]. Here, respondents judged a skill "in conducting vulnerability scans and recognizing vulnerabilities in security systems" to be the most important, which would be easy to automate. At the same time they judged that a skill "in the use of social engineering techniques" was less important. This skill would be significantly harder to automate.

The five models must be seen as gross simplifications that serve the purpose of representing recurring patterns, and not as a rigid method to exactly predict to what extent cybersecurity work can be automated. It is a bit surprising that the models, despite their fundamentally different constructions (e.g., linear vs. exponential, and minima vs. maxima), yield such a consistent ranking (as indicated by the heat map coloring in Tables 6, 7, and 8). One reason for this is that the values of the four criteria are correlated, i.e., high demands for creativity seldom come without equally high demands for another criterion, like perhaps social interaction. An advantage here is that the models display small differences, and that any model can be used. This, in turn, leads to the results of the study being, again, more robust, less susceptible to assumptions, and easier to interpret.

5.2   Other Important Variables

The results discussed this far have been about possibilities for automation as of *today*. This study can therefore provide some guidance about what role to automate first if there are several options to consider. There are, however, many other variables that also affect decisions about preferred automation solutions (as has been briefly touched upon in Sect. 2.1). In the following we discuss some of these.

5.2.1   Market Potential

It is reasonable to assume that the roles that are the easiest and most profitable to automate will be automated first [6]. Profitability can be reached in different ways, though. One could either automate jobs that are relatively simple, but occupy large groups of people, or more complicated jobs that occupy fewer, but better paid personnel. To roughly estimate the market potential for automation of various IT jobs, data from Statistics Sweden, the Swedish governmental agency for official statistics, has been used. Table 10 shows the grand sums of all monthly salaries that are paid out in various IT occupations.[3] As an example, it can be seen that the savings in salaries would be eight (8) times greater if the jobs of *Software- and system developers* were to be automated instead of *ICT operations technicians*, on the Swedish labor market. We did not, however, investigate if the allotment of portions of cybersecurity professions on the labor market is similar in other countries.

We used the data in Table 10 due to that we do not have access to statistics related to specific NICE roles, which means that the jobs displayed in the table do not fully relate to the jobs in the NICE framework. Comparisons are therefore hard to make. The website CyberSeek,[4] however, indicates the proportions of commonality of various IT jobs in terms of the NICE categories in the United States. There are great differences. In the beginning of April 2019 there were 207,190 jobs listed in the *Operate and Maintain* category, while a mere 49,825 were listed in *Collect and Operate*. To summarize, data from both Sweden and the United States suggest that the market potential for the various specialties in the NICE framework differ. The question of automation should therefore also be seen in light of this fact. Besides the number of specific jobs on the market—the *commonality* of jobs—as discussed, *competence requirements* also affect salaries [19]. Jobs with high demands yield high salaries and vice versa, and as mentioned jobs with high responsibility requirements appear to be difficult to automate.

---

[3] Compiled based on Statistics Sweden's table entitled "Employees 16–64 years at national level by occupation (4-digit SSYK 2012), sector, and sex. Year 2014–2017" in the Swedish occupational register, http://www.statistikdatabasen.scb.se/, and "Salary search", https://www.scb.se/en/finding-statistics/sverige-i-siffror/salary-search/.

[4] https://www.cyberseek.org/.

Table 10 IT jobs and the total amount of monthly salary paid out, based on average salaries and the number of people occupied within each job

Code	Name	Total salary (Swedish crowns, SEK)
2512	Software- and system developers	3,208,320,900
2511	System analysts and ICT-architects	666,564,200
3512	ICT support technicians	570,362,400
3514	Computer network and systems technicians	476,825,800
3511	ICT operations technicians	403,930,800
2614	Business and company lawyers	344,061,300
2515	System administrators	279,847,900
2514	System testers and test managers	249,895,000
3513	System administrators	154,556,200
2516	Security specialists (ICT)	93,998,000
3515	Webmasters and web administrators	77,634,000

5.2.2 Intent and Ability

Up til this point we have been reasoning about the feasibility of automation and market potential, but a few additional prerequisites also have to be fulfilled before automated solutions can be launched. There has to be a *will* to automate.

Already in 1957, Cowan noted that human resistance could be an obstacle to successful automation efforts [12]. Factors such as habit and fear were seen as prohibitive, including aspects related to, for example, personal complacency and the fear of losing a well paid or high status position. As a solution to turn people who felt threatened by automation, Cowan suggested either to seek their active involvement in the automation efforts, or extensive training. This would increase the chances for them to accept or even embrace automation [12]. These suggestions ring equally true today.

First, it seems to be hard to more precisely quantify the level of resistance towards machines by individuals in the cybersecurity field. Despite the quantification difficulties, this problem appears to be an important one for organizations to handle. We have previously put forth (see Sect. 2.1) that both usefulness and usability are important factors for prospective users when new technology is introduced [27]. All automation is probably not met with equal resistance, though; software testing is a task that may be perceived as less stimulating than, for example, systems architecture work, and may therefore encounter less resistance. A type of stronger resistance, where whole groups rather than individuals are united in "anti-automation" alliances, can also be imagined; on an organizational level, it is not too far-fetched that whole IT departments might fight efforts to outsource their tasks by, for example, buying cloud computing capabilities from an external supplier.

Second, both individuals and organizations have to be ready to not only accept automation changes, but also to *embrace* them. De Zan [15] argues that organizational changes generally follow when IT investments have been made, and new technology is introduced. Such changes can consist of restructured workflows and new ways of sharing data. Data can then be used for machine learning. A high degree of automation probably leads to a *more* data-intensive work environment. The increased amount of data could then lead to difficulties with the existing organizational structures and IT architecture. That is, it is no trivial task to actually make use of all (new) data to bring forth more efficient decisions [6].

5.2.3 Ethical and Legal Issues

Given the content of this chapter, one realizes that many tasks can be automated from a purely technical standpoint. Some of those tasks, however, will not be automated due to ethical or legal considerations. Self-driving cars is an example where the question of legal liability after an accident poses a great obstacle for automation: it is not permitted to abdicate the responsibility to a machine [23]. Other ethical and legal issues may also arise in cybersecurity, although the majority of cases are likely to be unproblematic. To have automated systems scan employees' e-mails for malware is probably not controversial. Such a solution, where no humans view personal information, may be preferred over a manual process. An investigation after abusive use of a company's IT resources, on the other hand, can probably not be fully automated. Decisions about filing formal criminal charges or firing an individual, cannot be delegated to a machine. For such cases there need to be humans in the loop. In line with this reasoning, it seems reasonable to believe that tasks in the NICE category *Investigate* are more suitable for automation than tasks that involve, e.g., executive leadership or judgmental components. It can also be speculated that there are probably considerably less ethical problems involved in tasks such as construction of new systems (e.g., *Systems Development*), than for tasks that involve collection of sensitive data related to systems already in use (e.g., *Collection Operations*).

Another example is the use of facial recognition technology. Such use would be perfectly feasible and serve a greater good by its ability to identify and catch criminals. There are, however, examples where use has been prohibited. The city of San Francisco chose to ban facial recognition in 2019 due to concerns regarding potential privacy issues and the possibility for abusive use.[5] Yet other aspects to keep in mind, are the introduction of potential biases in AI systems, and the opacity of the employed algorithms. Bias can be either deliberately or accidentally built into the algorithm itself, or arise from already biased training data [52]. Lack of algorithmic transparency can result in both ethical and practical problems. Research with the aim to interpret and explain *black box* decision support systems is ongoing [24].

It can be concluded that both laws and ethics are factors to be considered with regard to whether automation is allowed or not, but also with regard to whether it should be strived for or not. However, laws and ethics also affect the very *conditions* for creating automated solutions. The availability of data for research,

---

[5] https://www.nytimes.com/2019/05/14/us/facial-recognition-ban-san-francisco.html.

systems development, and alignment of automated solutions, can be regulated by laws. Mandatory reporting of cyber-related incidents, as an example, would greatly enhance the knowledge about cyberattacks, which could be used to extract knowledge for the benefit of cybersecurity efforts, not least for the handling of threat intelligence [45]. More restrictive laws related to personal integrity, on the other hand, would make the collection of large datasets for machine learning significantly harder.

5.3   Will Automation Improve Cybersecurity?

A highly relevant question to ponder is whether extensive AI automation of cybersecurity work actually improves the level of cybersecurity. In this section we speculate about possible outcomes. Coombs et al. [11] found no studies that evaluated changes in overall organizational performance even after extensive automation. We earlier brought up that it is more likely that specific tasks within a role are automated than all aspects of that role. Zhong et al. [53], for example, argue that cybersecurity work in security operations centers cannot be expected to be fully automated anytime in the near future. They stress that there are in principle two main paths to achieve increased efficiency in such centers. The first would be to identify areas that can be automated, and strive for the automation of those. The second would be to ensure viable coexistence conditions for humans and machines, so that maximum gains from the automated parts can be extracted. It is important to achieve synergies in man-machine teams and draw on the strengths of both.

There are factors that point towards improved cybersecurity due to automation. Automation will cut the time consumption for several tasks, and increased speed will be important against nonautomated adversaries. Another factor is that automation can help reduce the required amount of information that eventually needs to be considered by human analysts. A major (cognitive) problem for cybersecurity analysts is the need to process overwhelming amounts of information [13], e.g., to handle information overload [18]. Much time is spent on removing false positives from alert systems. At the same time it is important for human operators to maintain a high degree of attention and ability to focus over extended periods of time. Such "cyber vigilance" [35] has been shown to affect the results of maintaining good cybersecurity. Automation will, thus, help analysts to maintain their vigilance longer by removing tedious work and by reducing their cognitive load.

Hitherto we have discussed automation for cyber *defense*, which this chapter is about. It should be noted, though, that the potential for automation is equally present for other areas within the cyber domain. Technologies such as, e.g., automatic vulnerability scans [49], and machine learning approaches for improving intrusion detection systems [8], can just as well be used for offensive purposes. In fact, there are fears that ever-increasing use of AI for cybersecurity will lead to a "cyber arms race" that even risks to escalate into conventional war with actual physical attacks [44].

It is next to impossible to foresee the actual gains of future automation of cyber-security functions. The main factor that makes such predictions highly uncertain is that the underlying automation technology is available for potential adversaries as well. Potential improvements on the cybersecurity side therefore risk being levelled out by equal improvements on the adversarial side. But if this balance is tilted, and highly automated cybersecurity functions are up against nonautomated adversaries, chances are that the level of cybersecurity will be improved compared to today. The nature of cybersecurity work for humans may also change. If many tedious and time-consuming tasks are automated, the capabilities of human experts can be "saved" for particularly hard tasks.

5.4   Effects on the Labor Market

In this section we discuss possible effects on the (cybersecurity) labor market in an imaginary future scenario after most cybersecurity tasks have been automated.

It is evident that automation efforts this far have not resulted in a diminished need for IT work [15]. In 2014, it was reported that programmer was the most common profession in the (Swedish capital) Stockholm region [42], and that the need for programmers on the labor market remained at a high level. In 2019, *Software-and system developers* were ranked as the eighth largest profession in Sweden, according to Statistics Sweden.[6] In fact, the IT business as a whole continues to grow, and cybersecurity personnel are also in high demand [42]. Further, on the international level, multiple reports point to severe shortages of cybersecurity personnel. In addition, it has been reported that the shortage cannot be remedied in the near future, because the proposed solutions take time to implement [15].

Automation will increasingly affect work that is carried out in the cybersecurity field. The OECD [32] points out that personnel with the lowest level of training or salaries, are the ones that first risk being replaced by automated solutions. Here it is important to remember that whole professions are not necessarily going to be automated in their entirety [15]. What will remain are subtasks that computers (machines) are worse at solving than humans. These include unusual unscripted tasks, and tasks that require social interaction and problem-solving that cannot easily be described by algorithms.

In general, Brynjolfsson and McAfee [7] argue that technological advances have meant that the gap between the most competent part of the workforce, and those who perform on, or below, average, has increased. The most competent personnel tend to be more sought-after, indispensable, and therefore better paid, at the expense of the group that we here call the average performers. An indication of this phenomenon is that military commanders in the U.S. have been reported to claim that the most productive IT specialists produce up to a factor hundred more worth of effect, than

---

[6] https://www.scb.se/.

the least productive ones [7]. With this increased focus on specialized competencies and high productivity, it is therefore the average performers who risk being made redundant on the labor market. They will have to accept lowered salaries, or even permanent unemployment. In this chapter we have not dug into any details of this reasoning, but note that the same kind of reasoning probably applies to the cybersecurity labor market as well.

6 Conclusions

In this section we answer the three research questions that were outlined in Sect. 1. The reader should note that the answers represent the outcome of the analysis given the analytical process. That is to say that there are uncertainties regarding the universal validity of the conclusions. Moreover, the results apply for the wider cybersecurity field, that is, it is obviously possible to obtain better and more precise results for research questions targeting more isolated questions. For example, in the study presented by Sommer and Paxson [37] discussed in Sect. 2.2, the development of intrusion detection systems directly relates to automation of work performed specifically by the NICE framework role *Cyber Defense Incident Responder*.

6.1 What Variables Affect How Hard a Cybersecurity Role Is to Automate?

From the point of envisioning models for automation of generic work tasks, three variables of interest were identified. In the beginning of our analysis, however, four variables emerged: requirements for creativity, social interaction, physical work, and the availability of statistical data related to the role in question. These variables in themselves represent gross simplifications, as they can be described in many equally sensible ways. Creativity, as an example, can be seen both as having a capability to invent novel solutions (originality), and to identify viable (but already existing) solutions to problems. The latter seems more common. It is therefore a problem to isolate and succinctly define variables that affect the possibilities for automation. The exception is the requirement for physical work, which clearly involves physical movement. Out of the original four variables, physical work was determined to play an insignificant role (see Sect. 4.1), and was removed. The answer to the question is, thus:

- requirements for creativity,
- requirements for social interaction, and
- the availability of statistical data.

The importance of the variables vary with roles (see Table 4). There are also differences in the types of requirements for different roles. Tasks carried out by a *Program Manager* and an *IT Program Auditor* have requirements for creativity and for social interaction on roughly the same level, whilst a *Systems Developer* and a *Systems Security Analyst* are performing tasks that have significantly higher requirements for creativity than for social interaction. It could be noted that the requirements covary to a large extent, i.e., if there is a requirement for a high value for one variable (like creativity), there is often a similarly high requirement for another variable (like the availability of statistical data):

- requirements for social interaction and requirements for creativity for various skills and abilities have a correlation coefficient of 0.38,
- requirements for social interaction and availability of statistical data for various skills and abilities have a correlation coefficient of 0.58,
- requirements for creativity and availability of statistical data for various skills and abilities have a correlation coefficient of 0.73.

The covariation demonstrated above is not particularly unexpected. For example, social skills often require creative ways of communicating, and it is natural that tasks without documented historical examples/data to rely on, require creative solutions. This means, however, that the answer to the question becomes less clear, i.e., the fact that the variables covariate indicates that there are underlying variables that play a role, and that the criteria used for the study presented herein are in this sense not an optimal (orthogonal) breakdown of the variables that affect automation. What these underlying variables might be, and which criteria might be more suitable, is left for future research.

6.2   How Likely Is It That Current Cybersecurity Roles Will Be Automated?

The tables in Sect. 4 show significant differences between how hard it seems to be to automate various roles. They show that it is much easier to automate tasks that database administrators, data analysts, and network specialists perform, than those performed by intelligence analysts and senior executives. There are indicators that support this conclusion. For example, there are studies that show that the budgets allotted for database administrators decreased between 2013 and 2017.[7] However, as already mentioned in Sect. 5, it is unlikely that whole professions will be automated simultaneously, and the cybersecurity market as a whole does not necessarily seem to be moving in a direction where a majority of its personnel will be deemed redundant or need retraining. On the contrary, the U.S. Bureau of Labor Statistics,

---

[7] Computer Economics, Inc., "Database Administrator Ranks Show Steady Decline", https://www. computereconomics.com/article.cfm?id=2439.

for example, suggests that database administrators are heading towards a bright future, where the rate of increase is larger than that of the average profession.[8] This, in turn, might in part be explained by the increase of the whole IT sector, making it possible that database administrators face a bright future even if their relative percentage of the IT budget decreases.

6.3 What Variables Constrain the Potential for Automation of Today's Cybersecurity Roles?

As has been described in Sect. 6.1, the variables covary. This makes it hard to conclusively answer the question about the most constraining variables. However, some indications are that:

- the low demand for physical work, tells us that this requirement is not a significant obstacle (see, for example, Scenarios 3 and 12 in Table 9),
- the requirement for social interaction is a minor obstacle than the requirement for creativity and the lack of statistical data (see, for example, Scenarios 6, 7, and 9 in Table 9),
- the requirement for creativity and the need for existing statistical data covaries strongly (with a correlation coefficient of 0.73).

Based on the above remarks, a conclusion is that an ability to produce machines that suggest creative solutions to hard problems, would enable many roles to be automated. Another possibility to enhance the chances for automation would be to focus on collecting data to be used for machine learning. In practice, these suggestions are not mutually exclusive, though: recent creative advances in AI hinge upon the availability of historical data with correct solutions (labeled datasets), or the possibility to create relevant data by, for example, letting machines compete against each other. The lack of data, hence, seems to be a significant obstacle for further automation within the cybersecurity field.

Acknowledgments This work was originally commissioned to the Swedish Defence Research Agency, FOI, by the Swedish Civil Contingencies Agency, MSB. Some initial results were reported on in a short memo [38]. Stefan Varga was sponsored by the Swedish Armed Forces. The authors would like to acknowledge and thank Erik Zouave for his part in the assessment work.

---

[8] U.S. Department of Labor Bureau of Labor Statistics, Occupational Outlook Handbook, "Database Administrators and Architects", https://www.bls.gov/ooh/computer-and-information-technology/database-administrators.htm.

References

1. Arntz, M., Gregory, T., Zierahn, U.: Revisiting the risk of automation. Econ. Lett. **159**, 157–160 (2017). https://doi.org/10.1016/j.econlet.2017.07.001
2. Autor, D.H., Levy, F., Murnane, R.J.: The skill content of recent technological change: an empirical exploration. Q. J. Econ. **118**(4), 1279–1333 (2003). https://doi.org/10.1162/003355303322552801
3. Avgerinos, T., Cha, S.K., Rebert, A., Schwartz, E.J., Woo, M., Brumley, D.: Automatic exploit generation. Commun. ACM **57**(2), 74–84 (2014). https://doi.org/10.1145/2560217.2560219
4. Barr, E.T., Harman, M., McMinn, P., Shahbaz, M., Yoo, S.: The oracle problem in software testing: a survey. IEEE Trans. Softw. Eng. **41**(5), 507–525 (2015). https://doi.org/10.1109/TSE.2014.2372785
5. Borg, M., Wernberg, J., Olsson, T., Franke, U., Andersson, M.: Illuminating a blind spot in digitalization: software development in Sweden's private and public sector. In: Proceedings of the IEEE/ACM 42nd International Conference on Software Engineering Workshops (ICSEW 2020), pp. 299–302. ACM, New York (2020). https://doi.org/10.1145/3387940.3392213
6. Bresnahan, T.F., Brynjolfsson, E., Hitt, L.M.: Information technology, workplace organization, and the demand for skilled labor: firm-level evidence. Q. J. Econ. **117**(1), 339–376 (2002). https://doi.org/10.1162/003355302753399526
7. Brynjolfsson, E., McAfee, A.: The Second Machine Age: Work, Progress, and Prosperity in a Time of Brilliant Technologies. W. W. Norton & Company, New York (2014)
8. Buczak, A.L., Guven, E.: A survey of data mining and machine learning methods for cyber security intrusion detection. IEEE Commun. Surv. Tutorials **18**(2), 1153–1176 (2016). https://doi.org/10.1109/COMST.2015.2494502
9. Chen, T.R., Shore, D.B., Zaccaro, S.J., Dalal, R.S., Tetrick, L.E., Gorab, A.K.: An organizational psychology perspective to examining computer security incident response teams. IEEE Secur. Privacy **12**(5), 61–67 (2014). https://doi.org/10.1109/MSP.2014.85
10. Connell, J.: Kitanai, kitsui and kiken: the rise of labour migration to Japan. ERRRU Working Paper No 13, Economic and Regional Restructuring Research Unit, University of Sydney, Sydney (1993)
11. Coombs, C., Hislop, D., Taneva, S.K., Barnard, S.: The strategic impacts of intelligent automation for knowledge and service work: an interdisciplinary review. J. Strategic Inform. Syst. **29**(4), 1–30 (2020). https://doi.org/10.1016/j.jsis.2020.101600
12. Cowan, G.R.: The human side of automation. Electr. Eng. **76**(9), 768–771 (1957). https://doi.org/10.1109/EE.1957.6442704
13. D'Amico, A., Whitley, K., Tesone, D., O'Brien, B., Roth, E.: Achieving cyber defense situational awareness: a cognitive task analysis of information assurance analysts. Proc. Hum. Fact. Ergon. Soc. Annu. Meeting **49**(3), 229–233 (2005). https://doi.org/10.1177/154193120504900304
14. Dasgupta, P., Collins, J.B.: A survey of game theoretic approaches for adversarial machine learning in cybersecurity tasks. AI Mag. **40**(2), 31–43 (2019). https://doi.org/10.1609/aimag.v40i2.2847
15. De Zan, T.: Mind the gap: the cyber security skills shortage and public policy interventions. Tech. rep., Global Cyber Security Center, Rome (2019)
16. Deloitte: 2018 Luxembourg cyber security technology adoption survey (2018)
17. D'Silva, V., Kroening, D., Weissenbacher, G.: A survey of automated techniques for formal software verification. IEEE Trans. Comput.-Aided Design Integr. Circuits Syst. **27**(7), 1165–1178 (2008). https://doi.org/10.1109/TCAD.2008.923410
18. Eppler, M.J., Mengis, J.: The concept of information overload: a review of literature from organization science, accounting, marketing, MIS, and related disciplines. Inform. Soc. **20**(5), 325–344 (2004). https://doi.org/10.1080/01972240490507974

19. Erbacher, R.F., Frincke, D.A., Wong, P.C., Moody, S., Fink, G.: A multi-phase network situational awareness cognitive task analysis. Inform. Visualization **9**(3), 204–219 (2010). https://doi.org/10.1057/ivs.2010.5
20. Ferguson-Walter, K.J., Shade, T.B., Rogers, A.V., Niedbala, E.M., Trumbo, M.C., Nauer, K., Divis, K.M., Jones, A.P., Combs, A., Abbott, R.G.: The Tularosa study: an experimental design and implementation to quantify the effectiveness of cyber deception. In: Proceedings of the 52nd Annual Hawaii International Conference on System Sciences (HICSS 2019), pp. 7272–7281 (2019). https://doi.org/10.24251/HICSS.2019.874
21. Frey, C.B., Osborne, M.A.: The future of employment: how susceptible are jobs to computerisation? Technol. Forecasting Soc. Change **114**, 254–280 (2017). https://doi.org/10.1016/j.techfore.2016.08.019
22. Goodall, J.R., Lutters, W.G., Komlodi, A.: I know my network: collaboration and expertise in intrusion detection. In: Proceedings of the 2004 ACM Conference on Computer Supported Cooperative Work (CSCW 2004), pp. 342–345. ACM, New York (2004). https://doi.org/10.1145/1031607.1031663
23. Greenblatt, N.A.: Self-driving cars and the law. IEEE Spectr. **53**(2), 46–51 (2016). https://doi.org/10.1109/MSPEC.2016.7419800
24. Guidotti, R., Monreale, A., Ruggieri, S., Turini, F., Giannotti, F., Pedreschi, D.: A survey of methods for explaining black box models. ACM Comput. Surv. **51**(5), 1–42 (2018). https://doi.org/10.1145/3236009
25. Guo, M., Wang, G., Hata, H., Babar, M.A.: Revenue maximizing markets for zero-day exploits. Auton. Agents Multi-Agent Syst. **35**(2), 1–29 (2021). https://doi.org/10.1007/s10458-021-09522-w
26. Harreld, J.B.: Foreword: automation is at the center of human progress. In: Nof, S.Y. (ed.) Springer Handbook of Automation, Springer Handbooks, pp. XI–XII. Springer, Berlin/Heidelberg (2009). https://doi.org/10.1007/978-3-540-78831-7
27. King, W.R., He, J.: A meta-analysis of the technology acceptance model. Inform. Manag. **43**(6), 740–755 (2006). https://doi.org/10.1016/j.im.2006.05.003
28. Kordy, B., Piètre-Cambacédès, L., Schweitzer, P.: DAG-based attack and defense modeling: don't miss the forest for the attack trees. Comput. Sci. Rev. **13–14**, 1–38 (2014). https://doi.org/10.1016/j.cosrev.2014.07.001
29. Liu, B., Shi, L., Cai, Z., Li, M.: Software vulnerability discovery techniques: a survey. In: Proceedings of the 2012 Fourth International Conference on Multimedia Information Networking and Security (MINES 2012), pp. 152–156. IEEE, Piscataway (2012). https://doi.org/10.1109/MINES.2012.202
30. Manyika, J., Chui, M., Miremadi, M., Bughin, J., George, K., Willmott, P., Dewhurst, M.: A future that works: automation, employment, and productivity. Report, McKinsey Global Institute, San Francisco (2017)
31. Newhouse, W., Keith, S., Scribner, B., Witte, G.: National initiative for cybersecurity education (NICE) cybersecurity workforce framework. NIST Special Publication 800-181, National Institute of Standards and Technology, U.S. Department of Commerce (2017). https://doi.org/10.6028/NIST.SP.800-181
32. OECD: Artificial Intelligence in Society. OECD Publishing, Paris (2019). https://doi.org/10.1787/eedfee77-en
33. Parasuraman, R., Riley, V.: Humans and automation: use, misuse, disuse, abuse. Hum. Fact. **39**(2), 230–253 (1997). https://doi.org/10.1518/001872097778543886
34. Patton, R.D., Patton, P.C.: What can be automated? What cannot be automated? In: Nof, S.Y. (ed.) Springer Handbook of Automation, Springer Handbooks, chap. 18, pp. 305–313. Springer, Berlin/Heidelberg (2009). https://doi.org/10.1007/978-3-540-78831-7_18
35. Sawyer, B.D., Finomore, V.S., Funke, G.J., Mancuso, V.F., Funke, M.E., Matthews, G., Warm, J.S.: Cyber vigilance: effects of signal probability and event rate. Proc. Hum. Fact. Ergon. Soc. Annu. Meeting **58**(1), 1771–1775 (2014). https://doi.org/10.1177/1541931214581369

36. Scandariato, R., Walden, J., Joosen, W.: Static analysis versus penetration testing: a controlled experiment. In: 2013 IEEE 24th International Symposium on Software Reliability Engineering (ISSRE 2013), pp. 451–460. IEEE, Piscataway (2013). https://doi.org/10.1109/ISSRE.2013.6698898

37. Sommer, R., Paxson, V.: Outside the closed world: on using machine learning for network intrusion detection. In: Proceedings of the 2010 IEEE Symposium on Security and Privacy, pp. 305–316. IEEE, Piscataway (2010). https://doi.org/10.1109/SP.2010.25

38. Sommestad, T., Brynielsson, J., Varga, S.: Möjligheter för automation av roller inom cyber-säkerhetsområdet [Opportunities for automation of cybersecurity roles]. FOI Memo 6737, Swedish Defence Research Agency, Stockholm (2019)

39. Sommestad, T., Franke, U.: A test of intrusion alert filtering based on network information. Secur. Commun. Netw. **8**(13), 2291–2301 (2015). https://doi.org/10.1002/sec.1173

40. Sommestad, T., Hunstad, A.: Intrusion detection and the role of the system administrator. Inform. Manag. Comput. Secur. **21**(1), 30–40 (2013). https://doi.org/10.1108/09685221311314400

41. Sommestad, T., Sandström, F.: An empirical test of the accuracy of an attack graph analysis tool. Inform. Comput. Secur. **23**(5), 516–531 (2015). https://doi.org/10.1108/ICS-06-2014-0036

42. Stockholm Chamber of Commerce: Programmerare: vanligaste yrket i Stockholmsregionen [Programmer: the most common profession in the Stockholm region]. Analys 2014:3, Stockholms Handelskammare, Stockholm (2014)

43. Suta, C., Barbieri, L., May-Gillings, M.: Future employment and automation. In: Hogarth, T. (ed.) Economy, Employment and Skills: European, Regional and Global Perspectives in an Age of Uncertainty, pp. 17–43. Fondazione Giacomo Brodolini, Rome (2018)

44. Taddeo, M., Floridi, L.: Regulate artificial intelligence to avert cyber arms race. Nature **556**(7701), 296–298 (2018). https://doi.org/10.1038/d41586-018-04602-6

45. Tounsi, W., Rais, H.: A survey on technical threat intelligence in the age of sophisticated cyber attacks. Comput. Secur. **72**, 212–233 (2018). https://doi.org/10.1016/j.cose.2017.09.001

46. van de Weijer, S.G.A., Leukfeldt, R., Bernasco, W.: Determinants of reporting cybercrime: a comparison between identity theft, consumer fraud, and hacking. Eur. J. Criminol. **16**(4), 486–508 (2019). https://doi.org/10.1177/1477370818773610

47. van der Zande, J., Teigland, K., Siri, S., Teigland, R.: The substitution of labor: from technological feasibility to other factors influencing the potential of job automation. In: Larsson, A., Teigland, R. (eds.) The Digital Transformation of Labor: Automation, the Gig Economy and Welfare, Routledge Studies in Labour Economics, chap. 3, pp. 31–73. Routledge, London (2019)

48. Verendel, V.: Quantified security is a weak hypothesis: a critical survey of results and assumptions. In: Proceedings of the 2009 Workshop on New Security Paradigms Workshop (NSPW 2009), pp. 37–49. ACM, New York (2009). https://doi.org/10.1145/1719030.1719036

49. Wen, T., Zhang, Y., Wu, Q., Yang, G.: ASVC: an automatic security vulnerability categorization framework based on novel features of vulnerability data. J. Commun. **10**(2), 107–116 (2015). https://doi.org/10.12720/jcm.10.2.107-116

50. Werlinger, R., Hawkey, K., Beznosov, K.: An integrated view of human, organizational, and technological challenges of IT security management. Inform. Manag. Comput. Secur. **17**(1), 4–19 (2009). https://doi.org/10.1108/09685220910944722

51. Werlinger, R., Muldner, K., Hawkey, K., Beznosov, K.: Towards understanding diagnostic work during the detection and investigation of security incidents. In: Proceedings of the Third International Symposium on Human Aspects of Information Security & Assurance (HAISA 2009), pp. 119–132 (2009)

52. Wilner, A.S.: Cybersecurity and its discontents: artificial intelligence, the internet of things, and digital misinformation. Int. J. **73**(2), 308–316 (2018). https://doi.org/10.1177/0020702018782496

53. Zhong, C., Yen, J., Liu, P.: Can cyber operations be made autonomous? An answer from the situational awareness viewpoint. In: Jajodia, S., Cybenko, G., Subrahmanian, V.S., Swarup, V., Wang, C., Wellman, M. (eds.) Adaptive Autonomous Secure Cyber Systems, pp. 63–88. Springer, Cham (2020). https://doi.org/10.1007/978-3-030-33432-1_4

Artificial Intelligence for Cybersecurity Education and Training

Razvan Beuran, Zhenguo Hu, Youmeizi Zeng, and Yasuo Tan

1 Introduction

In the last decade Artificial Intelligence (AI) has found applications in many fields, and has changed our daily life in many ways, for example via the proliferation of virtual personal assistants. As it can be expected, AI techniques have also been applied to the field of cybersecurity, by putting to use the data analysis capabilities of AI and machine learning for tasks such as the detection of threats or incidents, risk prediction, endpoint protection, and so on [3].

The Cyber Range Organization and Design (CROND) NEC-endowed chair, which has been in place between April 2015 and March 2021 at Japan Advanced Institute of Science and Technology (JAIST), focused on research and development related to cybersecurity education and training. As part of this research activity we have investigated the use of AI techniques in the field of cybersecurity training, which has so far received less focus than other cybersecurity domains, and our results have revealed the promising potential that AI has for this field.

In this chapter we present two applications of AI to cybersecurity education and training that we developed at CROND, as follows:

1. *Deep Reinforcement Learning (DRL) for penetration testing training*: We implemented a penetration testing framework, AutoPentest-DRL, that employs DRL to recommend an attack path for a given target network, thus making it possible to study in a practical manner the mechanisms of penetration testing.
2. *Natural Language Generation (NLG) for security awareness education*: We implemented an awareness training platform, CyATP, that uses NLG to automatically generate training content based on data retrieved from Wikipedia and

R. Beuran (✉) · Z. Hu · Y. Zeng · Y. Tan
Japan Advanced Institute of Science and Technology, Nomi, Japan
e-mail: razvan@jaist.ac.jp; zhghu@jaist.ac.jp; s1910129@jaist.ac.jp; ytan@jaist.ac.jp

T. Sipola et al. (eds.), *Artificial Intelligence and Cybersecurity*,
https://doi.org/10.1007/978-3-031-15030-2_5

DBpedia, and includes both learning and gamification features, such as quizzes and crossword puzzles.

We note that both AutoPentest-DRL and CyATP were released as open source on GitHub, and can be used as such or extended if needed by any interested party [5].

The remainder of this chapter is organized as follows. In Sect. 2 we provide an overview of cybersecurity education and training. Sect. 3 introduces the manner in which we applied DRL techniques to penetration testing, and presents the AutoPentest-DRL framework that we implemented. Sect. 4 discusses the approach we took to apply NLG techniques to security awareness education, and the CyATP platform that we developed. The chapter ends with conclusions and references.

2 Cybersecurity Education and Training

An increasing number of security incidents affect all kinds of organizations, companies, and education institutions across the globe. To reduce the occurrence and impact of such incidents, it is necessary to actively conduct cybersecurity education and training for the employees of these organizations. Depending on the skill level of the participants, training activities can be divided into two classes (see Fig. 1):

- *Technical security training*, which aims to improve the technical knowledge and skills of security experts and IT professionals involved in security tasks, so that they can efficiently handle cybersecurity issues at their work place.
- *Security awareness training*, which focuses on providing the basic knowledge and skills to IT users and those IT professionals that are not involved in security tasks, so as to reduce the risks that they fall prey to cyberattacks while they carry out their daily activities.

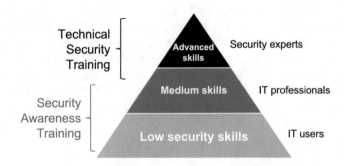

Fig. 1 Pyramid of cybersecurity skills—the type of security training depends on the participant skill level

2.1 Technical Security Training

Technical security training is aimed at developing the technical skills of the participants, therefore practical activities are often included in the training, such as hands-on practice on cyber ranges. Moreover, the content of the practical activities is structured so as to cover one or more of the three aspects of cybersecurity training, which are attack, forensics and defense [4].

One way of learning attack techniques is via penetration testing (also called *pentesting*) practice. Pentesting is an authorized simulated cyberattack on an organization network that is used to assess the cybersecurity posture of that organization. By using the perspective of penetration testers, trainees are able to deeply understand the practical mechanisms of cyberattacks. Furthermore, investigating the traces of an attack helps in developing forensics skills, and the knowledge about attack techniques is useful when designing defense mechanisms, hence penetration testing training can be considered as an entry point for cybersecurity training.

Consequently, one of our research areas was the penetration testing training aspect of cybersecurity education and training. In order to enable the study of its mechanisms in a practical manner, we propose the use of DRL to recommend a suitable attack path for a given target network. Trainees can then analyze this recommendation to understand its advantages, and even use the system we developed to experience how the attack can be put into practice. Details about this approach will be provided in Sect. 3.

2.2 Security Awareness Training

Security awareness training is not concerned with technical knowledge or skills, since the main target audience are regular IT users. Instead, basic knowledge about IT and security, sometimes called IT literacy, needs to be provided to a wide public, which may be less motivated than the technical staff. Therefore, a different approach must be taken to make the training more effective and attractive, and one possibility is to use the serious game approach for this purpose.

Serious games are games which incorporate pedagogic elements and that are not intended to be played primarily for amusement purposes. While the concept of serious games was initially introduced in the context of role playing in the 1970s [1], it has been since extended to computer games as well. By incorporating game elements into security awareness training via gamification, the motivation of the learners can be increased, and retention rate improvements are also to be expected.

Another challenge related to security awareness training is that typically the training content is created manually by educators, which is a time consuming process. This also means that the training content is potentially updated more rarely, which can become an issue in the quickly-evolving field of cybersecurity.

In order to address this challenge, we propose to use NLG techniques to automatically generate the awareness training content based on publicly available data from Wikipedia and DBpedia. In a first form this training content is used directly for studying, but we have also created training content for the serious game components of the platform, which are quizzes and crossword puzzles, thus making the overall learning process more enjoyable. This approach will be presented in Sect. 4.

3 Penetration Testing Training Using DRL

Attack techniques are an important component of security training, and learning how to conduct penetration testing is a basic way of studying attack techniques. In what follows we provide first a research background on penetration testing, then an overview of Deep Reinforcement Learning (DRL) and how we applied it in our research, and finally we introduce the AutoPentest-DRL penetration testing framework that we designed and implemented. For an in-depth discussion of this research, please refer to [10].

3.1 Research Background

Penetration testing is typically conducted manually by ethical hackers following standard frameworks or methodologies, such as the Penetration Testing Execution Standard (PTES), which outlines the steps to be carried out when executing pentesting [22]. When carrying out such activities, ethical hackers rely on standard tools, such as Nmap [12] or Metasploit [24] to conduct each step, and the sequence of their actions is decided based on the personal experience of each ethical hacker. However, there are no guarantees that such pentesting execution will be exhaustive, and over the years methods have been developed to improve the thoroughness.

One of the first approaches used in connection with analyzing the security of a system was the *attack tree*, which was proposed in 1999 by Schneier as a method of formal threat and risk analysis [29]. This method was generalized in 2002 by Sheyner to the case of *attack graphs*, thus improving the security analysis flexibility [30]. Several tools have been implemented to generate the attack graph corresponding to a given system topology, and one of the most widely used is MulVAL [20]. While these approaches are by themselves not sufficient for conducting penetration testing practically, they represent valuable stepping stones, and we have actually employed them in our approach, as it will be discussed in section "Attack Graph".

Attack path planning takes the above idea further towards the goal of practical penetration testing. One example in this area leverages the Plan Domain Definition Language (PDDL) as a way of applying planning methods to determine attack paths for penetration testing purposes [18]. This approach was further extended to use the so-called Probabilistic PDDL (PPDDL) in order to make it possible to handle the uncertainty involved in attack planning [28]. While such approaches are powerful, they are computationally intensive; moreover, the target system representation, including the full network topology and host configuration, must be known and set up in advance for these approaches to work.

In order to model the decisions that occur during pentesting execution it was also proposed to use a Markov Decision Process (MDP), which is a methodology for modeling problems of discrete decision making by taking into account uncertainty. This approach was used for automated pentesting by considering the possible outcomes of each action, with the goal of realistically simulating a human hacker [9]. However, this method did not take into account the actual system configuration, which is essential in pentesting execution. Our approach attempts to improve on the limitations of the above methods, including via the ability to automatically gather information about the target system and actually execute the pentesting activity. Moreover, we also rely on deep reinforcement learning, as it is described next.

3.2 Deep Reinforcement Learning Approach

The AI technique called Reinforcement Learning (RL) uses a model of an agent taking actions in an environment, and the goal of the training is for the agent to get a maximum cumulative reward for its actions [32]. This makes RL very suitable for sequential decision making, such as that involved in penetration testing [8].

Deep Reinforcement Learning (DRL) combines the reinforcement learning approach with deep learning. One of the most used types of DRL is Deep Q-Network (DQN), proposed as a way to provide human-level control for computer game playing [15]. DQN combines the Q-Learning model-free reinforcement learning technique with the Convolution Neural Network (CNN) algorithm for deep learning, thus creating a powerful DRL model. Figure 2 provides an overview on DQN operation.

In order to apply DQN to penetration testing, an appropriate representation has to be associated to the four main elements of reinforcement learning: the agent, the agent actions, the rewards for those actions, and the environment in which the agent operates. In our case the agent corresponds to the penetration tester, the agent actions are the decisions taken when conducting penetration testing, and the environment is the network environment in which the pentester operates. As for the rewards, they must be correlated with the value a certain action has from a pentesting point of view. The next subsections provide more details about these aspects.

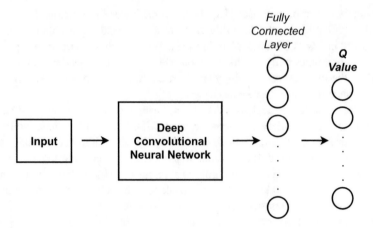

Fig. 2 Overview of the Deep Q-Network (DQN) approach for deep reinforcement learning

3.2.1 Attack Graph

Schneier proposed the use of an attack tree model to represent the interdependence between attack behaviors and attack steps in order to analyze the security threats regarding a given system [29]. The root node of the tree indicates the attack goal, and for each node in the tree its children represent the conditions that are needed to reach that stage in the attack, which can be either of *OR* or of *AND* type.

The idea of attack tree was extended by Sheyner, who proposed the use of an attack graph model to represent the actions of potential intruders [30]. The attack graph includes three kinds of vertices that are each used to represent: (i) system configurations, including security vulnerabilities; (ii) privileges that an attacker gains by exploiting given vulnerabilities; (iii) rules that link the preconditions for an attack step to its consequences.

In order to generate the attack graph for a given network environment, tools such as MulVAL (Multi-host, Multi-stage Vulnerability Analysis Language) can be used [20, 27]. The input of MulVAL is a representation of the network environment, such as the network topology and the vulnerabilities of each node. The output of MulVAL is the attack graph generated for a certain target node in that environment. An example of such an attack graph produced by MulVAL is given in Fig. 3.

3.2.2 Action Representation

While the attack graph is useful for the analysis of the attack paths for a given network topology, it is not an appropriate format for the DQN model. Therefore, we converted the attack graph into an action representation in matrix form that is suitable as input for DQN. In a first instance, this is basically a matrix representation of the attach graph, in which cell values are the rewards in the DQN algorithm.

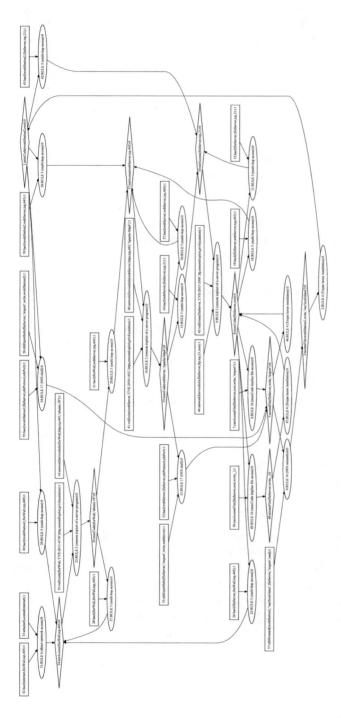

Fig. 3 Example of an attack graph generated by MulVAL

Fig. 4 Example of an attack
matrix created using the DFS
algorithm on the MulVAL
attack graph matrix
representation

$$
\begin{bmatrix}
0.01 & 4.6 & 2.5 & 1.6 & \cdots & -1 \\
0 & -1 & -1 & -1 & \cdots & 100 \\
0 & -1 & -1 & -1 & \cdots & 100 \\
0 & -1 & -1 & -1 & \cdots & 100 \\
\vdots & \vdots & \vdots & \vdots & \ddots & \vdots \\
0 & -1 & -1 & -1 & \cdots & 100 \\
-1 & 0 & 0 & 0 & \cdots & -1
\end{bmatrix}
$$

In order to assign rewards to penetration testing actions, we leveraged the
Common Vulnerability Scoring System (CVSS) v3.1, which provides numerical
values for each known vulnerability [16]. The CVSS values we used are the *base
score*, which quantifies how serious overall a vulnerability is, and the *exploitability
score*, which quantifies how easy it is to exploit it; both these scores range from
0 to 10. In particular, we defined the reward associated to exploiting a certain
vulnerability, $Reward_{vul}$, as follows:

$$
Reward_{vul} = Score_{base} \times \frac{Score_{exploitability}}{10}, \tag{1}
$$

where $Score_{base}$ is the base score of that vulnerability, and $Score_{exploitability}$ is its
exploitability score.

Given the definition above, we assign the following reward values to each cell of
the action representation matrix:

- For attack graph vertices that include vulnerabilities, we use the $Reward_{vul}$ value
  in Eq. 1 as reward.
- For the starting vertex of an attack path the reward value is 0.01, and for the end
  vertex (the attack goal), it is 100.
- For all the graph vertices that correspond to exploits, except for the end vertex,
  the reward value is 0.2.
- For any other vertex we assign the reward value 0 if it is accessible from another
  vertex, and -1 if it is not.

To speed up computation, we created an alternative representation matrix of a
smaller size by using the DFS (Depth First Search) algorithm. Specifically, we used
the DFS algorithm to search all the attack paths in the initial action representation
matrix and build a new matrix that only includes those paths. In the new matrix, the
cell value for each combination of start and end vertices of a valid attack path is the
sum of the intermediate vertex rewards. This new matrix represents the input of the
DQN model in our system. An example of such a matrix is shown in Fig. 4.

3.3 *AutoPentest-DRL*

AutoPentest-DRL is the automated penetration testing framework that we designed and implemented using DRL to determine the most appropriate attack path for a given logical network. AutoPentest-DRL can also be used to execute a penetration testing attack on a real network via tools such as Nmap [12] and Metasploit [24]. This framework is intended for educational purposes, and trainees can use it to study penetration testing attack mechanisms.

An overview of AutoPentest-DRL is shown in Fig. 5. The framework receives user input regarding the logical target network, including vulnerability information; alternatively, the framework can use Nmap to discover via network scanning the actual vulnerabilities in a real target network with known topology. MulVAL is then used to generate the attack graph for that topology, which is fed in a simplified matrix form into the DRL engine. The attack path that is produced as output can be used to study various attack mechanisms for a large number of logical networks. The framework can also use the attack path with the Metasploit penetration testing framework, making it possible for the user to examine how the attack is carried out in practice on a real target network.

3.3.1   Features

AutoPentest-DRL has several features that support training activities related to penetration testing techniques, as follows:

- *Real vulnerability data*: The Shodan search engine [13] was used to collect data about real hosts for several types of servers (web server, file server, etc.), and this data is used to populate with actual vulnerabilities the logical network topologies that are used to train the DRL engine.
- *Vulnerability dataset*: The National Vulnerability Database (NVD) [17] and the Microsoft vulnerability database [14] were used as sources of information about actual security vulnerabilities; in particular, the DRL engine employs the CVSS score to compute the reward for each exploit action in the attack graph.

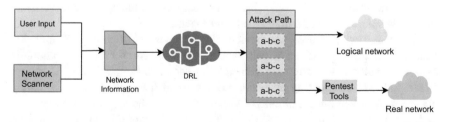

Fig. 5 Overview of the AutoPentest-DRL framework

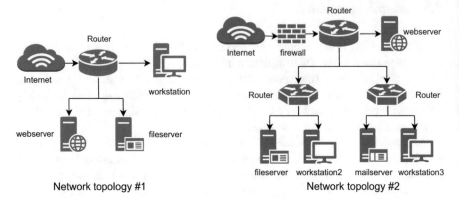

Fig. 6 Logical network topologies used to evaluate AutoPentest-DRL

- *Network scanning*: Nmap can be used to discover the actual vulnerabilities for the hosts of interest in a real target network; in this case, the IP addresses for the hosts to be scanned must be provided in advance via a configuration file.
- *Logical network pentesting*: When used in logical attack mode, the framework will output the recommended attack path for the input logical network; this attack path can be used to study the actions needed to conduct pentesting in the given logical network.
- *Real network pentesting*: When used in real attack mode, after generating the recommended attack path for the input real network, the framework will employ the Metasploit framework to attempt that attack in the given network; this is achieved by employing the RPC API of Metasploit to control it according to the actions in the recommended attack path.

3.3.2 Evaluation

We have evaluated AutoPentest-DRL both on logical and real networks. The logical network topologies we have used for evaluation are shown in Fig. 6. The first of them is very basic, with two servers and a workstation connected via a router, whereas the second one is somewhat more complex, including three servers and two workstations, but also a firewall and three routers.

For evaluation purposes we created 500 instances of topology #1 and 500 instances of topology #2 in which each server and workstation was randomly assigned a vulnerability from our vulnerability database. For each case the correct attack path was assessed by analyzing the results of the MulVAL deep trimming algorithm. We then ran AutoPentest-DRL to determine the recommended path for each topology, and concluded that the correct path was output in 932 cases and the wrong one in 68 cases, leading to an accuracy of 93.2%. The detailed results are shown in Fig. 7.

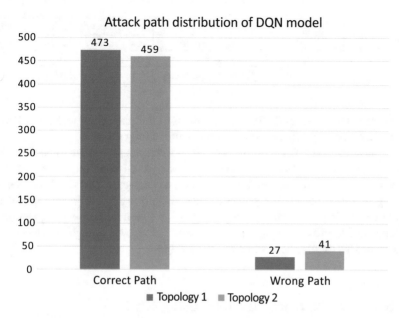

Fig. 7 Accuracy of AutoPentest-DRL for the two logical network topologies

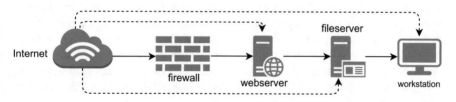

Fig. 8 Evaluation of AutoPentest-DRL with a real network create using virtual machines

We also evaluated AutoPentest-DRL on a real network topology created by means of virtual machines. In this case, we deployed the Nmap scanning and Metasploit attack features of the framework, and we confirmed that the framework is able to determine the correct attack path for that topology and conduct the attack as intended. The evaluation was conducted as shown in Fig. 8. For simplicity, we assumed that once a host is taken control of it becomes accessible from the Internet, so that all hosts can be accessed from the same Metasploit machine. A tunnel mechanism, for example, could be used to relax this constraint in future experiments.

Another type of evaluation was done by comparing certain aspects of the DRL approach used by the AutoPentest-DRL framework with path planning, which is a typical class of solutions for attack planning. In [18], for example, the authors use the Plan Domain Definition Language (PDDL), which was originally intended for planning representation, to plan attack paths using a deterministic planning

Table 1 Comparison of the attack planning and DRL approaches for attack path finding

Characteristics	Attack Planning	DRL Approach
Tuning flexibility	Low	High
Time efficiency	Low	High
Optimality guarantee	Yes	No

algorithm named Metric-FF. This allows them to find the attack paths in a PDDL representation of the network topology and vulnerability scenario.

One advantage of DRL is that by changing model parameters the same algorithm can be used to recompute the attack path according to different criteria, hence DRL has more parameter tuning flexibility. Another advantage of DRL is that while the training is a time consuming process, when actually using the trained model the results are provided very fast. On the other hand, a deterministic planning algorithm is guaranteed to provide the optimal result every time, even though this may take a long time. This discussion is summarized in Table 1.

4 Security Awareness Training Using NLG

As mentioned in Sect. 2.2, one main challenge related to security awareness training is content creation, and our approach is to use Natural Language Generation (NLG) techniques to address this challenge. In what follows we start with a research background on awareness training, then we provide an overview of NLG and how we applied it in our research, and finally we introduce the actual system that we designed and implemented, CyATP. For a more in-depth discussion of this research, please refer to [34].

4.1 Research Background

Traditionally, security awareness training is conducted via reading training materials and/or watching video content, sometime combined with classroom learning. However, such approaches lack interaction, leading to a "dry" learning experience, which reduces learner motivation. Game-based learning has been used as a cost-effective and low-risk approach to conduct training in an engaging manner, while also having the advantage that learners can easily transfer the knowledge into the real world [31].

Anti-Phishing Phil is a serious game that focuses on learning how to avoid phishing, and for which a positive impact on phishing susceptibility has been demonstrated [2]. Another game, named Internet Hero, was used to convey learning contents about the technical and social basics of using the Internet, and the game was shown to be engaging and effective [11]. We also use some gamification elements in our system, such as a crossword puzzle, thus leveraging the engaging nature of serious games.

Another key aspect of our approach is that we generate the *cloze questions*—also known as *embedded answers questions*—used when conducting the security awareness training. Natural Language Generation (NLG) is a subset of Natural Language Processing (NLP) that aims to produce human-understandable natural language output from a nonlinguistic information input. Generally, NLG systems use knowledge about language and application domains to automatically generate documents, reports, instructions, help messages, and other types of texts [26].

Generative Pre-trained Transformer 3 (GPT-3) is probably the most well-known NLG system, which given a text prompt, i.e., a phrase or sentence input by the user, returns a text completion in natural language [19]. While GPT-3 has high performance for general use, such as dialogue or translation, the current version only provides access via an API, hence it lacks control on the training process and data sources, and it also lacks programmability. These issues make GPT-3 not suitable for cloze question generation in our context, in which the questions should be generated based on the content used in the learning stage, and should have answers that are part of the concept set used during learning. Moreover, the proprietary closed-source nature of GPT-3 means end users cannot modify it, which we want to avoid.

The nature of cloze questions and the existence of already labeled training data make this problem suitable for supervised learning models. Linear support-vector machines (Linear SVMs) are an example of such a learning model that is appropriate for classifying linearly separable data. A decision tree is a decision support tool that can be also used for classification, and which uses a tree-like model for decisions and their possible consequences. Random forests are an ensemble learning method for classification that constructs a multitude of decision trees at training time; the output of the random forest is the class selected by most trees. Adaptive Boosting (AdaBoost) is a statistical classification meta-algorithm that uses predictions of several simple models, such as small decision trees, to produce a final prediction through a weighted majority vote. Naive Bayes classifiers are a family of probabilistic classifiers that operate by applying Bayes' theorem under the assumption of feature independence. All these models are available in the `scikit-learn` machine learning library for Python [21] that we used to compare them, as it will be explained next.

4.2 Natural Language Generation Approach

In this research, we use NLG techniques to generate the cloze questions that are part of our security awareness learning content by relying on supervised learning models to generate questions from unstructured text [6].

Cloze questions are used in our system to allow learners to select the missing words that best match a given text, thus reinforcing the knowledge they accumulated during the initial learning stage. Generating such cloze questions is a linear classi-

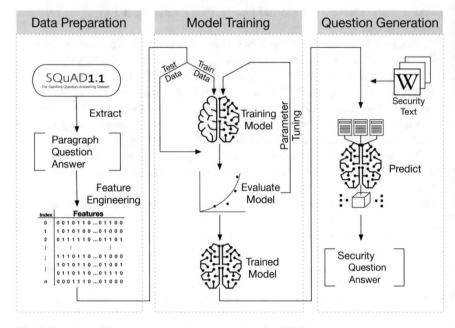

Fig. 9 Overview of the content generation process based on NLG

fication problem, and we conducted a comparative study by using Linear SVM, Decision Tree, Random Forest, AdaBoost, and Naive Bayes algorithms on several datasets available in the `scikit-learn` library. Our comparison has shown that Random Forest, AdaBoost and Naive Bayes had the highest classification accuracy for the linear dataset. Amongst them we selected Naive Bayes, as it has a short training time and a stable performance even with relatively little data for training.

An overview of the content generation process is shown in Fig. 9, and the next sections provide details about each of the three phases.

4.2.1 Data Preparation

In order to train the Naive Bayes model, we used the *Stanford Question Answering Dataset* (SQuAD v1.1) public dataset [23]. This dataset includes more that 100,000 question-answer pairs for over 500 articles from Wikipedia. The list of questions was created by crowdworkers based on those Wikipedia articles, and the answers to each of the questions is a fragment of text from the corresponding article.

Before using the data for training we did a consistency check to make sure we only use the data that is suitable for our purposes. Thus, we eliminated the questions that had missing answers, deleted the data for those questions for which we could not identify the paragraph they were based on, and deleted duplicated data entries.

Next we conducted feature engineering via the following steps:

Table 2 Features selected for Naive Bayes training

Feature Name	Feature Explanation
Is_Answer	Whether the word or noun chunk appear in the answer
TitleId	Article id of the word or noun chunk
ParagraphId	Paragraph id of the word or noun chunk
SentenceId	Sentence id of the word or noun chunk
InSentencePosition	Position of the word or noun chunk in the sentence
Word_Count	Count of words or noun chunks
NER	Named entity recognition
POS	Simple part-of-speech tag
TAG	Detailed part-of speech tag
DEP	Syntactic dependency
Is_Alpha	Whether the word or noun chunk is an alphanumeric character
Is_Stop	Whether the word or noun chunk is a stop word

	Words	Is_Answer	TitleId	ParagrapghId	SentenceId	InSentencePosition	Word_Count	NER	POS	TAG	DEP	Is_Alpha	Is_Stop
777	Ocarina	True	8	3	1	8	1	NP	PROPN	NNP	ROOT	True	False
287196	entrapment	False	364	26	5	5	1	None	NOUN	NN	dobj	True	False
352614	Mansoor Malangi	False	438	24	0	38	2	NP	None	None	None	False	False
140724	only 288,000 men	False	163	15	2	27	3	NP	None	None	None	False	False
32192	tidal forces	True	372	7	1	27	2	NP	None	None	None	False	False
395638	the capital city	False	479	1	1	9	3	NP	None	None	None	False	False
382293	ABC Entertainment	False	466	88	3	59	2	NP	None	None	None	False	False
113429	the original recording	False	112	32	0	18	3	NP	None	None	None	False	False
54445	seven state parks	False	11	52	0	2	3	NP	None	None	None	False	False
276041	the Cửa Lớn River	False	350	8	3	5	4	NP	None	None	None	False	False

Fig. 10 Sample data obtained from the SQuAD dataset via feature extraction

- *Feature selection*: Based on the specificities of cloze questions, and the way humans typically formulate questions using words such as *what*, *when*, and so on, we found that answers are often named entities or nouns. Consequently, we selected from the dataset the features shown in Table 2.
- *Feature extraction*: After deciding what features to use, the next step was to process the dataset to extract those features for each record in the database. Some sample data obtained via this feature extraction process is shown in Fig. 10.
- *Data encoding*: In order to be able to use the extracted data for Naive Bayes model training, features that have multiple discrete values, such as *NER* and *POS*, had to be encoded. For this purpose, we employed one-hot encoding by using N-bit status registers to encode features that have N states.

One issue with our initial training data was that it was imbalanced, since in our dataset the samples that are not the answer of a question are much more numerous than those that are. To address this issue, methods such as resampling (e.g., oversampling of minority samples, or undersampling of majority ones), or synthetic sample generation, such as via the SMOTE (Synthetic Minority Oversampling

Technique) or ADASYN (Adaptive Synthetic) algorithms, can be used, as discussed below.

4.2.2   Model Training

In order to be able to determine the best approach, we conducted model training with four Naive Bayes models, *Gaussian Naive Bayes*, *Bernoulli Naive Bayes*, *Multinomial Naive Bayes* and *Complement Naive Bayes*, and five datasets, *Original Data*, *Oversampled Data*, *Undersampled Data*, *SMOTE Data* and *ADASYN Data*. Furthermore, we conducted calibration via sigmoid scaling and isotonic regression. The computation was done using the Cray XC40 supercomputer at our university, JAIST. Each training job used four nodes to improve the training speed, with each node having an Intel Xeon E5-2695v4 2.1 GHz 36-core CPU and 128 GB RAM.

Due to space limitations we cannot present the comparison in detail, so we'll only mention that after evaluating all the combinations of the above settings we have concluded that the *Bernoulli Naive Bayes* model with isotonic regression calibration together with the SMOTE dataset provide the best performance, and were used in the later stages of our approach. For details about the evaluation, see [34].

4.2.3   Question Generation

In order to generate questions related to security knowledge, we needed a security dataset. To build this dataset we started by using the work in [33] and created a computer security concept map based on the public Linked Open Data (LOD) dataset called DBpedia [7].

Then, we retrieved descriptions for the concepts in the concept map from Wikipedia. Since descriptions could not be retrieved automatically for some of the concepts, our dataset currently consists of a total of 2640 concepts, out of which 2315 concepts have an associated description that can be used to study them.

The security dataset was first subjected to the same kind of preprocessing and feature engineering as mentioned in section "Data Preparation". Then it was used with the trained model discussed in section "Model Training" by following the next steps:

1. The trained model was used with the security dataset to generate cloze question and answer pairs for the quiz.
2. The Gensim Python library [25] was employed to generate incorrect answers that are similar to the correct one, to be used as alternative choices in the quiz.

Currently our training content includes a total of 278 quiz questions that were generated for the top 126 concepts in the concept map. The cloze questions with less than 25 words were selected to be crossword puzzles clues, so that the clues are easy to understand and also not too revealing. This lead to a crossword puzzle database of 28 clues related to some of the top 126 concepts in the concept map.

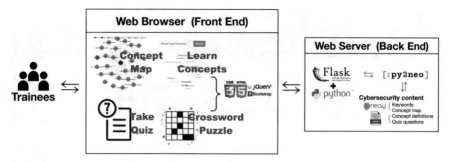

Fig. 11 Overview of the CyATP system features and implementation

4.3 CyATP

The NLG approach we described in Sect. 4.2 along with some gamification components were implemented into the CyATP (Cybersecurity Awareness Training Platform) system that we present here. An overview of the system features and implementation is shown in Fig. 11.

The front end of CyATP is a web application that uses the open-source framework Bootstrap and jQuery for page design. The back end of CyATP uses the lightweight Python web framework named Flask and the Jinja2 template engine. Our concept map data and concept descriptions are stored in a Neo4j relational database, and the generated quiz data and crossword puzzle clues are stored in JSON format.

4.3.1 Features

CyATP has the following features that support security awareness training activities:

- Learning activity components

  - *Concept map*: This component makes it possible for learners to visualize all the concepts related to a given target concept, and to understand their dependencies.
  - *Learn concepts page*: This component displays the description associated to a concept, and also visualizes all the related concepts for further learning.

- Serious game components

  - *Quiz game*: This is the main CyATP component that relies on the NLG content generation approach that we discussed. The game will present sequentially 10 questions selected randomly from our quiz database, and for each question a timer and the current score are also displayed (see Fig. 12).

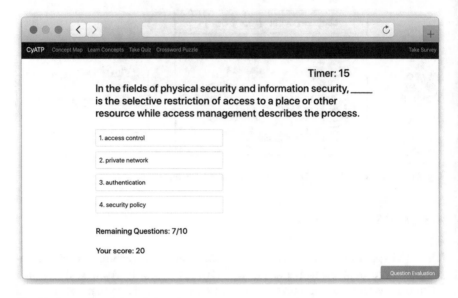

Fig. 12 Screenshot of the quiz interface

- *Crossword puzzle*: This component too uses content generated via NLG techniques, in particular the crossword puzzle clues that we mentioned. The learners must input in a crossword puzzle form the words missing from those clues, which is a more challenging task than the quiz game (see Fig. 13).

4.3.2 Evaluation

We evaluated our approach by asking 10 students from our university to use CyATP as a security awareness training platform. The assessment was conducted as follows:

- The training content was evaluated using a questionnaire with 8 questions related to the quality of the training content.
- The training platform was assessed both from a performance point of view (via web page performance testing), and also from a usability perspective (via the System Usability Scale).
- Serious game features were evaluated using a questionnaire with 29 questions related to factors such as enjoyment, learning effectiveness, and so on.

The above evaluations provided overall positive results, but due to space limitations we shall only discuss here the training content evaluation, which is most relevant to the topic of this chapter (for more details about the results, see [34]). The key insights are given below, with the scores being on a scale from 1 to 5:

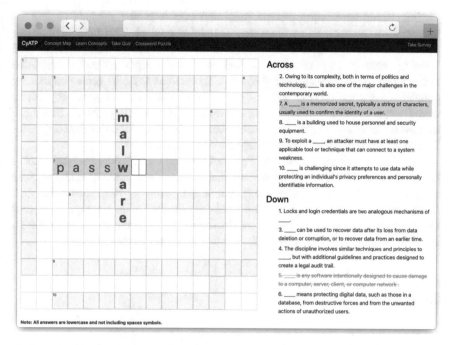

Fig. 13 Screenshot of the crossword puzzle interface

- Concept map content was evaluated with an average score of 4.75.
- Concept map descriptions were evaluated with an average score of 4.2.
- Quiz questions and crossword puzzle clues received an average score of 4.07.
- The overall quality of the learning content received an average score of 4.3.

5 Conclusion

In this chapter we have presented two applications of AI to cybersecurity education and training. The first of them uses Deep Reinforcement Learning for penetration testing purposes, so that the trainees can study attack techniques based on the recommendations of the system. This functionality was implemented in the form of an automated penetration testing framework, named AutoPentest-DRL. The evaluation of the framework showed that the accuracy for the tested logical networks exceeds 90%, and when used with a real network topology the framework is able to detect the actual security vulnerabilities, determine a suitable attack path, and carry out the attack on that network. Although we have only evaluated this framework with relatively small topologies, our work shows that this approach is promising, and we believe that its robustness and scalability can be improved in the future.

The second application that we presented uses Natural Language Generation techniques to generate security awareness training content. This functionality was implemented in the CyATP awareness training platform, which includes both learning (concept map visualization and concept descriptions) and gamification features (quiz game and crossword puzzle). The evaluation of the generated training content via a questionnaire with 10 respondents was generally positive, with an overall score of 4.3 out of 5. One significant strength of our approach is that it can be used for training in fields other than cybersecurity too, as the raw data originates from publicly available sources, Wikipedia and DBpedia.

The two systems presented, AutoPentest-DRL and CyATP, have been released as open source on GitHub, and we believe that making them publicly available is an important contribution to the research community. While we have shown that their functionality is good enough for immediate use, in the future we plan to conduct more detailed performance evaluations, including through comparison with similar methods, so that we can determine further ways to improve these systems.

References

1. Abt, C.C.: Serious Games. University Press of America, Lanham (2002)
2. Arachchilage, N.A.G., Love, S.: Security awareness of computer users: a phishing threat avoidance perspective. Comput. Hum. Behav. **38**, 304–312 (2014)
3. Belani, G.: The use of artificial intelligence in cybersecurity: a review. https://www.computer.org/publications/tech-news/trends/the-use-of-artificial-intelligence-in-cybersecurity
4. Beuran, R., Chinen, K., Tan, Y., Shinoda, Y.: Towards effective cybersecurity education and training. Tech. Rep. IS-RR-2016-003, Japan Advanced Institute of Science and Technology (2016)
5. Cyber Range Organisation and Design (CROND): CROND GitHub page. https://github.com/crond-jaist
6. Das, B., Majumder, M.: Factual open cloze question generation for assessment of learner's knowledge. Int. J. Educ. Technol. Higher Educ. **14**(1), 1–12 (2017)
7. DBpedia Association: DBpedia—Global and unified access to knowledge graphs. https://www.dbpedia.org/
8. Ghanem, M.C., Chen, T.M.: Reinforcement learning for efficient network penetration testing. Information **11**(1) (2020). https://www.mdpi.com/2078-2489/11/1/6
9. Hoffmann, J.: Simulated penetration testing: from "Dijkstra" to "Turing test++". In: Proceedings of the International Conference on Automated Planning and Scheduling, pp. 364–372 (2015)
10. Hu, Z.: Automated penetration testing using deep reinforcement learning. Master's Thesis, Japan Advanced Institute of Science and Technology (2021)
11. Kayali, F., Wallner, G., Kriglstein, S., Bauer, G., Martinek, D., Hlavacs, H., Purgathofer, P., Wolfle, R.: A case study of a learning game about the internet. In: Proceedings of GameDays 2014: Games for Training, Education, Health and Sports, pp. 47–58 (2014)
12. Lyon, G.: Nmap security scanner. https://nmap.org/
13. Matherly, J.: Shodan search engine. https://www.shodan.io/
14. Microsoft: Security update guide—vulnerabilities. https://msrc.microsoft.com/update-guide/vulnerability
15. Mnih, V., Kavukcuoglu, K., Silver, D., Rusu, A.A., Veness, J., Bellemare, M.G., Graves, A., Riedmiller, M., Fidjeland, A.K., Ostrovski, G., et al.: Human-level control through deep reinforcement learning. Nature **518**, 529–533 (2015)

16. National Institute of Standards and Technology: Common Vulnerability Scoring System (CVSS). https://nvd.nist.gov/vuln-metrics/cvss
17. National Institute of Standards and Technology: National Vulnerability Database (NVD). https://nvd.nist.gov/
18. Obes, J.L., Sarraute, C., Richarte, G.G.: Attack planning in the real world. Cryptogr. Secur. 3–6 (2013)
19. OpenAI: OpenAI API. https://beta.openai.com/
20. Ou, X., Govindavajhala, S., Appel, A.W.: MulVAL: a logic-based network security analyzer. In: USENIX Security Symposium, vol. 8, pp. 113–128 (2005)
21. Pedregosa, F., Varoquaux, G., Gramfort, A., Michel, V., Thirion, B., Grisel, O., Blondel, M., Prettenhofer, P., Weiss, R., Dubourg, V., Vanderplas, J., Passos, A., Cournapeau, D., Brucher, M., Perrot, M., Duchesnay, E.: Scikit-learn: Machine learning in Python. J. Mach. Learn. Res. **12**, 2825–2830 (2011)
22. Penetration Testing Execution Standard Group: Penetration testing execution standard. http://www.pentest-standard.org/index.php/Main_Page
23. Rajpurkar, P., Zhang, J., Lopyrev, K., Liang, P.: SQuAD: 100,000+ questions for machine comprehension of text (2016). arXiv preprint arXiv:1606.05250
24. Rapid7: Metasploit penetration testing framework. https://www.metasploit.com/
25. Rehurek, R.: Gensim: Topic modelling for humans. https://radimrehurek.com/gensim/
26. Reiter, E., Dale, R.: Building Natural Language Generation Systems. Cambridge University Press, Cambridge (2000)
27. RiskSense: MulVAL—Multi host, multi stage vulnerability analysis tool. https://github.com/risksense/mulval
28. Sarraute, C., Richarte, G., Obes, J.L.: An algorithm to find optimal attack paths in nondeterministic scenario. In: Proceedings of the 4th ACM Workshop on Security and Artificial Intelligence, pp. 71–80 (2011)
29. Schneier, B.: Attack trees—modeling security threats. Dr. Dobb's J. **24**, 21–29 (1999)
30. Sheyner, O., Haines, J., Jha, S., Lippmann, R., Wing, J.M.: Automated generation and analysis of attack graphs. In: Proceedings 2002 IEEE Symposium on Security and Privacy, pp. 273–284 (2002)
31. Squire, K.: Video games in education. Int. J. Intell. Simul. Gaming **2**(1), 49–62 (2003)
32. Sutton, R.S., Barto, A.G.: Reinforcement Learning: An Introduction, 2nd edn. The MIT Press, Cambridge (2018)
33. Tan, Z., Beuran, R., Hasegawa, S., Jiang, W., Zhao, M., Tan, Y.: Adaptive security awareness training using linked open data datasets. Educ. Inform. Technol. **25**, 5235–5259 (2020)
34. Zeng, Y.: Content Generation and Serious Game Implementation for Security Awareness Training. Master's Thesis, Japan Advanced Institute of Science and Technology (2021)

Offensive Machine Learning Methods and the Cyber Kill Chain

Hannu Turtiainen, Andrei Costin, Alex Polyakov, and Timo Hämäläinen

1 Introduction

Machine learning (ML), deep learning (DL), reinforcement learning (RL), and artificial intelligence (AI) technologies[1] have been among the most tackled and even controversial talking points in information technology for the past decade. Some view these technologies as a panacea for cybersecurity problems. Others are, however, more sceptical yet, and see additional issues arising, mainly due to the bias and non-transparent nature of such technologies, which is unfortunately common and the norm in many present implementations. As these technologies are slowly being adopted within the cybersecurity tools space, the attacking side has also been productive and advancing in this matter.

MLsec technologies bring several crucial benefits for more efficient and productive (ethical) hacking: the increase of capable actors, extensive increase in the possible attack frequency, and an increase in the variety of possible targets. These feats are possible due to the considerable scalability of MLsec systems and the ease of deployment in a cost-efficient and time-saving manner when compared to the classical "army of skillful humans." In addition, target selection benefits greatly

---

[1] Due to the breadth and depth of various definitions related to ML/DL/RL/AI and cybersecurity, throughout this paper we will refer to these technologies simply as MLsec.

H. Turtiainen · A. Costin (✉) · T. Hämäläinen
University of Jyväskylä, Jyväskylä, Finland
e-mail: hannu.ht.turtiainen@jyu.fi; ancostin@jyu.fi; timoh@jyu.fi

A. Polyakov
Adversa.AI, Tel Aviv, Israel
e-mail: alex@adversa.ai

from MLsec technologies as larger numbers of diverse data can be gathered and analyzed in almost real-time [11].

Complex systems such as smart Cyber-Physical Systems (sCPS) are particularly vulnerable to MLsec attacks due to their complex inter-connectivity via smart sensor networks, clouds, and the Internet of Things (IoT) [44]. Kaloudi and Li [44] compare the possible attacks to these systems to the Butterfly Effect, in which small, seemingly inconsequential incidents may have large, catastrophic effects, such as the global effect of the infamous Mirai botnet [6].

As MLsec methods are being used more and more in the cybersecurity space, they may also cause further unforeseen issues. ML methods rely on predetermined features, which can be biased or otherwise compromised or unrepresentative of the current threat landscape. DL and AI methods, although better suited for constant learning, can be "poisoned" (i.e., undetectable alterations with malicious intents) during training with poisoning samples to render them ineffective or considerably "crippled." They can also be fooled at the inference stage with the help of so-called adversarial examples, which can bypass AI-driven systems [51]. Researchers agree that as MLsec models get increasingly more efficient in their function, and as more and more data are generated, the MLsec tools will play a vital role in future cybersecurity "wars." From the (ethical) attacker's perspective, the reconnaissance, target infiltration, data exfiltration, and privilege escalation stages seem particularly advantaged with the addition of MLsec tools and techniques [89].

At the same time, offensive MLsec can pose serious threats to organizations' cybersecurity. In comparison to human attackers, offensive MLsec improves coverage, as the MLsec methods can scale virtually without limits. The speed of execution of such attacks is also significantly increased, thus considerably reducing the time available to defenders to respond. The success rate of the attacks can increase with the use of MLsec models as more data can be processed with each step and therefore, more knowledge is available to the attacker [58].

This paper is organized as follows. In Sect. 2, we exhibit the Cyber Kill Chain phases and present relevant MLsec related works respectively. Section 3 introduces ideas and suggests works on how ML and AI can be used against MLsec models. Finally, we conclude in this chapter in Sect. 4.

2   Cyber Kill Chain Phases

MLsec technologies are already entrenched in the cyberattack space in most of the phases of the Cyber Kill Chain. Today, MLsec methods are predominantly applied in the reconnaissance, infiltration, lateral movement, and act on objectives parts of cyberattacks. However, advances in the MLsec field bring the technologies to other phases and parts of the cyberattack taxonomy thanks to more use-cases being developed and showcased [12].

In this work, we try to map the current state-of-the-art in offensive MLsec by employing the seven steps of Lockheed Martin's original Cyber Kill Chain [54]

Recon	Weapon-ization	Delivery	Exploit-ation	Installation	C2	Act on Objecties

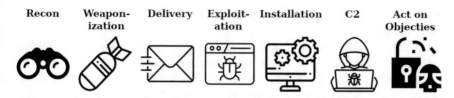

Fig. 1 The main phases of the traditional Cyber Kill Chain (as introduced by Lockheed Martin [54])

(see Fig. 1). We also highlight, whenever relevant, a more granular and differing version of the Cyber Kill Chain, presented as the MITRE ATT&CK framework [83]. Even though the MITRE ATT&CK kill chain framework presents 14 steps for more granularity, we feel that the work we present is not large enough in scope to warrant the use of the more granular frameworks at this time.

2.1 Reconnaissance

Reconnaissance is the first step in infiltrating a target, and can be broken down into three steps: identifying, selecting, and profiling the target. Target identification is a passive reconnaissance method, meaning that the target is unaware of the proceedings. It involves checking the domain names and web assets of the potential target from Internet address registries. Target profiling can be done on system and social levels. Social profiling is also a passive method, and it means crawling through social networks and public websites and documents. System profiling, on the other hand, is usually an active approach, meaning that the target is most likely aware of it. It includes fingerprinting and scanning the open ports and services on the target systems [88]. MITRE ATT&CK [83] convey similar steps and techniques in the reconnaissance phase. Profiling the victim through all possible sources (closed/open sources, domains, websites, phishing, etc.) is crucial. Active scanning may also be necessary in order to adequately fingerprint and identify the network target.

In order to successfully infiltrate a target without a zero-day exploit, many data about the target should be gathered. However, these data are meaningless without proper analysis and the transformation from data to real actionable insights. Algorithmic data gathering such as web crawling and automatic social engineering are fast and produce an abundance of data to be analyzed.

MLsec opportunities in the reconnaissance phases can be summarised as targeting AI. The tasks of MLsec models in this phase are identifying the best targets and learning their standard behavior [44]. As MLsec methods work well in pattern detection, common vulnerabilities in, for example, front-end PHP code can be found by tokenizing the entire available front-end code and feeding them through a model, therefore extracting matching patterns. Database enumeration through numerous database function executions can also be a suitable task for MLsec technologies [80].

As ML is a great tool for handling large nubmers of data, ML for information gathering/reconnaissance is a great fit. Nowadays, people expose and post a lot of information about themselves online, and the reconnaissance towards people (and not just towards information technology systems) has become more feasible. Classifiers can be used to scout out potential victims from social media. For example, one can root out any IT professionals from the potential victim list as one could make an assumption that they might not be as gullible targets as some other average or unaware users. Online service vendors such as PimEyes [65] offer this type of service. Other clustering and classification methods such as K-means, random forests, and neural networks can be employed on top of Natural Language Processing (NLP) analysis for analyzing social media posts to learn about targets. Image and object recognition can be of use, as well as social media is full of pictures. Certain objects and types of images can be of use in identifying and classifying potential targets [66].

Tools for network scanning and sniffing have been around for a long time. However, modern Software-Defined Network (SDN) implementations can prove to be too tricky for simple tools as targets may not be as clearly defined; therefore, more complex tools are required. Machine learning aids in this process in several ways. The attacker must probe the network, trigger arbitrary flows, and gather information about the network policies, rules, and filters in place. This is traditionally an arduous task; however, with ML methods, it can be made more manageable and feasible. Know Your Enemy (KYE) [15] is an attack method that provides a stealthy way of gathering valuable information about a target SDN. This intelligence can vary from network policies to security tool configuration options.

Phishing, and its variations such as vishing and smishing, are fraud attacks in which the target is contacted by the conman via some means of communication, such as email, voice phone calls, or SMS. The attackers represent themselves as a reputable entity in order to gain trust or induce some sort of reaction in the target to make them give up sensitive information, such as passwords or banking information about themselves [45]. Phishing is a common way to gain access to a target system, and protecting against it can be so resource-heavy that affects day-to-day proceedings. DeepPhish is an experimental MLsec-driven phishing URL creator. It learns effective patterns from previous attacks and adapts the URL generation strategy, which greatly increases the chances of false negatives from phishing detectors [8].

Social media is also a good venue for phishing because of its wide-spread use, although the public nature of it could prove problematic. Still, using automated and intelligent target-aware spear phishing frameworks is proving to be more productive than large-scale phishing attacks [72]. SNAP_R [71] is an AI spear phishing framework that enables target discovery and message customisation in relation to the target for Twitter phishing. Using SNAP_R, the attacker can launch automated spear phishing campaigns that seem to be comparable to large-scale manual phishing efforts [71].

Phishing detection is a common research topic in the MLsec field. Attackers can benefit from defensive research as well, because ML for detection avoidance is one of the key features of a good and successful phishing campaign. Some efforts, such as that of Khan et al. [45], experiment with a variety of algorithms and datasets, exposing strengths and weaknesses in them. Thus, this information can be used to further evolve and improve the phishing campaigns as well as the detection algorithms. All in all, it is an arms race between the attackers and the defenders.

2.2 Weaponizing

After the reconnaissance phase, the target has been selected and possible vulnerabilities, security holes, backdoors, etc. have been identified. The information gathered from the reconnaissance phase is now used to construct the payload containing a malware or a Remote Access Trojan (RAT) and the exploit in order to infiltrate the target [54, 43]. The steps during this phase in MITRE ATT&CK [83] focus on attack preparation through capability and infrastructure development but also compromising target infrastructure and accounts. Kaloudi et al. [44] sets the most important MLsec tasks for this phase as acquiring information about the standard behavior of the target and generating abnormal behavior based on that information, as well as new vulnerability discovery and payload generation. They refer to these steps as "AI-aided."

A common way to discover vulnerabilities in software is to use fuzzing. It is a method in which the input to the target (e.g., software, system) is tested with a huge variety of uncommon and carefully manipulated inputs, while the target is monitored for crashes and anomalous behavior. Machine learning can be beneficial for fuzzing in two ways: generation of new samples, and ranking of resulting crashes. If an algorithm can create smarter input for the fuzzer, it means valuable time can be saved in trying to crash the target under test. At the same time, not all crashes lead to a vulnerability discovery. Therefore, an MLsec-driven ranking algorithm can sort out the most exploitable-relevant crashes for researchers to look at first [66].

For malware creation, the way that ML is used can be thought of as counterintuitive. As malware detection heavily uses ML models, these models can be used as testbeds for new malware. For example, the attacker takes a known malware, introduces changes, and then tests the malware against malware detectors such as VirusTotal. On the other hand, many MLsec methods can be used to create initiation triggers for malware. For example, a sleeper malware in a system can wait for a certain facial recognition event to occur until it initializes [66], or other similar "secret knock" computer vision signals [16].

Initial access and malware delivery methods can be categorized in two types: "attacker-controlled" and "attacker-released" delivery methods. The "attacker-controlled" methods involve directly attacking the web services of the target, while the "attacker-released" methods make use of the users who have access to the target to deliver their payload. This can happen via email, USB sticks, social media interactions, and other means [54]. MITRE ATT&CK [83] proposes several methods for initial access, such as exploiting public-facing applications and services, compromised account usage, supply-chain compromise, phishing, hardware additions, insider access, etc. For MLsec methods, phishing, compromised accounts, and public services are the venues to look into.

One example of a stealthy spyware was presented by Zhang et al. [93]. They developed a proof-of-concept app that recorded users' phone calls after infiltrating an Android phone. The voice data were then used to synthesise Android voice assistant activation keyword ("OK Google") via Natural Language Processing (NLP). As the voice assistant is naturally granted high privileges in the phone, gaining such an access level is of high value. The attack might be detected by the user if it was launched in an arbitrary time; therefore, more data from the phone's sensors are collected and a more appropriate noisy attack time is selected [93]. This approach could be used to further gather information about some target, or to gain more privileges within the phone or the networks it connects to.

Spamming and phishing are old techniques for information gathering. They have become such an everyday phenomenon that today, spam and phishing filters in services are common ground. To circumvent them, the attackers must create better examples that mimic human activity. In order to train an algorithm to mimic authority, training samples are needed. As social media is public, the amount of training samples one can acquire can be vast, and therefore, the results can be surprisingly good (see Sect. 2.1). For emails, however, if the attacker does not have an insider within the target organization, getting examples of private email correspondence can be challenging [66].

Spoofing has seen huge leaps of improvement with MLsec contributions over the last decade. Fake pictures, voice, and videos are a real threat. Lybebird [20] showcase their audio-mimicking capabilities, while Van den Oord et al. [62] propose WaveNet, a waveform-level audio data model built around GANs. With MLsec technologies, the Internet could be filled with fakes in the not-too-distant future. As an example, voice cloning was used in a bank heist resulting in $35 million in losses [10]. Spoofing related to AI is discussed separately in Sect. 3.

Last but not least, numerous papers have been published over the last decade on variations of Automatic Exploit Generators (AEG) [7, 41, 42, 86, 3]. These developed tools are essentially signature-based detectors for exploits from source code and binaries. These tools employ static and dynamic analysis (some including their extensive vulnerability databases) to root out issues in the execution of the code or in the source code itself. Some tools also apply fuzzing tools to increase the bug yield by possibly triggering unknown vulnerabilities. Grieco et al. [31] resorted to ML algorithms in order to solve the AEG task. Their goal was to make vulnerability discovery easily scalable by using light-weight analysis components and automated by utilizing MLsec capabilities in having plenty of features from a large dataset instead of hand-picked features specialized for a certain task.

2.3   Delivery

In the delivery phase, the attacker launches their operation towards the target. The intent is to deliver the malware to the target system or endpoint. In controlled delivery, the attacker is attacking directly towards the target's web services; however, in released delivery, the attacker uses an auxiliary to deliver the malware. The auxiliary can be a phishing email, USB stick, or some other means of malware transportation not via the network [54]. In the delivery phase, "AI-concealed" steps are the ability to remain undetected and conceal the attacker's malicious intent [44]. MITRE ATT&CK [83] defines delivery as the initial access phase and it features methods such as phishing, supply chain compromise, hardware additions, etc.

Although denial-of-service (DoS) attacks are thought to be quite simple attacks; common detection and prevention systems are very effective against them [49, 92]. To fool these prevention mechanisms, ML algorithms can create arbitrary differing data packets, in turn, making detection much harder to differentiate from the real traffic. An even better approach is to sniff real traffic and train a neural network to generate legitimate packets to the target, albeit in a malicious manner.

Crowd-turfing, the malicious use of crowd-sourcing services, also benefits heavily on ML. The creation of fake reviews, news, accounts, etc, is tedious work for people and can be too complex for simple algorithms. There is an abundance of training material available online for creation of high-performing crowd-turfing ML models [66].

Botnets are the backbone of some of the most well known cyberattacks such as the Mirai-botnet [6]. The use of vast resources, even unsofisticated ones such as DVRs and CCTV cameras, can be technologically devastating. Although, as the name "botnet" suggests, the features of attacks are not sophisticated, as individually utilizing system resources of the bots is an impossible task for humans. Smart botnets, such as Hivenets [56], can identify the individual nodes of the botnet and put its resources to full use, making the threat of botnets even greater [66].

The "Completely Automated Public Turing test to tell Computers and Humans Apart" (CAPTCHA) is intended to restrict malicious attack attempts on websites and other graphical user interface services by disabling the possibility for automation. However, the advancements in MLsec technology have proven standard CAPTCHAs essentially broken [17, 78]. For example, Yu et al. [91] showcased their automated approach to cracking popular open-source Python CAPTCHAs using an MLsec-based chosen-plaintext attack. Further, Alqahtani and Alsulaiman [4] set several MLsec models (especially their CNN model) against Google's reCAPTCHA [29] with over 50% of the challenges successfully solved. With these developments, newer types of CAPTCHAs are being developed [30, 63].

2.4   Exploitation

Exploitation (or the attack and exploit execution) stage means gaining access to the target system using the vulnerabilities and weaknesses found earlier [54]. There are numerous ways this can be achieved in classical scenarios. MITRE ATT&CK [83] proposes ways such as using valid user credentials, API abuse, malicious scheduled tasks, container deployment, system services, etc. MLsec methods can aid in this step, for example, by ensuring proper environment, selecting proper execution time, and automating execution ("AI-automated") [44]. However, currently this topic has not gained much academic attention as there has been plenty of work done in more influential topics in the Weaponizing (see Sect. 2.2), Delivery (see Sect. 2.3), and Installation (see Sect. 2.5) stages, where the exploits and payload are in the spotlight.

This phase can also be a representative example of how tools meant for security may have implications against it. Bleeding edge technology such as Darktrace [19], a real-time security incident AI analyst modeled on the human immune system, is one example of this. It is supposed to detect deviation from the norm in an ICS environment. However, such tools, if plausible to enable in the target system, could benefit the attackers greatly in defining the norm of the system operation and possibly being used as an alert system for testing the limits; for example, data exfiltration methods (see Sect. 2.7).

2.5   Installation

Installation phase means that the attacker has reached a state where they are in control of some part of the system. Typically, this stage involves installing a persistent backdoor to maintain the access to the server for an extended period of time. Methods can vary from webshells, system backdoors, adding services and making malware appear as standard system files [54]. This stage is referred to as "AI evolved" by Kaloudi et al. [44] and the MLsec task is the (ideally stealth) self-propagation of the malware and persistence. MITRE ATT&CK [83] has this step divided into several more specific steps. Persistence requires the attacker to establish some ground on the target system by acquiring accounts or setting up some services for further use. Privilege escalation means gaining elevated access in the system, endpoint, or service, where the attack has originated. This can be achieved by using exploits or by the means of gaining superior credential access in the system. Defence evasion implies obfuscating or masquerading the malicious behavior in the target entity and fooling defence systems. After the initial installation, the attackers might require access to other systems or endpoints in the network; thus, network discovery and lateral movement in the network are required.

Installation can be a difficult phase for the attacker. Operating and security systems usually have systems in place where unwanted installations can be detected and prevented. MLsec-based evasive malware, such as DeepLocker [79], make this task easier by hiding behind benign, everyday software and only activating the payload once the conditions are met (e.g., precise target are reached). These conditions are determined by the deep neural network that is trained for the target specifications, as deep neural networks are essentially black boxes, and DeepLocker is able to hide the trigger conditions behind such smokescreens [79].

Another way to bypass MLsec-based malware detectors is to create malware examples that are benign to the detector itself. MalGAN [40] is an algorithm that generates adversarial malware examples, using the black-box detection algorithm employed in the defending end, in order to bypass it undetected [40]. The author's algorithm shows great promise and further fuels the MLsec technology war between the offensive and defensive actors. Vidal et al. [55] presented two MLsec models to masquerade detection bypassing. The models were based on action pruning and noise generation, and they were highly successful.

The accessed entity in the target's system is usually not the intended target, or if it originally was, a more attractive or valuable target may present itself when the first target is penetrated. Therefore, privilege escalation and lateral movement are required. Brute-force password guessing via generated password rules is resource intensive and time consuming and with proper security policies in place, it might be redundant as well. To address these issues, Hitaj et al. [38] presented PassGAN, a MLsec-based method for password guessing. The idea behind it is to generate better samples, with GAN models, based on password characteristics and structures, thus, being able to guess between 51% and 73% additional unique passwords in comparison to HashCat run with standard password generation rules and dictionary attacks.

Along with gaining access through MLsec-driven credential cracking [47], privilege escalation can be established through exploit use as well. Individually checking all the services and software within the breached target is tedious and stagnant, thus, requiring automation. However, testing every possible option is again quite a noisy and resource intensive procedure. To further develop this strategy (for white hat penetration testing purposes), MLsec-based smarter penetration testing frameworks have been researched.

Network discovery within the target's network may be noisy and alert the defenders easily. On the other hand, passive network discovery may be slow and yield less results. Network traffic analysis can be used to accomplish this task and discover hosts and services within a network automatically, thus, generating knowledge about the network, potential additional targets, and possible data exfiltration channels as well as establishing information about the standard network activity. The attackers may use methods meant for defenders in their activities. Works from Pacheco et al. [64] and Shafiq et al. [73] are some of the few examples of network traffic classification by capturing traffic and using MLsec models to refine it and gaining higher understanding of it.

Automated exploitation is a less-researched topic in the MLsec field possibly due to the high interpretability and high number of impacting factors in the decision. Still, Valea and Oprisa [85] used data from the popular penetration testing training platform Hack The Box [37] to train their MLsec models. The intention of their framework was to obtain root shell on the breached machine by first scanning the target, then search for vulnerabilities for the found services, and lastly, exploit the vulnerability to obtain root shell. Within their tests on the Hack The Box platform, they were able to successfully exploit seven out of ten test machines, clearly showcasing the ability to automatically exploit machines with known exploits with great success when using MLsec approaches. On the other hand, Fang et al. [22] developed an automatic MLsec-based exploitability metrics model for determining the real-world usability of recent exploits, which can be used to minimize the time wasted on lesser exploits with poor success rate.

As network data are often encrypted even in local networks, Man-in-the-Middle (MITM) attacks by themselves are less useful. Tools such as SSLStrip and SSLStrip2 can be used to set plain text data transfer between the victim and the attacker while preserving the perceived encrypted data transfer between the victim and the server (between the attacker and the server in reality). However, this type of attack is noticeable and can be hindered by the use of HTTP Strict Transport Security (HSTS). Nonetheless, a MITM attack can be useful even with encrypted data. Al-Hababi and Tokgoz [2] demonstrated how MLsec models can be trained to classify encrypted network traffic and determine which applications or services are being used. The attackers can use this technique for example to establish standard network behavior, or to prospect possible C2 solutions (see Sect. 2.6).

Keylogging is an old technique that can be used legitimately, for example, as a parental control in a child's computer or as an attack software, for example, to steal credentials. Essentially, if the tool can be installed on a desktop endpoint, the keylogger saves all the keyboard inputs and sends them to the attacker. The attackers can use this information mostly to yield credentials from the user or to gather personal or company secrets. To combat this, random noise can be inserted to the internal memory of the keyboard in order to obfuscate real data [90]. However, MLsec models can be used to counter this defence. Lee and Yim [50] proposed MLsec models to filter out the noise generated by the defence tools and yield the actual keystrokes from the keylogger. Their best model resulted in up to 96.2% accuracy, making the attack significantly more feasible than without such filtering.

2.6   Command and Control

As the attack and the malware has established a beachhead in the target system, the intent is to establish a Command-and-Control (C2 or C&C) infrastructure to remotely observe and manipulate the target. The C2 communication channel can be established in many different ways to mask it as standard traffic [54]. Kaloudi et al. [44] defines tasks for the C2 phase as "AI multilayered." MLsec is required to self-destruct the initial access processes and set up new layers for the campaign to move forward towards its end goal. MITRE ATT&CK [83] characterizes this step with means of creating the C2 network. There are many means to this end such as proxies, non-standard port use, communication through removable media, encrypted channels, protocol tunneling, etc.

Chung et al. [14] proposed a self-learning malware targeting Cyber-Physical Systems (CPS), as their security is often overlooked in the overall system. At first, their malware gathers data from the target CPS and learns patterns. The data are then used with statistical methods to select a strategy of attack that has the lowest probability of detection and the highest chance of success by emulating random incidents in the CPSes. The malware injects the CPS logic with their malicious code to start the attack. The malfunctioning part of the system in many cases causes a cascading effect that affects the system as a whole [14].

One way to establish an undetected C&C connection is to use Domain Generation Algorithms (DGAs). DGAs are typically used in many malware types; however, there are detectors set up by the network administrators in order to root out these fake domain names. In that vein, DeepDGA [5] is a DL architecture for creating hard-to-detect pseudo-random domains, for example, for C2 purposes. DeepDGA uses the GAN algorithm to generate domain names, which are sufficiently effective and efficient in confusing the MLsec-based DGA classifiers [5].

2.7 Actions on Objectives

The attackers have reached the final stage of the operation and their goal is accomplished. The attackers can now choose what to do next. They can, for example, destroy systems, exfiltrate and collect data and credentials, overwrite or corrupt data, escalate privileges further, and move laterally across the environment [54]. In this stage, the real damage can be done. MLsec tasks for this can be described as "AI massive." These tasks can vary from data destruction to victim extortion [44]. In this context, the collection, exfiltration, and impact steps from the MITRE ATT&CK [83] fit here. Data collection can be as effective as the attackers' access and lateral movement allow. The data can be collected from databases, emails, microphones, and cloud servers, and via screen, keyboard, or clipboard capture, with Man-in-the-Middle attacks, etc. After data capture, they need to be exfiltrated safely and unnoticed from the victim's system. At present, there are many ways to exfiltrate data, including unconventional methods covering air-gapped networks [35, 34, 36, 33]. Data exfiltration can be achieved by obfuscating it, timing it to fit regular behavior, done through a physical medium, set up via a web service, conducted through the C2 channel, as well as employing other sophisticated steps. MITRE defines impact steps as the destructive phase in the scenario. Possible impact of the attack can vary greatly and can include storage wipes, defacement, account removal, data corruption, DoS, data destruction and theft, and resource hijacking. At this time, we were unable to find any major work on MLsec data exfiltration methods. In theory, MLsec models could be a decidedly superior choice for selecting and generating data exfiltration traffic and steps based on the target's and network's standard behavior and current defence mechanisms.

Machine learning can be useful for the attack itself as well. When the attackers have breached their target, they may have one or more of the following goals: espionage, fraud, and sabotage. The attacks are performed with malicious programs such as malware, spyware, or ransomware. The most common way to infect a host nowadays is using phishing tactics to con legitimate users to download the malicious program [1]. Uploading the malicious program with the use of software vulnerabilities is also a prolific way to accomplish an attack. Denial-of-service attacks are also quite common mischievous attacks that could cause serious harm. An example of some of the less known attacks is crowd-turfing, which means the generation of fake news, fake reviews, mass following, and other exploits for social media and crowd-sourcing efforts. Machine learning is especially well adapted for crowd-turfing attempts [66].

3   Adversarial Machine Learning

Unsurprisingly, the MLsec technology can be attacked, as with any technology developed at present. As the use of MLsec models increases, so does the desire to influence them. The models themselves are in many cases essentially black-boxes; therefore the attacker's influence on them can be left unseen by the defenders.

In the logistics industry, autonomous vehicles can be tricked into misinterpreting signs and other triggers for action. The method for spoofing image classification algorithms has been proven already [26], and will certainly cause issues in this field. For AI in the cybersecurity space, MLsec methods are abundant in email spam filters and malware detection systems. These systems are not impenetrable and can be bypassed [81]. Facial recognition is used in many places, such as smart devices and laptops, as a credential replacement (i.e., identification feature). As with the logistics example, face recognition uses similar technology and can be fooled in many, sometimes arbitrary, ways [74]. This spoofing logic can be applied to voice recognition as well. Research shows [13] that, for example, Amazon Echo devices can be tricked into executing commands by adding minimal, inaudible noises to a voice recording. These arbitrary commands can be used to hack the devices. In the finance industry, MLsec-driven fraud detection systems and user behavior analysis are in place; however, hackers can still manipulate and trick these systems as well [67].

MLsec-driven systems can be attacked in many ways, but the attacks can be boiled down to three distinct goals that the attackers have: espionage (Privacy), sabotage (Availability), and fraud (Integrity) [67].

3.1 MLsec Attack Goals

The attackers can weaponize a defensive MLsec model against itself, by creating well-crafted inputs to the system in order to gain information about it. There are examples of anonymous data in a dataset being identified, such as the Netflix dataset case [59]. This information can be used to further enhance later attacks or used directly as-is [67].

The defender's MLsec models can also be sabotaged. Some typical attacks, such as flooding, also work on MLsec models. However, some specialized attacks are also available. For example, the trustworthiness of a model can be deteriorated by submitting many misclassified data to it and even aiding in the retraining of the model with this intentionally bad data. Another attack is called adversarial reprogramming of a MLsec model, and it means using the model for one's own purposes to solve one's tasks instead of the model holder's intended use for the model [67]. Another example of sabotage is resource denial, which is effectively a DoS-attack. Hong et al. [39] proposed DeepSloth, a multi-exit architecture targeting adversarial slowdown attack. The authors showcased how their attack can essentially render popular multi-exit architecture models, such as MobileNet, unable to perform tasks properly. With DeepSloth, the attacker can create adversarial perturbations, which are indistinguishable to humans, but result in far more complex calculations than a regular sample, thus, creating slowdowns [39].

Fraud is intentional task misclassification in MLsec model terms. This means that the model interprets it's environment or inputs incorrectly and possibly does something inaccurate or harmful. This can be done using poisoning or evasion. Poisoning means interacting with the system during the training phase and poisoning the dataset in order to make the model behave unintentionally [46]. Evasion is a term used for model vulnerability exploitation in order to achieve misoperation [67].

3.2 Adversarial Attacks

The scope of attacks against MLsec is extensive. MLsec models require specific hardware and environments with ML libraries and frameworks and they all have their own vulnerabilities. Nevertheless, the most important and underestimated part of AI security is the algorithm-specific vulnerabilities unique to ML.

There are three main approaches an attacker can take to affect a MLsec model:

- **Manipulation**. The attacker corrupts the logic of the MLsec model with a specially generated input. This approach includes such attacks as adversarial examples, adversarial reprogramming, scaling, and others.
- **Extraction**. The attacker extracts data from the MLsec model. The data can be data about the model or the dataset itself. Attacks in this section are model inversion, membership inference, model extraction, and others.

- **Injection**. The attacker injects data into a training process aiming to corrupt the model. Attacks such as poisoning, backdoors, and Trojans are part of this approach.

Similarly to OWASP Top-10 for Application Security [87], below we summarize an unofficial Top 10 list of adversarial attacks on AI solutions.

1. **Evasion attacks** involve inputs for MLsec that result in an incorrect output and cause models to make false predictions or behave in an unexpected manner [82]. As an example from the real world, we can take an AI-driver malware detection engine, which can be bypassed using an adversarial attack by changing binary in such a way that it will not be recognized as a malware.
2. **Poisoning attacks** involve injecting data into the training dataset to make MLsec models produce an incorrect output [70]. Such an attack can be performed, for example, against a spam filter by poisoning the ML classifier with non-spam data, which looks like spam to retrain the classifier.
3. **Model inversion** relates to retrieving information about the samples used in the dataset [25]. This type of attack can be used against NLP algorithms, such as GPT-3 [24], to retrieve critical information on how the system was trained. These data can contain credit card information, passwords, or any other private information.
4. **Backdoor attacks** affect training models in such a way that they behave anomalously when fed a particular input but work as intended with other inputs [32]. For example, AI applications, especially devices, may be developed by multiple vendors. The outsourced AI algorithm developer can insert a backdoor into their AI model and sell it to an IoT vendor as a smart speaker model. These types of backdoors can, for example, have some undocumented voice commands for accessing the device.
5. **Model extraction** implies gaining knowledge about the ML model and its parameters with the help of model extraction attacks [61]. For example, if someone wants to steal an API-provider's model, the attackers could use legitimate API requests in a specially-crafted manner so that it leads to model extraction after a finite number of API calls.
6. **Membership inference** is a privacy attack that is intended to determine whether certain data points were in the training dataset or not [75]. The healthcare industry could be affected by these types of attacks as their datasets contain private medical data.
7. **Trojan attacks** are direct modifications to a trained model. The intention is to enable the model to perform additional tasks [53]. In comparison to the *backdoor attack* above, the attacker does not have access to the dataset; however, the attacker has access to the MLsec model stored or transmitted insecurely. Many AI applications were trained with the help of transfer learning, therefore, most of the time the model base is publicly available. Attackers may hack the model hosting and inject trojans into the base model and affect models derived from that as well.

8. **Presentation attacks** are methods where the attacker generates and constructs new objects to fool the MLsec model [21]. Face recognition applications are the most common target for such an attack.
9. **Attribute inference** is an attack that is performed to get information about dataset attributes [27]. With this attack, the hackers may find information about the dataset attributes and guess what parameters are favored by the model. Recommendation systems may be a good example of a target for attribute inference attack.
10. **Slowdown attack** implies performing various types of DoS attacks [39], as some ML-related operations are resource intensive (e.g., re-training a model, transfer learning, inference on complex models). Any publicly available AI-driven API can be vulnerable to this type of attack.

3.3   Attacks on Various MLsec Methods

Adversarial samples are slightly altered versions of originals that cause MLsec models to misclassify the sample [28]. Adversarial samples are few and far between when it comes to ML models. Every classification algorithm [18] and regression algorithm [84] that the MLsec models are based on is vulnerable to some sort of adversarial input. Generative models such as auto-encoders and GANs are also prone to attacks [48].

Fast Gradient Sign Method (FGSM) [28] is one heavily utilized method for creating adversarial samples. In essence, FGSM calculates the gradients of a loss function in regards to the input sample and utilizes the sign of these gradients in order to generate a new adversarial input [28].

Clustering differs from classification, as the classes of the data are not known in advance. Clustering is heavily used in cybersecurity for malware detection, and commonly, new training data for it comes from the Internet. If this is somehow known, the attacker can manipulate the training data, effectively worsening the model from the start. Other attacks against clustering are available. For example, an attack against a common algorithm, k-nearest neighbor, was presented [77].

With complex systems and multi-featured data, dimensionality reduction is often required. Although this category is not nearly as popular as some of the others, there have been attacks performed for dimensionality reduction [68, 69]. For example, Rubistein et al. [69] showcased their attack on Principal Component Analysis (PCA), where they poisoned training data in order to decrease DoS attack detection rate significantly.

Reinforcement learning can also be tricked with adversarial attacks even though there is no training data gathered beforehand. Behzadan and Munir [9] demonstrated that the action-based and reward-based training of RL algorithms can be fooled, and thereby the policies can be affected by injecting adversarial inputs to the environment.

As MLsec-based Intrusion Detection Systems (IDSs) are one of the most implemented systems for MLsec in the cybersecurity space, it makes sense that those systems are being tested with new types of attacks. For example, Lin et al. [52] developed IDSGAN, a GAN-model-based adversarial malicious traffic generating system, to attack IDSs. The authors managed to reduce the detection rates of black-box IDS models to almost zero for several different attacks. Similarly, Shu et al. [76] demonstrated their Generative Adversarial Active Learning (Gen-AAL) method for adversarial attacks against IDSs without previous knowledge about the target system. They also require minimal number queries to the target to gain adequate numbers of training data for their GAN model.

Martins et al. [57] conducted a review on adversarial ML applied to malware and system intrusion cases. They concluded that adversarial attacks can deteriorate the efficacy of all normal classifiers. Nonetheless, the most effective defence against such attacks is adversarial training (i.e., including adversarial samples in training).

Catching encrypted C2 traffic is essential when dealing with attackers who have previously established a beachhead into a system. However, detection avoidance of C2 traffic can be improved by applying MLsec techniques, for example, Novo and Morla [60] generated C2 traffic adversarial samples by employing FGSM and adding TCP/IP flow delays (padding). They set the samples against their own detector and reached highly successful avoidance when the detector was not trained with a dataset containing adversarial samples.

4 Conclusion

In this chapter, we addressed the innovations in ML, DL, RL, and AI within the offensive cybersecurity fields. We structured this chapter inline with the Lockheed Martin's Cyber Kill Chain taxonomy in order to cover adequate grounds on this broad, growing, and hot topic.

At the time of this writing, the offensive MLsec is quite well represented and mature. On the one hand, Reconnaissance, Delivery, and Installation phases of the Cyber Kill Chain are most advanced in terms of technology maturity, number of state of the art works, and the coverage of possible scenarios. However, Exploitation and Acting on objectives phases are in incipient stages, and require more intensive research and innovation efforts. In addition to the use of MLsec for cybersecurity offensive scenarios, we have also explored the offensive technologies against MLsec technologies themselves. As the presented research has shown, the MLsec systems have weaknesses that can (and most certainly will) be exploited by attackers, which sets an increasingly worrying trend for future attacks as well as the defensive capabilities based on MLsec.

In this sense, we also conclude that besides the defenders, the attackers most certainly can and will (ab)use the MLsec technologies for nefarious purposes, and there is evidence that the attackers are often one step ahead. Very likely, it will be impossible to completely embargo or restrict the MLsec use to ethical use only (similarly to kitchen knives being easily available in many stores). However, the research and practitioner communities can minimize the abuse of MLsec for offensive purposes by developing MLsec technologies and models in a way that is easy out of the box to inspect, verify, and explain such as "eXplainable AI" (XAI).

Acknowledgments The authors would like to thank the technical team of Adversa.AI for valuable feedback and insights throughout the draft stages of this chapter. Hannu Turtiainen would like to thank the Finnish Cultural Foundation / Suomen Kulttuurirahasto (https://skr.fi/en) for supporting his Ph.D. dissertation work and research (grant decision 00211119), and the Faculty of Information Technology of University of Jyvaskyla (JYU), in particular Prof. Timo Hämäläinen, for partly supporting his PhD supervision at JYU in 2021–2022.

The authors acknowledge icon authors Gregor Cresnar, Freepik, and Good Ware (courtesy of https://flaticon.com [23]) for their royalty-free icons that are used in Fig. 1.

References

1. Abbate, P.: Internet Crime Report 2020. Tech. rep., Federal Bureau of Investigation (2021). https://www.ic3.gov/Media/PDF/AnnualReport/2020_IC3Report.pdf
2. Al-Hababi, A., Tokgoz, S.C.: Man-in-the-middle attacks to detect and identify services in encrypted network flows using machine learning. In: 3rd International Conference on Advanced Communication Technologies and Networking (CommNet). IEEE, Piscataway (2020)
3. Alhuzali, A., Gjomemo, R., Eshete, B., Venkatakrishnan, V.: {NAVEX}: precise and scalable exploit generation for dynamic web applications. In: 27th {USENIX} Security Symposium (2018)
4. Alqahtani, F.H., Alsulaiman, F.A.: Is image-based CAPTCHA secure against attacks based on machine learning? An experimental study. Comput. Secur. **88**, 101635 (2020)
5. Anderson, H.S., Woodbridge, J., Filar, B.: DeepDGA: adversarially-tuned domain generation and detection. In: ACM Workshop on Artificial Intelligence and Security. ACM, New York (2016)
6. Antonakakis et al., M.: Understanding the Mirai Botnet. In: 26th USENIX Security Symposium. USENIX Association (2017)
7. Avgerinos, T., Cha, S.K., Rebert, A., Schwartz, E.J., Woo, M., Brumley, D.: Automatic exploit generation. Communications of the ACM **57**(2), 74–84 (2014)
8. Bahnsen, A.C., Torroledo, I., Camacho, L.D., Villegas, S.: DeepPhish: simulating malicious AI. In: APWG Symposium on Electronic Crime Research (eCrime) (2018)
9. Behzadan, V., Munir, A.: Vulnerability of deep reinforcement learning to policy induction attacks (2017). https://arxiv.org/abs/1701.04143
10. Brewster, T.: Fraudsters Cloned Company Director's Voice In $35 Million Bank Heist, Police Find (2021). https://www.forbes.com/sites/thomasbrewster/2021/10/14/huge-bank-fraud-uses-deep-fake-voice-tech-to-steal-millions/?sh=1456cb187559
11. Brundage, M., Avin, S., Clark, J., Toner, H., Eckersley, P., Garfinkel, B., Dafoe, A., Scharre, P., Zeitzoff, T., Filar, B., et al.: The malicious use of artificial intelligence: forecasting, prevention, and mitigation (2018). https://arxiv.org/abs/1802.07228
12. Chomiak-Orsa, I., Rot, A., Blaicke, B.: Artificial intelligence in cybersecurity: the use of AI along the cyber kill chain. In: International Conference on Computational Collective Intelligence. Springer, Berlin (2019)
13. Chung, H., Iorga, M., Voas, J., Lee, S.: Alexa, can I trust you? IEEE Comput. Mag. **50**(9), 100–104 (2017)

14. Chung, K., Kalbarczyk, Z.T., Iyer, R.K.: Availability attacks on computing systems through alteration of environmental control: smart malware approach. In: 10th ACM/IEEE International Conference on Cyber-Physical Systems. ACM, New York (2019)
15. Conti, M., De Gaspari, F., Mancini, L.V.: Know your enemy: stealth configuration-information gathering in SDN. In: International Conference on Green, Pervasive, and Cloud Computing. Springer, Berlin (2017)
16. Costin, A.: Security of CCTV and video surveillance systems: threats, vulnerabilities, attacks, and mitigations. In: 6th International Workshop on Trustworthy Embedded Devices (TrustED) (2016)
17. Cruz-Perez, C., Starostenko, O., Uceda-Ponga, F., Alarcon-Aquino, V., Reyes-Cabrera, L.: Breaking reCAPTCHAs with unpredictable collapse: heuristic character segmentation and recognition. In: Mexican Conference on Pattern Recognition. Springer, Berlin (2012)
18. Dalvi, N., Domingos, P., Sanghai, S., Verma, D.: Adversarial classification. In: 10th ACM SIGKDD International Conference on Knowledge Discovery and Data Mining (2004)
19. Darktrace: Darktrace Cyber AI Analyst: Autonomous Investigations (White Paper)
20. Descript: Lyrebird AI. https://www.descript.com/lyrebird
21. Fang, M., Damer, N., Kirchbuchner, F., Kuijper, A.: Real Masks and Fake Faces: On the Masked Face Presentation Attack Detection (2021). https://arxiv.org/abs/2103.01546
22. Fang, Y., Liu, Y., Huang, C., Liu, L.: FastEmbed: predicting vulnerability exploitation possibility based on ensemble machine learning algorithm. PLOS ONE 15(2), e0228439 (2020)
23. Flaticon.com: (2021). https://www.flaticon.com/
24. Floridi, L., Chiriatti, M.: GPT-3: Its nature, scope, limits, and consequences. Minds Mach. 30(4), 681–694 (2020)
25. Fredrikson, M., Jha, S., Ristenpart, T.: Model inversion attacks that exploit confidence information and basic countermeasures. In: Proceedings of the 22nd ACM SIGSAC Conference on Computer and Communications Security (2015)
26. Gitlin, J.M.: Hacking street signs with stickers could confuse self-driving cars (2017). https://arstechnica.com/cars/2017/09/hacking-street-signs-with-stickers-could-confuse-self-driving-cars/
27. Gong, N.Z., Liu, B.: You are who you know and how you behave: attribute inference attacks via users' social friends and behaviors. In: 25th {USENIX} Security Symposium (2016)
28. Goodfellow, I.J., Shlens, J., Szegedy, C.: Explaining and harnessing adversarial examples (2014). https://arxiv.org/abs/1412.6572
29. Google: What is reCAPTCHA? https://www.google.com/recaptcha/about/
30. Gossweiler, R., Kamvar, M., Baluja, S.: What's up captcha? A captcha based on image orientation. In: 18th International Conference on World Wide Web (2009)
31. Grieco, G., Grinblat, G.L., Uzal, L., Rawat, S., Feist, J., Mounier, L.: Toward large-scale vulnerability discovery using machine learning. In: 6th ACM Conference on Data and Application Security and Privacy (2016)
32. Gu, T., Dolan-Gavitt, B., Garg, S.: BadNets: Identifying vulnerabilities in the machine learning model supply chain (2017). https://arxiv.org/abs/1708.06733
33. Guri, M., Bykhovsky, D.: air-jumper: covert air-gap exfiltration/infiltration via security cameras & infrared (IR). Comput. Secur. 82, 15–29 (2019)
34. Guri, M., Kachlon, A., Hasson, O., Kedma, G., Mirsky, Y., Elovici, Y.: Gsmem: data exfiltration from air-gapped computers over {GSM} frequencies. In: 24th {USENIX} Security Symposium (2015)
35. Guri, M., Kedma, G., Kachlon, A., Elovici, Y.: AirHopper: bridging the air-gap between isolated networks and mobile phones using radio frequencies. In: 9th International Conference on Malicious and Unwanted Software: The Americas (MALWARE). IEEE, Piscataway (2014)
36. Guri, M., Zadov, B., Elovici, Y.: LED-it-GO: leaking (a lot of) Data from Air-Gapped Computers via the (small) Hard Drive LED. In: International Conference on Detection of Intrusions and Malware, and Vulnerability Assessment. Springer, Berlin (2017)
37. HackTheBox: A Massive Hacking Playground. https://www.hackthebox.eu/

38. Hitaj, B., Gasti, P., Ateniese, G., Perez-Cruz, F.: Passgan: a deep learning approach for password guessing. In: International Conference on Applied Cryptography and Network Security. Springer, Berlin (2019)
39. Hong, S., Kaya, Y., Modoranu, I.V., Dumitraş, T.: A Panda? No, It's a Sloth: Slowdown Attacks on Adaptive Multi-Exit Neural Network Inference (2020). https://arxiv.org/abs/2010.02432
40. Hu, W., Tan, Y.: Generating adversarial malware examples for black-box attacks based on GAN (2017). https://arxiv.org/abs/1702.05983
41. Huang, S.K., Huang, M.H., Huang, P.Y., Lai, C.W., Lu, H.L., Leong, W.M.: Crax: software crash analysis for automatic exploit generation by modeling attacks as symbolic continuations. In: IEEE 6th International Conference on Software Security and Reliability. IEEE, Piscataway (2012)
42. Huang, S.K., Huang, M.H., Huang, P.Y., Lu, H.L., Lai, C.W.: Software crash analysis for automatic exploit generation on binary programs. IEEE Trans. Reliab. **63**(1), 270–289 (2014)
43. Hutchins, E.M., Cloppert, M.J., Amin, R.M., et al.: Intelligence-driven computer network defense informed by analysis of adversary campaigns and intrusion kill chains. Leading Issues Inform. Warfare Secur. Res. **1**, 80 (2011)
44. Kaloudi, N., Li, J.: The AI-based cyber threat landscape: a survey. ACM Comput. Surv. **53**, 1–34 (2020)
45. Khan, S.A., Khan, W., Hussain, A.: Phishing attacks and websites classification using machine learning and multiple datasets (a comparative analysis). In: International Conference on Intelligent Computing. Springer, Berlin (2020). https://arxiv.org/abs/2101.02552
46. Khurana, N., Mittal, S., Piplai, A., Joshi, A.: Preventing poisoning attacks on AI based threat intelligence systems. In: IEEE 29th International Workshop on Machine Learning for Signal Processing (MLSP). IEEE, Piscataway (2019)
47. Knabl, G.: Machine Learning-Driven Password Lists. Ph.D. Thesis (2018)
48. Kos, J., Fischer, I., Song, D.: Adversarial examples for generative models (2017). https://arxiv.org/abs/1702.06832
49. Kotey, S.D., Tchao, E.T., Gadze, J.D.: On distributed denial of service current defense schemes. Technologies **7**, 19 (2019)
50. Lee, K., Yim, K.: Cybersecurity threats based on machine learning-based offensive technique for password authentication. Appl. Sci. **10**, 1286 (2020)
51. Li, J.H.: Cyber security meets artificial intelligence: a survey. Front. Inform. Technol. Electron. Eng. **19**, 1462–1474 (2018)
52. Lin, Z., Shi, Y., Xue, Z.: Idsgan: Generative adversarial networks for attack generation against intrusion detection (2018). https://arxiv.org/abs/1809.02077
53. Liu, Y., Ma, S., Aafer, Y., Lee, W.C., Zhai, J., Wang, W., Zhang, X.: Trojaning attack on neural networks (2017)
54. Lockheed Martin Corporation: Gaining the advantageapplying cyber kill chain® methodology to network defense. https://www.lockheedmartin.com/content/dam/lockheed-martin/rms/documents/cyber/Gaining_the_Advantage_Cyber_Kill_Chain.pdf
55. Maestre Vidal, J., Sotelo Monge, M.A.: Obfuscation of malicious behaviors for thwarting masquerade detection systems based on locality features. Sensors **20**, 2084 (2020)
56. Manky, D.: Rise of the 'Hivenet': Botnets That Think for Themselves (2018). https://www.darkreading.com/vulnerabilities-threats/rise-of-the-hivenet-botnets-that-think-for-themselves
57. Martins, N., Cruz, J.M., Cruz, T., Abreu, P.H.: Adversarial machine learning applied to intrusion and malware scenarios: a systematic review. IEEE Access **8**, 35403–35419 (2020)
58. Mirsky, Y., Demontis, A., Kotak, J., Shankar, R., Gelei, D., Yang, L., Zhang, X., Lee, W., Elovici, Y., Biggio, B.: The Threat of Offensive AI to Organizations (2021). https://arxiv.org/abs/2106.15764
59. Narayanan, A., Shmatikov, V.: How to break anonymity of the netflix prize dataset (2006). https://arxiv.org/abs/cs/0610105
60. Novo, C., Morla, R.: Flow-based detection and proxy-based evasion of encrypted malware c2 traffic. In: 13th ACM Workshop on Artificial Intelligence and Security (2020)

61. Oh, S.J., Schiele, B., Fritz, M.: Towards reverse-engineering black-box neural networks. In: Explainable AI: Interpreting, Explaining and Visualizing Deep Learning. Springer, Berlin (2019)
62. van den Oord, A., Dieleman, S., Zen, H., Simonyan, K., Vinyals, O., Graves, A., Kalchbrenner, N., Senior, A., Kavukcuoglu, K.: WaveNet: A Generative Model for Raw Audio (2016). https://arxiv.org/abs/1609.03499
63. Osadchy, M., Hernandez-Castro, J., Gibson, S., Dunkelman, O., Pérez-Cabo, D.: No bot expects the DeepCAPTCHA! Introducing immutable adversarial examples, with applications to CAPTCHA generation. IEEE Trans. Inform. Forensics Secur. **12**, 2640–2653 (2017)
64. Pacheco, F., Exposito, E., Gineste, M., Baudoin, C., Aguilar, J.: Towards the deployment of machine learning solutions in network traffic classification: a systematic survey. IEEE Commun. Surv. Tutorials **21**, 1988–2014 (2018)
65. PimEyes: PimEyes: Face Recognition Search Engine and Reverse Image Search. https://pimeyes.com/en
66. Polyakov, A.: Machine learning for cybercriminals 101 (2018). https://towardsdatascience.com/machine-learning-for-cybercriminals-a46798a8c268
67. Polyakov, A.: Ai security and adversarial machine learning 101 (2019). https://towardsdatascience.com/ai-and-ml-security-101-6af8026675ff
68. Ringberg, H., Soule, A., Rexford, J., Diot, C.: Sensitivity of PCA for traffic anomaly detection. In: ACM SIGMETRICS International Conference on Measurement and Modeling of Computer Systems (2007)
69. Rubinstein, B.I., Nelson, B., Huang, L., Joseph, A.D., Lau, S.h., Rao, S., Taft, N., Tygar, J.: Stealthy poisoning attacks on PCA-based anomaly detectors. ACM SIGMETRICS Perform. Eval. Rev. **37**, 73–74 (2009)
70. Schwarzschild, A., Goldblum, M., Gupta, A., Dickerson, J.P., Goldstein, T.: Just how toxic is data poisoning? A unified benchmark for backdoor and data poisoning attacks. In: International Conference on Machine Learning. PMLR (2021)
71. Seymour, J., Tully, P.: Weaponizing data science for social engineering: automated e2e spear phishing on twitter. BlackHat USA **37**, 1–39 (2016)
72. Seymour, J., Tully, P.: Generative models for spear phishing posts on social media (2018). https://arxiv.org/abs/1802.05196
73. Shafiq, M., Yu, X., Laghari, A.A., Yao, L., Karn, N.K., Abdessamia, F.: Network traffic classification techniques and comparative analysis using machine learning algorithms. In: 2nd IEEE International Conference on Computer and Communications (ICCC). IEEE, Piscataway (2016)
74. Sharif, M., Bhagavatula, S., Bauer, L., Reiter, M.K.: Accessorize to a crime: real and stealthy attacks on state-of-the-art face recognition. In: ACM SIGSAC Conference on Computer and Communications Security (2016)
75. Shokri, R., Stronati, M., Song, C., Shmatikov, V.: Membership inference attacks against machine learning models. In: 2017 IEEE Symposium on Security and Privacy (SP). IEEE, Piscataway (2017)
76. Shu, D., Leslie, N.O., Kamhoua, C.A., Tucker, C.S.: Generative adversarial attacks against intrusion detection systems using active learning. In: 2nd ACM Workshop on Wireless Security and Machine Learning (2020)
77. Sitawarin, C., Wagner, D.: On the robustness of deep k-nearest neighbors (2019). http://arxiv.org/abs/1903.08333v1
78. Sivakorn, S., Polakis, J., Keromytis, A.D.: I'm not a human: breaking the Google reCAPTCHA. BlackHat (2016)
79. Stoecklin, M.P.: Deeplocker: how AI can power a stealthy new breed of malware. Secur. Intell. **8** (2018)
80. Stone, G., Talbert, D., Eberle, W.: Using ai/machine learning for reconnaissance activities during network penetration testing. In: International Conference on Cyber Warfare and Security. Academic Conferences International Limited (2021)

81. Subramaniam, T., Jalab, H.A., Taqa, A.Y.: Overview of textual anti-spam filtering techniques. Int. J. Phys. Sci. **5**, 1869–1882 (2010)
82. Szegedy, C., Zaremba, W., Sutskever, I., Bruna, J., Erhan, D., Goodfellow, I., Fergus, R.: Intriguing properties of neural networks (2013). https://arxiv.org/abs/1312.6199
83. The MITRE Corporation: MITRE ATT&CK Matrix for Enterprise. https://attack.mitre.org/
84. Tong, L., Yu, S., Alfeld, S., Vorobeychik, Y.: Adversarial regression with multiple learners (2018). https://arxiv.org/abs/1806.02256
85. Valea, O., Oprişa, C.: Towards pentesting automation using the metasploit framework. In: IEEE 16th International Conference on Intelligent Computer Communication and Processing (ICCP). IEEE, Piscataway (2020)
86. Wang, M., Su, P., Li, Q., Ying, L., Yang, Y., Feng, D.: Automatic polymorphic exploit generation for software vulnerabilities. In: International Conference on Security and Privacy in Communication Systems. Springer, Berlin (2013)
87. Wichers, D., Williams, J.: OWASP TOP-10 2017. OWASP Foundation (2017)
88. Yadav, T., Rao, A.M.: Technical aspects of cyber kill chain. In: International Symposium on Security in Computing and Communication. Springer, Berlin (2015)
89. Yamin, M.M., Ullah, M., Ullah, H., Katt, B.: Weaponized AI for cyber attacks. J. Inform. Secur. Appl. **57**, 102722 (2021)
90. Yim, K.: A new noise mingling approach to protect the authentication password. In: International Conference on Complex, Intelligent and Software Intensive Systems (2010)
91. Yu, N., Darling, K.: A low-cost approach to crack python CAPTCHAs using AI-based chosen-plaintext attack. Appl. Sci. **9**, 2010 (2019)
92. Zargar, S.T., Joshi, J., Tipper, D.: A survey of defense mechanisms against distributed denial of service (ddos) flooding attacks. IEEE Commun. Surv. Tutorials **15**, 2046–2069 (2013)
93. Zhang, R., Chen, X., Lu, J., Wen, S., Nepal, S., Xiang, Y.: Using AI to hack IA: a new stealthy spyware against voice assistance functions in smart phones (2018). https://arxiv.org/abs/1805.06187

Defensive Machine Learning Methods and the Cyber Defence Chain

Hannu Turtiainen, Andrei Costin, and Timo Hämäläinen

1 Introduction

The amount of research, results, and innovation in Machine Learning (ML), Deep Learning (DL), Reinforcement Learning (RL), and Artificial Intelligence (AI)[1] show that such technologies thrive in the Natural Language Processing (NLP) and Computer Vision (CV) fields. In the cybersecurity field, however, the situation is not as clear cut. Although many common tasks can be improved and automated with these technologies, they can also introduce new and even worse challenges to security if the defenders are over-committed to them. In the worst case, the attackers can also harness the MLsec technologies to their advantage [52], as discussed in the previous chapter, Offensive Machine Learning Methods and the Cyber Kill Chain.

Today's advanced cyberthreats are elaborate, sustainable, and exploit all of the possible openings in a target. Moreover, they have become affordable to deploy with new and advanced tools available to everyone [37]. As presented in the previous chapter, the attackers can and, most certainly, will deploy and use the offensive (or manipulate the defensive) MLsec models and techniques to their advantage. They have all to gain from the technology. In order to keep up with the arms war, the defensive side must leverage MLsec technology, keeping in mind the possible downsides and new attack surfaces that the technology can bring [37]. In any case, a successful use of MLsec in cybersecurity or any other comparable field requires

---

[1] Due to the breadth and depth of various definitions related to ML/DL/RL/AI and cybersecurity, throughout this paper we will refer to these technologies simply as MLsec.

H. Turtiainen · A. Costin (✉) · T. Hämäläinen
University of Jyväskylä, Jyväskylä, Finland
e-mail: hannu.ht.turtiainen@jyu.fi; ancostin@jyu.fi; timoh@jyu.fi

high quality training data, sufficient resources for model creation, and *effective algorithms* [28].

In layman's terms, ML is a pattern recognition approach to data analysis working through examples. It reduces time and effort put into handling simple or repetitive tasks required for large sets of data. Recent advances of ML and the exponentially increasing cybersecurity incidents lead to the fact that current methods for cybersecurity leverage ML a lot. Artificial Intelligence is a concept for machines to perform human tasks such as visual recognition, i.e., CV, or NLP. For example, it is not just machine learning or necessarily smart things, but can be something as simple as an edge detector on a robot. Deep Learning leverages ML to learn to recognize patterns of patterns. Deep Learning is a sizable field of study with several approaches and algorithms developed [52]. The basis of RL is that correct and encourageable actions of the trained generation are rewarded and bad actions lead to disciplinary actions [37].

Polyakov [52] classifies the ML opportunities for defensive cybersecurity into three dimensions—why, what, and how.

- *The Why-dimension* can be presented with Gartner's predict, prevent, detect, respond -models. Gartner developed their PPDR-model [51] to ease the communication of security program strategies. They assert that all security tasks can be set into five distinct categories: prediction, prevention, detection, response, and monitoring.
- *The What-dimension* consists of all the things in need of security features. Networks need Network Intrusion Detection Systems (NIDS) and Network Traffic Analysis (NTA), endpoints (workstations, servers) need anti-malware software, Applications require firewalls such as Web-Application Firewall (WAF) and database firewalls and Users should be protected with User behavior Analytics (UBA) and processes that benefit from anti-fraud functionalities. Each of these categories have their subcategories and even more specific functionalities are required.
- *The How-dimension* answers the question of how to check the security of an area. This denotes the concept of time and/or state of the environment in regards to the data to be analyzed. It can be real-time, at rest, historically, and others.

According to Polyakov [52], some tasks require looking into all of the dimensions, while other tasks may have no relevance in some of the dimensions. Nevertheless, every dimension has its quirks and features, but for MLsec technologies, the "What-dimension" might just be the predominant one.

This paper is organized as follows. Section 2 showcases MLsec technologies research that we feel is novel and relevant in cyber defence. Section 3 highlights some points on cybersecurity competitions in relation with MLsec that we feel fuels in part the research on MLsec-enabled cybersecurity. Lastly, we conclude the paper on Sect. 4 with future foreshadowing.

2 Cyber Defence Functions

The OWASP's Cyber Defense Matrix [46] is a functional checklist for organizations to ensure that their cybersecurity measures and program coverage are adequate. It employs the five NIST Cybersecurity Framework [42] functions in conjunctions with five classes of assets in need of being cybersecured. Our work is structured based on these five functions and the appropriate asset classes for each function.

The asset classes are set in the matrix [77] as follows:

- *Devices*: Workstations, servers, phones, tablets, storage, network devices, IoT infrastructure, etc., or endpoints generally speaking
- *Apps*: Software, interactions, and application flows on the devices
- *Networks*: Connections and traffic flowing among devices and apps
- *Data*: Content at rest, in transit, or in use by the resources above
- *Users*: The people using the above resources

MITRE's D3FEND [66] is a similar framework for cybersecurity and it proposes cybersecurity measures in an all-inclusive structural matrix form. It sections these measures into five distinct segments—harden, detect, isolate, deceive, and evict. The harden section proposes encryption, validation, authentication, and update tasks. The Detect section includes all forms of detection and analysis for networks, files, platforms, processes, and users. The isolation part consists of network and process isolation in forms of access and privilege control and proper network control via several forms of traffic filtering. The deceive section focuses on wasting attackers' time on decoy assets and possibilities, as well as generally observing and learning attackers' Tactics, Techniques, and Procedures (TTP). The Evict chapter concludes the matrix by introducing credential and process eviction policies. D3FEND can be perceived as a checklist or a proposal list, and a tool for cybersecurity experts and researchers.

2.1 Identity

In the Cyber Defense Matrix, the operations in the identity section are focused on asset recognition and risk management. Asset holders should be aware of all of their assets and the risks and threats that they possess and can manage, but they should also recognize normal operation [77].

People and companies have a lot of information about them available publicly at all times. This information is gathered with passive reconnaissance performed by the attacking parties. Therefore, managing the information available online is crucial and mostly in the hands of the users and companies themselves. Limiting information that you put out is crucial for privacy and security. It is also true for employees giving out information about the company; therefore, a proper information sharing policy and user education program are necessary for effective information security. These procedures alone limit the attractiveness of the target in the eyes of the attackers and they can aid in lowering the yield the attackers gained from the reconnaissance activities and can also reduce the effectiveness of automated reconnaissance methods.

Active reconnaissance is an attackers' information-gathering method that the defenders can be aware of: probing the network, sending phishing emails, etc. Dialogue and team work between web- and network administrators about visitor analytics and network logs is key in order to limit the attack surface and create historical data for incident responses and alerts [39].

As phishing is the most successful cybercrime in 2020 in terms of victim count [1], it is of the utmost importance to acquire protection from it. Although it is valuable to educate users in identifying phishing attempts, it is not an absolute solution and the results can vary significantly [71, 25]. Automated technical solutions can alleviate the issue by blocking the attempts before they reach a human target. Multiple researchers have studied MLsec-driven phishing detection [32, 33, 58].

Jain and Gupta [33] exhibited their hyperlink-based ML phishing detection. The model detects phishing URLs (even zero day ones) with high accuracy and can be deployed to in the front-end. The model utilized 12 distinct features to analyze the input data and determine phishing attempts. The authors chose logistic regression (LR) as a binary classifier for its accuracy in this task. They created and appropriated a labeled dataset consisting of 2544 websites of which 1428 were true positives. Supervised learning utilized in the model creation and the model caught 98.39% of the phishing sites in the testing dataset [33]. The results indicate the usefulness of hyperlink-based phishing detection through careful and knowledgeable feature selection.

Sahingoz et al. [58] proposed an URL-based phishing detector, a large training dataset containing 36.400 legitimate and 37,175 phishing URLs, respectively, and NLP, word vector, and hybrid feature sets. They tested seven different classification algorithms (Naive Bayes, Random Forest, K-Nearest Neighbour ($n = 3$), Adaboost, K-star, Sequential Minimal Optimization, and Decision Tree) ultimately reaching 97.98% detection accuracy with random forest classifier accompanied with NLP features. As with Jain and Gupta's [33] work, the authors model also can be implemented independently without third party services on the client side and can also detect zero-day phishing URLs [33].

Continuous risk assessment is a hot commodity in modern day information security management for combatting the changing threat environment. Paltrinieri et al. [48] proposed a Deep Neural Network (DNN) model to determine risk based on risk indicators and demonstrated it with an offshore oil and gas industry case study. The authors used Tensorflow's DNN classifier with their indicator datasets and for comparison, they also applied the Multiple Linear Regression (MLR) model to the dataset. The authors' DNN model achieved higher accuracy and precision, but lower recall than the equivalent MLR model. Many things affect the overall performance of the model. For example, the model is highly susceptible to input data quality and unsatisfactory data may affect the results in the long term, and also indicators are not distributed evenly, thus resulting in lack of dynamicity by the model. Due to the uncertainties in risk assessment and in the DNN model, the results from the ML risk assessment require an expert opinion to be fully utilized [48]. As risk assessment requires knowledge about the threat, Datta et al. [19] introduced a MLsec model for determining the consequences of cyberattacks for systems in order to reduce the cognitive load of experts focusing on risk assessment. Although initially they reached 60% accuracy, the groundwork for the technology is generally developed.

2.2 Protect

The Protect function covers pre-emptive countermeasures that can be applied to prevent or disrupt attacks. These measures include software patching, network segmentation, endpoint hardening, access management, vulnerability mitigation, etc. [77]. From MITRE's D3FEND [66], the hardening steps for applications, credentials, messages, and platform especially fit this stage.

2.2.1 Machine Learning for Endpoint Protection

The most modern anti-virus software relies on endpoint detection and response, which are based on learnt features of executables and process behavior. Issues can emerge when dealing with different kinds of endpoints, whether it is a workstation, server, or anything else, as the behavior of a process will change depending on the environment. To utilize ML in endpoint protection, you can, for example, use regression for system call prediction and compare the results with calls from normal operation. Classification can be used to categorize programs such as malware and clustering could be beneficial, for example, in protecting email by separating malicious attachments from legitimate ones [52].

Raff et al. [53] took a raw bytes static analysis approach to malware detection in their research. They took a dataset of 400.000 malicious and benign files, trained their neural network with it, and reached beyond 90% accuracy on malware detection on their testing dataset. The authors found improvements on their raw bytes-based model in comparison to byte n-gram-based model due to the n-gram model over-focusing on the headers and its frail features. The authors argue that ML-based malware detection is superior to signature-based models as the environments of the endpoints differ greatly, and therefore, specifying the signatures individually is not feasible [53].

Le et al. [35] turned a malware detection problem into a classification problem reaching detection accuracy above 98% with their nine malware classes. They used malware data from the Microsoft Malware Classification Challenge [57] dataset, scaled each raw binary malware file to 10.000 bytes, and represented these binary streams as sequences of 10.000 values, where one value represents one byte of data. This data was used to train three distinct models. The results were excellent and the model performed malware detection at a fast rate (0.02s per binary), which is a merit to a possible real-world implementation [35].

As malware detection for endpoints is a highly researched topic in numerous security publications [30, 54, 61, 23, 80, 27, 59, 38], the results from these closed environments can be biased or misleading as Pendlebury et al. [49] discovered with many Android malware detection papers. Other domains are likely to be affected as well. Pendlebury et al. [49] claim that the issues most likely arise due to the representational deficit of the datasets to real-world application and due to the incorrect time splits of training and testing datasets.

Ransomware attacks have made headlines over the years, not necessarily due to the financial losses, but due to the crippling effects of the attacks. As many industries rely on their IT infrastructure, having it in lockdown means huge business losses. In the research community, MLsec-based ransomware detection has been a widely researched topic over the last few years [2, 5, 13, 16, 31, 36, 43, 60, 79]. Deep learning is the method of choice for ransomware detection as Hwang et al. [31] cautioned that signature-based detectors lack longevity in ransomware detection as the rate of ransomware evolution is so high. Therefore, they proposed a two-model approach, where a Markov model and a Random Forest model detect ransomware from Windows API calls in a "sensor fusion" manner. Alhawi et al. [2] utilized several MLsec algorithms to detect ransomware from network traffic. Ultimately, their Detection Tree (J48) classifier performed the best with a 97.1% True Positive rate. Bae et al. [5] focused on distinguishing benign files, malware, and ransomware from each other with several different models. Cusack et al. [16] leveraged Software Defined Networks (SDN) to create a Random Forest ransomware classifier. Lee et al. [36] applied MLsec models to detect ransomware from file systems (e.g., big-data use) based on file entropy analysis.

Ransomware is certainly a threat to availability of data and services on the web and MLsec techniques can help alleviate the issue. However, even though researchers have reached exceptional results, as Chen et al. [13] demonstrated, many of the MLsec-based ransomware detectors they tested failed to detect their GAN-generated adversarial samples.

2.2.2 Machine Learning for Application Security

Applications vary a lot, as do the ways to secure them. It is unfeasible to build an universal model to secure applications. However, ML can be useful in several ways in application security: anomalies in HTTP requests can be detected with regression, known attacks can be classified, and Distributed Denial-of-Service (DDoS) attacks could be detected using clustering [52].

One could argue that proper application security stems from proper code. MLsec can be useful in this regard. For example, Zhou et al. [82] proposed the Deving (Deep Vulnerability Identification via Graph Neural Networks) model, which is a C programming language vulnerability detector for source code. The authors trained their model on their self-gathered and labeled dataset from four popular C libraries. At the time, the authors reported state-of-the-art performance with significant margins on any comparable static analyzers.

Web Intrusion Detection Systems (IDS) analyze web traffic in order to protect users from malicious activity. According to Dong and Zhang [20], Web IDSs usually combine signature-based and anomaly-based detections in order to increase the True Positive (TP) detection rate, which is common in anomaly-based methods, while preserving a low False Positive (FP) rate of the signature-based methods [20]. The authors argued that most of the anomaly-based Web IDSs are immutable since their training data is collected once and the model is based only on that data. Since the methods for web attacks are in constant evolution, the models rapidly become obsolete. The authors exhibit their adaptive solution, AMODS, which selectively picks new and important web request query strings and incorporates them to the model, hence improving the overall performance of web attack detection.

Stokes et al. [64] proposed their malicious JavaScript and VBScript deep recurrent neural classification system called ScriptNet in 2018. The system harnesses static and dynamic analysis methods in a sandbox environment to analyze and dissect the scripts. Malicious code can be hidden as an element (child-script) inside a script that scans as benign. Therefore, it is paramount to extract all of these scripts within scripts as well as possible. Stokes et al.'s [64] system scans the input scripts with Windows Defender and takes note of any child-scripts that the script-in-test might run. The child-scripts are also unpacked and analyzed similarly. This process goes on until no more unidentified scripts are found or launched. The text in the unknown scripts are normalized to the US-ASCII character set and sent through the trained models. The classifiers reached up to 67.2% TP rate with a FP rate of only 1% [64]. As mentioned previously (in Sect. 1), these types of hybrid detectors are effective, widely-adopted, and complement each other well [74].

Malicious URLs accomplish many tasks for the attackers: they can be used for identity thefts, malware installations, identify thefts, and other attacks. Traditional malicious URL lists are ineffective in today's rapid evolution of attacking means and methods; therefore, learning systems are required. URLNet by Le et al. [34] tackles the malicious URL detection task with ML.

The "Completely Automated Public Turing test to tell Computers and Humans Apart"s (CAPTCHAs) are widely used in web services and everyone using web services has at some point come across some type of CAPTCHA. As many types of CAPTCHAs have been deemed "broken" [3, 15, 76], new ideas for CAPTCHAs are required. Osadchy et al. [44] proposed DeepCAPTCHA, a CAPTCHA scheme utilizing adversarial examples. As adversarial examples are proven to be problematic to MLsec models, for example, with classification [17], the proposed method has legitimacy in previous work. With the addition of the adversarial noise to the image CAPTCHAs, the image to the user is more or less the same and at least very distinguishable; however, for the MLsec model cracking CAPTCHAs, the image is very different and it fools the automated systems completely. Similarly, Gosseweiler et al. [26] present their approach to CAPTCHAs, which tasks the user to set the image they are seeing in upright position. This is a simple task for humans, but MLsec models need special circumstances (attention in the dataset, special labeling, etc.) in order to solve these tasks [70, 81].

2.2.3 Machine Learning for User Behavior

A typical method for analyzing user behavior is the Security Information and Event Management (SIEM) software suite. However, more modern advanced attacks could outclass a SIEM; therefore, more modern systems are required. User and Event Behavior Analytics (UEBA) tools are a step in the right direction, although even they are not omnipotent to cover all user types and environments as user behavior analysis is one of the most complex subjects in Polyakov's technology driven What-dimension. Machine learning aid in user behavior analysis as well. Technologies such as regression can be used to detect unusual user actions, peer-analysis can be conducted using classification, and clustering can root out outliers in user groups [52].

Sun et al. [65] proposed an isolation forest algorithm derived from an anomalous user detection system. The system parses user activity logs and calculates an anomaly score for each activity using the isolation forest trees. These scores are compared to a baseline. Activities scoring over the set threshold are presumed anomalous activities and flagged as such. The authors chose the isolation forest algorithm because of some of its benefits such as small sample size requirement, there's no need for anomalous samples beforehand, and non-correlation of anomaly distance threshold (based on tree depth) and data set dimensions. The extension to the original isolation forest algorithm that the authors proposed introduces the ability to process categorical data (non-continuous dimensions on the dataset) [65].

Tuor et al. [69] approached user behavior analysis with DNN and Recurrent Neural Network methods (RNN). Their system employed a feature extractor, which accumulates raw user events and outputs a single vector for each user each day. This vector is fed into their trained neural networks models. The authors' DNN model and their Long Short-Term Memory (LSTM) RNN model both outperform the basic algorithm-based counterparts such as Isolation Forest, Support-Vector Machines (SVMs), and Principal Component Analysis (PCA) [69].

2.3 Detect

Detection is needed when attacks have passed the deterrents and protections and malicious events are occurring. The functions for this section are event discovery, triggers on anomalies, analyzing security events, and intrusion awareness [77]. MITRE's D3FEND [66] detect section points out similar analysis steps for many entities in the cyber-physical system such as files, messages, network traffic, user behavior, and processes.

Keeping up with the threat landscape with adequate threat intelligence can reduce the efficacy of the attackers' malware. Analyzing and detecting previously used methods and toolkits can help identify and mitigate current attacks if the attackers use parts of older technology even if the malware is mostly tailored to the attack [39].

Machine learning can aid in evaluating the risks in one's network. These ML models are trained on cyber-attack datasets and have imprinted generalized features of these attacks. The features are based on the previously discovered Indicators Of Compromise (IOC). Using the models, one can discover areas of weaknesses and can focus on hardening these sections of the network. Other routine security checks such as analyzing security reports and logs can also be done automatically. With the MLsec models, the security analysts can amass and process larger amounts of meaningful data and yield better results [55].

2.3.1 Machine Learning for Network Monitoring

Intrusion Detection Systems have been deployed for network security for ages and if they have had any ML components on them, they were usually some signature-based units embedded into the system. The most modern approach is the Network Traffic Analysis, which is an in-depth analysis of all traffic in all of the OSI layers and the function is to detect misconduct, attacks, anomalies, and other malicious activity. Machine learning can be used in many ways with Network Traffic Analytics (NTA). Regression can be used to compare normal packets and predicted network packet parameters of current traffic. Classification is useful in identifying known attacks and clustering is an avid tool in forensic analysis [52].

There are a myriad of intrusion detection papers based on NTA with different kinds of algorithms used and for many environments such as enterprise, 5G, and IoT networks. For example, Yulianton et al. [78] deployed the Adaboost algorithm for IDS use, Alrawashdeh et al. [4] experimented with the Restricted Boltzmann Machine (RBM)-algorithm for anomaly intrusion detection system, Maimó et al. [41] trained the Deep Belief Networks model for 5G network IDS with self-adaptive capabilities, and Eskandari et al. [22] focused on the IoT field with their Passban IDS using Isolation Forest and Local Outlier Factors models.

Many of today's IDS MLsec models are trained on KDD Cup 99 dataset from 1999. It's undoubtedly a large dataset with a wide variety of classes, but many were misrepresented in the papers [47]. Arguments can also be made about the dataset's descriptivity of today's traffic anomalies and attack techniques. However, the protocols in use today are still the same. Revathi and Malathi [56] compared and analyzed multiple MLsec techniques in conjunction with the NSL-KDD and KDD Cup 99 datasets. In their conclusion, the authors find Random Forest-based models highly accurate when trained on the NSL-KDD dataset. More recently, Otoum et al. [45] compared IDSs in Wireless Sensor Networks (WSN). They concluded that adaptive ML-based IDSs are comparable to DL-based IDSs, at least in WSN use in terms of detection accuracy; however, the ML-based IDSs performed their tasks much quicker.

Log monitoring can be crucial in dealing with network-based and insider attacks. Foriadou et al. [24] proposed LSTM and Convolutional Neural Network (CNN)-based models dealing with log monitoring. Long Short-Term Memory is widely adopted in multivariate time-series analysis and text-classification tasks becoming ideal for log monitoring. However, CNNs extract representative features from even complex datasets and in automatic fashion. The log events gathered for the dataset are from Suricata intrusion detection software running on pfSense router software. They gathered around 700.000 network events for their dataset. Both of the models achieved detection accuracy above 97% across the event classes, surpassing other classifiers such as random forests [24]. On the other hand, Du et al. [21] and Brown et al. [8] focused on system log analysis via RNN language models. Du et al.'s [21] DeepLog was trained using supervised training and Brown et al.'s [8] model was trained without labelled data (unsupervised). They both applied online training, which means that their algorithm predicts and learns simultaneously (two models, which are synced by a set time period) and posted state-of-the-art results for their time.

2.3.2 Machine Learning for Process Behavior

Process behavior analysis requires a great deal of domain knowledge as processes vary significantly. Nonetheless, ML has use cases in this discipline as well. In finance, regression can be used to detect credit card fraud by predicting user actions. Classification is useful in the search for known fraud behavior in the logs and clustering can detect outliers by process comparison [52].

Fraud detection, in financial, medical, and other fields, via the means of ML techniques has been researched considerably over the last couple of decades (such as [7, 11, 40, 50]). Recently, more work has been conducted on researching real-time fraud detection, instead of more traditional means of data-mining old transactions. Ye et al. [75] used Graphics Processing Units (GPUs) to increase the workload capabilities of e-commerce real-time fraud detections systems. Tran et al. [68] employed the One Class Support Vector Machine (OCSVM) algorithm and T2 control chart methods to achieve real-time fraud detection in the credit card fraud detection space. For online transaction fraud detection, Cao et al. [10] proposed TitAnt, an end-to-end system for fraud detection in a case study platform. As commerce and finance continue to embrace the online space, these types of fraud detection methods are in ever increasing demand, especially with real-time detection.

2.4   Respond

Respond functions are necessary reactions to the detect functions (i.e. certain detection functions lead to certain respond functions). These actions can be damage assessments, intruder eradication, forensic reconstructions, etc. [77].

At this point, the defenders should catch the threat before the attackers install any persistent backdoors or webshells. Identifying abnormal installations and behavior is key here as the attackers are now using regular system or users accounts to do their bidding and cannot be easily identified. Deceive and evict stages from MITRE's

D3FEND [66] taxonomy set the tasks for this stage. As the attacker has already penetrated the defences, the defenders are on damage control. Deceive sets tasks for wasting the attackers' time on "too good to be true" fake targets that are specifically set for that reason and contain nothing of value despite looking valuable. Evicting the attackers and containing the vulnerable or malicious credentials and processes are also crucial in this step.

Cybercrime forensics involves three phases: collecting, examining, and handling the evidence. During evidence collection, it is paramount to identify and preserve the evidence properly. Afterwards, the evidence is validated, analyzed, and interpreted in regards to the crime committed. Lastly, the evidence and findings are documented in a manner suited for further proceedings [14]. Machine learning can aid these phases of cybercrime forensics. Research has been conducted on the matter (e.g., Chhabra et al. [14] in the Internet-of-Things (IoT)-space); however, due to the nature of the problem, model accuracy can become a major limitation to a fully-developed system.

2.5 Recover

After events have been responded to and dealt with properly, recovery functions such as normal operations, service restoration, resiliency improvements, and incident documentation can commence [77].

In the MLsec research field, recovery can be one of the most overlooked areas in terms of research, technology, and awareness. Prevention and detection are the preferred approaches, but these days according to the statistics [1], cyberattacks do get through the defences. Therefore, recovery is paramount to the health of the systems and networks. Dramatic examples of poor recovery policies can be found in the many cases of severe ransomware attacks to the infrastructure [67] and the health care sector [12]. These examples and trends showcase the harsh consequences of simple ransomware attacks on unprepared systems, inadequate defenses and crucially nonexistent recovery steps.

Examples of successful MLsec techniques applicable at the recovery stage are extremely limited. Baek et al. [6] present SSD-insider as one example of local endpoint ransomware recovery. They incorporated ransomware detection and fault recovery into the NAND-flash of Solid-State Drives (SSDs). They achieved fast and perfect recovery of data in their experiments. For ransomware attack detection, they designed six hardware level features and trained their detection model using the "Iterative Dichotomiser 3" algorithm. Similarly, Huang et al. [29] introduced FlashGuard, an SSD firmware level ransomware recovery system with little to no performance or drive lifetime degradation impact.

As for normal operation restoration, there has been research conducted on MLsec strategies, for example, for sensor measurements [73] and smart grid power infrastructure [72]. However, research for normal operation recovery in cyberattack events for endpoints and networks is largely lacking attention. We feel that this area requires more research and innovation, both in the short and in the long term.

In any case, attacks will certainly continue to happen, and the defending parties need to learn from them. Having decent recovery policies and methods is essential in recovering back-to-normal operation in a swift manner. However, documenting the issue and recovery steps properly will aid in future incidents, and it might also prevent others from being attacked.

3 Machine-vs-Machine Cybersecurity Competitions

Machine-vs-machine cybersecurity competition is one of the positive technological drivers for advancing MLsec techniques and technologies, both from ethical offensive and defensive perspectives. Therefore, in this section, we also provide a short overview of the MLsec advancements in this area.

The Defense Advanced Research Projects Agency (DARPA) [18] launched their Cyber Grand Challenge (CGC) in 2014. It was a competition for automatic defensive systems, which should be capable of reasoning about flaws and overcoming bugs in the services when set against automated cyber-threat-hunting software. The final was held in 2016 and the game was set up with a typical Capture-the-Flag (CTF) -style setting that continued for eight hours straight without any humans intervening with competing machines.

The CGC offered an unique outlook on machine-operated cybersecurity. The competitors needed to disassemble, patch, recompile, and resume operation of binaries on the fly [62], which on the outside sounds ground-breaking. However, in today's world, the deployment of such tools would most likely result in breaking services and business logic in a production or industrial environment. Therefore, these types of MLsec tools would have ideal use-cases in software production and applied research.

For many of the competitors [62, 63, 9], the challenge clearly highlighted the differences between human- and computer-handled security. On the one hand, humans deal with abstract details well, they have intuition, and can look outside the box. On the other hand, machines have precision, brute-force, speed, and deal with complex issues as fluently as lesser ones. Most of all, computers have scaling by their side [9]. Moreover, one can deploy MLsec software anywhere in the world and have the same capabilities globally and instantly; however, human skill varies a great deal and can be scarce.

4 Conclusion

In this chapter, we addressed the innovations in ML, DL, and AI within the defensive cybersecurity fields. We mainly structured this chapter in line with the OWASP Cyber Defense Matrix in order to cover adequate grounds on this broad, growing, and hot topic.

At the time of this writing, the defensive MLsec is relatively well represented. As expected, the MLsec state-of-the-art for Identity and Detection/Protection phases is quite mature and well represented. However, the MLsec in Respond and Recover phases are generally not covered by state-of-the-art techniques. This lack of technology and innovation in Respond and Recover could be one explanation for the current ransomware "pandemic" where organizations are unable to effectively respond and recover from ransomware attacks despite the fact that many of them employ state-of-the-art detection/prevention technologies as well as Managed Security Providers (MSP). Overall, defensive MLsec (unsurprisingly) lags considerably behind both offensive MLsec and adversarial AI technologies as presented in the previous chapter. In addition to using MLsec for cybersecurity offensive scenarios, we have also explored the offensive technologies against MLsec technologies themselves. As the presented research has shown, the MLsec systems have weaknesses that attackers can, and certainly will, exploit, which sets an increasingly worrying trend for future attacks as well as the defensive capabilities based on MLsec. As also presented in the previous chapter, adversarial AI is an increasingly worrying issues that is poised to affect the defensive MLsec technologies as well. This will require more fundamental research rather than hot-patch solutions to current attacks. The MLsec technologies can be seen as a two-way street. In part, the latest innovations in the MLsec field can provide quick and consistent results in the short term; however, they can cause unforeseen issues and threats themselves. In this sense, we also conclude that, at present, the trust put into AI for cybersecurity is unwarranted, and the only safe way to move forward with AI in the defensive cybersecurity space is by developing AI technologies, algorithms, and models that are trustworthy, transparent, reliable, and resilient to cyberattacks.

Acknowledgments The authors would like to thank Alex Polyakov (CEO/co-founder of Adversa AI) for valuable feedback and insights throughout the draft stages of this chapter. Hannu Turtiainen would like to thank the Finnish Cultural Foundation/Suomen Kulttuurirahasto (https://skr.fi/en) for supporting his Ph.D. dissertation work and research (grant decision 00211119), and the Faculty of Information Technology of University of Jyvaskyla (JYU), in particular Prof. Timo Hämäläinen, for partly supporting his PhD supervision at JYU in 2021–2022.

References

1. Abbate, P.: Internet Crime Report 2020. Tech. rep., Federal Bureau of Investigation (2020). https://www.ic3.gov/Media/PDF/AnnualReport/2020_IC3Report.pdf
2. Alhawi, O.M., Baldwin, J., Dehghantanha, A.: Leveraging machine learning techniques for windows ransomware network traffic detection. In: Cyber Threat Intelligence. Springer, New York (2018)
3. Alqahtani, F.H., Alsulaiman, F.A.: Is image-based captcha secure against attacks based on machine learning? An experimental study. Comput. Secur. **88**, 101635 (2020)
4. Alrawashdeh, K., Purdy, C.: Toward an online anomaly intrusion detection system based on deep learning. In: 15th IEEE International Conference on Machine Learning and Applications (ICMLA). IEEE, New York (2016)

5. Bae, S.I., Lee, G.B., Im, E.G.: Ransomware detection using machine learning algorithms. Concur. Comput. Pract. Exp. **32**, e5422 (2020)
6. Baek, S., Jung, Y., Mohaisen, A., Lee, S., Nyang, D.: Ssd-insider: internal defense of solid-state drive against ransomware with perfect data recovery. In: IEEE 38th International Conference on Distributed Computing Systems (ICDCS). IEEE, New York (2018)
7. Bauder, R.A., Khoshgoftaar, T.M.: Medicare fraud detection using machine learning methods. In: 16th IEEE International Conference on Machine Learning and Applications (ICMLA). IEEE, New York (2017)
8. Brown, A., Tuor, A., Hutchinson, B., Nichols, N.: Recurrent neural network attention mechanisms for interpretable system log anomaly detection. In: 1st Workshop on Machine Learning for Computing Systems (2018)
9. Brumley, D.: The Cyber Grand Challenge and the future of cyber-autonomy. USENIX Login **43** (2018)
10. Cao, S., Yang, X., Chen, C., Zhou, J., Li, X., Qi, Y.: Titant: online real-time transaction fraud detection in ant financial (2019). http://arxiv.org/abs/1906.07407
11. Carneiro, N., Figueira, G., Costa, M.: A data mining based system for credit-card fraud detection in e-tail. Dec. Support Syst. **95** (2017)
12. Center, H.S.C.C.: Ransomware Trends 2021. Tech. rep., Health Sector Cybersecurity Coordination Center (2021). https://www.hhs.gov/sites/default/files/ransomware-trends-2021.pdf
13. Chen, L., Yang, C.Y., Paul, A., Sahita, R.: Towards resilient machine learning for ransomware detection (2018). https://arxiv.org/abs/1812.09400
14. Chhabra, G.S., Singh, V.P., Singh, M.: Cyber forensics framework for big data analytics in iot environment using machine learning. Multimedia Tools Appl. **79** (2020)
15. Cruz-Perez, C., Starostenko, O., Uceda-Ponga, F., Alarcon-Aquino, V., Reyes-Cabrera, L.: Breaking reCAPTCHAs with unpredictable collapse: heuristic character segmentation and recognition. In: Mexican Conference on Pattern Recognition. Springer, New York (2012)
16. Cusack, G., Michel, O., Keller, E.: Machine learning-based detection of ransomware using sdn. In: ACM International Workshop on Security in Software Defined Networks & Network Function Virtualization (2018)
17. Dalvi, N., Domingos, P., Sanghai, S., Verma, D.: Adversarial classification. In: 10th ACM SIGKDD International Conference on Knowledge Discovery and Data Mining (2004)
18. DARPA: Cyber Grand Challenge (2016). https://www.darpa.mil/about-us/timeline/cyber-grand-challenge
19. Datta, P., Lodinger, N., Namin, A.S., Jones, K.S.: Predicting Consequences of Cyber-Attacks. In: IEEE International Conference on Big Data (Big Data). IEEE, New York (2020)
20. Dong, Y., Zhang, Y.: Adaptively Detecting Malicious Queries in Web Attacks (2017). http://arxiv.org/abs/1701.07774
21. Du, M., Li, F., Zheng, G., Srikumar, V.: Deeplog: anomaly detection and diagnosis from system logs through deep learning. In: ACM SIGSAC Conference on Computer and Communications Security (2017)
22. Eskandari, M., Janjua, Z.H., Vecchio, M., Antonelli, F.: Passban IDS: an intelligent anomaly-based intrusion detection system for IoT edge devices. IEEE Internet Things J. **7**, 6882–6897 (2020)
23. Fang, Y., Huang, C., Liu, L., Xue, M.: Research on malicious JavaScript detection technology based on LSTM. IEEE Access **6**, 12284–12294 (2018)
24. Fotiadou, K., Velivassaki, T.H., Voulkidis, A., Skias, D., Tsekeridou, S., Zahariadis, T.: Network traffic anomaly detection via deep learning. Information **12** (2021). https://www.mdpi.com/2078-2489/12/5/215
25. Ghazi-Tehrani, A.K., Pontell, H.N.: Phishing evolves: analyzing the enduring cybercrime. Victims Offenders **16**, 28 (2021)
26. Gossweiler, R., Kamvar, M., Baluja, S.: What's up captcha? a captcha based on image orientation. In: 18th International Conference on World Wide Web (2009)

27. Grace, M., Zhou, Y., Zhang, Q., Zou, S., Jiang, X.: Riskranker: scalable and accurate zero-day android malware detection. In: 10th International conference on Mobile Systems, Applications, and Services (2012)
28. Hoffman, W.: AI and the future of cyber competition. CSET Issue Brief (2021)
29. Huang, J., Xu, J., Xing, X., Liu, P., Qureshi, M.K.: Flashguard: leveraging intrinsic flash properties to defend against encryption ransomware. In: ACM SIGSAC Conference on Computer and Communications Security (2017)
30. Huang, X., Ma, L., Yang, W., Zhong, Y.: A method for windows malware detection based on deep learning. J. Signal Process. Syst. **93**, 265–273 (2021)
31. Hwang, J., Kim, J., Lee, S., Kim, K.: Two-stage ransomware detection using dynamic analysis and machine learning techniques. Wireless Personal Commun. **112**, 2597–2609 (2020)
32. Jain, A.K., Gupta, B.: Comparative analysis of features based machine learning approaches for phishing detection. In: 3rd International Conference on Computing for Sustainable Global Development (INDIACom). IEEE, New York (2016)
33. Jain, A.K., Gupta, B.B.: A machine learning based approach for phishing detection using hyperlinks information. J. Amb. Intell. Human. Comput. **10**, 5 (2019)
34. Le, H., Pham, Q., Sahoo, D., Hoi, S.C.: URLNet: Learning a URL representation with deep learning for malicious URL detection (2018). http://arxiv.org/abs/1802.03162
35. Le, Q., Boydell, O., Namee, B.M., Scanlon, M.: Deep learning at the shallow end: Malware classification for non-domain experts (2018). https://arxiv.org/abs/1807.08265
36. Lee, K., Lee, S.Y., Yim, K.: Machine learning based file entropy analysis for ransomware detection in backup systems. IEEE Access **7**, 110205–110215 (2019)
37. Li, J.H.: Cyber security meets artificial intelligence: a survey. Front. Inf. Technol. Electron. Eng. **19**, 1462–1474 (2018)
38. Likarish, P., Jung, E., Jo, I.: Obfuscated malicious javascript detection using classification techniques. In: 4th International Conference on Malicious and Unwanted Software (MALWARE). IEEE, New York (2009)
39. Lockheed Martin Corporation: GAINING THE ADVANTAGE: Applying Cyber Kill Chain®Methodology to Network Defense (2015). https://www.lockheedmartin.com/content/dam/lockheed-martin/rms/documents/cyber/Gaining_the_Advantage_Cyber_Kill_Chain.pdf
40. Maes, S., Tuyls, K., Vanschoenwinkel, B., Manderick, B.: Credit card fraud detection using bayesian and neural networks. In: 1st International NAISO Congress on Neuro Fuzzy Technologies (2002)
41. Maimó, L.F., Gómez, Á.L.P., Clemente, F.J.G., Pérez, M.G., Pérez, G.M.: A self-adaptive deep learning-based system for anomaly detection in 5g networks. IEEE Access **6**, 7700–7712 (2018)
42. NIST: NIST Cybersecurity framework (2018). https://www.nist.gov/cyberframework
43. Noorbehbahani, F., Rasouli, F., Saberi, M.: Analysis of machine learning techniques for ransomware detection. In: 16th International ISC (Iranian Society of Cryptology) Conference on Information Security and Cryptology (ISCISC). IEEE, New York (2019)
44. Osadchy, M., Hernandez-Castro, J., Gibson, S., Dunkelman, O., Pérez-Cabo, D.: No bot expects the DeepCAPTCHA! Introducing immutable adversarial examples, with applications to CAPTCHA generation. IEEE Trans. Inf. Forensics Secur. **12** (2017)
45. Otoum, S., Kantarci, B., Mouftah, H.: A comparative study of ai-based intrusion detection techniques in critical infrastructures. ACM Trans. Internet Technol. **21**, 1–22 (2021)
46. OWASP Foundation: OWASP Cyber Defense Matrix. https://owasp.org/www-project-cyber-defense-matrix/
47. Özgür, A., Erdem, H.: A review of kdd99 dataset usage in intrusion detection and machine learning between 2010 and 2015. PeerJ Preprints **4**, e1954v1 (2016)
48. Paltrinieri, N., Comfort, L., Reniers, G.: Learning about risk: machine learning for risk assessment. Safe. sci. **118**, 475–486 (2019)
49. Pendlebury, F., Pierazzi, F., Jordaney, R., Kinder, J., Cavallaro, L.: TESSERACT: eliminating experimental bias in malware classification across space and time. In: 28th USENIX Security Symposium (USENIX Security) (2019)

50. Perols, J.: Financial statement fraud detection: An analysis of statistical and machine learning algorithms. Audit.: J. Pract. Theory **30**, 19–50 (2011)
51. Perry Carpenter: Using the Predict, Prevent, Detect, Respond Framework to Communicate Your Security Program Strategy (2016). https://www.gartner.com/en/documents/3286317/using-the-predict-prevent-detect-respond-framework-to-co
52. Polyakov, A.: Machine Learning for Cybersecurity 101 (2018). https://towardsdatascience.com/machine-learning-for-cybersecurity-101-7822b802790b
53. Raff, E., Barker, J., Sylvester, J., Brandon, R., Catanzaro, B., Nicholas, C.: Malware detection by eating a whole exe (2017). Preprint. arXiv:1710.09435
54. Ravi, C., Manoharan, R.: Malware detection using windows API sequence and machine learning. Int. J. Comput. Appl. **43**, 17 (2012)
55. Rege, M., Mbah, R.B.K.: Machine learning for cyber defense and attack. Data Analytics **2018**, 73–78 (2018)
56. Revathi, S., Malathi, A.: A detailed analysis on NSL-KDD dataset using various machine learning techniques for intrusion detection. Int. J. Eng. Res. Technol. **2** (2013)
57. Ronen, R., Radu, M., Feuerstein, C., Yom-Tov, E., Ahmadi, M.: Microsoft malware classification challenge (2018). https://arxiv.org/abs/1802.10135
58. Sahingoz, O.K., Buber, E., Demir, O., Diri, B.: Machine learning based phishing detection from URLs. Exp. Syst. Appl. **117**, 345–357 (2019)
59. Sahs, J., Khan, L.: A machine learning approach to android malware detection. In: European Intelligence and Security Informatics Conference. IEEE, New York (2012)
60. Shaukat, S.K., Ribeiro, V.J.: Ransomwall: A layered defense system against cryptographic ransomware attacks using machine learning. In: 10th International Conference on Communication Systems & Networks (COMSNETS). IEEE, New York (2018)
61. Singh, P., Tapaswi, S., Gupta, S.: Malware detection in pdf and office documents: a survey. Inf. Secur. J.: Global Perspect. **29**, 134–153 (2020)
62. Song, J., Alves-Foss, J.: The DARPA cyber grand challenge: a competitor's perspective. IEEE Secur. Priv. **13**, 72–76 (2015)
63. Song, J., Alves-Foss, J.: The DARPA cyber grand challenge: a competitor's perspective, part 2. IEEE Secur. Priv. **14**, 71–81 (2016)
64. Stokes, J.W., Agrawal, R., McDonald, G.: Neural classification of malicious scripts: a study with javascript and vbscript (2018). http://arxiv.org/abs/1805.05603
65. Sun, L., Versteeg, S., Boztas, S., Rao, A.: Detecting anomalous user behavior using an extended isolation forest algorithm: an enterprise case study (2016). http://arxiv.org/abs/1609.06676
66. The MITRE Corporation: MITRE D3FEND Framework. https://d3fend.mitre.org/
67. Tidy, J.: Colonial hack: How did cyber-attackers shut off pipeline? https://www.bbc.com/news/technology-57063636
68. Tran, P.H., Tran, K.P., Huong, T.T., Heuchenne, C., HienTran, P., Le, T.M.H.: Real time data-driven approaches for credit card fraud detection. In: International Conference on e-Business and Applications (2018)
69. Tuor, A., Kaplan, S., Hutchinson, B., Nichols, N., Robinson, S.: Deep learning for unsupervised insider threat detection in structured cybersecurity data streams (2017). http://arxiv.org/abs/1710.00811
70. Vailaya, A., Zhang, H., Yang, C., Liu, F.I., Jain, A.K.: Automatic image orientation detection. IEEE Trans. Image Process **11**, 746–755 (2002)
71. Weaver, B.W., Braly, A.M., Lane, D.M.: Training users to identify phishing emails. J. Educ. Comput. Res. **59**(6), 1169–1183 (2021)
72. Wei, F., Wan, Z., He, H.: Cyber-attack recovery strategy for smart grid based on deep reinforcement learning. IEEE Transactions on Smart Grid **11**, 2427–2439 (2019)
73. Wu, Z., Chen, S., Rincon, D., Christofides, P.D.: Post cyber-attack state reconstruction for nonlinear processes using machine learning. Chem. Eng. Res. Des. **159**, 248–261 (2020)
74. Xin, Y., Kong, L., Liu, Z., Chen, Y., Li, Y., Zhu, H., Gao, M., Hou, H., Wang, C.: Machine learning and deep learning methods for cybersecurity. IEEE Access **6**, 35365–35381 (2018)

75. Ye, C., Li, Y., He, B., Li, Z., Sun, J.: Gpu-accelerated graph label propagation for real-time fraud detection. In: International Conference on Management of Data (2021)
76. Yu, N., Darling, K.: A low-cost approach to crack python captchas using AI-based chosen-plaintext attack. Applied Sciences **9**, 2010–8574 (2019)
77. Yu, S.: Cyber defense matrix. https://cyberdefensematrix.com/
78. Yulianto, A., Sukarno, P., Suwastika, N.A.: Improving adaboost-based intrusion detection system (IDS) performance on CIC IDS 2017 dataset. In: Journal of Physics: Conference Series. IOP Publishing, Bristol (2019)
79. Zhang, H., Xiao, X., Mercaldo, F., Ni, S., Martinelli, F., Sangaiah, A.K.: Classification of ransomware families with machine learning based on n-gram of opcodes. Future Generation Computer Systems **90**, 211–221 (2019)
80. Zhang, J.: MLPdf: an effective machine learning based approach for PDF malware detection (2018). https://arxiv.org/abs/1808.06991
81. Zhang, L., Li, M., Zhang, H.J.: Boosting image orientation detection with indoor vs. outdoor classification. In: 6th IEEE Workshop on Applications of Computer Vision. IEEE (2002)
82. Zhou, Y., Liu, S., Siow, J., Du, X., Liu, Y.: Devign: Effective vulnerability identification by learning comprehensive program semantics via graph neural networks (2019). https://arxiv.org/abs/1909.03496

Part II
Privacy and Ethics

Differential Privacy: An Umbrella Review

Minna Kilpala, Tommi Kärkkäinen, and Timo Hämäläinen

1 Introduction

The decline of data storage costs, continuous growth of the computing speed, advances in processing heterogeneous datasets, and development of big data processing platforms has made data a stronger asset than ever [47]. Open data can, e.g., boost open innovation and creativity, foster private-public partnership between multiple bodies and actors, and inflow and outflow existing or new knowledge even at early stages of higher education [28]. Exploitation of open and big data allows assessment of the impacts of population growth and combating the climate change [52, 25]. The significance of open data to monitor and restrain the global expansion of COVID-19, and to discover novel therapeutics, has been widely recognized [2, 59].

Indeed, especially in public healthcare, the population-based information can be of utmost value in planning and decision-making [58]. However, sensitive personal information on citizens can not be made open for secondary purposes as such: protection of individual privacy must be guaranteed. Continuing with the ongoing COVID-19 epidemic, to be useful, the privacy preservation techniques and methods should not, however, change the underlying characteristics of a dataset [26]. This illustrates the two, constradicting targets of privacy preservation, the privacy–utility tradeoff: maximization of the confidentiality of individuals and minimization of the distortions on data. In addition to the technical aspects, this theme has a widespread and versatile social dimension including vivid public debate and derivation of legislative measures and frameworks [45].

M. Kilpala (✉) · T. Kärkkäinen · T. Hämäläinen
University of Jyväskylä, Jyväskylä, Finland

© The Author(s), under exclusive license to Springer Nature Switzerland AG 2023
T. Sipola et al. (eds.), *Artificial Intelligence and Cybersecurity*,
https://doi.org/10.1007/978-3-031-15030-2_8

1.1 Basic Definitions

The dawn of actionable conceptualization of privacy and differential privacy is described in [45], where the original contributions of Tore Dalenius and Ivan Fellegi on privacy, and Cynthia Dwork, Frank McSherry, Kobbi Nissim, and Adam Smith on differential privacy were mentioned (see also [12]).

Privacy is a challenging term to define exactly because its meaning is context and person dependent. In this article, we consider privacy as individual's right to not share her/his private data publicly or to make it available so that the individual can be recognized. Private data is also context specific but usually it refers to personally identifiable information (PII) meaning any data that can been used to identify a specific individual. European privacy law (General Data Protection Regulation, GDPR) protects all data that can be directly or indirectly connected to an individual. Sufficiently wide definition is needed to exclude, for example, use of a combination of different data sources in order to identify a person. Here, it is also important to distinguish between common personal data and personal data that can be used to identify a person. Common personal data is just data that is not person specific, i.e., it can not be used to identify a person.

Dwork defined Differential Privacy in [10]. The central idea was that instead of giving a privacy guarantee with maximal coverage, a strong enough, relative one could be given. This was formulated in [10] as follows:

> any given disclosure will be, within a small multiplicative factor, just as likely whether or not the individual participates in the database.

Later in [11], this is restated as:

> the removal or addition of a single database item does not (substantially) affect the outcome of any analysis.

Nowadays differential privacy can be seen as the *de facto* standard for privacy protection.

The definitions above do not prevent an individual to be disclosed, but they enforce that this does not happen because of his/her presence in data. For example, there may be certain attributes (like smoking) in data which correspond to certain consequences (like cancer) and that information can be used with additional information about an individual (from other sources), but this does not dependent on whether an individual was in database or not. The definition of Differential Privacy says that if a participant removes her/his data from a data set, then no output would become significantly more or less likely. This is formalized in the next theorem.

Differential Privacy definition *A randomized function K gives ε-differential privacy if for all data sets D_1 and D_2 differing on at most one element, and for all $S \subseteq Range(K)$,*

$$Pr[K(D_1) \in S] \le exp(\epsilon) \times Pr[K(D_2) \in S]$$

The value of ε is not exactly defined as it is treated as case specific, social question, but it should be some small value.

1.2   Research Scope and Questions

The focus of this study is how to take care of privacy in connection with, for example, use of personal data in machine learning or data mining algorithms. In other words, anywhere, where personal data needs to be processed in order to create models and achieve analysis results but where individuals, whose data are being used, should not be identifiable in order to prevent any harm to be done.

Processing in this context means processing in a big scale, where the aim is to draw some conclusions based on statistical techniques or when using unsupervised or supervised machine learning methods. We do not include cases where there are only one or a few individuals involved, for example, when a doctor is looking for a suitable cure of a patient based on a recommendation by some AI agent. Instead, we are interested how to make information used by the agent available while protecting privacy of the participants.

To this end, we address the following research questions

1. How has Differential Privacy evolved since it was defined?
2. How widely is Differential Privacy used?
3. In which domains is Differential Privacy used?

2   Description of the Study

In this section, we introduce the umbrella review as a systematic method for secondary literature reviews and provide details about the search protocol.

2.1   Method: The Umbrella Review

To know what is already known is essential when developing new knowledge. The amount of research and the number of scientific articles and reports has been rapidly expanding during the twenty-first century. Already a decade ago it was noticed how much primary and secondary research appears on a daily basis, e.g., in medicine in the article entitled as "Seventy-five trials and eleven systematic reviews a day: how will we ever keep up?" [5]. Indeed, information overload of research knowledge is a real challenge both in healthcare [36] and in science [37].

This is the landscape where all sorts of literature reviews on scientific knowledge have increased their popularity. There exists multiple types and forms of literature reviews. For instance, in [22], fourteen different types of reviews were defined: critical review, literature review, mapping review, meta-analysis, mixed studies review, overview, qualitative systematic review, rapid review, scoping review, state-of-the-art review, systematic review, systematic search and review, systematized review, and umbrella review. Additionally, there exists, e.g., narrative reviews [29] and many general [46] as well as domain-specific [51] guidelines and recommendations in order to realize a proper review, Different forms of reviews differ from each other on the following perspectives: (i) how the literature has been searched, (ii) is there a formal quality assessment of the included articles, (iii) how the body of knowledge in the articles is being synthesized, and (iv) how the analysis is being presented and concluded.

Another main aspect that separates different kind of reviews is their level of abstraction concerning the empirical research to be analyzed: up-to-date knowledge of evidence-based practices is sought by systematically collecting and reviewing primary studies, whereas the secondary meta-analysis level is concerned with addressing the already made surveys and reviews. On the meta-meta, i.e., tertiary level, these reviews themselves are being summarized (see, e.g., [27]). Here we focus on the meta-level by carrying out an umbrella review to address the development and forms of differential privacy through the reviews and surveys that have been published since 2014.

The purpose of an umbrella review is to systematically locate and summarize possibly competing views and perspectives on a broad area of interest [22]. In doing so, one ends up knowing what is known and what recommendations can be given for practice. With equal importance, one can conclude what remains unknown to raise evidence-based recommendations for future research. Concerning the research process [4], an umbrella review should be based on a priori defined protocol with detailed inclusion criteria and should apply a structured search process of the existing reviews, in order to present a critical appraisal of the included reviews. The first phase of the research process explicating the protocol by means of sources of research knowledge and inclusion/exclusion criteria are depicted next.

2.2   Search Protocol and Inclusion/Exclusion Criteria

We were searching for reviews or surveys on differential privacy written in English. Therefore, the common parts in the search string specifying the non-numeric inclusion criteria were "differential privacy" AND ("'review' OR 'survey' OR 'overview'") AND "'language' = 'English'". To ensure sufficient coverage of the umbrella review, we used seven general repositories of scientific articles with wide scope in the search: *Ebsco, ProQuest, Sage Journals, ScienceDirect, Scopus, Taylor&Francis, and Wiley.* Comments on the search strings, due to different search possibilities and interfaces of different repositories, and the numbers of the retrieved

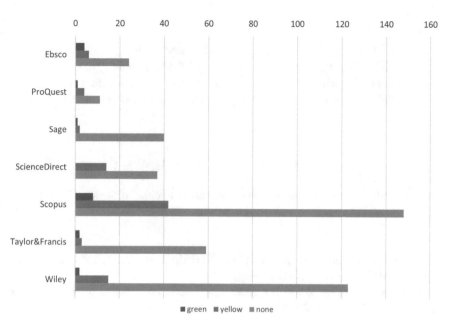

Fig. 1 Search result amounts per category per repository

articles are given next. Concerning the latter, we first report the number of qualified articles after the search. This set is then further reduced into "green" and "yellow" indicating numbers of those articles that were selected to be included with at least half of the article as differential privacy review and those, which were identified to have a small differential privacy review part, but where Differential Privacy was not the main focus of the article. In the first phase, inclusion/exclusion was based on article's abstracts and in an unclear case, the text was read until the decision was confirmed. The common exclusion criteria were considered in the following order: (i) not in English, (ii) not about differential privacy, or (iii) not a differential privacy review. Amount of articles per category (green, yellow, none) per repository is depicted in Fig. 1.

Ebsco

> **Search:** "differential privacy" AND (""review" OR "survey" OR "overview"")
> **Results:** 10 articles of which 4 green and 6 yellow (total 34).

ProQuest

> **Search:** "differential privacy" from all sources where type is "review" OR "literature review" AND language is "English"
> **Results:** 5 articles of which 1 green and 4 yellow (total 16); most the same than obtained from *Ebsco*, though, only 1 novel yellow.

Sage Journals

> **Search:** With "differential privacy" AND "review" 36 hits of which 2 novel ones; With "differential privacy" AND "survey" 23 hits of which 0 novel ones; With "differential privacy" AND "overview" 12 hits of which 0 novel ones
> **Results:** 3 articles of which 1 new green and 2 yellow, of which 1 novel (total 43)

ScienceDirect

> **Search1:** "differential privacy" AND ""article type" = ("review" OR "mini review")"
> **Results1:** 14 articles of which no green ones, 14 yellow of which 13 novel ones (total 51)

Scopus

> **Search:** ALL("differential privacy") AND (LIMIT-TO(DOCTYPE, "re")) AND (LIMIT-TO(LANGUAGE, "English"))
> **Results:** 50 articles of which 8 green with 4 novel ones and 42 yellow ones with 27 novel ones (total 198).

Taylor&Francis

> **Search:** [All: "differential privacy"] AND [[All: review] OR [All: survey] OR [All: overview]]
> **Results:** 5 articles of which 2 novel green and 3 yellow ones with 2 novel (total 64 plus 4 'Comment' articles that were excluded right away).

Wiley

> **Search:** 140 results for "differential privacy" anywhere AND "review" anywhere; 106 results for "differential privacy" anywhere AND "survey" anywhere; 9 results for "differential privacy" anywhere AND "survey" in Title; 3 results for "differential privacy" anywhere AND "overview" in Title anywhere
> **Results:** 17 articles of which 2 novel green and 15 yellow ones with 10 novel ones (total 140).

In total, 487 different articles were found of which 13 were categorized as green ('real review') and 58 as yellow ('small part depicts a review'). As the overall number of the articles was large, we decided to include articles only in the green category to the umbrella review. All included articles were between years 2013 and 2020 (1 at 2013, 2 at 2014, 1 at 2017, 1 at 2019 and 5 at 2020). What was also notable is that most of the articles were found only from one library, 50 articles from two libraries and 4 articles from three libraries. Of the last four, one was included in the actual review and two in the yellow category.

In the second cycle, a set of three articles originally tagged as green were excluded. One [50] because it was not an actual differential privacy review but a common presentation of the topic, one [20] because it was more an introduction to differential privacy, and one [49] because it was a clarification of differential privacy and focused on it's own model. Therefore, 10 review articles were included in the umbrella review.

3 Chronologial Review

In this section, we summarize the included reviews in a chronological order to see, how the concept of differential privacy has evolved—therefore answering to the first research question as stated in Sect. 1. We will focus on key points and when they have appeared.

3.1 Differential Privacy Is Defined

Cyntia Dwork defined Differential Privacy 2006 [10] as a solution for problem, how to get useful information on a population level from a database while securing participants' privacy well enough. Definition included first Differential Privacy models: interactive and non-interactive. The former model has a trusted data collector, who provides interface to data queries, and in the latter model, one data collector just publishes a "sanitized" version of data.

Dwork herself worked with the interactive model of data privacy, where the security mechanism was based on adding random noise to an individual answer. She defined sensitivity of the query function as magnitude of noise that corresponded to the largest change that a single participant could have in the output of the function. Histogram query was used as an example, why noise should be added to the result of the query function.

Dwork continued her work with the interactive model of differential privacy and in [11] she presented two basic techniques for achieving it. Her scenarios were in a statistical database. She presented a Laplace based technique that fits especially to histogram queries and mentioned the exponential mechanism by McSherry and Talwar [40] where auction was used as a good example of use of differential privacy. She also presented differentially private algorithms for three different tasks. Conclusion was that the required amount of noise should grow along with the complexity of the query sequence.

3.2 Reviews of Differential Privacy Start to Emerge

First review of Differential Privacy was made on 2013 in the healthcare domain [7]. Available mechanisms for achieving Differential Privacy in the interactive model at that time were the Laplace noise, in case of not real outcome (number) the exponential mechanism, median mechanism, and multiplicative weights mechanisms.

One challenge identified in this time was the value of ε. There were no rules for it, so the choices were data set depended. Another identified limitations were that differential privacy assumes that individuals are independent from each other, there is only one data holder, and mechanisms are restricted to certain data types. Differential privacy started from statistical database, histogram was mentioned in Dworks's work, so those limitations were to be expected.

At this point there existed (i) relaxed version of differential privacy (ε, δ)-differential privacy, where ε-differential privacy is achieved with a probability of at least $1 - \delta$ [31] and (ii) approximate differential privacy where additional small value is added in allowed privacy probability difference $(+\tau)$.

Commonly used utility definition for differential privacy was also missing, so this text defines (α, δ)-useful definition, where every query output is within α of the correct output with a probability of at least $1 - \delta$. Non-interactive model has also started it's life and now it's split to two main mechanisms: noise-based ones and other ones. However, it is still seen as a challenge to release a non-synthetic dataset that accurately answers any query.

Some practical limitations were also found but potential for the adoption of differential privacy in healthcare was concluded. So we were on a promising track for differential privacy.

3.3   Definitions of Differential Privacy Are Widened

Next, differential privacy was widened to different data release categories [54]. There are three different data release strategies: (1) noise to raw data & possible postprocessing, (2) first conversion & compression, then add noise, and (3) noise to raw data with ε-privacy budgets.

Base definitions are ε-differential privacy & (ε, δ)-differential privacy, which seemed to be standardly used in all reviews. Laplace and exponential mechanism were part of differential privacy standard with division to non-interactive and interactive models. What was new here was the division of the noise mechanism into global, local, and smooth sensitivity.

Combination properties, like sequential and parallel composition, were mentioned. One important aspect identified was how to budget the privacy parameter ε.

At this time, several differential privacy algorithms existed for different individual data release categories: histogram, tree structure release, time series release, graph release, and pattern mining release. There were already many strategies for many different approaches and one was still covering only certain areas where privacy needed to be conserved. Differential privacy has found it's place as a interesting study target and started to establish it's place as a standard for privacy guarantee.

Distributed Differential Privacy (DDP) was mentioned in [15] and it can be split into fully distributed or server-based approach. Same challenges as before are still valid: (i) trade-off between privacy and utility, (ii) the answer pollution problem, (iii) a significant computational effort, and (iv) tailoring of existing solutions to individual datatypes and perturbation mechanisms. It was noted that solutions depended on the area where DP was used (smart metering etc.) and there were different assumptions on the participants in different areas.

3.4 Differential Privacy Goes to Data Analysis

At 2017 in [60] differential privacy was approached from data analysis and data publishing point of views. Now data publishing was connected with interactive and non-interactive models while data analysis was based on machine learning. Interactive data publishing contained transaction, histogram, stream, and graph data publishing, but also non-interactive publishing was based on two models: batch query and synthetic dataset publishing. Also anonymization appeared inside differential privacy. Machine learning methods based on supervised, unsupervised, online, deep, and private learning were mentioned, with the ongoing studies on how differential privacy could be ensured. A new term Local Differential Privacy was introduced and, when combined with machine learning, the combination got its own differential privacy reviews three years later.

Two years later, another survey [19] focused solely on the integration of decision tree classification with differential privacy. The focus was clearly on how this type of a machine learning algorithm can be differentially private.

Issues to be considered when designing differentially private machine learning algorithm were identified as following: (i) total privacy budget needed, (ii) how many times data needs to be queried, (iii) sensitivity of the queries, and (iv) the size of data set. Here sensitivity was defined to Dvork's definition on 2006 [10] and privacy budget was split to ε values for each query. The selection of privacy budget (and parameter) was still seen as a problem, but some studies working with that were identified.

Two kind of decision trees were considered: Greedy Decision Trees and Random Decision Trees. Their differences and similarities in implementing differential privacy and using privacy budged were discussed. It was also noted that the attribute schema is considered as public information. Privacy mechanisms used were familiar from the previous studies: Laplace and Exponential mechanisms. For sensitivity, global, local and smooth sensitivity were considered, where local sensitivity is not seen to be enough for privacy, but making it smooth one gives privacy with privacy budget ε. The text focused on how to implement different decision tree tasks and classifiers (like counting queries, splitting functions, termination criteria, pruning and amount of trees) in order to minimize usage of privacy budged, reduce sensitivity, and keep differential privacy.

Above review also mentioned tradeoff between knowledge discovery and prediction accuracy (like privacy and utility), so that a user needs to know what s/he is looking for. New weakening definition from Rana et al. [48] was mentioned: this definition prevented finding values of individual, but allowed figuring out their presence in a dataset. An unexpected benefit of privacy was designing for as few data queries as possible to save privacy budged and thus also computational complexity.

3.5   2020—Year of Differential Privacy Reviews

Activity on year 2020 showed clearly, how differential privacy had taken it's place and had spread to many application and research areas. [55] and [35] focused their study in local privacy, [21] in machine learning, [18] in private regression for healthcare research, and [24] in usage of differential privacy in cyber physical systems. In [24], the review was focused on different cyber physical systems: energy, transportation, healthcare, and medical systems, and industrial internet of things. Also different privacy techniques in these domains were explored. Each area had an own section of how to implement differential privacy. Differential privacy was seen as a low complexity and adjustable method (compared to encryption and anonymization) for privacy protection. Same challenges (privacy budget, choosing ε value, sensitivity, data utility vs. privacy) were still mentioned from related surveys, but also data correlation problem was identified as a challenge for differential privacy algorithms.

At this point, differential privacy was divided to two major branches: (1) methods with differential privacy and (2) noise addition mechanisms. In addition to the Laplace and the Exponential mechanisms, also the Gaussian mechanism was explained within data perturbation mechanisms. Sequential and parallel composition theorems were given as part of basic definitions for differential privacy. New privacy preservation strategy 'information-theoretic privacy', which utilized entropy based techniques, had appeared. Now it was not only utility vs. privacy, but also different privacy models to choose from. From the milestone table in [24] it was visible, how first some applications appeared after Dwork published differential privacy and then 2015, 2017, and 2018 there were 4–5 examples of using differential privacy in cyber physical systems.

In machine learning the main privacy risk is leaking of private information in training data. In [21] 'differentially private machine learning', especially deep learning techniques, were surveyed. Within machine learning, differential privacy was categorized based on where the perturbation is done: (i) Laplace/Gaussian/Exponential mechanism where noise is added to the non-private model and (ii) output/objective perturbation mechanisms where output or the objective function gets random noise. Each machine learning area (traditional divided to supervised, unsupervised and online learning, ERM (the empirical risk minimization), distributed optimization, sample complexity and deep learning divided to centralized and distributed training algorithms, long short-term memory networks, generative neural networks, deep auto encoders, convolutional deep belief networks and deep walk) was attached with an explanation of available differential privacy possibilities based on the mentioned two categories. However, the conclusion was that more exploration is needed in order to design effective differentially private algorithms in machine learning. In addition to differential privacy, the definitions included sequential and parallel composition theorem, global and local sensitivity, and Laplace, Gaussian, and Exponential mechanisms.

The approach in [35] was a bit different, as it reviewed differential privacy as one of two options for anonymization techniques with social networks. Another option in review was a graph modification technique, but that part is omitted here. Differential privacy was split in global and local privacy, so also that division started to stabilize as part of basic definitions. In global privacy, a trusted curator adds noise to the answers and in local privacy, each each person adds noise before sharing their data.

In [55] the focus was completely on local differential privacy (LDP) in data statistics and analysis. At the latest, it was now clear that differential privacy had taken its place and evolved further. The original differential privacy was now seen as centralized, global differential privacy in contrast to distributed, local differential privacy. LDP-based algorithms were deployed in many real life systems and several fields have their own ongoing research efforts. Survey covered LDP in frequency estimation, mean value estimation, and machine learning, and it listed many algorithms for each area. Sequential composition theorem was especially important to LDP. Also a new basic mechanism, Randomized Response, was presented for LDP.

Now, interactive and non-interactive models were defined in a different way because LDP does not have a trusted curator model anymore. In the interactive morel, there is correlation between the output results which is missing in the non-interactive model. LDP had also started its life and developed further and there existed several variations of it too. Some are similar like in DP, some not and some are combining both. Basic example of variants were different relaxations or case specific definitions, where due to context or some other issue, privacy requirement could be slightly loosened or formulated differently. For the machine learning algorithms with LDP, supervised, unsupervised, deep, reinforcement, federated learning, and empirical risk minimization (ERM) were presented.

In [18], differential privacy was studied for regression modelling tool in a clinical and epidemiological research. Regarding definition of differential privacy, bounded and unbounded neighbouring databases were mentioned. In the first one, the difference is replacement of a single, arbitrary record and in later one, addition or removal of a single record. Two relaxations in addition to (ε, δ)-differential privacy were mentioned: (1) Rényi differential privacy [42], which is another quite new relaxation for differential privacy, stated to be stronger privacy guarantee than traditional (ε, δ)-differential privacy relaxation. (2) Zero-concentrated differential privacy (zCDP) [6], which uses privacy loss random variable probability (to quantify how much information is leaked about an individual) and Rényi divergence.

Conclusion was, however, that in this context more work is needed to be able to guarantee privacy due to the high stakes in this application area.

4 Analysis—Different Views and Definitions of the Research Field

Next, we will conclude some basic categorizations of differential privacy based on the chronological review of the previous section. The detailed definitions and mathematical formulations are left to original studies as our purpose is consider the results in a general level according to the scope of an umbrella review.

As the number and orientation of the found articles and reviews shows, it is clear that differential privacy is a popular study area and the amount of studies is increasing. From the included reviews we can see that some domains are characterized by several published differential privacy reviews. The reason for this is likely the large demand on protecting personal data but, on the other hand, needs to use such data sources in statistics, publications and analysis. So some basic definitions and categorizations are needed in order create starting place and to structure studies.

4.1 Basic Definitions

There are two basic composition theorems for differential privacy: sequential and and parallel [41]. In the sequential composition, the ε values need to be summed and in the parallel composition, the largest value of ε is selected to ensure ε-differential privacy.

Most generally, the basic variations of differential privacy are global and local differential privacy. Global differential privacy refers to the original differential privacy as defined by Dwork, where a trusted data collector that acts as proxy for data exists. In the local differential privacy [32], each user run randomization procedure locally before sharing their data for publication, so that they do not need to trust the data collector. This model can also be called a randomized response or an input perturbation model. Similarly to local differential privacy also distributed differential privacy was introduced [14]. It was defined through a non-interactive model with untrusted server, where each user responds with an perturbed version of their true answer.

Interactive and non-interactive models were defined already in the beginning of (global) differential privacy. In the former one, the trusted data collector provides interface which can be used for data queries and, in the latter case, the data collector just publishes a differentially private version of data. In the local differential privacy, the terms are slightly different due to absence of trusted data collector: in the non-interactive model, there is just one round of interaction with each user, and, in the interactive model, there can be more than one round [32] or correlations between the outputs [9].

Three basic mechanisms are usually mentioned for differential privacy: the Laplace, the exponential, and the Gaussian mechanisms. For local differential privacy, the Randomized Response is mentioned as a basic mechanism [55, 32]. The Laplace mechanism [13] adds random noise based on the Laplace distribution and it is used for numerical values. The exponential mechanism [40] uses scoring function to select a random output for nonnumerical values. It is used, for example, to pick best response for categorical values. The Gaussian mechanism [38] is similar to the Laplace mechanism but is only (ε, δ)-differentially private. The randomized response is also mentioned as early privacy process in [12] and refers to very basic randomization [57].

Sensitivity defines how much noise needs to be added in order to protect individuals. Its definition depends on a used function and mechanism. It can be a global sensitivity [10], when it needs to be considered through the whole domain (for example all databases) but is only treated as the sensitivity of the used function. In the local sensitivity [44], the noise magnitude is decided based on both, the function and the database. The smooth sensitivity uses the local sensitivity to scale noise and this is preferred because it remains less informative on the database itself.

Most common relaxation for differential privacy is (ε, δ)-differential privacy [31]. It says that ε-differential privacy is achieved with probability of $1-\varepsilon$, so it allows some loosening compared to the basic model, where δ would be 0 if so defined.

4.2   Research and Application Areas

From the included reviews we can conclude some basic, high level research areas. First one is in statistics and databases, where differential privacy was first defined. In this area, different methods with different data and different purposes are studied and there exists many different solutions [7, 54, 60, 55].

Next, differential privacy extended to analysis and algorithms in machine learning areas [60, 21, 55]. There basic mechanisms can be used in learning models directly or noise can be added to the objective function or to the output of the results. Another approach in machine learning is the private learning framework [56], where it is stated that in order a problem to be privately learnable there must exists an algorithm that is differentially private and asymptotically minimizes the empirical risk.

The most popular usage areas of differential privacy based on the reviews included in this umbrella are energy, transportation, healthcare and medical systems, internet of things, internet of vehicles, location-based services, recommender systems, and graphs on genetic data and social networks. Differential privacy has spread to a wide area of applications.

There were also some real life examples of the use of differential privacy:

- 2008: U.S. Census Bureau used differential privacy within their synthetic data model in OnTheMap [39] and in 2020 it was adopted in Population and Housing area [1].
- 2014: Google used RAPPOR to protect privacy of users who have opted-in to report statistics [16] and said to be continually expanding it's usage for example in Google Maps [23]. RAPPOR is built on randomized responses idea so it can be categorized as local differential privacy model.
- 2017: Apple protected their users with local differential privacy for collecting information on how people used their devices [3]. It was stated that this was one of the first large scale implementation of differential privacy.
- 2017: Microsoft used local differential privacy mechanism to collect telemetry across millions of devices [8]. Differential privacy seems to be active area in Microsoft.
- 2018: Uber implemented a practical approach for differential privacy in SQL queries based on [30]. This was used in their internal data analytics, but its current usage is unsure; the development project looks to be deprecated.
- 2019: SAP HANA implemented k-anonymity and local differential privacy as their offered privacy methods [33].
- 2020: Facebook used differential privacy when providing data for researcher [43] through a system that allows construction of differentially private analysis [34]. They seem to be actively working with differential privacy [53] and [17].

One common characterization of these real life examples is that many are local: they protect end user privacy so that she/he is able to share some statistics that device or software vendor would like to utilize.

5   Conclusion

In this umbrella review, we elaborated first how differential privacy has been evolving from the first mathematically sound definition of relative privacy to a wide range of different additional definitions and their implementations. Next, we concluded some basic categorizations and application areas of differential privacy. Based on all this, it is clear that there was a big need for a mathematically sound privacy definition. However, the need is still there, because not all areas are yet covered or have good enough and usable solutions developed. Privacy requirements (like GDPR, U.S. Privacy laws, HIPAA) need to be satisfied and these are likely to get more attention in the future when even larger amounts of data are utilized in different contexts.

Overall conclusion of this work was created as a mind map, which is available at https://minnakilpala.fi/research/DP_mindmap.pdf. All ten reviews are separated by color and/or number. Numbering was used to separate reviews, if it was possible to combine categorizations in one branch. In some cases, the same categorizations were under a bit different titles or the contents was divided slightly differently, so that some almost equal branches were kept. Please note that this mind map does not try to be complete mapping of differential privacy. It just helps to structure contents in this umbrella review.

References

1. Abowd, J., et al.: Census TopDown: Differentially Private Data, Incremental Schemas, and Consistency with Public Knowledge (2019). https://systems.cs.columbia.edu/private-systems-class/papers/Abowd2019Census.pdf.
2. Alamo, T., et al.: Covid-19: open-data resources for monitoring, modeling, and forecasting the epidemic. Electronics **9**(5), 827 (2020)
3. Apple Differential Privacy Team: Learning with Privacy at Scale (2017). https://docs-assets. developer.apple.com/ml-research/papers/learning-with-privacy-at-scale.pdf
4. Aromataris, E., et al.: Summarizing systematic reviews. Int. J. Evidence-Based Healthcare **13**(3), 132–140 (2015). ISSN: 1744-1609. https://doi.org/10.1097/XEB.0000000000000055
5. Bastian, H., Glasziou, P., Chalmers, I.: Seventy-five trials and eleven systematic reviews a day: how will we ever keep up? PLoS Med **7**(9), e1000326 (2010)
6. Bun, M., Steinke, T.: Concentrated differential privacy: simplifications, extensions, and lower bounds, pp. 635–658 (2016). https://doi.org/10.1007/978-3-662-53641-4_24
7. Dankar, F.K., El Emam, K.: Practicing differential privacy in health care: a review. Trans. Data Privacy **6**, 35–67 (2013). https://www.researchgate.net/profile/Fida_Dankar/publication/288417434_Practicing_Differential_Privacy_in_Health_Care_A_Review/links/5889c07ea6fdcc9a35c3b516/Practicing-Differential-Privacy-in-Health-Care-A-Review.pdf?origin=publication_detail&fbclid=IwAR
8. Ding, B., Kulkarni, J., Yekhanin, S.: Collecting telemetry data privately. Adv. Neural Inform. Proc. Syst **2017**, 3572–3581 (2017)
9. Duchi, J.C., Jordan, M.I., Wainwright, M.J.: Local Privacy, Data Processing Inequalities, and Minimax Rates. Tech. rep. 2014
10. Dwork, C.: Differential privacy. In: Bugliesi, M., et al. (ed.), Automata, Languages and Programming. Springer, Berlin Heidelberg, pp. 1–12 (2006). ISBN: 978-3-540-35908-1
11. Dwork, C.: Differential privacy: a survey of results. In: Agrawal, M., et al. (ed.), Theory and Applications of Models of Computation. Springer, Berlin Heidelberg, pp. 1–19 (2008). ISBN: 978-3-540-79228-4
12. Dwork, C., Roth, A.: The algorithmic foundations of differential privacy. Found. Trends®Theor. Comput. Sci. **9**(3–4), 211–407 (2014). ISSN: 1551-305X. https://doi.org/10. 1561/0400000042
13. Dwork, C., et al.: Calibrating noise to sensitivity in private data analysis. In: Halevi, S., Rabin, T. (eds.) Theory of Cryptography. Springer, Berlin Heidelberg, pp. 265–284 (2006). ISBN: 978-3-540-32732-5
14. Dwork, C., et al.: Our data, ourselves: privacy via distributed noise generation. In: Vaudenay, S. (ed.) Advances in Cryptology—EUROCRYPT 2006. Springer, Berlin Heidelberg, pp. 486–503 (2006). ISBN: 978-3-540-34547-3
15. Eigner, F., et al.: Achieving optimal utility for distributed differential privacy using secure multiparty computation. In: Land, P., Kamm, L. (eds.) Applications of Secure Multiparty computation, Chap. 5, pp. 81–105. IOS Press BV (2015). ISBN: 978-1-61499-532-6. https:// doi.org/10.3233/978-1-61499-532-6-81
16. Erlingsson, Ú., Pihur, V., Korolova, A.: RAPPOR: randomized aggregatable privacy-preserving ordinal response. In: Proceedings of the 2014 ACM SIGSAC Conference on Computer and Communications Security. CCS '14. Association for Computing Machinery, New York, pp. 1054–1067 (2014). ISBN: 9781450329576. https://doi.org/10.1145/2660267.2660348

17. Facebook: What Are Privacy-Enchancing Technologies (PETs) and How Will They Apply to Ads? (2021). https://about.fb.com/news/2021/08/privacy-enhancing-technologies-and-ads/
18. Ficek, J., et al.: A Survey of Differentially Private Regression for Clinical and Epidemiological Research. Int. Stat. Rev. (2020). ISSN: 03067734. https://doi.org/10.1111/insr.12391
19. Fletcher, S., Zahidul Islam, Md.: Decision tree classification with differential privacy. ACM Comput. Surv. **52**(4), 1–33 (2019). ISSN: 0360-0300. https://doi.org/10.1145/3337064
20. Gehrke, J.: Quo vadis, data privacy? Ann. N. Y. Acad. Sci. **1260**(1), 45–54 (2012). ISSN: 00778923. https://doi.org/10.1111/j.1749-6632.2012.06630.x
21. Gong, M., et al.: A survey on differentially private machine learning [Review article]. IEEE Comput. Intell. Mag. **15**(2), 49–64 (2020). ISSN: 1556-6048. https://doi.org/10.1109/MCI. 2020.2976185
22. Grant, M.J., Booth, A.: A typology of reviews: an analysis of 14 review types and associated methodologies. Health Inform. Lib. J. **26**(2), 91–108 (2009)
23. Guevara, M.: How we're helping developers with differential privacy (2021). https:// developers.googleblog.com/2021/01/howwere-helping-developers-with-differential-privacy. html
24. Hassan, M.U., Rehmani, M.H., Chen, J.: Differential privacy techniques for cyber physical systems: a survey. IEEE Commun. Surv. Tutorials **22**(1), 746–789 (2020). ISSN: 1553-877X. https://doi.org/10.1109/COMST.2019.2944748
25. Hassani, H., Huang, X., Silva, E.: Big Data and climate change. Big Data Cogn. Comput. **3**(1), 12 (2019)
26. Hauer, M.E., Santos-Lozada, A.R.: Differential privacy in the 2020 Census will distort COVID-19 rates. Socius **7**, 2378023121994014 (2021)
27. Hoda, R., et al.: Systematic literature reviews in agile software development: a tertiary study. Inform. Softw. Technol. **85**, 60–70 (2017)
28. Isomöttönen, V., Kärkkäinen, T.: Project-based learning emphasizing open resources and student ideation: how to raise student awareness of IPR? In: International Conference on Computer Supported Education, pp. 293–312. Springer, Berlin (2015)
29. Jahan, N., et al.: How to conduct a systematic review: a narrative literature review. Cureus **8**(11) (2016)
30. Johnson, N., Near, J.P., Song, D.: Towards practical differential privacy for SQL queries. Proc. VLDB Endow. **11**(5), 526–539 (2018). ISSN: 2150-8097. https://doi.org/10.1145/3187009. 3177733
31. Kasiviswanathan, S.P., Smith, A.: On the 'semantics' of differential privacy: a Bayesian formulation. J. Privacy Confidentiality **6**(1), 2575–8527 (2014). https://doi.org/10.29012/jpc. v6i1.634
32. Kasiviswanathan, S.P., et al.: What can we learn privately? SIAM J. Comput. **40**(3), 793–826 (2011). ISSN: 0097-5397. https://doi.org/10.1137/090756090
33. Kessler, S., Hoff, J., Freytag, J.C.: SAP HANA goes private: from privacy research to privacy aware enterprise analytics. Proc. VLDB Endow **12**(12), 1998–2009 (2019). ISSN: 2150-8097. https://doi.org/10.14778/3352063.3352119
34. Kifer, D., et al.: Guidelines for implementing and auditing differentially private systems (2020). http://arxiv.org/abs/2002.04049
35. Kiranmayi, M., Maheswari, N.: A review on privacy preservation of social networks using graphs. J. Appl. Secur. Res. 1–34 (2020). ISSN: 1936-1610. https://doi.org/10.1080/19361610. 2020.1751558
36. Klerings, I., Weinhandl, A.S., Thaler, K.J.: Information overload in healthcare: too much of a good thing? Zeitschrift für Evidenz, Fortbildung und Qualität im Gesundheitswesen **109**(4–5), 285–290 (2015)
37. Landhuis, E.: Scientific literature: information overload Nature **535**(7612), 457–458 (2016)
38. Liu, F.: Generalized Gaussian mechanism for differential privacy. IEEE Trans. Knowl. Data Eng. **31**(4), 747–756 (2019). ISSN: 1558-2191. https://doi.org/10.1109/TKDE.2018.2845388
39. Machanavajjhala, A., et al.: Privacy: theory meets practice on the map. In: 2008 IEEE 24th International Conference on Data Engineering, pp. 277–286 (2008). https://doi.org/10.1109/ ICDE.2008.4497436

40. McSherry, F., Talwar, K.: Mechanism design via differential privacy. In: 48th Annual IEEE Symposium on Foundations of Computer Science (FOCS'07), pp. 94–103 (2007). https://doi.org/10.1109/FOCS.2007.66

41. McSherry, F.D.: Privacy integrated queries: an extensible platform for privacy-preserving data analysis. In: Proceedings of the 2009 ACM SIGMOD International Conference on Management of Data. SIGMOD '09. Association for Computing Machinery, New York, pp. 19–30 (2009). ISBN: 9781605585512. https://doi.org/10.1145/1559845.1559850

42. Mironov, I.: Rényi differential privacy. In: 2017 IEEE 30th Computer Security Foundations Symposium (CSF), pp. 263–275 (2017). https://doi.org/10.1109/CSF.2017.11

43. Nayak, C.: New privacy-protected Facebook data for independent research on social media's impact on democracy (2020). https://research.fb.com/blog/2020/02/new-privacy-protected-facebook-datafor-independent-research-on-social-medias-impact-on-democracy/

44. Nissim, K., Raskhodnikova, S., Smith, A.: Smooth sensitivity and sampling in private data analysis. In: Proceedings of the Thirty-Ninth Annual ACM Symposium on Theory of Computing. STOC '07. Association for Computing Machinery, New York, pp. 75–84 (2007). ISBN: 9781595936318. https://doi.org/10.1145/1250790.1250803

45. Oberski, D.L., Kreuter, F.: Differential privacy and social science: an urgent puzzle. Harvard Data Sci. Rev. 2(1) (2020)

46. Page, M.J, et al.: PRISMA 2020 explanation and elaboration: updated guidance and exemplars for reporting systematic reviews. BMJ 2021, 372 (2021)

47. Perrons, R.K., Jensen, J.W.: Data as an asset: what the oil and gas sector can learn from other industries about "Big Data". Energy Policy 81, 117–121 (2015)

48. Rana, S., Gupta, S.K., Venkatesh, S.: Differentially private random forest with high utility. In: 2015 IEEE International Conference on Data Mining, pp. 955–960 (2015). https://doi.org/10.1109/ICDM.2015.76

49. Sarwate, A.D., et al.: Sharing privacy-sensitive access to neuroimaging and genetics data: a review and preliminary validation. Front. Neuroinform. 8. ISSN: 1662-5196. https://doi.org/10.3389/fninf.2014.00035

50. Snoke, J., Bowen, C.M.: How statisticians should grapple with privacy in a changing data landscape. Chance 33(4), 6–13 (2020). https://doi.org/10.108/09332480.2020.1847947

51. Snyder, H.: Literature review as a research methodology: an overview and guidelines. J. Bus. Res. 104, 333–339 (2019)

52. Tatem, A.J.: WorldPop, open data for spatial demography. Sci. Data 4(1), 1–4 (2017)

53. Testuggine, D., Mironov, I.: Introducing Opacus: a high-speed library for training PyTorch models with differential privacy (2020). https://ai.facebook.com/blog/introducingopacus-a-high-speed-library-for-training-pytorch-modelswith-differential-privacy/

54. Wang, J., Liu S., Li, Y.: A review of differential privacy in individual data release. Int. J. Distrib. Sensor Netw. 2015, 1–18 (2015). ISSN: 1550-1329. https://doi.org/10.1155/2015/259682

55. Wang, T., et al.: A comprehensive survey on local differential privacy toward data statistics and analysis. Sensors 20(24), 7030 (2020). ISSN: 1424-8220. https://doi.org/10.3390/s20247030

56. Wang, Y.-X., Lei, J., Fienberg, S.E.: Learning with differential privacy: stability learnability and the sufficiency and necessity of ERM principle. J. Mach. Learn. Res. 17(1), 6353–6392 (2016). ISSN: 1532-4435

57. Warner, S.L.: Randomized response: a survey technique for eliminating evasive answer bias. J. Am. Stat. Assoc. 60(309), 63 (1965). ISSN: 01621459. https://doi.org/10.2307/2283137

58. Wennberg, J., Gittelsohn, A.: Small area variations in health care delivery: a population-based health information system can guide planning and regulatory decision-making. Science 182(4117), 1102–1108 (1973)

59. Zeng, X., et al.: Repurpose open data to discover therapeutics for COVID-19 using deep learning. J. Proteome Res. 19(11), 4624–4636 (2020)

60. Zhu, T., et al.: Differentially private data publishing and analysis: a survey. IEEE Trans. Knowl. Data Eng. 29(8), 1619–1638 (2017). ISSN: 1041-4347. https://doi.org/10.1109/TKDE.2017.2697856

AI in Cyber Operations: Ethical and Legal Considerations for End-Users

Kirsi Helkala, James Cook, George Lucas, Frank Pasquale, Gregory Reichberg, and Henrik Syse

1 Introduction

In December 2020, the European Union's Agency for Cyber Security released a detailed assessment of the security threats posed by artificial intelligence [10]. The report noted that AI and cybersecurity have a multi-dimensional relationship and a series of interdependencies. The authors identified three broad threat categories: (1) providing cybersecurity for AI itself when used in a range of other operations (e.g., autonomous combat weapons and logistical systems, driverless cars, and a range of devices connected within the Internet of Things); (2) using artificial intelligence to enhance cybersecurity operations, both offensive and defensive; and (3) the malicious use of AI by adversaries to create and launch ever more sophisticated, malicious, and destructive cyberattacks.

This chapter focuses primarily upon the ethical and legal challenges posed by pursuing the *second* of these threat categories. Here we consider only cyber

K. Helkala (✉)
Norwegian Defence University College/Cyber Academy, Lillehammer, Norway
Peace Research Institute Oslo, Oslo, Norway
e-mail: khelkala@mil.no

J. Cook
United State Air Force Academy, Colorado Springs, CO, USA
e-mail: james.cook@afacademy.af.edu

G. Lucas
United State Naval Academy, Annapolis, MD, USA

F. Pasquale
Brooklyn Law School, Brooklyn, NY, USA

G. Reichberg · H. Syse
Peace Research Institute Oslo, Oslo, Norway
e-mail: greg.reichberg@prio.org; syse@prio.org

© The Author(s), under exclusive license to Springer Nature Switzerland AG 2023
T. Sipola et al. (eds.), *Artificial Intelligence and Cybersecurity*,
https://doi.org/10.1007/978-3-031-15030-2_9

operations that are conducted and defended within cyberspace exclusively. This means that we exclude from this chapter the social and cognitive domain operations that also are enabled by cyber measures. Invoking this demarcation implies, for example, that discussion of malware incidents such as SolarWinds or NotPetya would fall within the purview of our study as having transpired exclusively within the cyber domain, while campaigns of disinformation, for example, using social media to disrupt real-world political activities, would not. We recognize the latter category of operations as equally significant, but perhaps better suited for treatment in a separate discussion. More specifically, as NATO alliance members alongside the USA and the nations of the European Union seek to enhance their own individual and collective security through such measures, the authors of this chapter examine the ethical and legal concerns they may well confront, and how these might be resolved to the satisfaction of the controlling governments and societies. In particular, we consider which tactical alternatives pose the least risk of legal liability or moral injury to the individual citizens of those nations and alliances who will be most closely involved in designing and carrying out these AI-enhanced cyberspace operations.

We distinguish between two distinct categories of ethical challenges: those arising from deliberate or wantonly reckless misuse of such technology, and a wholly separate and more widespread admonition that end-users attempt, in good faith, to guard against carelessness, negligence, or the emergence of unintended consequences arising from their otherwise justifiable and presumably beneficial uses of AI.

2 Background: AI and Cyber Operations

2.1 Artificial Intelligence

There are several definitions of artificial intelligence, no one of which is definitive. High-level doctrine in the European Union [11] defines AI systems as

> software (and possibly also hardware) systems designed by humans that, given a complex goal, act in the physical or digital dimension by perceiving their environment through data acquisition, interpreting the collected structured or unstructured data, reasoning on the knowledge, or processing the information, derived from this data and deciding the best action(s) to take to achieve the given goal.

NATO has not issued joint doctrine pertaining specifically to use of AI in cyberspace. However, NATO's Allied Joint Doctrine for Cyberspace Operations [31], cited extensively below, in all relevant respects appears fully compatible with the EU doctrine ([11], p.1.), in which the high-level description of the operations and capacities of AI systems

> either use symbolic rules or learn a numeric model, and . . . can also adapt their behaviour by analysing how the environment is affected by their previous actions.

As a scientific discipline, AI includes several approaches and techniques [32], including various degrees of machine learning (ML) (of which deep learning and reinforcement learning are specific examples), machine reasoning (which includes planning, scheduling, knowledge representation and reasoning, search, and optimization), and robotics (which includes control, perception, sensors and actuators, as well as the integration of all other techniques into cyber-physical systems).

Currently AI applications are all around us; we use them on a daily basis whether we are aware of them or not. Easy examples are online searches, product recommendations, and the vast array of algorithms enabling self-driving cars and similar machines. In cybersecurity, common examples are malware detection and classification, network intrusion detection, file type, network traffic and SPAM identification, insider threat detection and user authentication [2, 5].

These AI-supported applications are examples of modular AI [3] (narrow or weak AI are alternatives that frequently appear in the literature on AI). This mode of AI can be phenomenally good at single tasks in strictly defined environments— like winning at chess or Go; but it is useless where more general intelligence is needed in broader contexts and unfamiliar environments [13]. General artificial intelligence (often termed strong AI) is closer to human intelligence in operating across a variety of cognitive tasks. A key element of general AI is the ability to improve its knowledge and performance on its own. Unsupervised ML systems, for instance, do not merely follow a pre-determined algorithm. Instead, they generate their own algorithms from information they gather. While general AI has not yet been attained in any of its envisioned forms (let alone embedded in cybersecurity systems at present), there are a variety of approaches that fall somewhere between modular and general AI, reflecting distinct paradigms of ML [1, 42].

AI systems (including those used to provide defensive cybersecurity) are vulnerable to attacks, failures, and accidents. The list of the possible threat actors conducting AI adversarial attacks is the same for traditional cyberattacks; these actors vary from the unsophisticated (script kiddies) to the sophisticated (state actors and state-paid actors), including cyber criminals, terrorists, hacktivists, as well as malicious and non-malicious insiders [10].

The European Union's Agency for Cyber Security categorizes threats into eight main categories [10]: *nefarious activity/abuse*, namely malicious action to disrupt the functioning of AI systems; *surveillance/interception/hijacking* involves actions whose goal is to eavesdrop or otherwise control communications; *physical attacks* sabotage the components or infrastructure of the system; *unintentional damages* are accidental actions harming systems or persons; *failures/malfunctions* happen when a system itself does not work properly; *outages* are unexpected disruptions of service; *disasters* are natural catastrophes or larger accidents; and *legal threats* occur when a third party uses applicable law, domestic or international, to constrain the cyber operations of an opponent.

Adversarial input attacks and poisoning attacks [7, 16] are examples of abuse. In input attacks, the input is manipulated in ways that may go unnoticed by the human eye, as, for instance, when tape is affixed to a road sign [7]. Poisoning attacks, by contrast, target the design process of AI and the learning process itself. Poisoning can be done both to algorithms and to the massive data sets upon which machine learning is based [7]. In addition to nefarious activity, Hartmann and Steup [16] discuss techniques that can be used in eavesdropping on different neural networks and support-vector networks. The entry and exit points (not all applicable for each method) include input, labelling, pre-processing, feature extraction, classifiers, and weights. Noise generator and selector points are included simply to illustrate that AI methods are vulnerable both to actions with unintentionally destructive consequences and to deliberately malicious actions. When data sets are corrupted or algorithms are biased, the conclusions AI reaches will likewise be distorted or biased. And here lies the core of the problem: to what extent can we trust the results and decisions recommended by AI?

2.2 Cyberspace Operations

AI solutions vary in complexity, and the context where they are used sets unique demands regarding both the requirements for flawlessness of decisions and the degree of autonomy delegated to AI. This applies especially with respect to AI tools used in cyberspace. NATO, the USA, and allies (such as members of the Five Eyes) currently use AI to shrink critical timelines for cyber threat situational awareness. AI use in cyber operations enhances the capability to detect threats and malicious activities at a rate that is not humanly possible. Suspicious events, behaviors, and anomalies can be rapidly identified for cyber professionals and operators to further investigate and deploy mitigation strategies. This decreases the likelihood of adversaries gaining access to NATO and US-DoD networks, infrastructure, and weapon systems [21].

According to NATO's operational doctrine for cyberspace ([31], p.2),

> Cyberspace is not limited to, but at its core consists of, a computerized environment, artificially constructed and constantly under development.

NATO doctrine ([31], p.3) divides cyberspace into three layers: physical (e.g., hardware), logical (e.g., firmware, protocols) and cyberpersona (virtual identities, e.g., emails, net-profiles). The logical layer is always involved in cyberspace operations (COs), but effects of those operations can also impact both the physical and cyberpersona layers of cyberspace. Furthermore, NATO doctrine recognizes that COs can affect human senses, decision-making, and behavior. Similarly, COs can have an impact on other physical elements that are directly included within or connected to cyberspace. Activities outside of cyberspace that have an effect on cyberspace (e.g., the physical sabotage of hardware components), are not, however, considered COs.

In general, the basic principles applicable to NATO joint operations apply to cyberspace operations just as they do to operations in the kinetic domain (a separate document governs targeting in this domain). However, the concept of time and reach can be somewhat different in different situations. Cyberspace operations doctrine [31] lists some direct and indirect effects that cyberspace operations can have. The first five (1–5) are effects that defensive operations normally have in one's own communication and information systems (CIS), while the remaining (6–10) are effects that offensive operations can have on the other's (adversary's) network.

1. **Secure** against compromise of CIA (confidentiality, integrity and availability) of our own CIS, as well as the data they store.
2. **Isolate** the communication between adversaries and our own affected systems.
3. **Contain** the spread of the malicious activity.
4. **Neutralize** malicious activity permanently from our own CIS.
5. **Recover** quickly from the effects of malicious activity (network resilience).
6. **Manipulate** the integrity of an adversary's CIS.
7. **Exfiltrate** the information of adversaries through unauthorized access to their own CIS.
8. **Degrade** an asset of an adversary to a level below its normal capacity or performance.
9. **Disrupt** an asset of an adversary for an extended period of time.
10. **Destroy** an asset of the adversary.

From a legal perspective, cyber operations are expected to conform to international law (such as the United Nations Charter, Laws of Armed Conflict and human rights law) as well as to applicable domestic law (i.e., the laws of the nation carrying out COs). A specific cyber operation plan should include a description of the rules of engagement (ROE), as well as define the standing authority and expected effects of COs. Estimation of effects on dual-use objects (e.g., network infrastructure), other prospective collateral damage, as well as likelihood of attribution for the operation can be difficult [31] to determine.

Instruments of international law, as mentioned above, are extrapolated to cyberspace operations in the *Tallinn Manual 2.0* [40], while treaties and legislation pertaining to conventional armed conflict were extrapolated to the cyber domain in the initial *Tallinn Manual 1.0* [39]. The manuals are not presented as binding international law, but like many other manuals (e.g., the *San Remo Manual on International Law pertaining to Armed Conflicts at Sea* [37]), are intended to provide guidance in applying existing law to specific complex or novel situations. In this chapter, we purposely leave out of the discussion the specifics on who in the organization has responsibility for conducting such operations, and which type of cyber operations are intended, as these specifics obviously vary from one state jurisdiction to another.

2.2.1 Some Examples of AI-Supported Cyberspace Measures

A useful listing of defensive and offensive COs can be found in Truong, Diep and Zelinka [41]: On the defensive side of AI-based cyber applications, they list malware detection (PC malware, Android malware), network intrusion (intrusion detection, anomaly detection), phishing/spam detection (web phishing, mail phishing, spam on social media, spam mail) and other, similar measures (countering advanced persistent threats (APTs), identifying domain names generated by domain generation algorithms). For malicious use of AI, they list autonomous intelligent threats (strengthening malware and social engineering) and tools for attacking AI models (adversarial inputs, poisoning training data and model extraction).

Kaloudi and Li [22] have made a similar survey to the one above, but they focus chiefly on the offensive side with examples that they also map onto the cyber targeting chain that is often used when attack vector vulnerabilities are estimated. This chain contains three main phases and seven subphases: the *planning* (reconnaissance and weaponization), *intrusion* (delivery, exploitation, and installation) and *execution* phase (remote command and control, and actions). AI methods are used in the *reconnaissance* phase for selecting targets and learning targets' standard behavior. In the *weaponization* phase, AI can be thought to generate attack payloads, aid password guessing or brute force attacks, generate abnormal behavior and find new vulnerabilities. In the *delivery* phase, AI methods help attacks to remain undetectable and conceal malicious intent. Automated methods establish means of distributing disruptive content in the *exploitation* phase. AI methods that can evolve and self-propagating malicious code are both used in the *installation* phase. In the *remote command and contol* phase and *action* phase, AI activates the malicious code and harvests the outcomes of the actions. Kaloudi and Li also discuss using AI-based methods on the defensive side. In their framework, methods for behavioral and risk analysis are to be used in the *planning* phase. Methods that are suited to detect anomalies and offensive AI patterns are suited for the *intrusion* phase. In the *execution* phase, AI methods should handle real-time response and configuration management.

Some AI methods used in real-time response against cyberattack fall within a "gray zone" between defensive and offensive tools. James Pattison [33] speaks of active cyber defense when the organization that is first to be attacked attacks or hacks back. Pattison's contrast appears to discriminate between offensive measures as a tactic of active defense (i.e., both repelling an initial attack and simultaneously taking up the initiative of retaliation within the initial attack framework), and the more conventional meaning of offensive as initiating the conflict (strategic offense). The definition of passive and active cyber defense is based on where the action occurs. When the cyber measures are initiating activity only inside the targeted organization's network, they are called passive defensive measures (e.g., firewalls). If the defensive activity extends beyond the targeted organization's network, it is classified under active defensive measures. The disruptiveness and intrusion level of these methods varies. Examples of these are honeypots, botnet takeouts, and entering the attackers' network to gain information or rescue stolen information.

Some measures that are used in defensive work (such as penetration testing within one's own network in order to patch the security breaches when found) can be used in another's network, making use of the same testing measures this time in an offensive cyberspace operation. It is also worthy of mention that the examples of AI-supported methods discussed in [22] and labeled as offensive operations can also be classified as malicious use of AI, as in [10].

3 Background: Ethical Considerations of AI Usage

Concern for recognizing and adhering to relevant ethical norms and standards is often voiced by national and military leaders. The U.S. Department of Defense Joint Artificial Intelligence Center (JAIC), established in 2018, for example, lists leadership in military ethics and AI safety as among its five pillars of AI strategy [20]. Interestingly, neither the above-mentioned ENISA AI cybersecurity challenges report [10] nor NATO's cyberspace operation doctrine [31] includes explicit ethical questions or challenges among the otherwise vital issues targeted for closer research. Although much has now been written on the ethics of cyber operations generally, the ethics of AI use itself in cyber operations to date has largely gone unaddressed. What exactly such vague and generalized expressions of concern mean in practice is thus far from clear. And efforts to operationalize or otherwise use ethical norms in the development and use of AI-enhanced military technologies generally are not obviously apparent.

One recent study of ethics aimed at both AI lifecycle actors and end users [36] enumerates normative implications of existing AI ethics guidelines for developers and organizational users of AI generally. They describe eleven principles, which comprises 91 guidelines, most of which (82) are drawn from a general ethics overview by Jobin et al. [19].

1. **Transparency** in all facets of AI technology (data, algorithms and decision making) throughout the phases of development and use.
2. **Justice and fairness** guaranteed by developers and users so that AI does not discriminate against any groups or provide unfair outcomes.
3. **Non-maleficence** to avoid AI harming human beings.
4. **Responsibility** for AI actions and their consequences must always be traceable to a legal person.
5. **Privacy** should be ensured by AI-supported tools; the GDPR should apply.
6. **Beneficence.** AI use should be beneficial for humans.
7. **Freedom and autonomy.** AI use should strengthen democratic values and personal self-determination.
8. **Trust.** Developers and users of AI should demonstrate their trustworthiness, and the reliability of their AI systems.
9. **Sustainability.** Development and use of AI technology should be sustainable.
10. **Dignity.** AI use should not violate fundamental human rights.
11. **Solidarity.** AI use should promote social welfare and security.

Here we focus our ethical perspective on the end users of AI-supported cyberspace operations. Each of the effects of cyberspace operations (shown in Sect. 2.2) pose delicate, and sometimes non-apparent ethical and legal dilemmas. Despite AI's comparative advantages in pursuing these objectives, its utilization as a tool within cyber operations has exacerbated three problems: (i) inadvertent *escalation*, insofar as AI-enabled autonomous interactions without "humans in the loop" are resistant to normal measures of supervision and control; (ii) *proliferation*, insofar as AI reduces the human personnel needed for cyber operations, thereby decreasing the cost of these operations; and (iii) these lowered costs, in turn, permit more actors (state and non-state) to acquire the capacity to engage in cyber operations, and with that consequent multiplication of actors, the *attribution problem* grows proportionately more difficult.

Here the term *proliferation* (see ii above) is invoked in the sense that arms control analysts use the term, i.e., the spread of a deadly weapon. An offensive cyber capability can cause severe damage. Until recently only certain states that possessed large and dedicated cyber programs, with many personnel working together, were able to launch effective cyberattacks. But by using AI, smaller actors can enter the game. An example of this cyber proliferation (although not specifically with AI) is the spate of ransom incidents whereby municipalities and businesses have been locked out of their computer systems. The program being used for this purpose, Wanna Cry, is reported to have been developed by the National Security Administration [15], and was somehow exfiltrated and released on the web (perhaps by a disgruntled employee) [6]. There it was obtained and used by cyber criminals, until it was detected and removed. This weapon has unfortunately proliferated. Our concern is that AI usage may only exacerbate this problem.

We do not mean to imply that current and future uses of AI have only ethical downsides. One obvious upside of AI is to strengthen defensive cyber capabilities via earlier detection and appropriate defensive response while easing the strain and manual workload of the human defenders. Another ethical upside in the war context is the enhanced ability to bring force to bear on an adversary with less destructiveness. One party might opt to shut down rather than physically destroy an adversary's power grid, for example, allowing services to resume when the conflict has been resolved.

3.1   GDPR for Cybersecurity AI Included

Before examining the ethics of AI from the end-user perspective (Sect. 4), we need to discuss the ramifications for AI-enhanced cyber operations of the General Data Protection Regulation (GDPR). GDPR is among the most stringent privacy and security laws in the world at present, and although it was drafted and passed by the European Union, it imposes legal and ethical obligations on organizations and states throughout the world who might be involved in targeting the security of, or collecting data about, citizens in EU countries [43]. This broad discussion, in turn, provides the background for consideration of this regulation's impact on the specific, case-by-case activities of end-users.

Cutting-edge cybersecurity systems will be increasingly data-driven [27]. As such, they will also risk running afoul of data protection regimes, such as the GDPR, as well as other laws restricting the use of AI. Ethical deployment of such systems thus should include some consultation with competent professionals capable of mapping the complex domain of requirements and exceptions characteristic of this body of law. This section will touch on basics, noting first the fundamental divide between state and non-state actions in this realm.

The GDPR applies to all companies, organizations, and government agencies that

> process [personally identifiable information] on individuals residing in the European Union ... regardless of where the entity is located [23].

State actors involved in the realm of policing enjoy great latitude under the GDPR [8]. When such actors collect data to prevent crimes or threats to public safety, the GDPR does not restrict their activities ([12], Art. 23). To the extent that defensive military cybersecurity is akin to crime prevention (prevention of harm to citizenry), the armed forces enjoy similar freedom from GDPR privacy restrictions. There are also specific derogations that Member States can apply in areas such as security and defense [8].

Cybersecurity reporting requirements may also fall under GDPR exemptions or derogations. For example, in some situations Member States require a wide range of entities to distribute information to other entities. Those entities required to engage in such information distribution remain exempt from the requirements of the GDPR so long as sufficient safeguards for the data are in place.

Moreover, Article 23 of the GDPR authorizes a Member State to, "when necessary and proportionate," restrict the scope of the obligations under the GDPR ([12], Article 23). Nevertheless, private entities developing cybersecurity systems should be mindful of GDPR protections. As U.S. Department of Defense attorney (and Professorial Lecturer in Law at George Washington University Law School) Brandon W. Jackson [18] has observed:

> Autonomous cybersecurity systems are driven by data, and the European Union General Data Protection Regulation (GDPR) is an unavoidable moderator in this regard. The GDPR places significant restraints on the collection and use of data in Europe. Moreover, the extraterritorial nature of the regulation compounds the impact it has on global industries.

While Jackson concludes that current AI-based cybersecurity systems are likely capable of complying with the GDPR, he also cautions that maintaining compliance will be difficult as these systems achieve greater autonomy [18]. These challenges will become more salient as AI components of cybersecurity systems become more important in the private sector.

4 Cyberspace Operations and AI Ethics Guidelines for End-Users

In general, the ethical principles we recognize are easier to apply when our moral situation is relatively uncomplicated. Living by them will be challenged when we face situations of uncertainty, ambiguity, or great complexity. It is important to identify in advance some of the likely situations in which ethical dilemmas might surface and prepare ourselves through advance discussion of representative cases.

When, for example, might the ethical principles that we normally follow need to be altered or even set aside? We may understand how moral rules apply in peacetime, but what do we do when we find ourselves in a complex and wholly unfamiliar crisis, such as war or equivalent forms of armed conflict?

In Sect. 2, we purposely omitted discussion of who might be conducting cyberspace operations, as these assignments vary depending upon national context. However, from the ethical point of view, we argue that all who are engaged in defensive cyber operations should also consider the ethical dilemmas that can arise in offensive cyber operations. As noted above, the roles, authorities, and responsibilities might change based on the situation, especially during a transition from peacetime to war. A civilian defensive cyberspace operator, for example, might be recruited by the military into an offensive cyber operation, much as during World War II civilians were called to duty as code breakers or to calculate bombing trajectories. To simplify and for purposes of the discussion that follows, we presume the end-user to be a *military* cyber operator, as offensive cyber operations are usually carried out by defense forces. As the cyber operator inherits an occupation, we consider the two forms of occupational ethics that apply in this domain: military ethics and engineering ethics.

Transparency in AI-Supported COs Transparency can be understood in several different ways. Rather than attempt to offer an exhaustive catalog, it might help to think of undesirable and desirable transparencies, also including platforms other than cyber and AI-supported CO. In general, transparency in any domain and with respect to any weapon system or supporting technology or doctrine is something policy makers and their militaries are well advised to avoid. A similar logic applies to cyberspace operations, along with the specific tools and procedures that might be utilized in carrying them out [whether AI-supported or not], as these must remain organizational secrets.

Undesirable transparency comes in several forms, the most important of which in our context being the undesirable revelation of information that should be kept out of the wrong hands. In general, law professor David Pozen [35] has argued that demands for transparency became more and more threatening to public institutions' functioning and legitimacy as they are expected to comply with the policies of openness and accountability.

An even more direct threat is a real or potential adversary's ability to discern enough about a Blue team's (the term used for the "good" side in cyber exercises) capabilities, training, and doctrines, alongside intentions to neutralize some or all advantages those would confer. For examples, if the opposing Red team knows Blue's catalog of zero-day exploits useful for disabling currently-fielded AI, and also knows under what circumstances each zero-day exploit would be deployed and therefore revealed, Red team has an advantage.

In both offensive and defensive operations, the capabilities of AI-supported COs are rarely revealed intentionally. Occasionally, a nation might decide to send a message of national will or technological superiority in order to control Red team's psychology and motivate them to act in certain ways. But this is relatively rare.

The plan for a cyber operation must be issued in advance and approved by the relevant authority, and this requires some level of transparency. The plan should include a description of the rules of engagement (ROE), as well as define the standing authority and expected effects of COs [24]. The plan should also comply with applicable international law. Here the two *Tallinn manuals* provide guidance to end-users in determining when, where, and how compliance with relevant international law impacts their anticipated operations. (e.g., *Tallinn Manual 2.0* [40]: Rule 103).

Transparency has another meaning in the realm of development as well as in testing, evaluation, verification, and validation (TEVV) [30]. The essence of transparency here is that governments and their militaries should acquire and field only technologies with known or at least knowable effects under given sets of conditions. Similarly, industries and other organizations that develop systems which then pass TEVV regimens should emerge as open books; there should be no surprises once the systems are fielded. This sense of transparency could require a degree of flexibility with respect to strong AI.

It is conceivable that some aspects of a system's or weapon's transitions through sense-think-act iterations will not be fully understood, even when the TEVV process reveals regularity sufficient to engender the confidence a nation needs to field the system. Explainable AI, however, helps increase transparency between AI and its users. It incorporates four principles [34]: explanation, meaning, accuracy, and limits of applicable knowledge. By following these principles in designing AI-systems, the point is to ensure that they operate only within the context for which they are designed such that the outputs are accompanied with reasoning that is understandable to the different user groups.

Desirable transparency can also be presented to all sides as a shared acknowledgment of unsafe practices that all should avoid for their mutual benefit. As with nuclear weapons, states have agreed on some desirable safety practices. Work is ongoing to establish similar practices also for use of AI (e.g. the Global partnership of artificial intelligence [14]).

Thus we have two distinct kinds of transparency: one that pertains to weapon developers and the other that pertains to end users in the cyber battlespace. The first (developers) must demonstrate (be transparent about) the efficacy and safety of the systems they have designed. The second group (cyber operators) ordinarily aim to surprise; in this sense transparency (vis-à-vis the enemy) is inimical to their mission. Sometimes, however, cyber weapons are put to deterrent use; in this instance, a military will deliberately reveal details about its capabilities to dissuade an enemy from some line of action. In this context, transparency will be militarily appropriate. Moreover, apart from transparency toward enemies, military personnel who use AI-based cyber weaponry must, on demand, reveal to their superiors and others engaged in post-battle assessments what exactly happened when these weapons were deployed. In this sense, a strict obligation of transparency exists. To sum up, the transparency appropriate to the battlespace falls within the purview first and foremost of military ethics, while the transparency incumbent on developers mainly pertains to engineering ethics. There are evidently areas of overlap; for instance, engineers have an ethical mandate, clearly recommended by their code of ethics, not to field weapon systems incorporating military decision-algorithms (such as the US Air Force's Arachnid) unless the TEVV process has ensured there will be no surprises once the AI-supported technologies are finally deployed. Cyber operators, likewise, must acquire a basic understanding of the safety constraints of the systems they use, constraints that pertain chiefly to engineering ethics.

There should be something less than full transparency between state-security organizations that conduct cyberspace operations and the general public. The same applies for the individual users of the AI. Trade and national security secrets (particularly offensive cyber capabilities), must never be disclosed to friends, family, or the public. In another sense, however, the engineering-based transparency between the AI-supported tool developer and the end-users requires that the staff of the client security agency or organization understand how the AI technology they are using really works, such that their decision-making about its employment is fully informed. In this instance transparency is desirable and even required.

Justice and Fairness in AI-Supported COs Concerns regarding justice and fairness often focus on implicit bias in databases that might result in unjust discrimination in operational outcomes. AI development depends on having sufficient data necessary to achieve optimal performance. We know that biased data sets can create problems in AI algorithms: e.g., the well-known discovery that some facial-recognition programs have failed to recognize Black women more often than they have failed to recognize White men. This phenomenon has obvious ethical implications. One solution is to increase the amount of data available to the AI as it learns to do its tasks. However, the quest to acquire the greatest possible volume of data can threaten individual privacy and corporate security.

Furthermore, while the problem of bias in data sets and among designers, testers, and operators is important, the general concerns for justice and fairness in a military setting might encompass even more. The sorts of calculations implied by the *in bello* principle of proportionality, and the kind of deontic work that underlies the principle of discrimination, require an underlying conception of justice. Lacking such a conception, how would one know what to count as good or bad in a proportionality calculation, and how would one judge the aptness of rules for determining who is a combatant and who not as prerequisite to applying the principle of discrimination?

Consider the following three situations in which an AI-enhanced CO might introduce more complications than the human-controlled CO is causing today. The first one is the pace of move-countermove. Already today, the need for countering a cyberattack in cyberspace can be too time-limited to leave room for ethical considerations. Therefore, these considerations should be discussed and established within the ROEs beforehand, prior to any conduct of specific cyber operations. This requirement is also specified in NATO's cyberspace operation doctrine. Once AI-enhanced tools are introduced, however, cyber-cyber interactions can take place even faster, affording little or no chance of detecting errors before disaster occurs, resulting in an outcome ranging from an error in discrimination to a grave war crime.

A second situation arises from our basic ignorance of why attacks and counter-attacks unfold as they do. Suppose that an accidental but destructive attack occurs using AI-supported CO. It is hard, if not impossible, to reverse engineer from effect to algorithmic cause [26]. It is one thing to ask for lenience at the state level while providing a clear explanation of what transpired, and quite another only to be able to state: "We didn't intend for those bad things to happen, and we don't know how they happened."

The third situation arises from the ease of introducing multi-dimensional distancing. Much has been written about the moral dangers of standoff weapons. The foundational concern is that as the spatial or temporal distance between a would-be shooter and her intended victim increases, the shooter is less likely to suffer the visceral horror that would discourage her from taking another human life. To take just one possible example, an AI-supported CO can be psychologically tailored to avoid the qualms of legislatures, command authorities, and operators, and thereby encourage approving or doing violence that otherwise would not be countenanced. In the cyber domain, and especially with the aid of AI, tailoring a weapon to combine different types of distancing would be relatively simple.

Non-maleficence in AI-Supported COs It is tempting to say that with respect to non-maleficence and benevolence, AI-supported cyber defense and offense are not significantly different than operations in other domains fought with non-cyber means. Indeed, there are many enlightening similarities and analogies among domains and weapons.

The *Tallinn Manual (2.0)* [40], for example, states that similar to other dual-use objects, "Cyber infrastructure used for both civilian and military purposes is a military objective" (Rule 101) and therefore constitutes a legitimate military target. The manual, however, forbids the use of cyber booby traps associated with objects specified in the law of armed conflict (e.g., medical help) (Rule 106), giving a specific example of malware embedded in fake emails from medical personnel causing physical illness (Rule 106, Explanation 4).

Like traditional warfare, offensive cyber operations can be used to harm civilian noncombatants: indirectly, by affecting the systems they use, but also directly (for example through malware embedded in digital medical devices). Collateral damage is also possible with offensive CO due to the connectivity of different systems and networks. Dual-use targets are likewise an issue of concern in cyber operations just as in conventional or kinetic operations. For example, disrupting traffic in networks which might be used for both military and civilian purposes will have an impact on civilian operations, and not just on the military.

But there is one curious pattern in cyber operations that is closer to ancient than modern 3-D warfare, a pattern one might describe in terms of reusability. In ancient times, many if not most weapons were recyclable. Thus, if a Greek hoplite dropped his dory, an enemy soldier could pick it up and use it, perhaps after modification. Even some arrows (or at least their heads) could be recycled. In each of these cases, the artifact that does direct harm in war can be reused if captured or found. At a certain point in history, however, as weapons technology (and perhaps a facet of human psychology) made standoff combat preferable, most of war's artifacts of direct harm could no longer be recycled. By the twentieth century, the most traumatic killing was done by projectiles or other means—bombs and missiles and shells and bullets and poison gasses—that could not be recovered and reused. (The means of delivery of these artifacts of direct harm could be reused, but not the things that penetrated flesh and bone or respiratory systems.)

Many defensive and offensive cyber weapons at present are conceivably reusable if stolen or recovered after they are "fired," with the caveat that many are context-specific. The Stuxnet/Olympic Games code was useful to penetrate an industrial control system fronting centrifuges and creating a man-in-the-middle deception. Defensive measures such as coded encryption algorithms are likewise reusable in certain contexts. The WannaCry software weapon cited above constitutes another example. Aside from its use after having been stolen, it is unclear whether the same weapon, if it had been used by the US first, would have been recoverable, and if so, whether it could subsequently have proven useful in attacking US interests (a prospect that should motivate us to reflect further on symmetry).

The point is that once a nation develops an offensive cyber weapon, it is important that a blend of pessimism and humility motivate it to build defenses against any capture or reuse of its own innovation. And if this proves to be impossible, it must seriously consider whether the weapon should be built at all. Similarly, once a nation finds a potent defensive cyber tool, it behooves it to envision possible offensive means to overcome it. In general, a nation cannot be sure its offensive and defensive weapons will not be stolen [6] or otherwise turned against it by malicious users. In this sense, cyber weapons, though standoff, have conceivably returned us to a problem last prevalent in ancient combat.

From the non-maleficence and benevolence perspective, we need to accept the fact that cyber weapons will often leak beyond their intended targets (as Stuxnet did), and that they can be recovered and possibly be re-used or reverse-engineered for unintended malevolent purposes. Therefore, there is a need to think hard about proportionality and discrimination not only with respect to the weapons' effects on our adversary but also on ourselves and our allies (Stuxnet, for example, was famously designed to limit the useful prospects of capture or reuse ([29] p.58-60)). Similarly, when developing and fielding cyber defenses, we must think of our activities not only in terms of benevolent results on our own and our allies' behalf but also on the harm they might cause if the adversary appropriates them through theft or inference, aided perhaps by observing the effects of multiple, probing attacks.

What does this mean for the end-user? Based on NATO's cyberspace operation doctrine, offensive operations are not conducted without a decision from the highest decision level. It is ordinarily teams of cyberspace operators, however, that will in the end carry out the commands. They are therefore in a position not unlike platoons of conventional combatants, concerned with determining when it is ethically acceptable to attack or destroy an adversary. Other issues discussed above likewise fall finally to individual cyber operators (usually working in small teams), such as the responsibility for carefully developing, deploying and storing cyber weapons. The end-user at the tactical level can also serve as a knowledgeable advisor to command, offering input on the risks, as well as benefits gained from using specific cyber tools. All these factors conspire to place a burden of responsibility on cyber end-users (just as conventional combatants) to be knowledgeable about the ethical dilemmas attendant upon their own actions in carrying out the orders they might receive.

Responsibility in AI-Supported COs In the military setting, all missions have an assigned leader and therefore the ultimate responsibility for effects of specific CO's utilized falls by law to the mission commander. *Tallinn Manual 2.0* [40], Rule 85, specifically states the following: (a) Commanders and other superiors are criminally responsible for ordering cyber operations that constitute war crimes; (b) Commanders are also criminally responsible if they knew or, owing to the circumstances at the time, should have known their subordinates were committing, were about to commit, or had committed war crimes and failed to take all reasonable and available measures to prevent their commission or to punish those responsible.

To avoid criminal activities, NATO's doctrine specifically states that, prior to an offensive cyberspace operation being carried out, the discussion at higher decision levels, including legal experts, must have taken place. Thus, before the end-user proceeds to undertake an action, the decisions to carry out the specified action have been reached higher up in the appropriate chain of command.

However, accidents may yet occur and ignorance of relevant software design or operational procedures can still bring about the unfortunate result that the end-users actually conducting the cyber operations are discovered to have acted wrongly. In these cases, it is for digital forensic investigation to bring forth the evidence, and of the judicial system to use that evidence to prove guilt [9].

But what happens if or when an AI-enhanced system itself haphazardly runs amok? Absent a thoughtful advance notion of collective or systemic responsibility (and liability), such accountability is likely to be assigned arbitrarily or by rote (as described above) to the ranking member military unit directly implicated in the damage caused by AI. It might not make sense, let alone seem altogether just, however, simply to assign blame to the ranking officer or commander when AI-enhanced cyber activities go awry. But would not the threat of doing so, at least, serve as a catalyst to crack open any black boxes and demand AI systems that are fully explainable, knowing in advance who otherwise will ultimately be "on the hook" in the worst case?

An additional wrinkle regarding responsibility is compartmentalization. A familiar bureaucratic principle in defense and security operations requires, for example, that one have not only the appropriate clearance to be read in on any given highly-classified topic, but also the demonstrable need to know. The dual requirement leads naturally to the compartmentalization that stovepipes whole communities in order to keep the information they need more secure than it would otherwise be. Compartmentalization increases the risk of accidents, as linkages between parts of an interlocking system are poorly understood by its individual operators, who focus solely on their specific tasks, thereby ignoring the ramifications for the overall system (see [28], p. 103–167), on a friendly-fire incident that took place in Northern Iraq in 1994).

A leader at any level of the command hierarchy will probably be too busy (and perhaps also lack the specific expertise) to evaluate the ethical aspects of any complex weapon system, cyber or not, such that assigning responsibility for technical failures to that leader would be somewhat arbitrary in any case. But if one adds the black-box aspect of AI and the compartmentalization that is common in the entire cyber operations realm, individual leadership responsibility for tech-based failures of discrimination or proportionality will seem increasingly far-fetched. The inevitable conclusion is that responsibility will often be systemic in nature, rather than traceable to specific individuals (see [28]).

Responsibility for deploying and using AI that subsequently runs amok is not crystal clear and will most likely vary dramatically from case to case. What does this factor mean for the end-user? This likely transcends military ethics questions related to responsibility in operations, but also invokes purely personal values. How willing is any given operator to utilize a tool whose functionality he or she is unsure of? How much effort will the individual operator expend to learn and understand the tool she is using? How much autonomy is the individual operator willing to delegate to an AI-enhanced cyber weapon or system itself, if it is they (rather than it) who will nonetheless be held responsible in the end for its proper functionality? Yet again, how willing is the individual operator likely to be to confess his or her own mistakes, or even to report incriminating activity by others, in cases where that operator has either authorized or used AI-supported tools even before official permission has been given, or in contexts where the AI-supported tools were not intended to be used?

Privacy in AI-Supported COs When conducting defensive and offensive COs, the full privacy of the user cannot be given. Both defensive and offensive CO employ AI-enhanced tools for network and system monitoring and analysis; however, the sensitivity and level of detail vary. AI-supported tools will obviously make the monitoring and analysis of information faster. The problem with guaranteeing individual identity or privacy during such operations is that everything will be stored, thereby offering the possibility of use of stored data for illegal purposes.

Similarly, as discussed under the category of transparency above, private information that a nation has stored on its own equipment can be used against it by any adversary if that information is exfiltrated or stolen. Such data can also be misused by one's own operators when, for example, while monitoring the networks that one is assigned to protect also affords a possibility for spying on one's own colleagues. It is therefore both an operational and engineering-related question to determine what kind of information is relevant to monitor, store and analyze in each operation.

Another hypothetical ethical dilemma arises when ongoing criminal activity is inadvertently discovered, but when reporting or acting on this discovery might also compromise the primary mission. For example, when spying on adversaries' networks, one might notice ongoing criminal activities (e.g., child pornography). What would the appropriate individual choice or organizational ethical decision be:

to save a child but "blow the cover," or decide instead to ignore the discovery and continue the operation? Which good is the greater good?

This raises the additional specter of what has come to be called *lawfare* i.e., using provisions of relevant law as weapons against an adversary [25]. For example, the New York Times reported that the SolarWinds attackers had used US-based servers to stage their efforts in order to avoid NSA scrutiny, which would in that case be prohibited by statute 215 of the Patriot Act from surveillance of American citizens [38]. Why wouldn't a hostile actor twist any tool at hand, including the Fourth Amendment guaranteeing freedom of expression, into a useful weapon in the cyber arena?

Intelligence expert Jim Baker [4] worries about the vast amounts of information concerning the behavior of US citizens that can be gleaned from emerging 5G networks, an ever-enlarging IoT, and other sources. Hostile powers could utilize AI to mine such data to gain the ability to understand, then predict, and finally manipulate behaviors in the US to suit their ends. Presumably a primitive version of this tactic was utilized in the Russian disinformation and voter manipulation efforts during the 2016 US elections. Baker concludes, however, by pointing out that US counterintelligence will be an obvious target: ominously, undermining the efforts of the security guardians by understanding them, predicting their next moves, and finally manipulating them through information operations.

Even though such information operations themselves are not part of this chapter, the worries outlined by Baker are relevant for end-users to understand. Variation in internal laws and compliance of international rules between nations differentiates possibilities of methods used in defensive and offensive COs. GDPR mentioned in Sect. 3.1 is an example, where there are major differences in compliance required between nations. A cyber incident or a conflict (or even war) is not considered fully fair when opposing sides are constrained by law in different ways. Those final examples point in turn to the characters of the individual operators. How willing is an end-user to adhere to legal restrictions applying to her or to the methods she uses, if the adversary is not likewise bound by them?

Beneficence in AI-Supported COs AI use should, on balance, promise at least to prove beneficial for individual well-being. It should be used for securing the common good, social good and peace. Here, in general, the ethical dilemma is to define whose well-being warrants consideration. In cyberspace operations, there is always *us* and *them*: the Blue team versus the Red team, the nation and its adversaries and competitors. But who finally is us and who constitutes them? An individual user is likely to find herself belonging to several different legitimate groups of stakeholders. She will be part of an organization, such as a cybersecurity unit, to be sure. But there might be internal conflict inside the organization itself dividing it into separate, competing teams, each of which also includes other individuals with disparate goals, each one worrying "what does this mean for me?" Also, an organization's goals might sometimes fail to align with its supervening nation's goals. Whose overall welfare then has the highest priority? And even more to the point: which standpoint enjoys the higher priority, the individual operator's own nation's welfare or interest, or the standpoint of international humanitarian laws and rights of others, even including the enemy?

The use of AI decreases the manual workload in cyberspace operations, for instance, by analyzing net traffic and disclosing anomalies or scanning for system weaknesses, all of which benefit the end-user. AI can also provide a vastly enhanced background for decision-making based on predictions (for example mapping possible collateral damage), allowing cyber operators to discern which offensive cyber operations would lessen the harm done to the enemy, but still prove of maximum benefit for us. In this fashion, AI allows concern for beneficence to be looked at comparatively with reduction of maleficence to adversaries, thereby significantly improving compliance with the requirement of proportionality of means and ends during conflict.

Freedom and Autonomy in AI-Supported COs China's current efforts aimed at finding ethnic minorities and categorizing them as potential threats [17] is an example of a large-scale use of AI-supported tools in cyber domain in which individual freedom is severely threatened. Methods and tools used in the cyber operations discussed in this chapter could, in theory, likewise be used in finding and categorizing people according to some threat assessment. However, the regulations and laws stemming from the GDPR set well-defined limits to the use of data collection for such purposes. First the persons whose data would be collected must give their prior, informed consent. Second, access rights to the data are also limited—meaning, for example, that military units do not automatically have authorized access to the personal finance data or phone traffic data of civilians. Likewise, police units do not have access to individual health records without either prior permission or legal warrants.

Surveillance can also be carried out within an organization's own network, however, as well as blocking access to information flow. In some organizations, for example, social media sites are blocked during working hours via organizational tools whose use is perfectly legal. Similarly, as discussed with respect to terms of individual privacy, employee preferences can be catalogued and may even be used against them inside an organization. Hence, the risk of discrimination and of overriding individual freedom and autonomy exists internally.

For the end-user perspective, two familiar ethical questions can arise. One is the same as in privacy discussions generally: namely, whether to use the confidential information of one's colleagues for one's own purposes. The second question is, what does working under the prospect of such constant surveillance do to the individuals surveilled?

Trust in AI-Supported COs Trust is closely related to the first principle, transparency, inasmuch as both have individual, organizational and state levels. Trust develops over time, and that applies to both human relationships and relationships between humans and their technologies. Consider the smart phone. We use it for a variety of purposes and our trust in its safety has been established. We are aware of the downsides (for example, that it is constantly collecting data on us) but its utility in enabling our manifold daily routines and especially its instant connectability simply outweigh these well-known downsides.

Transparency regarding how AI functions is one of the key points for maintaining public trust (as noted above). However, there are other trust-related issues in using AI tools that pose ethical questions for end-users to consider. One such question, also related to transparency, is the degree to which end-users credit the results given by AI tools. One might say that the higher the level of engineering education the user has, the more the consequent trust in the results of AI-assisted operations can be grounded confidently in knowledge, rather than in mere faith. Perhaps a person possessing a high degree of knowledge is better suited than others, for example, to challenge the results and decisions given by AI.

Being a trustworthy person is also often cited as a chief virtue of a good person. What does trustworthiness mean in cyber operations? Is it a loyalty to your unit, to your people, to a state, or to humankind? Here there are once again several layers of significance to ponder, but at least two are straightforward to identify: viz., being a whistle blower, and being an insider threat. Where does one draw the line between staying loyal and remaining silent instead of becoming a whistle blower by bringing attention to ongoing misuse of a cyber tool? Or when does one decide to become an insider threat to one's organization or government, either to exact personal revenge, or from having been influenced by others?

Sustainability, Dignity and Solidarity in AI-Supported COs Obviously, cyber operations need energy. However, it is difficult to generalize whether energy use is less or more with AI-supported tools than without. Nonetheless, sustainability from the energy perspective is something that developers of AI tools should factor into the design of their systems. Offensive cyberspace operations, however, can have environmental effects. For example, disturbing the functionality of a dam can cause a flood. However, the use of cyberattacks for delivering disturbing effects need not destroy the system itself; the goal can rather be to disable it for a particular time. In this sense, cyberattacks are less harmful to society than kinetic operations (bombing raids, for example) and in this sense are more sustainable.

Dignity means respecting human rights and recognizing that each person has inherent value. In general, AI supported tools should be used in such a way that dignity is preserved. Similarly, use of AI should promote social security and cohesion, and not undermine solidarity. Cyberspace operations that we focus on in this chapter do not target specific individuals directly. Neither are they used to create, manipulate, and spread false information. Those are instead means that pertain to Information Operations. However, the effect on dignity of the cyberspace operations we consider in this chapter can be indirect. AI-supported tools can be used, for example, to extract sensitive information from a database owned by an organization, a company for instance, that is to be harmed. If the data is subsequently leaked, thereby damaging the reputation of the company, its customers, whose personal data has now been publicly released, are the surrogate victims, collateral damage, as it were.

Similarly, solidarity might be indirectly affected. For example, offensive cyber operations can be used to degrade, disrupt, and destroy supply chains of the enemy. Even if the direct effect is on those supply-chain systems, the indirect effect can fall upon civilian groups needing humanitarian help. Here again, the rules of engagement should also be discussed with and among the tactical-level end-users of the AI, both from the military-ethical point of view but also from a personal point of view. With which commands is the end-user ultimately willing to comply? What can AI decide alone, and where should a human be part of the process?

5 Conclusion

In this chapter, we have attempted to enumerate and describe many of the benefits, as well as some of the moral challenges, that end-users in AI-enhanced cyber operations, both offensive and defensive, are likely to face. Many of these challenges have to do with individual and collective accountability for any negative or unintended consequences of such operations, coupled with the thorny problem of transparency and attribution of those consequences. These dilemmas are particularly intractable when gauged asymmetrically: between operators and their agencies, who are tasked with promoting ethically responsible operations in cyber conflict, on the one hand, and those, on the other hand, who decline to become encumbered by any such scruples. It helps to restore balance between parties to cyber conflicts if the ethical challenges can be identified in advance, and morally responsible considerations baked into the strategies formulated in response. Thereby, one avoids the need to introduce moral considerations on the fly as additional constraints to be imposed upon decision-making and time-sensitive action in the midst of conflict. This essay intends to initiate, if nothing else, a serious discussion about the important task of anticipating and developing strategic responses to cyberattacks and intrusions; responses that are reasonably guaranteed, in themselves, to uphold the values of our respective nations and allies, even while we are engaged in the complex and time-sensitive tasks of providing security for our citizens' lives and property in the cyber domain.

References

1. Akram, A., Lowe-Power, J.: The Tribes of Machine Learning and the Realm of Computer Architecture (2020). arXiv
2. Apruzzese, G., Colajanni, M., Ferretti, L., Guido, A., Marchetti, M.: On the effectiveness of machine and deep learning for cyber security. In: 10th International Conference on Cyber Conflict (CyCon), Tallinn, pp. 371–390 (2018). https://doi.org/10.23919/CYCON.2018.8405026
3. Ayoub, K., Payne, K.: Strategy in the age of artificial intelligence. J. Strategic Stud. **39**(5–6), 793–819 (2016)
4. Baker, J.: Counterintelligence Implications of Artificial Intelligence—Part III (2018). https://www.lawfareblog.com/counterintelligence-implications-artificial-intelligence-part-iii. Cited by 8 May 2021
5. Berman, D.S., Buczak, A.L., Chavis, J.S., Corbett, C.L.: A survey of deep learning methods for cyber security. Information **10**(4), 122 (2019). https://doi.org/10.3390/info10040122
6. Buchanan, B.: The Hacker and the State. Harvard University Press, Cambridge, MA (2020). https://doi.org/10.4159/9780674246010-004
7. Comiter, M.: Attacking Artificial Intelligence-AI's Security Vulnerability and What Policymakers Can Do About It. Belfer Center for Science and International Affairs (2019). https://www.belfercenter.org/publication/AttackingAI. Cited 3 May 2021
8. Council on Foreign Relations: Ctrl + Shift + Delete: The GDPR's Influence on National Security Posture. Net Politics (2019). https://www.cfr.org/blog/gdpr-influence-national-security-posture
9. Crootof, R.: War Torts: Accountability for Autonomous Weapons. 164 University of Pennsylvania Law Review 1347 (2016)
10. ENISA ad hoc Working Group on Artificial Intelligence: AI CYBERSECURITY CHALLENGES-Threat Landscape for Artificial Intelligence (2020). https://www.enisa.europa.eu/publications/artificial-intelligence-cybersecurity-challenges
11. EU High-Level Expert Group on Artificial Intelligence: A Definition of AI: Main Capabilities and Disciplines (2019). https://ec.europa.eu/digital-single-market/en/news/definition-artificial-intelligence-main-capabilities-and-scientific-disciplines
12. European Commission: General Data Protection Regulation (GDPR) (2018)
13. Gilli, A., Gilli, M., Leonard, A.S., Stanley-Lockman, Z.: "NATO-Mation": Strategies for Leading in the Age of Artificial Intelligence. NDC Research Paper 15 in NATO Defense College "NDC Research Papers Series" (2020)
14. Global partnership of artificial intelligence (GPAI): Working group on responsible AI (2020). https://gpai.ai/projects/responsible-ai/. Cited by 26 May 2021
15. Harley, N.: North Korea behind WannaCry attack which crippled the NHS after stealing US cyber weapons, Microsoft chief claims. The Telegraph (2017). Cited 3 May 2021
16. Hartmann, K., Steup, C.: Hacking the AI-the next generation of hijacked systems. In: 12th International Conference on Cyber Conflict (CyCon), Estonia, pp. 327–349 (2020). https://doi.org/10.23919/CyCon49761.2020.9131724
17. Human Rights Watch (HRW): China: Big Data Fuels Crackdown in Minority Region (2018). https://www.hrw.org/news/2018/02/26/china-big-data-fuels-crackdown-minority-region. Cited 8 May 2021
18. Jackson, B.W.: Cybersecurity, Privacy, and artificial intelligence: an examination of legal issues surrounding the european union general data protection regulation and autonomous network defense. Minnesota J. Law Sci. Technol. **21**(1), 169 (2020)
19. Jobin, A., Ienca, M., Vayena, E.: The global landscape of AI ethics guidelines. Nat. Mach. Intell. **1**(9), 389–399 (2019). https://doi.org/10.1038/s42256-019-0088-2
20. Joint Artificial Intelligence Center (JAIC) (2018). https://www.ai.mil/about.html
21. Joint Artificial Intelligence Center (JAIC): Integrating AI and Cyber into the DoD (2019). https://www.ai.mil/blog.html. Cited 3 May 2021

22. Kaloudi, N., Li, J.: The AI-based cyber threat landscape: a survey. ACM Comput. Surv. **53**(1) (2020). https://doi.org/10.1145/3372823
23. Kawamoto, D.: Will GDPR Rules Impact States and Localities? Government Technology (2018). https://www.govtech.com/data/Will-GDPR-Rules-Impact-States-and-Localities.html. Cited 3 May 2021
24. Kehler, C.R., Lin, H., Sulmeyer, M.: Rules of engagement for cyberspace operations: a view from the USA. J. Cybersecur. **3**(1) (2017). https://doi.org/10.1093/cybsec/tyx003
25. Kittrie, O.F.: Lawfare. Oxford University Press, Oxford (2016)
26. Knight, W.: The Dark Secret at the Heart of AI (2017). https://www.technologyreview.com/2017/04/11/5113/the-dark-secret-at-the-heart-of-ai/. Cited by 8 May 2021
27. Kontzer, T.: What Does the Near Future of Cyber Security Look Like? A Roomful of RSAC Attendees Considered That, and Here Are the Takeaways. In: RSA Conference Blog (2019). https://www.rsaconference.com/library/blog/what-does-the-near-future-of-cyber-security-look-like-a-roomful-of-rsac-attendees. Cited 25 May 2021
28. Leveson, N.G.: Engineering a Safer World. MIT Press, Cambridge, MA (2011)
29. Lucas, G.: Ethics and Cyber Warfare: The Quest for Responsible Security in the Age of Digital Warfare. Oxford University Press, New York (2017)
30. MITRE: Verification and Validation, Systems Engineering Guide (2013). https://www.mitre.org/publications/systems-engineering-guide/se-lifecycle-building-blocks/test-and-evaluation/verification-and-validation
31. NATO: Allied Joint Doctrine for Cyberspace Operations AJP-3.20 (2020)
32. Nilsson, N.J.: The Quest for Artificial Intelligence. Cambridge University Press, Cambridge (2010)
33. Pattison, J.: From defence to offence: The ethics of private cybersecurity. Eur. J. Int. Secur. **5**(2), 233–254 (2020). https://doi.org/10.1017/eis.2020.6
34. Phillips, P.J., Hahn, C.A., Fontana, P.C., Broniatowski, D.A., Przybock, M.A.: Four Principles of Explainable Artificial Intelligence, NISTIR 8312 (2020). https://doi.org/10.6028/NIST.IR.8312-draft
35. Pozen, D.E.: Transparency's ideological drift. Yale Law J. **128**, 100 (2018)
36. Ryan, M., Stahl, B.C.: Artificial intelligence ethics guidelines for developers and users: clarifying their content and normative implications. J. Inform. Commun. Ethics Soc. (2020). https://doi.org/10.1108/JICES-12-2019-0138/full/html
37. San Remo Manual on International Law Applicable to Armed Conflicts at Sea, 12 June 1994 (1994). https://ihl-databases.icrc.org/ihl/INTRO/560
38. Sanger, D.E., Perlroth, N., Barnes, J.E.: As Understanding of Russian Hacking Grows, So Does Alarm, New York Times. New York Times (2021). https://www.nytimes.com/2021/01/02/us/politics/russian-hacking-government.html. Cited by 26 May 2021
39. Schmitt, M.N. (ed.): Tallinn Manual 1.0-On the International Law Applicable to Cyber Warfare. Cambridge University Press, Cambridge (2013)
40. Schmitt, M.N., Vihul, L. (eds.): Tallinn Manual 2.0—On the International Law Applicable to Cyber Operations, 2nd edn. Cambridge University Press, Cambridge (2017)
41. Truong, T.C., Diep, Q.B., Zelinka, I.: Artificial intelligence in the cyber domain: offense and defense. Symmetry **12**(3), 410 (2020). https://doi.org/10.3390/sym12030410
42. Vaccaro, L., Sansonetti, G., Micarelli, A.: An empirical review of automated machine learning. Computers **10**(1:11) (2021). https://doi.org/10.3390/computers10010011
43. Wolford, B.: What is GDPR, the EU's new data protection law? GDPR.EU (2019). https://gdpr.eu/what-is-gdpr/. Cited 26 May 2021

Part III
Applications

Android Malware Detection Using Deep Learning

Stuart Millar, Niall McLaughlin, Jesus Martinez del Rincon, and Paul Miller

1 Introduction

Malware detection is a growing problem, especially in mobile platforms. Given the proliferation of mobile devices and their associated app-stores, the volume of new applications is too large to manually examine each application for malicious behavior. The Android OS from Google is widely used with over 2.5 billion active Android devices, including smartphones, wearables and in-car implementations. This creates a plethora of attack opportunities for malware authors, and consequently a need for effective Android malware detection techniques.

Malware detection has traditionally been based on manually examining the behavior and/or de-compiled code of known malware programs in order to design malware signatures by hand. This process does not easily scale to large numbers of applications, especially given the static nature of signature based malware detection, meaning that new malware can be designed to evade existing signatures.

Consequently, there has recently been a large volume of work on automatic malware detection using ideas from machine learning (ML). Various methods have been proposed based on examining the dynamic application behavior [59, 62], requested permissions [39, 57, 60] and the n-grams present in the application byte-code [33, 31, 11]. However, expert Android malware knowledge is regularly required to hand-craft input features to such detectors. This also leaves them potentially more vulnerable to zero-day attacks, until such time as the new malware

S. Millar (✉)
Rapid 7 LLC, Boston, MA, USA
e-mail: stuart_millar@rapid7.com

N. McLaughlin · J. M. del Rincon · P. Miller
CSIT, Queen's University Belfast, Belfast, Northern Ireland, UK
e-mail: n.mclaughlin@qub.ac.uk; j.martinez-del-rincon@qub.ac.uk; p.miller@qub.ac.uk

© The Author(s), under exclusive license to Springer Nature Switzerland AG 2023   209
T. Sipola et al. (eds.), *Artificial Intelligence and Cybersecurity*,
https://doi.org/10.1007/978-3-031-15030-2_10

can firstly be detected and reverse-engineered, after which features for detection are updated.

In this chapter, we show how to decouple these domain insights from the input features and the learning process. As a result our method is attractive in terms of real-world use and maintenance, particularly from a zero-day perspective. We propose a deep neural network incorporating convolutional methods, with multiple views learning from three raw input feature sets of low-level opcodes, app permissions and proprietary Android API packages, all of which are extracted from each app directly.

Recently, convolutional networks have been shown to perform well on a variety of tasks related to natural language processing. Thus, we investigate the application of convolutional networks to malware detection by treating the disassembled byte-code and API calls of an application as a text to be analyzed, in combination with the permissions requested by the app. This approach has the advantage that three complementary feature sets are automatically learned from raw data, and hence removes the need for malware signatures to be designed by hand. The usefulness of each feature set is tested to show its effectiveness despite not requiring domain insight for feature ranking or selection. We provide evidence that these feature sets in combination with a multi-view architecture outperform the state-of-the-art, both in a zero-day scenario and for the conventional detection case.

Our proposed malware detection method is computationally efficient as training and testing time is linearly proportional to the number of malware examples. The detection network can be run on a GPU, which is now a standard component of many mobile devices, meaning a large number of malware files can be scanned per-second. In addition, it is expected that as more training data is provided the accuracy of malware detection will improve because neural networks have been shown to have a very high learning capacity, and hence can benefit from very large training-sets in the future.

2 Related Work

2.1 Traditional ML Techniques

Learning based approaches using hand-designed features have been applied extensively to both static analysis, using derived signatures with no code execution, and dynamic analysis, where an attempt is made to execute malware in real-time for behavioural study. Traditional ML approaches were adopted in early work, including SVMs [7, 79, 43], naive Bayes [73], kNN, k-means clustering [58, 63] and decision trees [73, 13, 22, 1, 14]. Such methods tend to have hand-crafted, manual rankings or selections of input features [73, 1, 5, 17]. These include pre-selected APIs [63, 79, 1, 61, 50, 42], permissions [61, 56, 3], network traffic [37, 67], network addresses [7], malicious system call traces [9], and embedded call graphs

[23]. The drawback to this prior work is that depending on expert knowledge for feature engineering makes a detector more vulnerable to change, rather than if such knowledge was encapsulated inside the detector itself and learned end-to-end. There is also a problem with the use of too small or unbalanced datasets, giving rise to some uncertainty regarding effectiveness in the wild. Almost none of these methods have been thoroughly tested in arguably the toughest of scenarios, that is, a comprehensive zero-day situation where the task is to detect never-before-encountered malware.

2.2 Neural Network Techniques

Recently, detection methods have begun to implement deep learning neural networks, following the state-of-the-art performance that convolutional neural networks (CNNs) have shown for object recognition in images and natural language processing (NLP). Techniques such as CNNs have huge potential to be applied in the field of malware detection, inspired by those methods originally developed for NLP. These systems benefit from a data-centric approach where features are learned from training examples rather than being manually derived by experts. This allows creation of models that are easier to train, update and maintain when new malware samples are available, and they may also be able to extract discriminative features not immediately obvious to human experts.

A variety of approaches to malware detection using other neural network architectures have been proposed. Yuan et al. [75] was an early neural net detector using a series of autoencoders in a deep belief network. Xu et al. [70] built a neural network that included a long short-term memory unit (LSTM), though with 18 million learnable parameters in three hidden layers alone, there is a questions over its generalisation capability given the amount of training data was many orders of magnitude smaller. Kim et al. [35] also presented a network to include multi-modal features such as opcodes or APIs, though seemingly offered no significant improvement over their baseline. Oak et al. [49] experimented with both an LSTM and a BERT model for the malware detection task, showing promising results, however the dataset used was a set of dynamic analysis traces produced by Palo Alto Networks using their Wildfire [51] tool. These are not easily reproducible given Wildfire is not open-sourced and the apps used are not publicly available.

Few approaches have used CNNs effectively in Android malware detection. McLaughlin et al. [45] presented a CNN to learn solely from opcode patterns, and [44] built a CNN to learn from system calls extracted via dynamic analysis. Ding et al. [15] pre-selected 245 sensitive APIs as input to their system but only reported results on part of a benchmark dataset. Evaluations in [34] showed strong detection performance though their CNN had several hundred thousand trainable parameters plus an arbitrary API dictionary with one hundred thousand entries that could be viewed as brittle. Lee et al. [38] used stacked RNNs and CNNs with packages, permissions, certificate info and intent actions as input features. Nix and Zhang [48]

Table 1 Related work summary for detection techniques

Author	Year	Approach	Features	Zero-day
Burguera et al. [9]	2011	k-means	Malicious system call traces	N
Sanz et al. [56]	2012	Trees	Pre-selected APIs, permissions	N
Aafer et al. [1]	2013	Trees	Pre-selected APIs	N
Arp et al. [7]	2014	SVM	Various hand-crafted	Y
Yerima et al. [74]	2015	Bayesian, trees	Hand-crafted APIs	N
Zhu et al. [79]	2015	SVM	Pre-selected APIs	N
Faruki et al. [17]	2015	Bloom filter signatures	Hand-crafted entropy features	N
Chen et al. [13]	2016	Trees	Various dynamic and static	N
Chen et al. [14]	2016	Trees	Hand-crafted semantics	N
Yuan et al. [75]	2016	Deep belief network	Various static, dynamic features	N
Mariconti et al. [43]	2017	SVM	Hand-crafted APIs	N
Sun et al. [63]	2017	k-means	Pre-selected APIs	N
Alzaylaee et al. [5]	2017	SVM, Bayesian, trees	Hand-crafted dynamic	N
Skovoroda et al. [61]	2017	Model matching	Pre-selected APIs, permissions	N
Maiorca et al. [42]	2017	Trees	Pre-selected APIs	N
Maiorca et al. [37]	2017	KNN, trees	Network traffic	N
McLaughlin et al. [45]	2017	CNN	Opcodes	N
Martinelli et al. [44]	2017	CNN	System calls	N
Saracino et al. [58]	2018	k-means	Kernel, app, user, packages	N
Garcia et al. [22]	2018	Decision trees	APIs, reflection, native code	N
Onwuzurike et al. [50]	2018	Trees	Pre-selected APIs	N
Ding et al. [15]	2018	CNN	Pre-selected APIs	N
Karbab et al. [34]	2018	CNN	Arbitrary APIs	N
Wang et al. [67]	2018	SVM	Network traffic	N
Raff et al. [54]	2018	CNN	Windows PE byte sequences	N
Xu et al. [70]	2018	LSTM	XML resources, bytecode	N
Kim et al. [35]	2019	Neural network	Inc. permissions, APIs, strings	N
Oak et al. [49]	2019	BERT	Wildfire activity	N
Lee et al. [38]	2019	CNN, RNN	Packages, permissions, certs, intents	N
Alazab et al. [3]	2020	Trees, kNN, Bayesian	Permissions and APIs	N

helped introduce recurrency using a CNN with an LSTM to learn program flows of system API call sequences.

Like the traditional ML models, neural network methods were also not rigorously tested in the zero-day scenario. A summary of these prior methods, both traditional and neural network based, are provided in Table 1.

2.3 API Features for Detection

It can be seen from the listing in Table 1 that APIs are regularly used as input features for Android malware detection, however they are heavily hand-crafted using expert knowledge. For example, an app can be statically scanned for a select number of predefined sensitive or malicious APIs [74], either for their presence, or to measure their frequency of use. Alternatively this analysis can be dynamic, for example when building sequences of temporal API call invocations [41]. However considering a benchmark dataset can have tens of thousands of apps, this is time-consuming, with upwards of several minutes execution time per app. In addition, anti-emulation and anti-sandbox techniques are used by malware authors to keep malicious functionality dormant if instrumentation is detected [5], so these dynamic sequences may not be as useful as expected.

Regarding static analysis of APIs, the Drebin detector [7] has a hand-engineered mapping of APIs in a total of eight feature sets, including suspicious API calls and restricted API calls. Many other state-of-the-art detectors used APIs in some form as features too. Chen et al. [13] built a group of 240 sensitive API calls that were then ranked to select a top 90. Skovoroda et al. [61] created a list of hand-engineered protected API calls plus a list of unprotected API calls, totalling 384 API features. Fan et al. [16] adopted a weighted sensitive API call-based matching approach to detection, with a pool of 26,322 sensitive API calls. Kim et al. [35] used method invocation within APIs as a feature, parsing apps for hand-chosen dangerous APIs, both for existence and frequency of use. Garcia et al. [22] also counted various API invocations as features, with a package-level count of occurrences, grouped into purpose, in addition to a method-level count. Yerima et al. [74] produced a listing of 56 malicious API calls, Android commands and Linux terminal commands, while [64] engineered sensitive Android-specific and Java-specific API features for detecting repackaged malware.

Of methods that adopt dynamic analysis of APIs, [41] focused on what APIs were used, their frequency and their dynamic sequence, forming one-hot vectors derived from control flow graphs. They considered all APIs both in the JDK and Android SDK, likely to run into the thousands. Cai et al. [10] engineered features from a behavioural characterisation study, using security-relevant APIs they described as sensitive. This involved hand-crafting 122 different features, with feature selection pruning this list to 70. Alzaylaee et al. [5] used API call signatures, part of a wider ranked list of 100 features, generated during dynamic instrumentation. However they admit anti-emulator techniques meant it was possible for some API calls not to be logged. Wong and Lie [69] used a list of 62 targeted Android APIs, whilst [2] traced invocations of APIs in specified lists, using call frequencies in classification, and [71] extracted API calls as a one-hot encoding using a heterogeneous information network, again requiring significant expertise.

Considering this previous work collectively, it is clear that in general the use of APIs as features in Android malware detection has required a significant amount of feature-engineering and domain insight.

2.4   Zero Day

In the Android domain this translates into circumstances where a given malware family has not been encountered before. Hence the research focus of zero-day detection is developing malware detectors that are effective in classifying apps that belong to new malware families never seen previously, i.e. not available in the training set. This contrasts the more general case of traditionally detecting an app belonging to a previously seen family as malicious, i.e. with samples belonging to that family in the training set.

The zero-day setting is therefore much more challenging and will expose the weaknesses of existing systems to real-world complexity and test the generality of a learned model to new and never-before-seen malicious attacks. In this setting, signature-based systems will likely be compromised since no signature has been yet derived to detect the new threat. Similarly, ML-based systems may suffer or fail to detect new threats since they were not been exposed to the new malware type during training. This fact is exacerbated if feature engineering based on obsolete data has been extensively used or over-fitting to the training data rather than generalisation has occurred.

3   Methodology

3.1   Motivation

Traditional ML systems learn from hand-crafted features engineered from raw data in order to make predictions or classifications. In order for this to be effective a significant level of domain knowledge is required, and previous methods often rely on a single feature set. For example, an Android app will make various API calls that can be statically extracted from reversed source code, or dynamically recorded, but thereafter malicious API sequences still need identified by hand. ML however can be extended beyond the prediction step to include automatic learning and encapsulation of information-rich encodings for raw input features, with minimal or sometimes even no manual feature-engineering. A multi-view approach can further decouple this expensive domain expertise by automatically creating a salient complex representation from several feature sets. Instead of individual features being hand-crafted externally to the model, relevant knowledge is acquired in the training phase by learning individual features and fusing them together. Moreover, this may result in features not obvious to human experts, and the multi-view model is easier to re-train and update when new apps are available, compared to repeating a costly feature-engineering stage. The presented Android malware detection model incorporates three views learning from raw input feature sets of low-level opcodes, app permissions and proprietary Android API packages. These individual raw feature sets are extracted from each app directly, per Fig. 1.

Fig. 1 Extracting raw input
features

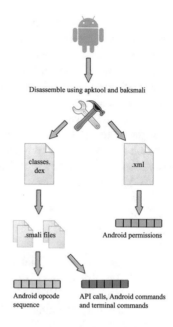

Separate extraction of each raw feature set allows the combination and fusing of these three sources of complementary information in the architectural design. Generalisation to unseen apps in the zero-day scenario may also benefit, as it is more difficult for new malware to avoid scrutiny. Note this is straight-forward raw feature extraction, with neither any feature-selection and ranking used by other approaches, nor statistical analysis to pre-categorise input features. Hence domain insight is not required, with the relative importance of these features and their contribution to classification learnt and encapsulated within the model during the learning process. The desire to decouple specialist knowledge, lessening the involvement of the human analyst, is key in this approach. Each app's *.dex* file is first disassembled into *.smali* files using baksmali [32] and apktool [6]. The following raw input feature sets are extracted from every app used in the study:

1. opcode instruction sequences.
2. Android permissions usage.
3. arbitrary API package usage.
4. proprietary Android API package [25] usage.

3.1.1 Opcodes

An opcode is the lowest level instruction used by the Android Dalvik run-time, with 218 possible opcode instructions. Each method in a *.smali* file is made up of a set of opcodes, for example *invoke*, *goto* or *move*, with arguments, also known as operands. These opcode instructions can include methods calls, changing program control flows or performing calculations. They are statically extracted from an app's *.smali* files and concatenated to give a sequence representing one single app. This sequence is a series of one-hot vectors, with each containing 218 elements to represent the range of all opcodes. To encode the opcode used at a given point in the sequence, the corresponding element in the one-hot vector is set to 1 and all the other elements are 0. The operands are discarded as they represent an unmanageable range of references to low-level aspects like floats, longs, objects and registers, compared to the limited set of 218 opcodes. Attempting to understand operands at such a granular level of machine or assembly code also requires expertise beyond the scope of this work, with the aim being to avoid this very type of costly, non-trivial knowledge.

3.1.2 Permissions

Permissions enable special access to mobile device functionality and must be requested by apps, potentially for sensitive purposes. For example, the permissions SENDSMS, RECEIVESMS, ACCESSNETWORKSTATE or INTERNET have been previously identified as being strongly associated with malware. An app contains an *AndroidManifest.xml* file that lists its requested Android permissions in order for the app to run correctly. Permissions are extracted for each app by parsing this manifest, generating a multi-hot vector representing 138 Android permissions. This extraction occurs for all apps, regardless of their release date, by matching against a predefined list which is a snapshot from 2016. In future, updating this list will automatically adapt the feature extraction to newly released apps.

3.1.3 Arbitrary API Packages

Android malware apps can be produced en-masse, with simultaneous development and packaging via a standardised process [4]. Large amounts of malware created at once using this batch compilation likely means recurring automatic injection of the same malicious code. Therefore the intuition in using API package feature sets is that there may be repeated invocation patterns across a dataset to indicate malicious behaviour which could be learned by the model without any manual analysis. Two variations of arbitrary API usage are selected for comparison to this study's choice of proprietary Android APIs. These feature sets are named *APIs* and *GoogleAPIs* respectively. *APIs* represents any and all APIs that are invoked in an app's methods, and has the broadest scope. *GoogleAPIs* differs by representing only only invocations of APIs written by Google, thus has somewhat more focus by disregarding any non-Google invocation. By treating APIs as a type of vocabulary, a dictionary-style approach is used to build each feature set separately, one for *APIs* and one for *GoogleAPIs*. These approaches are inspired by NLP methods for vocabulary selection, and bear similarities to others [34]. Details are as follows:

- *APIs*: A single Java class in an app has a corresponding *.smali* file containing the methods of that class. For each app in turn, all its *.smali* files are parsed line-by-line for API usage. Given a line of code, if the term *'invoke'* is present, the API invoked is extracted and added to a dictionary as a key-value mapping. In such a mapping, the key is a unique API, and its value a unique integer ID.
- *GoogleAPIs*: This is similar to the creation of the *APIs* feature set, except only invoked APIs that start with *'com.google.'* are added to the dictionary. These are parsed by matching against a predefined list in line with official Android documentation as of April 2020 [27].

Per Algorithm 1, when creating each of these feature sets the full dataset is scanned once to build an empty data structure of key-value mappings, with each key being a unique API, and the corresponding value being an integer ID between 1 and the total number of keys. A count is stored for each API to track how often it is invoked, initialised at 0 to begin with.

Algorithm 1 Generating an API dictionary $dict$

Require: Require: All *.smali* files $smaliFiles$, empty API dictionary $dict$, invocation condition $invocation$.

    procedure PROCEDURE: GENERATE DICTIONARY$((smaliFiles, dict, invocation))$
        for all $smaliFile \in smaliFiles$ **do**   ▷ for each smali file.
           for all $line \in smaliFile$ **do**   ▷ for each line of code.
               if $invocation \in line$ **then**   ▷ if the invocation condition is met.
                  parse $line$ for API ▷ extract the API from that line of code.
                  if not $API \in dict$ **then**   ▷ if the API is not in the dictionary.
                     add API to $dict$
                     create integer ID for API
                     initialise API count to 0
        for all $smaliFile \in smaliFiles$ **do**   ▷ for each smali file.
           for all $line \in smaliFile$ **do**   ▷ for each line of code.
               if $invocation \in line$ **then**   ▷ if the invocation condition is met.
                  parse $line$ for API
                  if $API \in dict$ **then**
                     increment API count by 1

Some APIs will be invoked often across a dataset, and some rarely, so a dictionary of relevant APIs can be created automatically by selecting the most frequently used APIs, being possible common malicious calls or perhaps indicators of normality, plus the less frequent as potential anomalous indicators. To do this, after the initial $dict$ is created from a given dataset, the total number of times each API was invoked can be calculated with a second scan, and the count of invocations for each API updated. To ensure such a dictionary systematically represents APIs used both often and seldom, a threshold T is set for a minimum number of invocations that must be reached for an API to be included. After setting T, a newly thresholded dictionary of size S is generated, containing the $S/2$ most used and $S/2$ least used APIs. Each app is scanned for a third time to build its API sequence, excluding the APIs that

invoke-virtual {v2, v0}, Landroid/util/Log;->i(Ljava/lang/String;Ljava/lang/String;)I

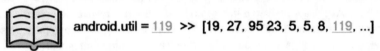

android.util = 119 >> [19, 27, 95 23, 5, 5, 8, 119, ...]

Fig. 2 *AndroidAPIs* sequence creation

are not in the dictionary. This API sequence is translated to a sequence of integers, where each value matches the original dictionary integer ID of the API invoked at a given point in the sequence. The dictionary size S and threshold T are later varied to study how this type of vocab selection impacts performance.

3.1.4   Proprietary Android API Packages

These are at the heart of the Android platform [25] and so it is logical to expect they may hold a degree of predictive power. Given proprietary Android APIs are less likely to change over time compared to the wider selection that is available to app developers generally, this may be of benefit in zero-day scenarios defending against future, unseen apps. This rationale, along with their lack of use in previous research, is the motivation to experiment with them, and avoids both arbitrary decisions about which APIs to consider from other vendors, as well as library dependency issues. During extraction, a dictionary data structure is first built using all 210 Android API packages, eliminating the need to define a dictionary size or a threshold compared to the previous API feature sets outlined. Each entry is once more a key-value mapping, where each key is a unique Android API, and its value an integer ID between 1 and 210. Again, for each app in turn all its *.smali* files are parsed line-by-line for API invocations. Android API usage is registered if in a given line of code the term *'invoke'* is used and the API matches one in the Android API dictionary. Like the arbitrary API feature sets, this results in a sequence of integers for each app, where each value matches the dictionary integer ID of the proprietary Android API invoked at a given point in the sequence, as illustrated in Fig. 2. This feature set is referred to as *AndroidAPIs* throughout.

3.2   Neural Architecture

An end-to-end, multi-view deep learning model is proposed for Android malware detection, both under zero-day conditions and for the conventional detection case, with domain insight decoupled. The architecture, illustrated in Fig. 3, consists of three views; one CNN learning from opcodes, a fully-connected neural net learning from permissions, and a second CNN learning from APIs. CNNs are selected for opcodes and APIs as these feature sets have a sequential nature that convolutional

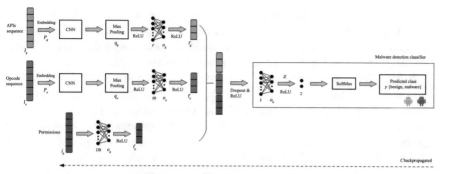

Fig. 3 Multi-view Deep Learning Network Architecture for Android malware detection

methods can learn sub-patterns from. In contrast, while relationships are envisaged between permissions, these associations are not sequential in nature. Therefore permissions are better suited to a fully-connected neural net, as each one is simply either present in an app, or not.

These feature sets are then combined together in a fully-connected network that gives a final classification as to whether an Android app is malicious or benign. The multi-view approach is adopted since the representations for each feature set are inherently different due to their modalities, and allows analysis of each part of the architecture separately. This design decision also enables more refined tuning of the model, and performance comparisons between each view permutation.

3.2.1 Opcodes CNN

Outside computer vision, many successful applications of convolutional architectures occur when the task can be modelled as a Natural Language Processing (NLP) problem using word embeddings [36, 46, 76]. This work is connected to these methods however instead of using pre-trained embeddings, a dense embedding layer is trained from the data simultaneously with the rest of the network parameters, considering each opcode as a word or a token whilst attempting to capture their semantics. The purpose of this CNN is to automatically learn salient patterns from each app's sequence of opcodes that discriminate between malicious and benign. In this way knowledge is encapsulated inside the architecture, rather than being provided by a human expert via feature engineering and ranking.

The CNN aims to learn discriminative patterns from each sample's sequence of raw opcode instructions that can be used to differentiate between malicious and benign. This decoupling of expert knowledge means these concepts are learnt directly and encapsulated inside the CNN. Thus, effort needed to handle changes introduced by opcode authoring variations over time is significantly less compared to repeating complex mathematical ranking and feature engineering. This is a differentiator between our method and previous work where more manual, hand-engineered features are required. We need only to extract the raw opcodes from each sample, which is purely an implementation task and needs no Android malware domain knowledge. The CNN does not need to be informed what the most malicious opcode patterns are, nor which ones are safe to be overlooked.

A raw input opcode sequence I_o for a single app is a series of one-hot vectors and can be written as $I_o = \{x_1 \ldots x_n\}$, where x_n represents the nth opcode in a sequence of length n_o. Each vector x is a one-hot vector, which has $d_o = 218$ elements to represent the range of all opcodes. The element corresponding to the opcode used at position n in I_o is set to 1, and all other elements are set to 0. CNN filters learn feature representations containing relationships between nearby opcodes, which enables learning of sub-patterns. However, due to the use of one-hot vectors, I_o has a degree of sparsity, reducing the amount of useful information for a filter to learn from without that filter being inefficiently large from a computational standpoint. To mitigate this sparsity and improve learning, the one-hot vectors are projected into a dense, information rich k_o-dimensional embedding space P_o. This is shown in Fig. 4.

In doing so, each vector in I_o is multiplied by an embedding weight matrix W_{E_o} of size $d_o \times k_o$. The weights in W_{E_o} are randomly initialised at the start of the training procedure and updated during the learning process. The resulting embedding projection P_o is a matrix of size $n_o \times k_o$, processed by one convolutional layer with r filters. Each filter has size $s_o \times k_o$, with s_o being the number of consecutive opcodes analysed by each filter. Each of the r filters perform a 1D convolution over the full embedding matrix P_o generating an activation map a_{o_r} of size n_o as follows:

$$a_{o_r} = ReLU(Conv(P_o)_{W_{r b_r}}) \qquad (1)$$

where W_r and b_r are the trainable weight and bias parameters of the rth filter. The rectified linear activation function $ReLU(x) = max\{0, x\}$ is used post-convolution. The activation maps produced from each filter are stacked to produce the activation matrix A_o of size $n_o \times r$, denoted as:

$$A_o = [a_{o_1} | a_{o_2} | \ldots | a_{o_r}] \qquad (2)$$

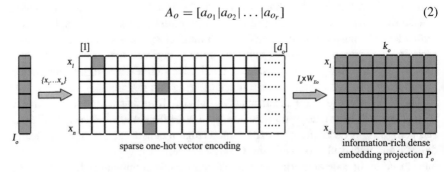

Fig. 4 Creating the embedding projection P_o

Global max-pooling subsamples A_o and produces a vector q_o of length r containing the maximum activation of each filter over the opcode sequence length n_o, written as:

$$q_o = [max(a_{o_1})|max(a_{o_2})|\ldots|max(a_{o_r})] \tag{3}$$

The static analysis in this study aims to highlight presence of malicious code that could be injected in any arbitrary location. Hence global max-pooling is a logical choice as it identifies sections of the opcode sequence that cause the maximum activation of each filter can be thought of those that model deems most important in classifying an app, regardless of the location of that section in the overall sequence. Max-pooling also ensures an input opcode sequence of arbitrary length is represented as a fixed-length vector ahead of being passed to the classification layer. q_o is fed through a fully-connected layer with o_o output neurons, producing the feature vector f_o:

$$f_o = ReLU(W_o q_o + b_o) \tag{4}$$

where W_o and b_o are the weight and bias parameters of the hidden layer learned during training.

3.2.2 Permissions Neural Net

The permissions contain useful information pertaining to malware detection that complements features derived from the opcodes CNN and the APIs CNN. For the permissions input, given an app and its manifest file, a multi-hot 1D array, or vector, of length 138 is generated. Each element maps to one of 138 Android permissions, with its value being 1 if a permission is in the manifest, or 0 if not. This permissions vector i_p is input to a fully-connected layer to allow the model to learn relationships between permissions for classification, giving the feature vector f_p, denoted as:

$$f_p = ReLU(W_p i_p + b_p) \tag{5}$$

where W_p and b_p are the learnable weight and bias parameters of the permissions input layer. The output layer in this neural net has o_p neurons.

3.2.3 APIs CNN

This CNN is concerned with learning discriminative patterns from API input sequences. Its architecture is similar to that of the opcodes CNN. Again, these API sequences are only extracted, with no ranking or feature-engineering being undertaken. There is no manual identification of individual APIs or patterns of APIs that are indicative of malware or benign apps. Like the opcodes CNN, a raw input API sequence I_g for an app is a series of one-hot vectors, $I_g = \{x_1 \ldots x_n\}$, representing a sequence of length n_g. In this case each x has length d_g elements to represent all potential APIs.

Similar to I_o, I_g also is a sparse matrix, and is projected into a k_g-dimensional embedding space P_g of size $n_g \times k_g$, processed by a single convolutional layer with m filters. Each filter has size $s_g \times k_g$, with s_g being the number of consecutive APIs analysed by each filter. Each of the m filters perform a 1D convolution operation over the full embedding matrix P_g generating an activation map a_{g_m} of size n_g as follows:

$$a_{g_m} = ReLU(Conv(P_g)_{W_m b_m})   \tag{6}$$

where W_m and b_m are the trainable weight and bias parameters of the mth filter. Again $ReLU$ is used post-convolution. The activation maps produced from each filter are stacked to produce the activation matrix A_g, of size $n_g \times m$, denoted as:

$$A_g = [a_{g_1}|a_{g_2}|\ldots|a_{g_m}]   \tag{7}$$

Global max-pooling subsamples A_g and produces a vector q_g of length m containing the maximum activation of each filter over the opcode sequence length n_g, written as:

$$q_g = [max(a_{g_1})|max(a_{g_2})|\ldots|max(a_{g_m})]   \tag{8}$$

q_g is fed through a fully-connected layer with o_g output neurons, producing the feature vector f_g:

$$f_g = ReLU(W_g q_g + b_g)   \tag{9}$$

where W_g and b_g are the weight and bias parameters of the hidden layer learned during training.

3.2.4   Classification Layer

Per Fig. 3, each feature vector is concatenated into a single feature representation f. The make-up of f depends on which permutation of input feature sets are used. It can be denoted as:

$$f = [f_g|f_o|f_p]   \tag{10}$$

Dropout is applied at a rate of 0.5, then f is input to a multi-layer perceptron (MLP) with an input layer of size $t=o_g+o_o+o_p$, a hidden layer h of size o_h neurons, and an output layer of size 2 neurons, since this malware classification problem is two-class, either malicious or benign. z can be denoted as:

$$z = ReLU(W_h f + b_h) \tag{11}$$

where W_h and b_h are the trainable weight and bias parameters of the hidden layer. This final output from the MLP, z, is a vector with each element giving a score that the app is associated with each class. z is passed to the SoftMax classification layer, which outputs the normalized probability of the app belonging to each class in the problem, formally:

$$p(y = i|z) = \frac{\exp(w_i^T z + b_i)}{\sum_{i'}^{I} \exp(w_{i'}^T z + b_i)} \tag{12}$$

where w_i and b_i are the trainable weight and bias parameters of the SoftMax layer learned for each of the i classes, $w_i^T z$ is the inner product of w_i and z, with y being the predicted label.

3.3 Cost Function

The model's cost function C to be minimized for a batch of B training samples, $\{I_{(1)}, \ldots, I_{(B)}\}$, can be written as:

$$C = -\frac{1}{B} \sum_{j=1}^{B} \sum_{i=1}^{c} 1\{y'_{(j)} = i\} \log p(y_{(j)} = i|z_{(j)}) \tag{13}$$

where c is the number of classes in the task, $y'_{(j)}$ is the ground truth for sample $I_{(j)}$ and $z_{(j)}$ is the resulting output after the forward pass of $I_{(j)}$ through the network. The function $1\{y'_{mal(j)} = i\}$ returns 1 if the condition is true, and 0 if false. Learning is performed by stochastic gradient descent which updates the network parameters via backpropagation after each sample is forwarded using the gradient of the cost function with respect to these parameters. A learning rate α is used in this process. During training the network is repeatedly presented with batches of training samples in random order until the parameters converge, and the cost function is minimized.

4 Experimental Setup

The experiments are presented in four stages. The first covers hyper-parameter tuning for the opcodes CNN and the APIs CNN, with the second an analysis of features learned by the permissions network. The third evaluates the single and multi-view settings for malware detection to prove the proposed model is effective in a conventional detection setting. The fourth is a series of zero-day experiments to recreate a challenging scenario where a malware detector is tested against a new family of malware it has never encountered before. To do this each family is excluded in turn from training, keeping it held out only for testing. State-of-the-art comparisons are provided throughout and the focus is on F1 score and false positive (or false alarm) rate, as per convention in previous work [7, 45, 34, 43, 47]. The false positive rate of a detector is particularly important as it allows further evaluation to select optimal models, especially in the case where several achieve similarly high or saturated F1 scores. Moreover, from a real-world standpoint false alarms should be minimised to reduce noise and alert fatigue. The F1 score and false positive rate are calculated formally as:

$$F1 = \frac{2 \times precision \times recall}{precision + recall} \tag{14}$$

$$precision = \frac{TP}{TP + FP} \tag{15}$$

$$recall = \frac{TP}{TP + FN} \tag{16}$$

$$false\ positive\ rate = \frac{FP}{FP + TN} \tag{17}$$

where TP, FP, TN, FN are true positives, false positives, true negatives and false negatives respectively, with the false positive rate expressed as a percentage in the results. The positive case is where an app is malicious, and the negative case is where an app is benign.

4.1 Datasets

Four different datasets are used (1) Malgenome [78], which contains 1260 malware apps across 49 different families, (2) an Intel Security dataset of 9902 malware apps from their own internal repository, (3) Drebin [7], with 5560 malware apps from 179 families, and (4) AMD [68], consisting of 24,553 malware apps from 71 families. The Malgenome dataset is only used for designing the initial architecture and hyperparameter tuning, not in the detection or zero-day experiments given its small size, and the Intel dataset is only used for investigating dictionary parameters since it is a proprietary set that does not allow comparison. For the evaluations and state-of-the-art comparison, the Drebin and AMD benchmark datasets are selected. This avoids overfitting and artificially inflated performance since neither Drebin or AMD are used in the tuning phase. These datasets are publicly available, and are chosen due to their continual use in the Android malware detection domain, allowing direct comparisons between the proposed approach and others, both in

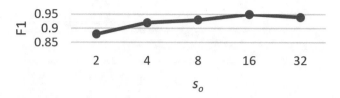

Fig. 5 Hyperparameter tuning for s_o

this work and in future. Every dataset is balanced with the addition of equivalent numbers of benign apps collected from Google Play, and then each dataset is split into 80% for training, 10% for validation, and 10% for testing, with the 50/50 balance of malware and benign apps maintained in each split. For the avoidance of doubt, these test apps are kept totally unseen and are not used in training or validation at any stage.

5   Experimental Results: Tuning and Learning Analysis

A thorough set of ablation experiments are performed to define the architecture design and investigate the influence of each of the hyperparameters. Architectures used in tuning the opcodes CNN and the APIs CNN have only a single convolutional layer, as in [45]. Given the relatively small datasets available, larger numbers of layers are likely to be prone to overfitting and have a greater amount of trainable parameters with little performance improvement [77].

5.1   Opcodes CNN

Hyperparameters for the opcodes CNN are empirically set applying ablation [18, 66, 12], where one parameter is varied while all others are held constant, and using the Malgenome dataset. In summary, the resulting settings are: $s_o = 8$, $r = 64$, $k_o = 8$ and $n_o = 8192$. These are the default settings unless specified otherwise in an ablation.

5.1.1   Filter Length s_o and Number of Filters r

The filter length s_o was varied from $s_o = 2$ to $s_o = 32$, while the number of convolutional filters was held constant at $r = 64$ and the filter stride held at 1. Longer filter lengths let the network learn longer patterns of opcodes and detect long-range dependencies between them. Figure 5 shows an increase in F1 using longer filters, until around $s_o = 8$.

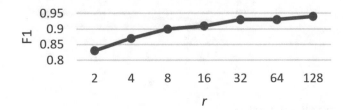

Fig. 6 Hyperparameter tuning for r

This result may be unsurprising, as very short opcode sequences are presumably statistically common and hence less discriminative, while very long sequences are too specific to a single sample. There likely exists an in-between length where opcode sequences both discriminate and generalise well. The filter length is set at $s_o = 8$, given the F1 improvement is marginal using filters twice or three times longer. In addition, since Dalvik is optimised for devices with constrained resources, it has a more powerful instruction set than conventional $\times 86$, meaning less use of the stack and registers. With over 1000×86 opcodes [30] compared to 218 opcodes in Dalvik [26], fewer instructions are likely to be needed by Dalvik for standard code constructs such as switch statements or for loops. These architectural differences are further motivation to select $s_o = 8$ over a unnecessarily longer filter length of 16 or 32.

The number of filters r affects the network's ability to learn a diverse set of features from the opcode sequences. This may be especially important if different malware families do not share many common characteristics, thus requiring different sequences of opcodes to be detected. All other network hyper-parameters are held constant while the number of filters is varied from $r = 2$ to $r = 128$ in powers of two. Note that regardless of the number of filters used, they are all of length $s_o = 8$. As per Fig. 6, the trend is an increase in F1 as the number of filters is increased. Approximately a 10% improvement in F1 is seen when moving from $r = 2$ to $r = 128$ filters. Performance plateaus at around 32 filters. Therefore, $r = 64$ filters are used to ensure satisfactory performance while keeping the number of parameters small, thus reducing the chance of overfitting.

5.1.2 Embedding Dimension k_o

The embedding layer takes a list of raw opcodes and learns to represent each opcode as a vector in an embedding space. The dimension of the embedding space k_o affects the network's internal representation of opcodes. In this experiment the dimension of the embedding space is varied from $k_o = 2$ to $k_o = 16$ in powers of two. Furthermore, to validate the use of the embedding layer, an experiment with no embedding layer is performed—note that in this case each opcode is simply

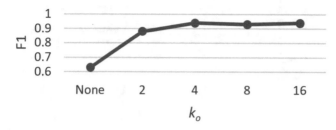

Fig. 7 Hyperparameter tuning for k_o

represented using its corresponding index value, i.e. a real number in the range 1 to 218, and thus filters of size $s_o \times 1$ are used. From Fig. 7 firstly it can be seen that use of the embedding layer is crucial to good performance. Once an embedding layer is used, there is only a weak correlation between increasing the embedding dimension and increasing F1.

This may be due to the fact that there are only a relatively small number of possible opcodes, with many opcodes representing similar underlying instructions. This contrasts with human language, where high dimensional embeddings are needed to encode the rich semantic relationships between words [46]. The results of this experiment indicate that, while using an embedding layer produces much better F1 performance, the use of a high-dimensional embedding is not required. Therefore a small embedding can be used, and k_o is set to 8, which in turn reduces the number of parameters in the opcodes CNN, and hence the network may generalize better to new data.

5.1.3 Number of Convolutional Layers *l*

In this experiment the number of convolutional layers, l, is varied from $l = 1$ to $l = 6$, while the number of convolutional filters and their length are held constant at $r = 64$ and $s_o = 8$ for all layers. Increasing the number of layers potentially allows the network to learn increasingly complex relationships between widely separated parts of the opcode sequence, by increasing the receptive field of the deeper filters.

However, the results in Fig. 8 show that performance does not significantly improve when adding more layers. This suggests that, at least in the Malgenome dataset being used for tuning, features based on sequences of consecutive opcodes are sufficient for the task of malware detection.

Higher level features, based on the combinations and ordering of sets of lower level features, appear not to be required. For static analysis this may be expected as the large-scale ordering of instructions, classes and other program constructs when coded originally is only loosely related to how those instructions are then executed at run-time after compilation. As a result of this experiment, only one layer in the opcodes CNN in used, since adding more layers will only increase the

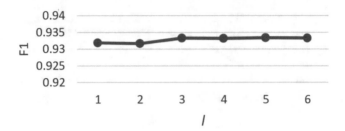

Fig. 8 Hyperparameter tuning for l

number of parameters, hence increasing the likelihood of over-fitting, while also reducing computational efficiency.

5.1.4   Effect of Max-Pooling Layer e

Using max-pooling after the convolutional layer serves two main purposes. Firstly, it allows any program, regardless of the length, to be represented as a fixed-length feature vector, which is a prerequisite to enable classification. Given that each Android app has a different number of instructions, this normalisation is required. Secondly, by only selecting the maximum activation of each convolution, the presence of a relevant sequence of opcodes can be detected anywhere in the program regardless of its location. However, compressing the full feature map, which gives magnitude of activation and location of each filter response, down to just the maximum activation value from each filter may discard too much potentially relevant information, such as the repetition of the relevant opcode sequence over the program length. To validate the max-pooling approach and explore alternatives that may retain additional information, a comparison is made between the performance of max-pooling over the full length, also known as global max-pooling, and max-pooling applied over regular program segments. This alternative max-pooling approach aims to preserve more information as well as enable the network to detect repetitions of filter activations.

For this experiment, the full program length is divided in a given number of segments e, where $e = 1$ is equivalent to the default of max-pooling over all instructions, and $e = n$ corresponds to dividing the full program length into n equal sized blocks, before applying max-pooling to each block. The length of the feature vector passed to the classifier is thus $e \times m$. Note each app has a different number of opcodes, and each program is divided into the same number of segments, therefore the segment length will vary depending on each individual program length. Figure 9 indicates changing the number of segments, e, does not significantly affect performance. Hence these results justify the architectural choice of applying the max-pooling over the full program length.

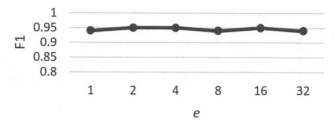

Fig. 9 Hyperparameter tuning for e

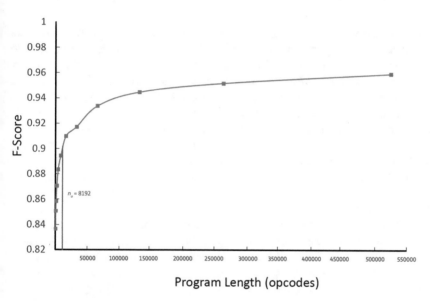

Fig. 10 Hyperparameter tuning for n_o

5.1.5 Input Length n_o

Accurate classification decisions may not require the entire sequence of an app's opcodes. Instead it may be possible to detect malware by examining only a short sample of contiguous instructions from the complete program. This improves computational efficiency and could be useful in the future design of a cascade classifier [65] where certain programs likely to be benign are quickly excluded from further consideration, while programs that appear malicious are examined more thoroughly. To study how performance is affected by limiting the number of opcodes n_o seen by the network, the maximum input length of the opcode sequence for each app is varied from $n_o = 256$ to $n_o = 524{,}288$, increasing two-fold for each step. Where the number of opcodes in an app is less than this maximum length, the full sequence is used. Figure 10 shows using longer lengths of opcode instructions improves performance.

However it can also be seen even relatively short opcode sequences can be used to detect malware effectively, which may be useful in resource constrained Android environments such as smartphones or in-vehicle systems. As much higher orders of magnitude do not produce a large enough corresponding improvement in performance, the setting $n_o = 8192$ provides an optimal balance of performance and computation.

5.2 APIs CNN

Similar ablation studies are performed for the APIs CNN. The *APIs* feature set is used in this tuning step as it is the broadest and most arbitrary compared to *GoogleAPIs* and *AndroidAPIs*. To avoid overfitting, the selected optimal hyper-parameter settings for *APIs* are then fixed and also used in the *GoogleAPIs* and *AndroidAPIs* CNNs in the later evaluations. Holding CNN hyperparameters constant for the architecture itself whilst varying the API features used allows fairer comparison between the discriminative capability of each API feature set. As with the opcodes CNN, the model hyperparameters are empirically set using the Malgenome dataset. In summary, the results are $s_g = 8$, $m = 64$ and $k_g = 8$, with the Intel dataset then used to empirically set the dictionary hyperparameters, resulting in $S = 250$, $T = 1$ and $n_g = 10,000$. These are the default settings unless specified otherwise in an ablation.

In the first of these experiments, API sequences created from an unthresholded arbitary dictonary are used, before then introducing S and T. It is interesting to note some of the final APIs CNN hyperparameter settings are the same as for the opcodes CNN, though it should be stressed both were tuned independently. Perhaps this is to be expected on reflection, given the opcodes sequences and API sequences used in these ablation studies are derived from the same .*smali* files. For this reason a single convolutional layer and global max-pooling were again used, as both were already varied when tuning the opcodes CNN and thus these experiments were not repeated for the APIs CNN.

5.2.1 Filter Length s_g and Number of Filters m

Like the opcodes CNN, increasing the length of the convolutional filters allows the network to learn longer patterns of APIs and learn long-range dependencies between APIs, while the number of filters impacts the diversity of features learnt from the API sequences. The Malgenome dataset is used in this experiment and a grid search performed. The range of hyper-parameters in the grid search are: $s_g = [4, 8, 16, 32]$ and $m = [4, 8, 16, 32, 64]$. The filter stride is held at 1, with $k_g = 4$ and $n_g = 50$. Figure 11 shows a noticeable F1 increase when s_g increases from 4 to 8, and when $m = 64$. Hence the settings are $s_g = 8$ and $m = 64$.

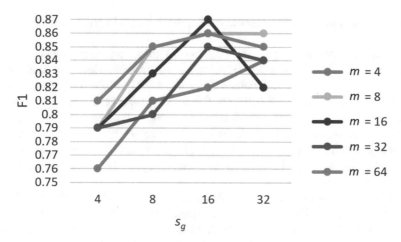

Fig. 11 Hyperparameter tuning for s_g and m

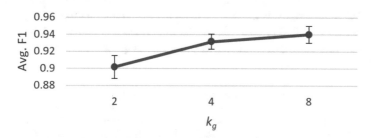

Fig. 12 Hyperparameter tuning for k_g, bars show σ over k_g

5.2.2 Embedding Dimension k_g

The embedding layer learns to represent each API as a vector in an embedding space and the dimension of this space affects the model's internal representation of APIs. Another grid search is performed using $k_g = [2, 4, 8]$ and $T = [1, 10, 50, 100, 250, 500]$. The dictionary size S is held at 250 and for each dictionary threshold T the APIs sequences are adjusted to remove APIs not present in each resulting dictionary. The average length of a sequence across both malware and benign samples in the Malgenome dataset is around 6500 APIs. Therefore the input length n_g is set to 10,000, including zero padding where needed. As per Fig. 12, when the F1 is averaged across all values of T, with the variability over k_g represented as a standard deviation bar around the mean, $k_g = 8$ performs best overall. Thus with a high-dimensional embedding not required, k_g is set to 8.

5.2.3 Dictionary Size S, Invocation Threshold T and Input Length n_g

In order to better investigate the influence of these hyperparameters, the Intel dataset is used as it is much larger than Malgenome. Here the grid search has the following hyper-parameters: $S = [125, 250, 500, 750, 1000]$ and $T = [1, 10, 50, 100, 250, 500, 1000, 1500]$. Figure 13 shows the average F1 across all values of S as T increases, with the variability over T represented as a standard deviation bar around the mean. There is no clear choice for T since the impact of varying it is minimal, so it is set as $T = 1$. The selection of $S = 250$ is also made as this is the closest size to the opcodes dictionary of $d_o = 218$ and saves computation compared to using a larger S.

With S and T then held constant, n_g is varied to study the effect of longer API input lengths. For the malicious samples in the Intel dataset, the average length of an API sequence varies from 8500 to 26,500 APIs, and for the benign samples the average length varies from 7000 to 20,200 APIs. The average length across both malware and benign samples varies from 8200 to 23,300 APIs. In this grid search $n_g = [10,000, 15,000, 20,000]$. Figure 14 shows the improvement for longer API input lengths is minimal, and incurs extra computational cost, hence the setting of $n_g = 10,000$ is made. Since the Intel dataset is real-world, it is asserted these dictionary and input length hyper-parameters are optimal for the experimental evaluations.

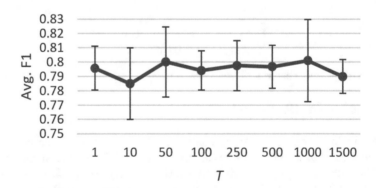

Fig. 13 Hyperparameter tuning for T, bars show σ over T

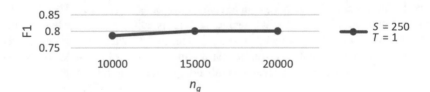

Fig. 14 Hyperparameter tuning for n_g

5.3 Analysis of Features Learned by the Permission View

No hyperparameters need tuned for the permissions network as all 138 specified permissions are used as input. However, an analysis is performed to validate the architecture has learned something meaningful and explore how the network's internal knowledge can inform the Android malware domain. Note doing the same for the opcodes CNN or APIs CNN is difficult as the input information is at a very low level—while reverting to the sequences of opcodes or APIs that max-activate each filter is possible, linking back that usage directly in a meaningful manner is highly challenging, so such CNN analysis as left as future work. By comparison, the permission view weights are easier to associate with each permission's importance for detecting malware or benign samples, and observations can be cross-referenced with previous literature. Each permission's importance for discriminating between malware or benign samples is ranked, giving insight into what the model has learned. This is also a sanity check for the approach, as important permissions can be checked against the literature. If the neural network is using features in a similar way to an expert human malware analyst, this builds confidence in the model's decisions. To create this ranking, each input neuron's weights are averaged. As the permissions input is an ordered vector, each input neuron corresponds directly to one single permission. Figure 15 lists all permissions ordered by average weight.

Averaging the weights in matrix W_p connected to each input neuron gives the importance of each permission. Stronger connections, i.e. larger weight values, mean the network ascribes more importance to a given permission. To prove the permissions view is learning meaningful features, the permissions deemed to be important by the model are compared with those from previous work. The permissions SEND_SMS and RECEIVE_SMS, ranked first and third most important by

Fig. 15 Android permissions ranked by relevance for malware classification

the model, have high mutual-information scores for malware detection [74, 72]. They are also ranked in the top-ten most important permissions in several other analyses [56, 40, 55, 80, 19, 28, 53]. Similarly, permissions with highly negative importance values according to the model are also found to be important in the literature: READ_PHONE_STATE and ACCESS_NETWORK_STATE [74, 72, 78, 52], CALL_PHONE [40, 52, 74, 72] and INTERNET [56, 78, 8, 52, 20, 53, 74, 72]. Finally, SYSTEM_ALERT_WINDOW, given the second largest value by the model, is linked to 'Cloak and Dagger' attacks [21].

6 Experimental Results: Final Model and State-of-the-art Comparisons

A thorough evaluation of the proposed multi-view approach is now performed using the two standard publicly available benchmark datasets Drebin [7] and AMD [68]. A state-of-the-art comparison is presented and a zero-day setting evaluates the network under challenging realistic conditions. Hyperparameter values used in all experiments are set as per previous, that is, $n_o = 8192$, $s_o = 8$, $k_o = 8$, $m = 64$, $o_o = 16$, $n_g = 10{,}000$, $s_g = 8$, $k_g = 8$, $r = 64$, $o_g = 16$, $S = 250$, $T = 1$, $o_p = 64$, and $o_h = 16$, plus $B = 1$, $\alpha = 0.001$ and a filter stride in both CNNs of 1. No further tuning is carried out, and each model is trained for 75 epochs. The metrics reported are on the unseen Drebin and AMD testing splits.

6.1 Single-View Model Detection Performance

The evaluations start with the performance of a series of single-view models learning from only one of the input feature sets. Similarly, the three presented API feature extraction methods are compared. This creates a baseline to compare the multi-view models to, and confirms to what degree each of these feature sets are useful in isolation. For Drebin and AMD separately, each single-view model is trained using the training set and then tested with the unseen testing set.

Results in Table 2 show each of the feature sets are indeed effective for malware detection, with Figs. 16 and 17 showing the F1 and FP% rate comparisons respectively.

For the Drebin apps, while performance is strong across the board, it can be seen that the APIs methods which use *GoogleAPIs* and *AndroidAPIs* give the best F1 scores and FP% rates. For the AMD apps, the *GoogleAPIs* and *AndroidAPIs* again perform best, with particularly low FP% rates. With the AMD dataset being five times larger than Drebin, it is perhaps to be expected the AMD metrics are better by comparison since there are more apps to learn from in the training phase. It is concluded each single-view model performs well on both the Drebin

Table 2 Detection performance and FP % rate of single-view models

Dataset	Model	F1	FP %
Drebin	Opcodes	0.9559	4.98
Drebin	Perms	0.9217	5.62
Drebin	APIs	0.9456	6.68
Drebin	GoogleAPIs	0.9688	4.57
Drebin	AndroidAPIs	0.9679	4.39
AMD	Opcodes	0.9745	1.03
AMD	Perms	0.9514	3.38
AMD	APIs	0.9653	2.58
AMD	GoogleAPIs	0.9928	0.49
AMD	AndroidAPIs	0.9922	0.76

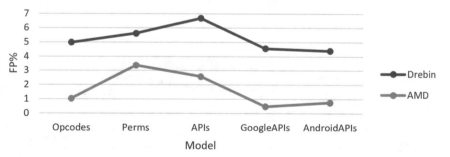

Fig. 16 Single-view F1 comparison

Fig. 17 Single-view FP% rate comparison

and AMD datasets. Interestingly these results show the discriminative power of the *AndroidAPIs*, despite using the limited proprietary set of only 210 APIs, much smaller than the other API methods, resulting in similar or better detection performance with lower computational cost. It is worth recalling too that the dictionaries used in *APIs* and *GoogleAPIs* need some arbitrary and/or empirical decision-making. The benefit of *AndroidAPIs* is that these decisions are avoided entirely, as there only are 210 APIs to start with.

6.2   Multi-View Model Detection Performance

Next the single-view features are combined in a multi-view model to assess how performance is impacted versus using only one feature set in isolation. Having established the input feature sets are of use individually in single-view, it is expected there may be some difference in performance if more than one is used, which would show the feature sets are complementary. Thus in this experiment the proposed feature sets are combined to see if detection can be improved and the FP rate reduced. Results in Table 3, Figs. 18 and 19 show that for both the Drebin and AMD datasets, combining feature sets always results in a performance improvement, since the network learns to use them in a complementary way during training.

Table 3 Detection performance and FP% rate of multi-view models

Dataset	Model	F1	FP %
Drebin	Opcodes + Perms	0.9759	3.51
Drebin	Opcodes + Perms + APIs	0.9837	1.23
Drebin	Opcodes + Perms + GoogleAPIs	0.9838	1.93
Drebin	Opcodes + Perms + AndroidAPIs	0.9928	1.05
AMD	Opcodes + Perms	0.989	0.53
AMD	Opcodes + Perms + APIs	0.9951	0.53
AMD	Opcodes + Perms + GoogleAPIs	0.9971	0.27
AMD	Opcodes + Perms + AndroidAPIs	0.9963	0.08

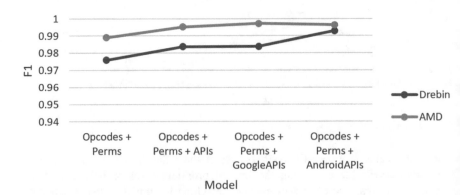

Fig. 18 Multi-view F1 comparison

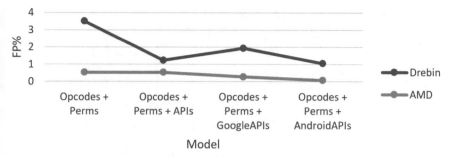

Fig. 19 Multi-view FP% rate comparison

Among the three API feature extraction methods, *AndroidAPIs* results in the most successful combination with a significant decrease in false positives, i.e. false alarms, which is a critical factor in real-world detector deployments. Again, *AndroidAPIs* also does not involve arbitrary decisions regarding API selection as it is a limited, pre-defined set of 210, reducing the number of hyperparameters to use and simplifying updates to the model, since the dictionary does not need to be revised or recalculated for new samples or datasets.

6.3 State-of-the-Art Comparison: Malware Detection

Table 4 shows a comparison of the proposed multi-view approach against state-of-the-art methods using the Drebin and AMD benchmark datasets in a conventional detection setting, where all families are in both training and testing. Direct comparisons are performed using the Drebin detector [7], Maldozer [34] and [74] (referred to as APIs56). It is ensured the same experimental setting and dataset splits used in the experiments thus far are also used to evaluate these other methods. Note the Maldozer paper does not disclose its model's input sequence length or batch size, and not enough detail is present to recreate their API dictionary of 100,000 APIs with embedding size 64. Thus the Maldozer network architecture for detection is replicated, including the use of word2vec [46] when training the embedding layer, with the input features being *AndroidAPIs*. In all other cases, comparisons are made versus the reported results in the respective papers.

On the Drebin dataset, the multi-view model achieves the highest F1 and the lowest FP rate of only 1.05%. This is 60% less than the Drebin FP rate, 50% less than the Maldozer FP rate, and 83% less than *APIs56*. The MaMaDroid [43] and DroidAPIMiner [1] F1 scores are 0.96 and 0.32 respectively, with [44] using only 10 of the Drebin families in evaluating their model, giving an accuracy of 0.78. These performance gains are due to the multi-view model learning better from the three input feature sets, and the fact there are no hand-crafted features, allowing the model to encapsulate internally its own representation of malware and benign characteristics without expert human analysis beforehand. With the AMD dataset,

Table 4 State-of-the-art comparison in conventional detection setting

Dataset	Model	F1	Acc.	Recall	FP %	Comment
Drebin	[44]	–	0.78	–	–	Hand-crafted feats. Only used 10 families
Drebin	[1]	0.32	–	–	–	Hand-crafted feats. Reported in [43]
Drebin	[43]	0.96	–	0.97	–	Hand-crafted feats
Drebin	[7]	0.9868	0.9866	0.9736	2.64	Hand-crafted feats e.g. *suspiciousAPIs*
Drebin	[34]	0.9875	0.9875	0.9964	2.11	word2vec embedding. 244,098 params
Drebin	[74]	0.9378	0.9385	0.9403	6.33	Hand-crafted feats e.g. API calls related
Drebin	*AndroidAPIs*	0.9679	0.9679	0.9801	4.39	No hand-crafted feats, 6922 params
Drebin	**Multi-view**	**0.9928**	**0.9929**	**0.9964**	**1.05**	No hand-crafted feats. 23,226 params
AMD	[41]	–	–	0.95	6.2	Hand-crafted feats. API usage, tree
AMD	[41]	–	–	0.97	9.1	Hand-crafted feats. API freq., neural net
AMD	[41]	–	–	0.99	2.9	Hand-crafted feats. API sequence, LSTM
AMD	[7]	0.9975	0.9928	0.988	1.2	Hand-crafted feats e.g. *suspiciousAPIs*
AMD	[34]	0.9936	0.9939	0.9914	0.38	word2vec embedding. 244,098 params
AMD	[74]	0.7458	0.8005	0.6104	2.43	Hand-crafted feats e.g. API calls related
AMD	*AndroidAPIs*	0.9922	0.9925	0.9926	0.76	No hand-crafted feats. 6922 params
AMD	**Multi-view**	**0.9963**	**0.9964**	**0.9934**	**0.08**	No hand-crafted feats. 23,226 params
Average	[7]	0.9922	0.9897	0.9808	1.92	Average of Drebin & AMD results
Average	[34]	0.9906	0.9907	0.9939	1.25	Average of Drebin & AMD results
Average	[74]	0.8418	0.8695	0.7754	4.38	Average of Drebin & AMD results
Average	*AndroidAPIs*	0.9801	0.9802	0.9864	2.58	Average of Drebin & AMD results
Average	**Multi-view**	**0.9946**	**0.9947**	**0.9949**	**0.57**	Average of Drebin & AMD results

Bold font signifies the best value for that metric

the multi-view model again achieves a near-perfect F1 whilst giving a FP rate of only 0.08%. This is a 79% reduction compared to the best performing other model in that regard, which is Maldozer, and compared to the neural net in [41], this is a 99% reduction. The FP rate is 97% lower than the best FP rate using the LSTM reported in [41]. Also, the multi-view model is likely to train faster than LSTMs, since recurrent architectures are known to be comparatively slow to train [24]. Notably, the F1 of APIs56 on AMD samples is lower than its F1 on the Drebin samples, and indeed much lower than the multi-view model. Given the Drebin dataset consists of samples discovered from 2010 to 2012, with the AMD dataset consisting of samples discovered from 2010 to 2016, it could be said APIs56 is a possible example of a detection system that, since it uses manually hand-crafted features from a snapshot in time, is vulnerable to aging and becoming out-of-date. Lastly, considering the average figures it can be seen the multi-view model achieves the highest F1 of 0.9947 and the lowest FP rate of 0.57%, which in relative terms is 77% less on average compared to the state-of-the-art.

In addition to this compelling quantitative performance, there are further qualitative comparisons to be made regarding the differences in the amount of human domain expertise used in creating the input feature sets. The use of opcodes, permissions and *AndroidAPIs* implicitly means malware domain expertise has been decoupled, since these three input feature sets are only extracted in their raw form, not statistically ranked, refined or pre-categorised by an expert. The *AndroidAPIs* feature set is very likely to perpetuate over time as they are intrinsically linked to the core of the Android platform—they are proprietary and are much less likely to change. By comparison, from the Drebin detector codebase there appears to be handcrafting of input features to create eight different feature sets: *suspicious API calls, restricted API calls, hardware features, requested permissions, app components, filtered intents, used permissions, and network addresses*. On the other hand, the presented multi-view approach does not require any such malware detection insights. Finally, with regards to a real-world implementation of this model, once this multi-view architecture has been trained, large numbers of files can be efficiently scanned using a GPU. The model can classify an app in 1 millisecond using an NVIDIA 1080TI GPU, eight times faster than using a standard Intel Core i7-8700 CPU, which can classify an app in 8 milliseconds. In addition, a mobile app of this malware detector, running on a Google Pixel device, has been developed [29].

6.4 Zero-Day Scenario Evaluation

Arp et al. [7] included a zero-day experiment where the top 20 largest families in the Drebin dataset were selected, with each in turn left out of the training process. That same unseen held-out family was then used in testing. Using both the Drebin and AMD datasets, this experiment is recreated using the same zero-day technique. The architecture used is the multi-view model using opcodes, permissions and *AndroidAPIs*. For the state-of-the-art comparison, the Drebin detector and Maldozer are selected. The original zero-day experiment is extended to evaluate not only the top 20 largest families per [7], but in fact all 178 families in the Drebin dataset, and all 71 families in the AMD dataset. The metric is the detection rate, calculated as the % of malicious samples in test correctly classified as malware. A weighted average is used when reporting results as the number of samples per family varies widely, shown in Figs. 20 and 21. The detection rate for each family is therefore weighted by the number of available samples for that family in relation to the total number of samples in the dataset.

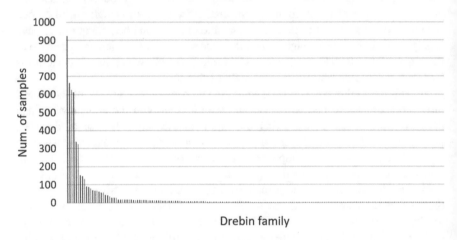

Fig. 20 Number of samples per family in the Drebin dataset

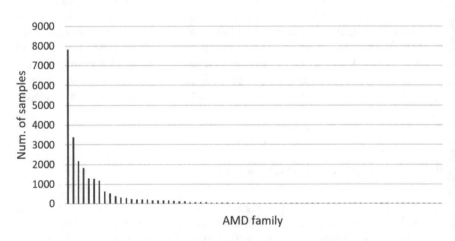

Fig. 21 Number of samples per family in the AMD dataset

6.5 State-of-the-Art Comparison: Zero-Day Scenario

6.5.1 Drebin Dataset Zero-Day Evaluation

Table 5 shows the results for the Drebin dataset, with detection performance calculated across the 20 largest families and also calculated across all 178 families.

For the largest 20 families, the multi-view model using opcodes, permissions and *AndroidAPIs* has a weighted detection average of 91%, a significant improvement on Drebin and Maldozer, scoring 53% and 86% respectively. Furthermore, when this experiment is expanded across the whole Drebin dataset of 178 families, strong performance is maintained and the multi-view model performs best when considering the variation in family size by using the weighted average.

6.5.2 AMD Dataset Zero-Day Evaluation

Table 6 contains the detection performance for the AMD dataset top 20 largest families and across the full 71 families.

It can be seen the multi-view model has a weighted detection rate of 81% for the largest 20 families, better than the Drebin detector and Maldozer. When considering all 71 families in the AMD dataset, this performance gain is maintained, with the multi-view model scoring a weighted detection rate of 81% compared to the Drebin and Maldozer scores, both of which are only 75%. The superior performance of the proposed system in this complex zero-day setting seems to confirm that the multi-view neural architecture extracts improved and more discriminative features during training with less over-fitting. This results in an approach that is able to generalise better against new threats and malware families that have never been seen, where signature-based systems will likely fail.

Table 5 Zero-day detection performance on Drebin dataset

Average	Drebin [7]	Maldozer [34]	Multi-view
Largest 20 families (weighted)	53%	86%	**91%**
All families (weighted)	58%	86%	**91%**

Bold font signifies the best value for that metric

Table 6 Zero-day detection performance on AMD dataset

Average	Drebin [7]	Maldozer [34]	Multi-view
Largest 20 families (weighted)	75%	75%	**81%**
All families (weighted)	75%	75%	**81%**

Bold font signifies the best value for that metric

7 Conclusions

This chapter presents a multi-view CNN for static Android malware analysis learning from opcodes, permissions and proprietary Android APIs. The experiments show several relevant conclusions. Firstly, the use of deep learning architectures makes it possible to reach state-of-art results in automatic malware detection, while reducing the dependency of feature engineering and domain expertise. This system can be better trained and be easily updated against new threats by simply collecting more samples. Secondly, using multi-view compared to single-view architectures improves performance since the model is exposed to simultaneous sources of information and can learn a more effective set of features. Finally, the model achieves state-of-the art detection performance in a challenging zero-day scenario compared to the Drebin and Maldozer detectors, with the key takeaway being this architecture can reduce over-fitting to the training set and generalise better to effectively detect unseen malware families. The presented model is able to protect better against these new malware families, where signature-based systems will almost certainly fail, and other more traditional ML approaches will struggle. Our method reduces false positives by 77% in relative terms on average compared to others, an important metric for potential real-world deployment, with the network also achieving state-of-the art performance in the conventional task of malware detection whilst decoupling domain insights.

References

1. Aafer, Y., Du, W., Yin, H.: Droidapiminer: Mining API-level features for robust malware detection in android. In: Security and Privacy in Communication Networks. 9th International ICST Conference, SecureComm 2013 (2014)
2. Afonso, V., Amorim, M., Grégio, A., Junquera, G., De Geus, P.: Identifying android malware using dynamically obtained features. J. Comput. Virol. Hacking Tech. 11, 9–17 (2014)
3. Alazab, M., Alazab, M., Shalaginov, A., Mesleh, A., Awajan, A.: Intelligent mobile malware detection using permission requests and API calls. Future Generation Computer Systems 107, 509–521 (2020)
4. Allix, K., Jerome, Q., Bissyandé, T.F., Klein, J., State, R., Traon, Y.L.: A forensic analysis of android malware—how is malware written and how it could be detected? In: 2014 IEEE 38th Annual Computer Software and Applications Conference, pp. 384–393 (2014)
5. Alzaylaee, M.K., Yerima, S.Y., Sezer, S.: Emulator vs real phone: android malware detection using machine learning. In: Proceedings of the 3rd ACM on International Workshop on Security And Privacy Analytics, IWSPA '17, pp. 65–72. ACM, New York (2017)
6. Apktool: Apktool—a tool for reverse engineering 3rd party, closed, binary Android aps. https://ibotpeaches.github.io/Apktool/. Accessed April 2020
7. Arp, D., Spreitzenbarth, M., Hubner, M., Gascon, H., Rieck, K.: Drebin: effective and explainable detection of android malware in your pocket. In: 24th Annual Network and Distributed System Security Symposium, NDSS 2014 (2014)
8. Barrera, D., Kayacik, H.G., van Oorschot, P.C., Somayaji, A.: A methodology for empirical analysis of permission-based security models and its application to android. In: Proceedings of the 17th ACM Conference on Computer and Communications Security, pp. 73–84. ACM, New York (2010)

9. Burguera, I., Zurutuza, U., Nadjm-Tehrani, S.: Crowdroid: Behavior-based malware detection system for android. In: Proceedings of the 1st ACM Workshop on Security and Privacy in Smartphones and Mobile Devices, SPSM '11, pp. 15–26. ACM, New York (2011)

10. Cai, H., Meng, N., Ryder, B., Yao, D.: Droidcat: Effective android malware detection and categorization via app-level profiling. IEEE Transactions on Information Forensics and Security **14**(6), 1455–1470 (2019)

11. Canfora, G., Mercaldo, F., Visaggio, C.A.: Mobile malware detection using op-code frequency histograms. In: Proc.of Int. Conf. on Security and Cryptography (SECRYPT) (2015)

12. Cashman, D., Perer, A., Chang, R., Strobelt, H.: Ablate, variate, and contemplate: Visual analytics for discovering neural architectures. IEEE Trans. Visualization Comput. Graph. **26**(1), 863–873 (2020). https://doi.org/10.1109/TVCG.2019.2934261

13. Chen, S., Xue, M., Tang, Z., Xu, L., Zhu, H.: Stormdroid: A streaminglized machine learning-based system for detecting android malware. In: Proceedings of the 11th ACM on Asia Conference on Computer and Communications Security, ASIA CCS '16, pp. 377–388. ACM, New York (2016)

14. Chen, W., Aspinall, D., Gordon, A.D., Sutton, C., Muttik, I.: More semantics more robust: improving android malware classifiers. In: Proceedings of the 9th ACM Conference on Security & Privacy in Wireless and Mobile Networks, WiSec '16, pp. 147–158. ACM, New York (2016)

15. Ding, Y., Zhao, W., Wang, Z., Wang, L.: Automaticlly learning features of android apps using CNN. In: 2018 International Conference on Machine Learning and Cybernetics (ICMLC), vol. 1, pp. 331–336 (2018)

16. Fan, M., Liu, J., Luo, X., Chen, K., Tian, Z., Zheng, Q., Liu, T.: Android malware familial classification and representative sample selection via frequent subgraph analysis. IEEE Trans. Inform. Forensics Secur. **13**(8), 1890–1905 (2018)

17. Faruki, P., Laxmi, V., Bharmal, A., Gaur, M., Ganmoor, V.: Androsimilar: Robust signature for detecting variants of android malware. J. Infor. Secur. Appl. **22**, 66–80 (2015). Special issue on Security of Information and Networks

18. Fawcett, C., Hoos, H.H.: Analysing differences between algorithm configurations through ablation. J. Heuristics **22**(4), 431–458 (2016).

19. Felt, A.P., Finifter, M., Chin, E., Hanna, S., Wagner, D.: A survey of mobile malware in the wild. In: Proceedings of the 1st ACM Workshop on Security and Privacy in Smartphones and Mobile Devices, pp. 3–14. ACM, New York (2011)

20. Felt, A.P., Greenwood, K., Wagner, D.: The effectiveness of application permissions. In: Proceedings of the 2Nd USENIX Conference on Web Application Development, p. 7 (2011)

21. Fratantonio, Y., Qian, C., Chung, S.P., Lee, W.: Cloak and dagger: from two permissions to complete control of the UI feedback loop. In: 2017 IEEE Symposium on Security and Privacy (SP), pp. 1041–1057 (2017)

22. Garcia, J., Hammad, M., Malek, S.: Lightweight, obfuscation-resilient detection and family identification of android malware. ACM Trans. Softw. Eng. Methodol. **26**(3), 11:1–11:29 (2018)

23. Gascon, H., Yamaguchi, F., Arp, D., Rieck, K.: Structural detection of android malware using embedded call graphs. In: Proceedings of the 2013 ACM Workshop on Artificial Intelligence and Security, AISec '13, pp. 45–54. ACM, New York (2013)

24. Goodfellow, I., Bengio, Y., Courville, A.: Sequence modelling: recurrent and recursive nets. In: Deep Learning, pp. 371–372. MIT Press, Cambridge (2016)

25. Google: Android API Developer Reference. https://developer.android.com/reference/packages. Accessed April 2020

26. Google: Dalvik. https://source.android.com/devices/tech/dalvik/dalvik-bytecode.html. Accessed April 2020

27. Google: Google APIs for Android. https://developers.google.com/android/reference/packages Accessed April 2020

28. Grace, M., Zhou, Y., Wang, Z., Jiang, X.: Systematic detection of capability leaks in stock android smartphones. In: NDSS Symposium 2012 (2012)

29. GSMA: Mobile Scholar 2019 Finalists. https://vimeo.com/325173012. Accessed July 2020

30. Intel Developer Zone: Intel 64 and IA-32 Architectures Software Developer's Manual: Volume 2. https://software.intel.com/en-us/download/intel-64-and-ia-32-architectures-sdm-combined-volumes-1-2a-2b-2c-2d-3a-3b-3c-3d-and-4. Accessed April 2020
31. Jerome, Q., Allix, K., State, R., Engel, T.: Using opcode-sequences to detect malicious android applications. In: 2014 IEEE Int. Conf. on Communications (ICC) (2014)
32. Jesus Freke: Baksmali. https://github.com/JesusFreke/smali. Accessed April 2020
33. Kang, B., Kang, B., Kim, J., Im, E.G.: Android malware classification method: Dalvik bytecode frequency analysis. In: Proc. of the 2013 Research in Adaptive and Convergent Systems (2013)
34. Karbab, E.B., Debbabi, M., Derhab, A., Mouheb, D.: Maldozer: Automatic framework for android malware detection using deep learning. Digital Invest. **24**, S48–S59 (2018)
35. Kim, T., Kang, B., Rho, M., Sezer, S., Im, E.G.: A multimodal deep learning method for android malware detection using various features. IEEE Trans. Inform. Forensics Secur. **14**(3), 773–788 (2019).
36. Kim, Y.: Convolutional neural networks for sentence classification. In: Proceedings of the 2014 Conference on Empirical Methods in Natural Language Processing (EMNLP), pp. 1746–1751. Association for Computational Linguistics (2014)
37. Lashkari, A.H., A.Kadir, A.F., Gonzalez, H., Mbah, K.F., A. Ghorbani, A.: Towards a network-based framework for android malware detection and characterization. In: 2017 15th Annual Conference on Privacy, Security and Trust (PST), pp. 233–23309 (2017)
38. Lee, W.Y., Saxe, J., Harang, R.: Seqdroid: Obfuscated android malware detection using stacked convolutional and recurrent neural networks. In: Deep Learning Applications for Cyber Security, pp. 197–210. Springer, Cham (2019)
39. Liu, X., Liu, J.: A two-layered permission-based android malware detection scheme. In: 2014 2nd IEEE Int. Conf. on Mobile Cloud Computing, Services and Engineering (MobileCloud) (2014)
40. Liu, X., Liu, J.: A two-layered permission-based android malware detection scheme. In: 2nd IEEE International Conference on Mobile Cloud Computing, Services, and Engineering (MobileCloud), pp. 142–148. IEEE, Piscataway (2014)
41. Ma, Z., Ge, H., Liu, Y., Zhao, M., Ma, J.: A combination method for android malware detection based on control flow graphs and machine learning algorithms. IEEE Access **7**, 21235–21245 (2019)
42. Maiorca, D., Mercaldo, F., Giacinto, G., Visaggio, C.A., Martinelli, F.: R-packdroid: Api package-based characterization and detection of mobile ransomware. In: Proceedings of the Symposium on Applied Computing, SAC '17, pp. 1718–1723. ACM, New York (2017)
43. Mariconti, E., Onwuzurike, L., Andriotis, P., Cristofaro, E.D., Ross, G.J., Stringhini, G.: Mamadroid: Detecting android malware by building Markov chains of behavioral models. In: 24th Annual Network and Distributed System Security Symposium, NDSS 2017 (2017)
44. Martinelli, F., Marulli, F., Mercaldo, F.: Evaluating convolutional neural network for effective mobile malware detection. Procedia Comput. Sci. **112**(C), 2372–2381 (2017)
45. McLaughlin, N., Martinez del Rincon, J., Kang, B., Yerima, S., Miller, P., Sezer, S., Safaei, Y., Trickel, E., Zhao, Z., Doupé, A., Joon Ahn, G.: Deep android malware detection. In: Proceedings of the Seventh ACM on Conference on Data and Application Security and Privacy, CODASPY '17. ACM, New York (2017)
46. Mikolov, T., Chen, K., Corrado, G.S., Dean, J.: Efficient estimation of word representations in vector space (2013). CoRR abs/1301.3781
47. Millar, S., McLaughlin, N., Martinez del Rincon, J., Miller, P., Zhao, Z.: Dandroid: a multi-view discriminative adversarial network for obfuscated android malware detection. In: Proceedings of the Tenth ACM Conference on Data and Application Security and Privacy, CODASPY '20 (2020)
48. Nix, R., Zhang, J.: Classification of android apps and malware using deep neural networks. In: 2017 International Joint Conference on Neural Networks, IJCNN 2017, Anchorage, AK, USA, May 14–19, 2017, pp. 1871–1878 (2017)
49. Oak, R., Du, M., Yan, D., Takawale, H., Amit, I.: Malware detection on highly imbalanced data through sequence modeling. In: Proceedings of the 12th ACM Workshop on Artificial Intelligence and Security, AISec'19, pp. 37–48. Association for Computing Machinery (2019)

50. Onwuzurike, L., Almeida, M., Mariconti, E., Blackburn, J., Stringhini, G., De Cristofaro, E.: A family of droids-android malware detection via behavioral modeling: Static vs dynamic analysis. In: 2018 16th Annual Conference on Privacy, Security and Trust (PST), pp. 1–10 (2018)
51. Palo Alto Networks: WildFire malware analysis service. https://docs.paloaltonetworks.com/wildfire.html. Accessed April 2020
52. Peiravian, N., Zhu, X.: Machine learning for android malware detection using permission and api calls. In: 2013 IEEE 25th International Conference on Tools with Artificial Intelligence, pp. 300–305 (2013)
53. Peng, H., Gates, C., Sarma, B., Li, N., Qi, Y., Potharaju, R., Nita-Rotaru, C., Molloy, I.: Using probabilistic generative models for ranking risks of android apps. In: Proceedings of the 2012 ACM Conference on Computer and Communications Security, pp. 241–252. ACM, New York (2012)
54. Raff, E., Barker, J., Sylvester, J., Brandon, R., Catanzaro, B., Nicholas, C.K.: Malware detection by eating a whole exe. In: Workshops at the Thirty-Second AAAI Conference on Artificial Intelligence (2018)
55. Rosen, S., Qian, Z., Mao, Z.M.: Appprofiler: A flexible method of exposing privacy-related behavior in android applications to end users. In: Proceedings of the Third ACM Conference on Data and Application Security and Privacy, CODASPY '13, pp. 221–232 (2013)
56. Sanz, B., Santos, I., Laorden, C., Ugarte-Pedrero, X., Bringas, P.G., Marañón, G.A.: Puma: Permission usage to detect malware in android. In: CISIS/ICEUTE/SOCO Special Sessions 2012, Advances in Intelligent Systems and Computing, vol. 189, pp. 289–298. Springer, Berlin (2012)
57. Sanz, B., Santos, I., Laorden, C., X. Ugarte-Pedrero, P.G.B., Alvarez, G.: Puma: permission usage to detect malware in android. In: Int. Joint Conf. CISIS'12-ICEUTE'12-SOCO'12 (2012)
58. Saracino, A., Sgandurra, D., Dini, G., Martinelli, F.: Madam: Effective and efficient behavior-based android malware detection and prevention. IEEE Trans. Dependable Secure Comput. 15(1), 83–97 (2018)
59. Shabtai, A., Kanonov, U., Elovici, Y., Glezer, C., Weiss, Y.: Andromaly: a behavioral malware detection framework for android devices. J. Intell. Inform. Syst. 38(1), 161–190 (2012)
60. Sharma, A., Dash, S.K.: Mining api calls and permissions for android malware detection. In: Cryptology and Network Security (2014)
61. Skovoroda, A., Gamayunov, D.: Automated static analysis and classification of android malware using permission and api calls models. In: 2017 15th Annual Conference on Privacy, Security and Trust (PST), pp. 243–24309 (2017)
62. Su, X., Chuah, M.C., Tan, G.: Smartphone dual defense protection framework: detecting malicious applications in android markets. In: 2012 Eighth Int. Conf. on Mobile Ad-hoc and Sensor Networks (MSN) (2012)
63. Sun, M., Li, X., Lui, J.C.S., Ma, R.T.B., Liang, Z.: Monet: A user-oriented behavior-based malware variants detection system for android. IEEE Trans. Inform. Forensics Secur. 12(5), 1103–1112 (2017)
64. Tian, K., Yao, D., Ryder, B.G., Tan, G., Peng, G.: Detection of repackaged android malware with code-heterogeneity features. IEEE Trans. Dependable Secure Comput. 17(1), 64–77 (2020)
65. Viola, P., Jones, M.J.: Rapid object detection using a boosted cascade of simple features. In: IEEE Conference on Computer Vision and Pattern Recognition, pp. 511–518. IEEE, Piscataway (2001)
66. Wang, C., Dong, S., Zhao, X., Papanastasiou, G., Zhang, H., Yang, G.: Saliencygan: Deep learning semisupervised salient object detection in the fog of IoT. IEEE Trans. Ind. Inform. 16(4), 2667–2676 (2020)
67. Wang, S., Yan, Q., Chen, Z., Yang, B., Zhao, C., Conti, M.: Detecting android malware leveraging text semantics of network flows. IEEE Trans. Inform. Forensics Secur. 13(5), 1096–1109 (2018)

68. Wei, F., Li, Y., Roy, S., Ou, X., Zhou, W.: Deep ground truth analysis of current android malware. In: International Conference on Detection of Intrusions and Malware, and Vulnerability Assessment (DIMVA'17), pp. 252–276. Springer, Bonn (2017)

69. Wong, M., Lie, D.: Intellidroid: A targeted input generator for the dynamic analysis of android malware. In: Proceedings of the 2016 Symposium on Network and Distributed System Security (NDSS) (2016)

70. Xu, K., Li, Y., Deng, R.H., Chen, K.: Deeprefiner: Multi-layer android malware detection system applying deep neural networks. In: 2018 IEEE European Symposium on Security and Privacy (Euro SP), pp. 473–487 (2018)

71. Ye, Y., Hou, S., Chen, L., Lei, J., Wan, W., Wang, J., Xiong, Q., Shao, F.: Out-of-sample node representation learning for heterogeneous graph in real-time android malware detection. In: Twenty-Eighth International Joint Conference on Artificial Intelligence, IJCAI-19, pp. 4150–4156 (2019)

72. Yerima, S., Sezer, S., McWilliams, G., Muttik, I.: A new android malware detection approach using bayesian classification. In: Advanced Information Networking and Applications (AINA), 2013 IEEE 27th International Conference on, pp. 121–128. IEEE, Piscataway (2013)

73. Yerima, S.Y., Sezer, S., Muttik, I.: Android malware detection using parallel machine learning classifiers. In: Proceedings of the 2014 Eighth International Conference on Next Generation Mobile Apps, Services and Technologies, NGMAST '14, pp. 37–42. IEEE Computer Society (2014)

74. Yerima, S.Y., Sezer, S., Muttik, I.: High accuracy android malware detection using ensemble learning. IET Inform. Secur. **9**(6), 313–320 (2015)

75. Yuan, Z., Lu, Y., Xue, Y.: Droiddetector: android malware characterization and detection using deep learning. Tsinghua Sci. Technol. **21**(1), 114–123 (2016)

76. Zhang, X., Zhao, J., LeCun, Y.: Character-level convolutional networks for text classification. In: Proceedings of the 28th International Conference on Neural Information Processing Systems—Volume 1, NIPS'15, pp. 649–657. MIT Press, Cambridge (2015)

77. Zhang, Y., Wallace, B.C.: A sensitivity analysis of (and practitioners' guide to) convolutional neural networks for sentence classification. In: IJCNLP (2015)

78. Zhou, Y., Jiang, X.: Dissecting android malware: characterization and evolution. In: 2012 IEEE Symposium on Security and Privacy (SP), pp. 95–109. IEEE, Piscataway (2012)

79. Zhu, J., Wu, Z., Guan, Z., Chen, Z.: Api sequences based malware detection for android. In: 2015 IEEE 12th Intl Conf on Ubiquitous Intelligence and Computing and 2015 IEEE 12th Intl Conf on Autonomic and Trusted Computing and 2015 IEEE 15th Intl Conf on Scalable Computing and Communications and its associated Workshops (UIC-ATC-ScalCom), pp. 673–676 (2015)

80. Zonouz, S., Houmansadr, A., Berthier, R., Borisov, N., Sanders, W.: Secloud: a cloud-based comprehensive and lightweight security solution for smartphones. Comput. Secur. **37**, 215–227 (2013)

Artificial Intelligence Enabled Radio Signal Intelligence

Zhechen Zhu and Asoke K. Nandi

1 Introduction

Radio signal intelligence (RSI) provides an intelligent insight into the radio signal transmission when the observer is not a part of the intended message transmission system. Due to the nature of radio frequency (RF) signals and their transmission medium, they are easy to be intercepted or eavesdropped on. Therefore, RSI can be implemented as long as a RF receiver can be installed in the proximity of the RF signal transmission range. The intercepted signal contains much valuable information including the transmitted message, timing of communications, the amount of data transmitted and specifications of the communication devices. With proper processing technology, one can make great use of this information.

An obvious example of radio signal intelligence application can be found in electronic warfare [1] where adversary radio transmission signals can be intercepted to recover the transmitted message, predict adversary activity, identify adversary units, and generate interrupting RF signal (jamming signal). In civil applications, signal intelligence provides a powerful surveillance tool for the law enforcement considering the reliance on wireless communication of also everyone nowadays.

On the other hand, techniques developed for RSI including AMC can also be employed to improve the performance of cooperative communications systems. When the transmitter or the receiver is capable of sensing the network environment intelligently, optimization is possible to improve the link reliability, transmission throughput or more efficient usage of limited RF spectrum resources [2]. Specifi-

---

Z. Zhu
School of Electronic and Information Engineering, Soochow University, Suzhou, China
e-mail: zczhu@suda.edu.cn

A. K. Nandi (✉)
Department of Electronic and Electrical Engineering, Brunel University London, London, UK
e-mail: Asoke.Nandi@brunel.ac.uk

T. Sipola et al. (eds.), *Artificial Intelligence and Cybersecurity*,
https://doi.org/10.1007/978-3-031-15030-2_11

cally for AMC, when paired with adaptive modulation, the transmitter is provided the freedom to deploy different modulation methods according to the channel condition or throughput demand. In the meantime, the receiver can intelligently identify the modulation type of the transmitted signal using AMC, therefore deploy the correct demodulation method. The advantage of AMC over broadcasting the modulation information over the control channel is that the amount of spectrum resource consumed by control information is reduced and spectrum efficiency is improved.

1.1   History of AMC Development

Modulation classification first became a subject of interest in the military scene due to the increased usage of wireless communications systems. The initial classification method relied on trained engineers interpreting signal characters using dedicated instruments. As faster and more accurate classification was desired, people started to turn to machines for automated classification which signaled the birth of automatic modulation classification. The first publication on AMC accessible by the public was written by C. S. Weaver in the 1969 Stanford Electronics Laboratories technical report [3]. Wider research effort from public research space only started to occur during the 1980s [4, 5, 6, 7, 8, 9] probably due to the advancement in civilian wireless communication applications. In the 1990s, more researchers started to work on AMC solutions [10, 11, 12, 13, 14, 15, 16]. During this time two groups of approaches started to emerge, namely feature based and likelihood based. Such categorization is still well accepted among the current AMC researchers.

The feature based approaches revolve around expert features that is designed to encourage discrimination between signals modulated in different ways [17, 18]. Normally, a single feature is only capable of distinguishing between two or few modulation types. Classification can normally be achieved by using a threshold value for the feature that is carefully optimized. When more number of modulation candidates have to be considered, a multi-class classifier is required to classify all possible modulation types. Feature based methods are often lower in computational complexity and suitable for low power and low specification devices where real-time classification is required. However, channel interferences are often not accounted for during classification, resulting in significant performance degradation when higher level of interference is present.

The likelihood based approaches [19, 20, 21], on the other hand, utilize the statistical likelihood of the received signal modulated under different hypothesized modulation candidates to reach a classification decision. The evaluation of likelihood requires a signal model that describes the relationship between the transmitted signal, interferences and the received signal. When a matching signal model can be established and accurate channel parameters are available to describe the interference, the likelihood based approaches can provide the upper bound of classification accuracy. However, these conditions are difficult to meet. Wireless communication channels are often very complex with interference difficult to model mathematically while changing over time and relative movement of the transmitters and receivers. Even if a matching model is achievable, the channel parameters are difficult and time consuming to estimate [22]. Not to mention that the estimation accuracy of these parameters can affect the classification accuracy greatly.

1.2   Significance of Machine Learning in AMC

With the introduction of machine learning algorithms, it is quickly adopted for AMC making use of the feature based approach. Methods like artificial neural network removes the need for manually crafted decision tree for classification. Multi-class classification can be handled with a single classifier instead of multiple two-class classifiers. The decision thresholds no longer need to be tuned for each case as the network is able to automate the process during training. Neither was a matching channel model or accurate channel parameters needed to accomplish classification. However some ML based classification methods can make use of the knowledge about channels to optimize classification performance. Feature selection can also be automated with algorithms such as genetic algorithm. In addition, with a fix set of features, further optimization is possible by combining features using techniques such as genetic programming.

On the other hand, recent development in deep learning (DL) provides a new way of approaching the AMC problem. Expert features are no longer required by the classifier since the algorithms are capable of extracting features from raw signal samples. Moreover, feature extraction in DL is adaptive to the changing channel condition. Features are derived from a fixed mathematical model but learnt by the network from training samples. In addition, channel estimation is no longer required since the network only relies on the training signal to understand the character of the transmission channel.

2   System and Signal Models

Wireless communications systems exist in vast variety of compositions. However, majority of them can be represented in a unified and relatively simple structure. The real difficulty of the processing and analysis of wireless communication signals lies in the channel effects that the radio signal has to endure. Different electromagnetic environment induces different channel effects. There is no one single mathematical signal model that can provide accurate presentation of wireless transmission channels in all application scenarios. Therefore, in this section, the aim is to provide the readers with some basic understanding of a wireless communication system and some commonly used mathematical signal models in the field of AMC research.

2.1 AMC in Communications Systems

Any wireless communication systems comprises an end that transmits radio signal and another end that receives the signal [2]. As depicted in Fig. 1, the source data is first processed via some type of source encoding and encryption for compression and security purposes. The resulting binary stream is then processed by a channel encoder for better immunity against certain channel effects. The base-band signal is then to be modulated and transmitted at a higher radio frequency. The selection of modulation type at this step would impact the signal in its amplitude, frequency and phase. It is with the knowledge of how signal is modulated can we proceed to construct a scheme to identify the modulation type that is selected at this stage. Therefore, Sect. 2.2 is dedicated to the subject of signal modulations. Continuing with the flow of signal in the transmitting end, the modulated signal is shifted in frequency to facilitate multiplexing of different frequency channels. At this stage the signal is emitted via the antennas and transmitted through the wireless channel.

As acknowledged in the previous section, when signal is travelling through the wireless channel, various channel effects will distort the signal in its amplitude, frequency and phase. The initial composition of the signal samples established in the modulation step is then altered to different levels. Without channel effects, there will be no need for sophisticated AMC algorithms since the original signal composition is preserved and can be easily identified. The subject of channel effects and how its modeled mathematically will be discussed in detail in Sect. 2.3.

AMC algorithms reside at the receiving end of the communication system. The signal is first collected by the receiving antennas. The analogue signal is then sampled and converted to digital signal samples. The amplitude, frequency and phase information can be extracted from each signal sample. These aforementioned steps at the receiving end requires several pre-conditions. First, the signal must be received and sampled at a matching frequency as the transmitting end. The knowledge of the carrier frequency in a radio signal intelligence scenarios is often not available to the receiver. Therefore, signal detection techniques are required to obtain this information. In the meantime, while signal amplitude is easy to measure, the phase information of each signal samples requires additional steps to be extracted [17]. As shown in Fig. 2, to demodulate (a matching reverse process to modulation), the signal has to be hold before the modulation information is

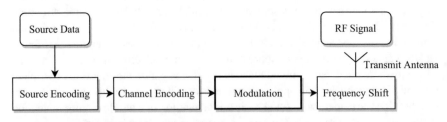

Fig. 1 The transmitting end of a wireless communication system

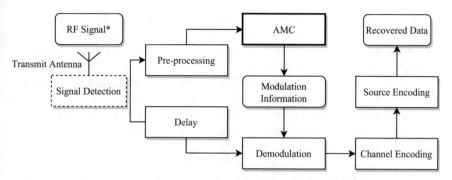

Fig. 2 The receiving end of a wireless communication system

recovered by the AMC module. In a cooperative communication system, this is unnecessary since the modulation information is agreed upon prior to system initialization. However, in a non-cooperative communication system, such information is not shared between the transmitter and receiver. Therefore, without an AMC module the signal will not be able to be demodulated and decoded correctly in the following steps, i. e. the data sent by the transmitter cannot be recovered.

2.2   Modulations

As stated in Sect. 2.1, the transmitter has the liberty to choose a modulation method for the signal to be transmitted. The number of modulations available for selection is quite large. Early analogue communication systems employed analogue modulations such amplitude modulation (AM) and frequency modulations (FM). Modern communication systems uses digital modulations almost exclusively. Among them, quadrature amplitude modulation (QAM), phase-shift keying (PSK) and pulse-amplitude modulation (PAM) are some of the most popular options. All modulation methods aim to make the radio signal more robust against interferences by shifting the base band (lower frequency) signal to a higher frequency. To achieve that, the modulator conveys the base band signal amplitude information in different aspects of a high frequency carrier signal. For example, AM alters the amplitude of the carrier frequency according to the amplitude of the input base band signal. Digital modulations such as QAM can embed information from base band signal in both the amplitude and phase of the carrier signal. Depending on how the amplitude and phase of the carrier signal is modulated, a single type of digital modulation can have different orders depending on the number of defined symbols. For QAM, there exists for example 4th order, 16th order and 64th order modulations. They are named as 4-QAM, 16-QAM and 64-QAM correspondingly. Different order of QAM can be generalized as M-QAM where "M" defines the order. Same applies to M-PSK and M-PAM modulations.

The selection of modulations depends on many factors. In a non-adaptive modulation system, a single modulation type is used and will not change over time. The modulation method is chosen when the communication system is designed. In an adaptive modulation system, the modulation method changes and can be selected based on channel conditions and the demand for transmission throughput. Generally speaking, lower order modulations are more robust against "noisy" channels but provides lower communication throughput. On the other hand, higher order modulations are more vulnerable against channel interferences while promising higher data rate when interferences are low.

In this chapter, the QAM and PSK modulations are discussed in details due to their popularity in modern wireless communication system designs and AMC research literature. Without learning the actual steps of manipulation the signal in a modulator, the modulation step can be easily grasped by understanding the relationship between the input data sequence and the output signal. Firstly, let us consider a binary data sequence. The modulation chosen has an order of M. For a QAM modulation if $M = 4$ then their exist 4 symbols where the data can be mapped to. If the signal is represented as complex values (as they normally are in communication system analysis), then the symbols and the subsequent modulated signal samples could be presented as complex valued data points. To visualize the symbols and the signal samples, a constellation plot is often used where the amplitude is taken as the radius and the phase taken as angular coordinate. An example of a constellation for a QPSK signal can be found in Fig. 3. The real part of the complex valued signal sample is often referred to as its in-phase component while the imaginary part being referred to as the quadrature component.

To map the data stream onto M symbols, different coding methods can be used. Among them Grey coding is one of the most popular one which minimized the bit error. With Grey coding, the data stream is broken down to blocks of $log_x M$ bits. All possible combination of the bits in a block is mapped to a unique symbol. The mapping is optimized to maximize the Euclidean distance between blocks which are different in one bit. Practically, one could easily convert the binary block into a modulation signal sample using reference equations from communication standards. For example, the 3GPP 5G physical channels and modulation specification defines the following modulation models [23]. BPSK signals are modulated as

$$s[n] = \frac{1}{\sqrt{2}}[(1 - 2b[n]) + j(1 - 2b[n])], \tag{1}$$

where $s[n]$ is the nth signal sample modulated from the nth binary block and $b[n]$ is the value of the nth bit in the binary stream. In the same fashion, the modulated signal sample can be calculated for QPSK as

$$s[n] = \frac{1}{\sqrt{2}}[(1 - 2b[2n]) + j(1 - 2b[2n + 1])], \tag{2}$$

16-QAM as

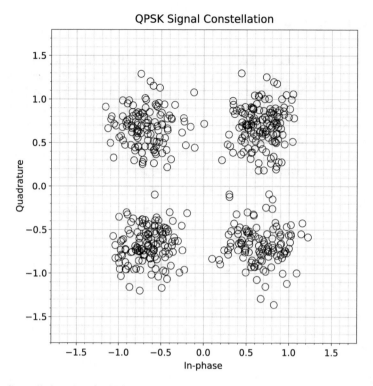

Fig. 3 Constellation plot of a QPSK signal at 10 dB

$$s[n] = \frac{1}{\sqrt{10}}\{(1 - 2b[4n])[2 - (1 - 2b[4n + 2])]$$
$$+j(1 - 2b[4n + 1])[2 - (1 - 2b[4n + 3])]\},$$

(3)

and 64-QAM as

$$s[n] = \frac{1}{\sqrt{42}}\{(1 - 2b[6n])[4 - (1 - 2b[6n + 2])[2 - (1 - 2b[6n + 4])]]$$
$$+j(1 - 2b[6n + 1])[4 - (1 - 2b[6n + 3])[2 - (1 - 2b[6n + 5])]]\}.$$

(4)

In simulated tests, the signal samples $s[n]$ are often treated as the transmitted signal foregoing the frequency shift and analogue-to-digital conversion. Although it does not reflect the real signal processing procedure in a real world system, it is still mostly valid for the purpose of AMC algorithm design.

2.3   Channel and Signal Models

The input signal for the modulation classifier can be very different from the signal that was transmitted due to interferences caused by the transmission channel. Although radio frequency transmission channels are affected by many environmental factors. It is still possible to create a simplified, unified and meaningful mathematical model for wireless signal analysis purposes. In this chapter, three major sources of interferences are considered, namely attenuation, additive noise and multi-path fading. As channel modeling is a rather complex subject, in this chapter, only the resulting signal model is presented with necessary explanations.

In most literatures on AMC to date, the received signal samples can be modeled generally as

$$r[n] = \alpha e^{j(2\pi f_o/f_c t + \theta_o)} s[n] + \omega[n]. \tag{5}$$

The positive scaler value $\alpha < 1$ denotes the attenuation of the radio frequency signal traveling over long distance. It is commonly considered to be inversely proportional to the square of the distance travelled. The frequency offset f_0 and phase offset θ_0 result from the change of relative position between the transmitter and the receiver (e.g. mobile communications) and signals reflecting of different surfaces in the transmission channel. Notably, the effect of frequency offset is determined by the ratio between the frequency offset and the carrier frequency. The last element in the equation above is the additive noise. Additive white Gaussian noise (AWGN) is often used under a more generally applicable assumption. However, non-Gaussian noises or impulsive noises has also been considered in AMC literatures [24, 25]. While the signal model is crucial for developing AMC algorithms, machine learning algorithms tend to make less use of the underlying relationship between the transmitted signal and received signal. In most cases, such relationship is learned by algorithms in training and does not need to be explicitly incorporated in the algorithm. On the other hand, if simulation tests are conducted, the signal model can provide an appropriate way of generating simulated test data. If more practical performance evaluation is required, there are also real world signal data available collected via physical experiments [26].

3   Expert Features

Raw signal samples are not easy to be understood. This applies to early human engineers who tried to identify signal modulation using instruments. More so for the computer algorithms that are designed to discriminate different modulated signals. To aid modulation classification in both scenarios, expert features were developed to summarize the characters of signals received. Different aspects of the signal can be used for formulate an expert feature. Same aspect of the signal can be formulated in different ways to create different expert features. Different expert features can be processed in different ways prior to be used for AMC. In this section, variety of expert features and feature processing techniques are discussed.

3.1 Spectral Features

As discussed in Sect. 2.2, the intrinsic difference between different modulation types is the way how information is conveyed in the carrier signal. An amplitude based modulation should exhibit a wider amplitude spectrum in its modulation signal with other aspects of the signal remaining largely consistent. A frequency based modulation on the other hand would introduce variance in the frequency spectrum without affecting the other aspects too much. It is not difficult to see that statistics on these signal spectrums should provide valuable information when distinguishing different signal modulations.

Fabrizi et al. [4], Chan and Gadbois [9], and Jovanovic et al. [10] laid the foundation for spectral signal features engineered for the classification of different modulations. Their work was later consolidated and updated by Nandi and Azzouz [17]. In this section, some of the key spectral features are examined and corresponding classification strategy is discussed.

The maximum value of the spectral power density γ_{max} of the received signal's instantaneous amplitude after normalization and centering is given by

$$\gamma_{max} = \max |DFT(A_{cn})|^2 / N, \tag{6}$$

where $DFT(-)$ is the discrete Fourier transform (DFT), A_{cn} is the normalized and centred instantaneous amplitude of the received signal r, and N is the total number signal samples. The normalization method can be found in [17].

The standard deviation of the absolute value of the non-linear component of the instantaneous phase σ_{ap} can be calculated as

$$\sigma_{ap} = \sqrt{\frac{1}{N_c} \left(\sum_{A_n[n] > A_t} \phi_{NL}^2[n] \right) - \left(\frac{1}{N_c} \sum_{A_n[n] > A_t} |\phi_{NL}[n]| \right)^2} \tag{7}$$

where N_c is the number of samples that meet the condition: $A_n[n] > A_t$. The variable A_t is a threshold value which filters out the low-amplitude signal samples because of their high sensitivity to noise. Term $\phi_{NL}[n]$ denotes the non-linear component of the instantaneous phase of the nth signal sample.

The standard deviation of the non-linear component of the direct instantaneous phase σ_{dp} is given by

$$\sigma_{dp} = \sqrt{\frac{1}{N_c}\left(\sum_{A_n[n]>A_t}\phi_{NL}^2[n]\right) - \left(\frac{1}{N_c}\sum_{A_n[n]>A_t}\phi_{NL}[n]\right)^2} \tag{8}$$

where all parameters remain the same as in the expression for σ_{ap}. However, it is noticeable that the absolute operation on the non-linear component of the instantaneous phase is removed.

An evaluation of the spectrum symmetry around the carrier frequency P, evaluated by

$$P = \frac{P_L - P_U}{P_L + P_U} \tag{9}$$

where P_L and P_U can be calculated correspondingly as

$$P_L = \sum_{n=1}^{f_{cn}}|X_c[n]|^2 \tag{10}$$

and

$$P_U = \sum_{n=1}^{f_{cn}}|X_c[n + f_{cn} + 1]|^2 \tag{11}$$

$X_c[n]$ is the Fourier transform of the signal $x_c[n]$. $(f_{cn} + 1)$ is the sample number corresponding to the carrier frequency f_c. f_s is the sampling rate. f_{cn} can be calculated as

$$f_{cn} = \frac{f_c N}{f_s} - 1 \tag{12}$$

The standard deviation of the absolute value of the normalized and centred instantaneous amplitude of the signal samples σ_{aa} is given by

$$\sigma_{aa} = \sqrt{\frac{1}{N}\left(\sum_{n=1}^{N}A_{cn}^2[n]\right) - \left(\frac{1}{N}\sum_{n=1}^{N}|A_{cn}[n]|\right)^2}. \tag{13}$$

The standard deviation of the absolute value of the normalized and centred instantaneous frequency σ_{af} is given by

$$\sigma_{af} = \sqrt{\frac{1}{N_c}\left(\sum_{A_n[n]>A_t} f_N^2[n]\right) - \left(\frac{1}{N_c}\sum_{A_n[n]>A_t} |f_N[n]|\right)^2} \qquad (14)$$

where the centred instantaneous frequency f_m is normalized by the sampling frequency f_s such that

$$f_N[n] = f_m[n]/f_s. \qquad (15)$$

The instantaneous frequency is centred using the frequency mean.

The standard deviation of the normalized and centred instantaneous amplitude σ_a is given by

$$\sigma_a = \sqrt{\frac{1}{N_c}\left(\sum_{A_n[n]>A_t} a_{cn}^2[n]\right) - \left(\frac{1}{N_c}\sum_{A_n[n]>A_t} a_{cn}[n]\right)^2}. \qquad (16)$$

The kurtosis of the normalized and centred instantaneous amplitude μ_{42}^a is given by

$$\mu_{42}^a = \frac{E\left\{A_{cn}^4[n]\right\}}{\left\{E\left\{A_{cn}^2[n]\right\}\right\}^2}. \qquad (17)$$

The kurtosis of the normalized and centred instantaneous frequency μ_{42}^a is given by

$$\mu_{42}^f = \frac{E\left\{f_N^4[n]\right\}}{\left\{E\left\{f_N^2[n]\right\}\right\}^2}. \qquad (18)$$

Each of these features can be used individually to distinguish between two types of modulations using an optimized threshold value. When classification of multiple modulations is required, a decision tree could be formed to reach a final classification decision through a chain of feature value evaluations. Figure 4 demonstrates how various analogue and digital modulations could be classification using the combination of spectral features and a decision tree classifier. More detailed explanation to the process can be found in [17] where the calculation of thresholds is also included. For a machine learning algorithm, it is much easier to devise a classification strategy and thresholds if needed. Although the machine is capable of learning to make use of the features, it is still valuable for the designer to understand the properties of these features.

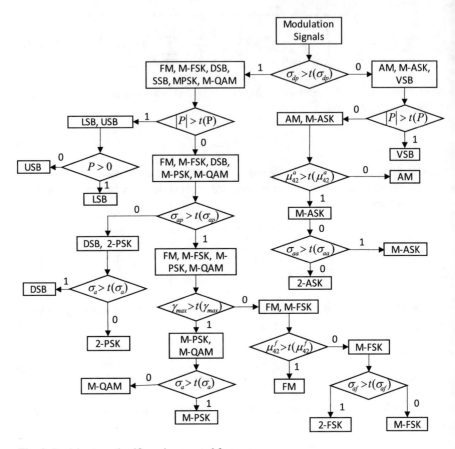

Fig. 4 Decision tree classifier using spectral features

3.2 High-Order Statistics Features

In the previous section, eight spectral features are presented along with some basic information regarding how they could be used for AMC. Taking a closer look at Fig. 4, it is not difficult to see that the modulations being classified are mostly analogue and digital modulation types that are fundamentally different in the way they modulated the carrier signal to convey messages. However, in modern communication systems where digital modulations are used primarily, the choice of modulations often differs in their order instead of their type. For example, QAM being a modulation type with high spectral efficiency, can be adopted for in different number of orders namely 4-QAM, 16-QAM, 64-QAM, etc. They are of the same type of modulation (QAM) but different in orders which also means that they cannot be demodulated in the same way. Thus, in this scenario, an AMC solution needs to be capable of distinguishing between modulations of the same type but different orders. It is for this reason, feature engineering in AMC has look towards high-order statistics for a solution. As of now, high-order moments and cumulants of the complex valued signal samples has been tested thoroughly and been established as some of the most effective features in solving this problem.

Hipp was the first to adopt the third-order moment of the demodulated signal amplitude as a modulation-classification feature [5]. However the need for demodulated signal does not fit the intended use case of radio signal intelligence. Soliman and Hsue later extended upon Hipp's work and proposed high-order moments of the signal phase for the classification of M-PSK signals [12]. The calculation of the kth order moment of the signal phase is defined as shown in Eq. 19.

$$\mu_k(\boldsymbol{r}) = \frac{1}{N} \sum_{n=1}^{N} \phi^k(n) \tag{19}$$

where $\phi(n)$ is the phase of the nth signal sample. It is concluded that the moments are a monotonically increasing function with respect to the order of the M-PSK modulation. Thus, high-order M-PSK modulations have higher moment values, which provide the condition for the classification of M-PSK modulations of different orders.

Azzouz and Nandi first proposed the the kurtosis of the normalized-centred instantaneous amplitude μ_{42}^a and the kurtosis of the normalized-centred instantaneous frequency μ_{42}^f for the classification of M-ASK and M-FSK modulations [15]. The calculation for each feature is listed in Eqs. 17 and 18 correspondingly. Hero and Hadinejad-Mahram generalized the moment-based features to include the high-order moment of signal amplitude, phase, and frequency [27] by evaluating the kth moment of the complex valued signal. The definition of such high-order moment is given as

$$\mu_{xy}(\boldsymbol{r}) = \frac{1}{N} \sum_{n=1}^{N} r^x[n] \cdot r^{*y}[n] \tag{20}$$

where $x + y = k$ and $r^*[n]$ is the complex conjugate of $r[n]$. The real and imaginary part of the signal is its in-phase and quadrature component following the definition in Sect. 2. Such features are capable of not only aiding the classification of one type of digital modulation in different orders but also digital modulations, such as M-FSK, M-ASK, M-PSK, or M-QAM.

Besides high-order moments, high-order cumulants are another set of powerful statistical features to provide discriminative ability toward multiple digital modulation types of different orders. Swami and Sadler proposed the second and fourth-order cumulant of the complex-valued signal as features for the classification of M-PAM, M-PSK and M-QAM modulations [18].

The second-order cumulants can be expressed in two different ways as

$$C_{20} = E\left\{r^2[n]\right\} \tag{21}$$

$$C_{21} = E\left\{|r[n]|^2\right\} \tag{22}$$

The fourth-order cumulants can be expressed in three different ways using different placements of conjugation as in Eqs. 23, 24 and 25,

$$C_{40} = \text{cum}(r[n], r[n], r[n], r[n]) \tag{23}$$

$$C_{41} = \text{cum}\left(r[n], r[n], r[n], r^*[n]\right) \tag{24}$$

$$C_{42} = \text{cum}\left(r[n], r[n], r*[n], r^*[n]\right) \tag{25}$$

where $cum(\cdot)$ is joint cumulant function defined by Eq. 26.

$$\text{cum}(w, x, y, z) = E(wxyz) - E(wx)E(yz) - E(wy)E(xz) - E(wz)E(xy) \tag{26}$$

Meanwhile, the estimation of the second and fourth cumulants is achieved by using the following equations.

$$\hat{C}_{20} = \frac{1}{N}\sum_{n=1}^{N} r^2[n] \tag{27}$$

$$\hat{C}_{21} = \frac{1}{N}\sum_{n=1}^{N} |r[n]|^2 \tag{28}$$

$$\hat{C}_{40} = \frac{1}{N}\sum_{n=1}^{N} r^4[n] - 3\hat{C}_{20} \tag{29}$$

$$\hat{C}_{41} = \frac{1}{N}\sum_{n=1}^{N} r^3[n]r*[n] - 3\hat{C}_{20}\hat{C}_{21} \tag{30}$$

$$\hat{C}_{42} = \frac{1}{N}\sum_{n=1}^{N} |r[n]|^4 - \left|\hat{C}_{20}\right|^2 - 2\hat{C}_{21}^2 \tag{31}$$

Table 1 Theoretical values of high-order cumulants for noise-free signals

	C_{20}	C_{21}	C_{40}	C_{41}	C_{42}
2-PAM	1.0000	1.0000	−2.0000	−2.0000	−2.0000
4-PAM	1.0000	1.0000	−1.3600	−1.3600	−1.3600
8-PAM	1.0000	1.0000	−1.2381	−1.2381	−1.2381
BPSK	1.0000	1.0000	−2.0000	−2.0000	−2.0000
QPSK	0.0000	1.0000	1.0000	0.0000	−1.0000
8-PSK	0.0000	1.0000	0.0000	0.0000	−1.0000
4-QAM	0.0000	1.0000	1.0000	0.0000	−1.0000
16-QAM	0.0000	1.0000	−0.6800	0.0000	−0.6800
64-QAM	0.0000	1.0000	−0.6191	0.0000	−0.6191

To provide some insight into how these features could be selected and used for the classification of different modulations, theoretical values of thess features for noise-free signals are listed in Table 1.

3.3 Cyclostationary Analysis-Based Features

Gardner first established the cyclostationary analysis techniques to utilize the periodic properties of a cyclostationary process [28]. The application of cyclostationary analysis in AMC is also proposed by Gardner [8] exploiting the difference between the cyclic spectrum patterns of different modulations. Detailed implementation can be found in an article by Ramkumar [29]. It is understood that the cyclic features are well suited for the classification of lower-order digital modulations. However, high-order modulations are easier to be distinguished with high-order moments and cumulants.

4 Machine Learning Based classifiers

Being a pattern recognition problem, AMC is well suited as an application for machine learning algorithms. Evidently, the development of AMC solutions has always evolved with the advancement of machine learning techniques. While unlikely to be the most popular option for real world deployment, machine learning has been the driving force behind recent development in AMC research. As establishing the fundamentals of various machine learning is not the object of this chapter, the main focus is on the implementation and performance comparison of difference techniques. Comments on the long-term and newly-found challenges for the ML based AMC solutions is also discussed at the end.

4.1 Signal Preprocessing

The implementation of a ML based AMC solution begins with signal preprocessing. Some of the preprocessing is universal for all classifier. The rest is unique to certain ML based method.

4.1.1 Normalization

Normalization is normally required by any type of classifiers. After passing through the transmission channel, attenuation of the signal strength is inevitable. The direct results is the amplitude of the signal being scaled down. If a classifier is to process the signal without the awareness of the attenuation, classification is likely to fail due to the condition these classifiers were designed under. Most classifier assume unite power for signal strength. Thus before feeding the signals into the classifier, it is necessary to scale the signal strength back up to unit power. On the other hand, certain level of DC offset may be added to the transmitted signal due to the channel interference or interference from the transceiver circuit. Such offset in signal amplitude is also detrimental to the classification performance. Therefore, it is also important to normalize the signal to have zero mean values for its in-phase and quadrature components. As the signal samples can be treated as complex valued numbers, the normalization process can be performed on its real component $\Re(r[n])$and imaginary component $\Im(r[n])$ separately as.

$$r_I[n] = \frac{\Re(r[n]) - \overline{\Re(r)}}{\sigma(\Re(r))}$$
$$r_Q[n] = \frac{\Im(r[n]) - \widetilde{s(r)}}{\sigma(\Im(r))} \qquad (32)$$

where $\Re(r)$ and $\Im(r)$ are the mean of the real and imaginary part of the signal samples with $\theta(\Re(r))$ and $\theta(\Im(r))$ being the standard deviation of the the signal samples. It is worth noting that the normalization process affects not only the transmitted signals but also the additive noises. To provide a more consistent way of quantifying the noise level, signal-to-noise (SNR) radio is used in most AMC related studies.The SNR in dB is defined as

$$\text{SNR} = 10 \log_{10} \frac{P(s)}{P(\omega)} \text{dB} \qquad (33)$$

where $P(s)$ and $P(\omega)$ represents the power of the transmitted signal and the additive noise correspondingly. Performance results over different SNR values will be used as a key factor in the evaluation of different AMC algorithm later in this chapter.

4.1.2 Spatial Representation

For deep learning algorithm such as CNN, two-dimensional matrices are commonly required as the input date format. However, the signal samples are one-dimensional array of scaler values. A fitting spatial representation of the signals is required to transform the signal samples into a fitting format for the network. There are two popular approaches to this transformation.

The first approaches creates a two-dimensional matrix by separating the in-phase and quadrature component of the signal samples [30]. As discussed in Sect. 2 each signal sample $r[n]$ could be expressed as a complex value with the real part $\Re(r[n])$ being the in-phase component and the imaginary part $\Im(r[n])$ being the quadrature component. For a signal with N number of signal samples, the resulting $2 \times N$ input matrix $\mathbf{x}$ after transformation can be expressed as

$$\mathbf{x} = \begin{bmatrix} \Re(r[1]) & \Re(r[2]) & \ldots & \Re(r[N]) \\ \Im(r[1]) & \Im(r[2]) & \ldots & \Im(r[N]) \end{bmatrix}. \tag{34}$$

This is a fairly easy way of creating a spatial representation of the signal. However, it does encourage effective feature extraction from the raw signal input. Since the samples are assumed to be independent and identically distributed (i.i.d), there is no obvious correlation between data points column-wise. In the meantime, the in-phase and quadrature components of each signal are often assumed to be independently distributed under normal conditions. Therefore, the row-wise correlation also does not provide much meaning for information for the network extract signal characters from. For this type of spatial representation, a kernel wider column-wise is needed to find meaningful patterns in the given signal.

A better approach of representation the signal spatially draws inspiration from the signal constellation. As can be seen from Fig. 3, the signal constellation clearly exhibits the spatial relationship between the signal samples and the symbol mapping of the underlying modulation scheme. However, a signal constellation is not a two-dimensional matrix. It is scatter plot generated with the in-phase component of each signal as its X axis coordinate and the quadrature component as the Y axis coordinate. On the given two-dimensional plane there is only binary representation of the signal where 1 corresponding to existence of signal sample at this location and 0 corresponding to non-existence of signal samples. To acquire a two-dimensional matrix, transformation is required to achieve the intended spatial representation.

One straightforward way of accomplishing this transformation is simply to take the plotted constellation as a bitmap matrix [31], where the pixels become elements in the two-dimensional array. However, there are several shortcomings to this method. First, the markers style and size of the scatter plot would introduce irrelevant information to the matrix. Second, the bitmap matrix is still a binary value matrix. Thus, when markers from two or more signal samples overlap with each other, such denser signal distribution character cannot be represented with a binary value. Meaningful information is lost in this case. Third, when certain input matrix size is required by the network, the bitmap needs to be resized. Depending

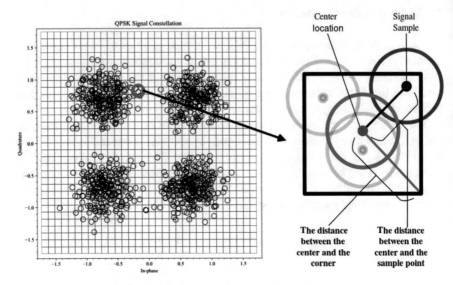

Fig. 5 Segmentation of the signal constellation for spatial representation

on the resizing approach, meaning for information can also be lost. To overcome these shortcomings, a distribution density based spectral transformation provides a better alternative [32]. Assume a signal with N number of sample, the goal of the transformation is to convert the one-dimensional array of complex vales into a matrix with I number of rows and J number of columns. The matrix element value at ith row and jth column representing the signal distribution density value at the corresponding location can be calculated as

$$G(i, j) = \frac{1}{N} \sum_{k=1}^{K(i,j)} \frac{d - \sqrt{(x(j) - \Re r(k))^2 + (y(i) - \Im r(k))^2}}{d}. \tag{35}$$

As shown in Fig. 5, the constellation plot is first segmented by a $(I+1) \times (J+1)$ grid with each segment representing an element in the matrix. The edge of the grid could be determined by the furthest sample from the origin. $x(j)$ is X axis coordinate of the jth column and $y(i)$ is the Y axis coordinate of the ith row. $K(i, j)$ is the numbers of signal samples located with the $(i, j)th$ segment. d is the distance between the center and the corner in each segment. The more number of samples are occupied in the segment and the closer samples are to the set center point, the greater value can be obtained. To visualized the end result, matrix values can be normalized to gray scale values. Figure 6 shows the converted matrix value form different modulations in gray scale.

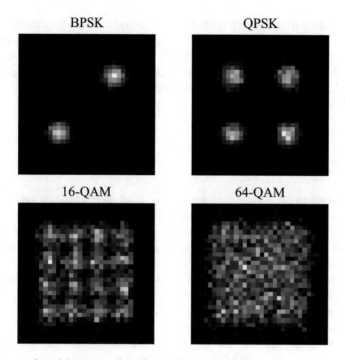

Fig. 6 Converted spatial representation of signal density distribution

4.1.3 Temporal Representation

Some network types such recurrent neural network are capable of handling sequential data inputs directly. Considering the signal samples are time-series data arranged sequentially, a temporal representation of signal for such networks seem most fitting. The actual conversion of signal for temporal representation is always identical to the spatial representation depicted in Eq. 34. However, instead of feeding the entire matrix into the network as a data block, it is fed as a column by column stream where a single sample is processed one at a time. Other type of temporal representation is also available in the form of a spectrograms where the signal spectrum acquired by FFT is fed to the network on sample timing at a time sequentially. The temporal representation alone does not always provide the best classification performance due to the same shortcoming of the first spatial representation approach in Sect. 4.1.2. Additional temporal representation could be obtained by taking the amplitude and phase of the signal samples. Similar to the handling of in-phase and quadrature components, amplitude and phase of the signal samples could also be arrange in a $2 \times N$ matrices matching the dimension of the matrix for in-phase and quadrature components [33, 34].

The temporal representation can provide input data for recurrent neural networks and form an AMC solution solely with this combination. However, when implemented together with the spatial representation it is able to provide additional temporal information to the classifier and improve the classification performance to various degrees [35]. One major benefit of a temporal representation based method is that classifier does not need to wait for an entire block to be processed before make a classification decision. If processing time is low enough, real-time online AMC decision make is possible with this approach.

4.2   Feature Based Methods

Features listed in Sect. 3 are very intuitive to work in conjugation with most ML algorithms to construct an AMC solution. Since the features have been engineered to encourage discrimination between different modulations, the goal of a ML algorithms is to select the proper features, enhance the selected features, create a feature space, and form a rule for classification.

For feature selection, genetic algorithm (GA) has been proven to be an effective measure [36, 37]. In GA, a set of preliminarily selected features are first mapped to a binary string of genetic encoding as demonstrated in Fig. 7. When a feature is coded with a value 1, it is selected for use during classification. A value 0 means that it is not selected. The algorithm starts with a randomly generated pool of binary string where each binary string represents a subset of selected features. Then each subset of features are used in the intended classifier to evaluate their performance. Based on the performance, better subsets of features are selected for reproduction, i.e., creating new subsets of features. The reproduction operations include crossover of two binary strings and mutation of a single binary string. The process is then repeated to evolve continuously the selection of features until the termination condition is meet. In the end, the subset of features that provides the best classification performance among all the tested subsets is used as the final selected features. Utilizing feature selection, a large pool of features could be considered without increased dimensionality of the feature space. Thus, a lower complexity classifier could be employed to accomplish the classification task.

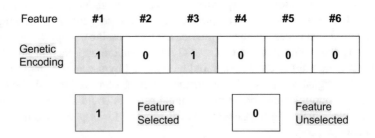

Fig. 7   Genetic encoding for GA based feature selection

Fig. 8 Tree structure in the
genetic genetic programming

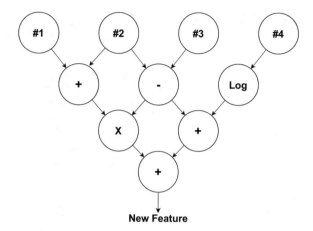

New Feature

For feature enhancement, it is essentially a symbolic regression problem. Among all the symbolic regression approaches genetic programming (GP) has been one of the best recognized options for AMC [38]. GP allows for nonlinear combination of features using an expression defined by a tree structure. As illustrated in Fig. 8, four features are selected for feature enhancement. The tree structure takes the four expert features as inputs. After several stages of mathematical operation, the tree structure produces a single output as the new feature. Similarly to GA, GP starts with a pool of randomly generated tree structures. At each generation, each tree structure/feature combination is evaluated for its AMC classification performance. The classification accuracy provided by each tree structure is assigned as the fitness value for it. Trees with higher fitness are selected for reproduction. In GP, the number of reproduction operations are much richer than the ones in GA. Besides crossover and mutation, GP can also employ combination of two tree structures and deletion of three branches in a single tree providing higher degree of freedom when controlling the evolution process. In the end a single new feature or a small set of new features can be passed on to the classifier as enhance feature sets. The enhanced feature inherits and improves the discrimination ability of the expert features while significantly reducing the feature space dimensions. However, the training process of GP is fairly complex and makes it a better matched with lower complex classifiers for improve training efficiency.

Creation of feature space and rule for classification are often embodied in the same algorithm. Artificial neural network (ANN) based AMC classifiers, for example, maps input features to several arbitrary target values each corresponding to a modulation candidate. Azzouz and Nandi were the first to propose an ML based modulation classifier using ANNs in 1997 [39]. Classification can be accomplish by measuring the difference between the network output and each target values [40]. The actual implementation of an ANN based AMC classified can be summarized by Fig. 9. Other forms of ANN classifiers has also been proposed [41]. Among them, a combination of decision tree for analogue modulations and ANN for digital

Fig. 9 ANN based AMC
classifier

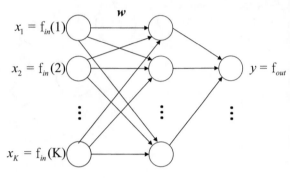

Fig. 10 SVM based AMC
classifier

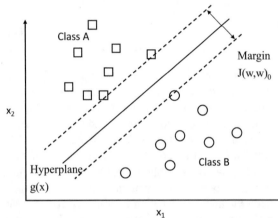

modulations has been proven to provide high efficiency and accuracy when both
classes of modulations are in the candidate pool [42].

For each signal, features f_{in} are calculated and feed to the network as input **x**.
For each modulation candidate, different target values are assigned as the targeted
output y. By training the network weights **w**, signals of specific modulation type
should produce network output value close to the assigned target value. Thus
classification can be achieved by measuring the difference between the output of
the network and each target values.

Another common ML based AMC classifier is the support vector machine (SVM)
[43]. With a given feature space, SVM is able to find the optimal boundary between
signal sample modulated in different ways. An example of two-class AMC using
two features is given in Fig. 10. The squares and circles represents signals in two
different modulations. The X and Y axis values of each sample correspond to the
the value of each feature. Jointly they create a two-dimensional feature space with
scattered data points. During training, reference signals from two modulation types
are placed in the feature space. A hyperplane $g(x)$ is trained iteratively to maximize
the margin $J(w, w_0)$ between two different class of signals. Once training ended
upon meeting the termination condition, the final hyperplane is used for classifying

new signals placed in the feature space. The common SVM implementation is not well suited as multi-class AMC classifier. However, multi-class implementation of the SVM classifier is available but not very intuitive.

4.3 Deep Learning Based Methods

Emergence of deep learning (DL) in the computer vision space has provided renewed interest for ML based AMC solutions [44]. One of the major reason why DL based AMC solutions are so popular nowadays is its ability to process raw signal inputs without the need for manually crafted expert features. This allows for the network to learn and extra features best suited for the given signal. As discussed in Sect. 3, expert features have fixed formulas independent of varying channel condition. They provide theoretical separation between different types of modulations. However, the actual feature values of signal in different channel conditions are likely to deviate from the theoretical value affecting the performance of these expert features. The features on their own is not designed to compensate for the change interferences. DL based approaches on the other is capable of adapting to the the changing characters of the training signal leading to improved robustness in classification performance. In this section, some of the most popular DL network implementations are discussed.

4.3.1 Convolutional Neural Network

Convolutional neural network has dominated the field of computer vision in recent years. Different network structures such LeNet, AlexNet, and GoogleNet have managed to achieve excellent performance in different image recognition tasks. Inspired by this this trend, efforts started to be made to apply these mature network structures in AMC. Among them AlexNet was the first to be adopted due to its better balanced classification accuracy and computational efficiency among the aforementioned structures. An illustration of a CNN based AMC solution is provide in Fig. 11. The complex valued one-dimensional signal sample arrays are first transformed to a spatial representation. For example, the two-dimensional distribution density spectral image in Sect. 4.1.2. It is worth mentioning that depending on the input size requirement of the network the grid size in the spatial transformation need to be adjusted accordingly. During training signals of each modulation type is indexed associated with the output of the CNN network. There are two major components in the CNN model. The first one includes multiple convolutional layers and pooling layers. The role of the convolutional layer is to extract different features from the signal. The second component is the fully connected layer. The goal of the fully connected layer is to formulate an output that reflects the likelihood of the input signal coming from each modulation candidates. The classification is accomplished in the classification layer where probabilities of all modulation candidate have a sum

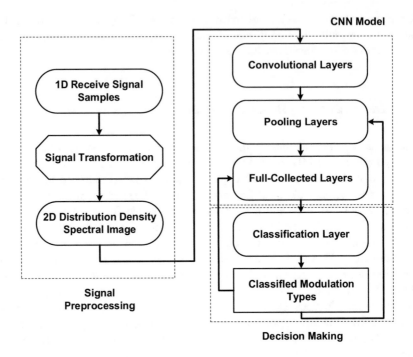

Fig. 11 CNN based AMC Solution

of 1. In the end, the modulation candidate with the highest probability associated is selected as the classification decision.

Although state-of-the-art network designs like AlexNet is capable of providing good classification performance. Such designs are mostly introduced for image processing purposes. Despite the signal preprocessing producing image-like matrices as inputs for the network. It is still a unique problem that is different from common image processing tasks. As CNN networks are highly configurable, network structures, key components and parameters can all be tuned to achieve better classification performance, i.e., higher accuracy and higher computational efficiency. For the network structure, the number of convolutional layers can be much smaller than the one for a conventional image recognition task.

Since the distributions of signal samples around each modulation symbol exhibit similar pattern, a convolutional layer to extract such local distribution feature should be included toward the beginning of the chain of layers. Such convolutional layer helps to identify possible locations of the underlying modulation symbols. Meanwhile, due to the predefined symbol mapping the spatial relationship of the symbol locations are consistent under different conditions. Therefore, an additional convolutional layer to extract the symbol mapping feature is useful for associating the mapping with the corresponding modulation scheme. Figure 12 shows an example of optimized network structure for AMC applications. It is worth noting

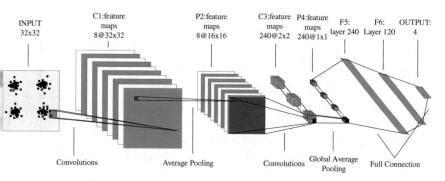

Fig. 12 CNN network structure for AMC

that such a network structure is much lower in complexity due to the reduce number of convolutional layers. Yet, it should still be able to provide adequate classification accuracy under commonly assumed AWGN channels. If other channel interference is present, more layers might be needed to learn extra features for improved robustness. For the rest of the network layers, there is no clear rule for setting the parameters. It vary from different modulation candidate pools and candidate modulations with difference difficulty to classify.

Due to the randomness of signal samples, batch normalization is preferred in most cases for improved training efficiency. Average pooling is favoured over other pooling methods for the same reason. Outlaying signal samples could create misinformation for the subsequent layers. Averaging the feature map helps to smooth out regions of abnormal distribution and also provide more information to the next layer. In terms of activation function, Tanh is recommended since negative input also contains meaningful information which contributes towards better classification accuracy. For the optimizer, Adam [45] provides several benefits that has received general recognition but also ones that improves the training efficiency for AMC specifically. The first is to do with the time-variant nature of the communication signals. Although modulated signal follows a generally fixed distribution pattern. Time-variant channel interferences such as phase offset could introduce shift in the distribution that could cause confusion for traditional gradient descent approaches. Moreover, at high SNR sample distribution is rather concentrated around the modulation symbols. In this case sparse gradient can occur and hinder the effectiveness of the training process.

4.3.2 Recurrent Neural Network

Recurrent neural network (RNN) differs from all the previously discussed ML algorithms that it processes temporal sequence instead of batch data. It provides several unique benefits that is unavailable from the other algorithms. It is still a relatively new territory for AMC development with handful of publication on

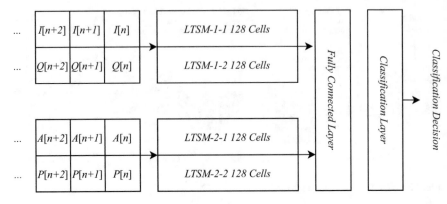

Fig. 13 LSTM network structure for AMC

the subject. The implementation of RNN among them are rather similar. First and foremost, the long-short-term memory (LSTM) is the obvious choice for architecture [46]. It cannot only processes temporal sequential data but also handle signal of varying length. The nature of the communication signal determines the sporadic distribution character between different time-series samples. Vanishing and exploding gradient, which can be solved by LSTM, are imminent problems in AMC. For the same reason, longer signal with more samples are normally required to establish discrimination between differently modulated signals which LSTM is better suited to handel. A common LSTM model is presented in Fig. 13.

The model takes two matrices as input for each channels of LSTM network. The top matrix with I an Q elements is the temporal sequential representation of signal in-phase and quadrature components as demonstrated in Sect. 4.1.3. The bottom matrix with A and P elements is the temporal sequentially representation of the signal amplitude and phase. Two LSTM channels are designated to handle each input matrix separately. Each channel of LSTM network consists of two layers each consisting 128 cells. A bigger number of cells are required due to the sparse correlation between the input signal samples. To achieve good classification accuracy, the number is should at least be greater than the highest order number of the modulation candidate. However, high cell numbers are also taxing on computational resources. The classification performance is not very sensitive to the other network parameters. Conventional network parameters selection guidelines could be used. The outputs of the dual-channel LSTM network is fed into a fully connected network to combine the features learned from different channel. A classifier at the end of the network chain provides the classification decision just as in the CNN network structure.

4.4 Performance Comparison

Selecting a ML algorithm for AMC can be difficult. The sheer number of ML algorithms available is staggering. Even limiting the range of algorithms to the ones that have been adapted and tested for AMC does not always yield a straightforward option. Therefore, to provide a general sense of performance metrics of different ML algorithms, this section is dedicated to the performance comparison of the aforementioned ML algorithms. Instead of cramping large amount quantitative results in this section, a qualitative summery of the performance character of each method is provided. It should provide some general sense as how these methods stack up against each other. Please be reminded that there is no single ML algorithm that is superior to every other algorithms. Selection of ML algorithm depends on the modulation pool, channel condition, computational power, accuracy requirement and processing time limit.

Table 2 provides an overview of the performance metrics for the ML algorithms discussed in this chapter. In case of AMC capability, expert feature based methods relies on the modulation discrimination capability of the features to achieve successful classification. Most of the commonly used modulation types have matching features in place for differentiation. However, if new modulation types are introduced to the pool, manual crafting of new features are needed to guarantee optimal classification performance. It then exceeds the scope of ML algorithms. Classifiers such as SVM supports only two-class classification. It can provide quick implementation for modulation pool with only two members. However, classification of multiple modulations requires extra setup. Deep learning based methods are better suited for cases in which no expert feature is available or the existing features fail to meet the required classification accuracy. If realtime online classification is required, the LSTM algorithm provides the only option within the scope of this chapter.

Classification accuracy is certainly the most important performance metric for an AMC solution. Although higher percentage of successful classification is a clear indication of the classification accuracy. There are other aspects that need to be considered. First, the accuracy under difference level of channel interferences may render classifier adequate for one application scenario but inadequate for another. Second, different algorithm require different size of signal samples to achieve optimal classification accuracy. Third, some algorithms can provide balanced accuracy for all members of the modulation pool while other algorithms have biased accuracy for different modulation types. Among the listed algorithms, CNN provides the best classification accuracy in most cases. While ANN and SVM can provide good classification accuracy with lower level of channel interference. Feature selection and enhancement using GA and GP can sometimes improve the accuracy of ANN and SVM classifier. However the improvement is limited. The LSTM provides subpar classification accuracy in noisy channels while high accuracy is still achievable in clear channels.

Table 2 Performance comparison between AMC based on different ML algorithms

Algorithms	Preprocessing	AMC Capability	Accuracy	Complexity
GA Feature select	Expert Features	Feature and classifier dependent	Trivial improvement	**Training:** Moderate **Testing:** Reduced
GP Feature enhance	Expert Features	Feature and classifier dependent	Significant improvement	**Training:** Complex **Testing:** Reduced
ANN	Expert Features	Feature dependent	Good	**Training:** Moderate **Testing:** Simple
SVM	Expert Features	Feature dependent Two-class only	Good	**Training:** Moderate **Testing:** Simple
CNN	Spatial Representation	Universal	Best	**Training:** Very complex **Testing:** Moderate
LSTM	Temporal Representation	Universal Online	Mediocre	**Training:** Moderate **Testing:** Simple

Computational complexity is another key aspect of AMC performance. Depending on the hardware that the algorithm is deployed on and the imposed processing time limit, simpler or more complex algorithm can be selected accordingly. For ML based AMC solution the matter is a bit more complex since a training stage is required to form the final classifier. ANN, SVM, and LSTM are mostly quick to train with CNN needing significantly more computational resource to complete the training process. GA and GP adds additional complexity to the training process. However, the amount of complexity added depends largely on the classifier that is used to evaluate the feature selections and combinations. When trained models are used for actual classification of unknown signals, the complexity is often trivial at the testing stage compared against the complexity of the training process and acceptable for most hardware platforms. Among different ML based AMC solutions and their specific design choices (e.g. network depth), the complexity in the training stage may vary significantly. However, once the classifier optimization is completed, the resulting mathematical models for the input signal and the output classification decision are rather straightforward and quick to solve. Therefore, the complexity difference during the actual classification task is fairly marginal. If long offline training time is not an issue, it is always favorable to choose the ML algorithm that provides the highest classification accuracy. For time critical system, algorithms such as LSTM provide a unique benefit of online per-sample processing.

5 Conclusion

Radio signal intelligence is a topic of wide spectrum with great potential for machine learning applications. This chapter focuses on using automatic modulation classification as an example of how ML can be implemented for the processing of wireless communication signals. Some basic understanding of communication systems and mathematical modeling of the signals is enough for a novice to understand the problem, data format, and performance metrics. The expert features are straightforward to implement and provides an easy transition between wireless signals and data that is easily understandable by ML algorithms. The ability to extract features from raw sample provided by deep learning method forgoes even the need for expert features. It is clear that different ML algorithms are suited for different application scenarios of AMC. Despite all the benefits ML algorithm promises, there still remains some challenges before wider adoption could be achieved in the real-world application scenarios.

5.1 Remaining Challenges

First, for supervised learning methods, labeled training data is not always available to the system. In cooperative communication systems, labeled training data could be transmitted in the form of pilot symbols during system initialization. In non-cooperative communications systems, training signal with known modulation types must be acquired prior to training in some ways. Additionally, ML algorithms require a large amount of training data to achieve expected classification performance.

Second, the training process could be time consuming and demand high computation power. Most communication systems do not have high computation power compared against other application scenarios of ML algorithms. Often signal processing is also expected to be completed in real-time. This is also why communications engineers and researchers raise questions regarding the practicality of implemented ML based AMC solution in common communications systems. Regarding this issue it is important to point out that the computation intensive and time consuming tasks only happens in the training stage. When deploying a ML based AMC solution, training could be performed offline on a separate device before transferring the final trained algorithm to the actual communication system. Most of the time, the trained algorithm has a relatively low computational complexity in a testing stage. Thus a trained algorithm is perfectly capable of real-time signal processing on a low power device. However, as mentioned previously, the channel condition may vary over time and will degrade the performance of a trained algorithm. Re-training the algorithm is necessary if such a condition occurs to guarantee expected classification performance.

Third, it is hard to incorporate understanding of the communication theory into the designing of a ML based algorithm. Meanwhile the resulting trained algorithm does not always provide improved theoretical understanding of a communication system. The former point may be perceived as an advantage from another point of view since it enables researchers from a non-communications background to start developing AMC solutions with little understanding of communication theories. Sometimes efforts from another domain could yield surprising results by introducing new techniques. On the other hand, the later point prevents the theoretical performance to be evaluated in a traditional fashion affecting the opinions of some that favours traditional deterministic approaches.

Last but not least, wireless communication systems are complex and continuously evolving. There are many channel interferences to be considered during the designing of a ML based AMC solution. New communication technologies also creates new problems that requires new approaches to the ML algorithm design.

References

1. Poisel, A.R.: Introduction to Communication Electronic Warfare Systems. Artech House (2008)
2. Goldsmith, A.: Wireless Communications. Cambridge University Press, Cambridge (2005)
3. Weaver, C.S., Cole, C.A., Krumland, R.B., Al, E.: The Automatic Classification of Modulation Types by Pattern Recognition. Stanford Electronics Laboratories (1969)
4. Fabrizi, P.M., Lopes, L.B., Lockhart, G.B.: Receiver recognition of analogue modulation types. In: IERE Conference on Radio Receiver and Associated Systems, pp. 135–140 (1986)
5. Hipp, J.E.: Modulation classification based on statistical moments. In: Military Communications Conference, pp. 20.2.1–20.2.6 (1986)
6. Aisbett, J.: Automatic modulation recognition using time domain parameters. Signal Process. **13**(3), 323–328 (1987)
7. Desimio, M.P., Prescott, G.E.: Adaptive generation of decision functions for classification of digitally modulated signals. In: IEEE Aerospace and Electronics Conference, pp. 1010–1014 (1988)
8. Gardner, W.A., Spooner, C.M.: Cyclic spectral analysis for signal detection and modulation recognition. In: Military Communications Conference, vol. 2, pp. 419–424 (1988)
9. Chan, Y.T., Gadbois, L.G.: Identification of the modulation type of a signal. Signal Process. **1**(4), 838–841 (1989)
10. Jovanovic, S.D., Doroslovacki, M.I., Dragosevic, M.V.: Recognition of low modulation index AM signals in additive Gaussian noise. In: European Association for Signal Processing V Conference, pp. 1923–1926 (1990)
11. Polydoros, A., Kim, K.: On the detection and classification of quadrature digital modulations in broad-band noise. IEEE Trans. Commun. **38**(8), 1199–1211 (1990)
12. Soliman, S.S., Hsue, S.-Z.: Signal classification using statistical moments. IEEE Trans. Commun. **40**(5), 908–916 (1992)

13. Lay, N.E., Polydoros, A.: Modulation classification of signal in unknown ISI environments. In: Military Communications Conference, pp. 170–174 (1995)
14. Yang, Y., Soliman, S.S.: An improved moment-based algorithm for signal classification. Signal Process. **43**, 231–244 (1995)
15. Azzouz, E.E., Nandi, A.K.: Automatic identification of digital modulation types. Signal Process. **47**(1), 55–69 (1995)
16. Azzouz, E.E., Nandi, A.K.: Procedure for automatic recognition of analogue and digital modulations. IEE Proc. Commun. **143**(5), 259–266 (1996)
17. Azzouz, E.E., Nandi, A.K.: Recognition of analogue modulations. In: Automatic modulation recognition of communication signals, pp. 42–76. Springer, Boston, MA (1996)
18. Swami, A., Sadler, B.M.: Hierarchical digital modulation classification using cumulants. IEEE Trans. Commun. **48**(3), 416–429 (2000)
19. Beidas, B., Weber, C.: Higher-order correlation-based approach to modulation classification of digitally frequency-modulated signals. Sel. Areas Commun. IEEE J. **13**(1), 89–101 (1995)
20. Sills, J.A.: Maximum-likelihood modulation classification, pp. 217–220 (1999)
21. Panagiotou, P., Anastasopoulos, A., Polydoros, A.: Likelihood ratio tests for modulation classification. In: Military Communications Conference, pp. 670–674 (2000)
22. Zhu, Z., Nandi, A.K.: Modulation classification in MIMO fading channels via expectation maximization with non-data-aided initialization. In: IEEE International Conference on Acoustics, Speech and Signal Processing—Proceedings, vol. 1, pp. 3014–3018 (2015)
23. TSGR: TS 138 211 - V15.2.0 - 5G; NR; Physical channels and modulation (3GPP TS 38.211 version 15.2.0 Release 15), vol. 0 (2018). https://portal.etsi.org/TB/ETSIDeliverableStatus. aspx
24. Chavali, V.G., da Silva, C.R.C.M.: Classification of digital amplitude-phase modulated signals in time-correlated non-Gaussian channels. IEEE Trans. Commun. **61**(6), 2408–2419 (2013)
25. Zhu, Z., Nandi, A.K.: Blind digital modulation classification using minimum distance centroid estimator and non-parametric likelihood function. IEEE Trans. Wirel. Commun. **13**(8), 4483–4494 (2014)
26. O'Shea, T.J., West, N.: Radio machine learning dataset generation with GNU radio. In: 6th GNU Radio Conference, pp. 1–6 (2016)
27. Hero, A.O., Hadinejad-Mahram, H.: Digital modulation classification using power moment matrices. In: International Conference on Acoustics, Speech, and Signal Processing, pp. 3285–3288 (1998)
28. Gardner, W.: Cyclostationarity in Communications and Signal Processing. IEEE Press (1994)
29. Ramkumar, B.: Automatic modulation classification for cognitive radios using cyclic feature detection. IEEE Circuits Syst. Mag. **9**(2), 27–45 (2009)
30. Shi, J., Hong, S., Cai, C., Wang, Y., Huang, H., Gui, G.: Deep learning-based automatic modulation recognition method in the presence of phase offset. IEEE Access **8**, 42831–42847 (2020)
31. Peng, S., Jiang, H., Wang, H., Alwageed, H., Yao, Y.D.: Modulation classification using convolutional neural network based deep learning model. In: 2017 26th Wireless and Optical Communication Conference, WOCC 2017, vol, 1, pp. 1–5 (2017)
32. Zhu, L., Gao, Z., Zhu, Z.: Blind modulation classification via accelerated deep learning. In: IEEE International Conference on Computer and Communications (ICCC), pp. 2102–2107. IEEE, Piscataway (2019)
33. Huang, L., Pan, W. Zhang, Y., Qian, L., Gao, N., Wu, Y.: Data augmentation for deep learning-based radio modulation classification. IEEE Access **8**, 1498–1506 (2020)
34. Guo, Y., Jiang, H., Wu, J., Zhou, J.: Open set modulation recognition based on dual-channel LSTM model. **2**(2), 2–5 (2020)
35. Zhang, H., Wang, Y., Xu, L., Aaron Gulliver, T., Cao, C.: Automatic modulation classification using a deep multi-stream neural network. IEEE Access **8**, 43888–43897 (2020)
36. Wong, M.L.D., Nandi, A.K.: Automatic digital modulation recognition using artificial neural network and genetic algorithm. Signal Process. **84**(2), 351–365 (2004)
37. Zhu, Z., Nandi, A.K.: Automatic Modulation Classification. Wiley Chichester (2014)

38. Aslam, M.W., Zhu, Z., Nandi, A.K.: Combination of Genetic Programming and KNN **11**(8), 2742–2750 (2012)
39. Nandi, A.K., Azzouz, E.E.: Modulation recognition using artificial neural networks. Signal Process. **56**(2), 165–175 (1997)
40. Azzouz, E.E., Nandi, A.K.: Automatic modulation recognition—Part II. J. Franklin Inst. **334B**(2), 275–305 (1997)
41. Jagannath, J., Polosky, N., O'Connor, D., Theagarajan, L.N., Sheaffer, B., Foulke, S., Varshney, P.K.: Artificial neural network based automatic modulation classification over a software defined radio testbed. In: IEEE International Conference on Communications, pp. 0–5 (2018)
42. Nandi, A.K., Azzouz, E.E.: Algorithms for automatic modulation recognition of communication signals. IEEE Trans. Commun. **46**(4), 431–436 (1998)
43. Zhu, Z., Aslam, M.W., Nandi, A.K.: Support vector machine assisted genetic programming for mqam classification. In: International Symposium on Signals, Circuits and Systems, pp. 1–6 (2011)
44. Jdid, B., Hassan, K., Dayoub, I., Lim, W.H., Mokayef, M.: Machine learning based automatic modulation recognition for wireless communications: a comprehensive survey. IEEE Access **9**, 1 (2021)
45. Kingma, D.P., Ba, J.L.: Adam: a method for stochastic optimization. In: 3rd International Conference on Learning Representations, ICLR 2015—Conference Track Proceedings pp. 1–15 (2015)
46. Gers, F.: Learning to forget: continual prediction with LSTM. In: International Conference on Artificial Neural Networks, pp. 850–855. IEEE, Piscataway (1999)

Deep Learning Quantile Regression for Robustness, Confidence and Planning

Dvir Ben Or, Michael Kolomenkin, Tanya Osokin, Gil Shabat, and Hanan Shteingart

1 Introduction

In many applications, it is sometimes required to predict a conditional quantile rather than the conditional mean or conditional median. Those use cases include applications for electricity consumption forecasting [9], short term power load forecasting [10], financial returns [19] and confidence intervals for risk assessment [4], to name some.

Perhaps the most known tool for tackling those problems is the quantile regression [11]. While regular least squares minimization estimates the conditional mean, quantile regression estimates the median or any other quantile. While the vanilla version of quantile regression, which is based on a linear model, can be viewed as a special case of linear regression, it can be extended to use non-linear models from machine learning. Therefore, non-linear quantile regression can be implemented using tree-based models [13] or using advanced neural network architectures that utilize modern deep learning algorithms to optimize a non-linear version of the quantile loss.

In this chapter, we present a different version of the deep learning quantile regression, that uses a different and more general loss function. In fact, it can be viewed as trying to optimize any loss function, while adding some "count" constraint, which forces a certain percentage (or amount) of samples from the training set to be above (below) the manifold learned by the neural network. Though this method is general, and can be implemented for many use-cases, the original motivation was for determining the "correct" difficulty level in games [14], where the goal was to optimize a loss function that describes the game experience of a

D. B. Or · M. Kolomenkin · T. Osokin · G. Shabat (✉) · H. Shteingart
Tel Aviv, Israel
e-mail: gil.shabat@cs.tau.ac.il

© The Author(s), under exclusive license to Springer Nature Switzerland AG 2023
T. Sipola et al. (eds.), *Artificial Intelligence and Cybersecurity*,
https://doi.org/10.1007/978-3-031-15030-2_12

player, while combining personalization with fairness. For cybersecurity, quantile regression methods are very effective to be used in anomaly detection frameworks [6, 20], so combining them with neural networks can yield a powerful approach. Though this chapter is built on [14] it is re-organized and re-modified to derive this generalization of neural network quantile regression as a general tool that can be used in many disciplines unrelated to the original motivation, which was difficulty levels in games.

2   Quantile Regression

This section gives a short overview on quantile regression and has two subsections: The first subsection, gives a short introduction to the linear quantile regression, while the second subsection describes how quantile regression can be used with modern machine learning techniques. In particular, it shows how neural networks can be used for nonlinear quantile regression models.

2.1   Linear Quantile Regression

Linear quantile regression, is a type of linear regression model, where the relation between the data and the prediction is assumed to be linear. Perhaps the most known linear regression model, is the linear regression for estimating the conditional mean (given a feature vector), which is computed by minimizing the least squares (LS) error between the data and the label,

$$\hat{\beta} = \operatorname{argmin} \|X\beta - y\|_2, \tag{1}$$

where $X \in \mathbb{R}^{n \times d}$ is the feature matrix, $y \in \mathbb{R}^n$ is the label vector and $\beta \in \mathbb{R}^d$ is the vector of the model parameters. Equation 1 is a linear model for minimizing the conditional mean, given a new test feature vector. Another well known regression model, is a linear model for predicting the conditional *median* given a feature vector. In this case, the loss function to minimize, is similar to the one in Eq. 1, except the l_2-norm is replaced by l_1-norm, i.e.

$$\hat{\beta} = \operatorname{argmin} \|X\beta - y\|_1. \tag{2}$$

Solving Eq. 2, can be done by linear programming techniques [8], gradient descent [17, 2], L-BFGS [12] and Iterative reweighted least squares (IRLS) [5], to name some. While Eq. 2 estimates the conditional median, which is the 50% percentile, it is sometimes needed to predict a different percentile (or quantile). This calls for a different formulation, which is called "Quantile Regression". Formally, linear quantile regression is also a linear model, which is designed to estimate (or predict) a conditional quantile. Similar to Eqs. 1 and 2, the formulation is given by

$$\hat{\beta} = \underset{\beta \in \mathbb{R}^d}{\text{argmin}} \left[(\tau - 1) \sum_{y_i < x_i^T \beta} (y_i - x_i^T \beta) + \tau \sum_{y_i \geq x_i^T \beta} (y_i - x_i^T \beta) \right], \quad (3)$$

where τ is the desired quantile to be estimated. Given a new test feature vector, Eq. 3 estimates the conditional quantile with respect to this input test feature vector. It creates a hyperplane that satisfies the following: a desired percentage of the data points is above the plane, and the rest of them are below the plane, in such a way that the sum of differences, between the data points and the plane is minimized. Solving Eq. 3 can be done in several ways, some of them are similar to the methods for solving Eq. 2.

2.2 Neural Network Quantile Regression

In addition to linear quantile regression models as in Eq. 3, it is possible to solve the quantile regression using neural networks [16, 21, 3, 15]. In this case, Eq. 3 is modified to have a neural network instead of a linear model

$$\hat{\Theta} = \underset{\Theta \in \mathbb{R}^d}{\text{argmin}} \left[(\tau - 1) \sum_{y_i < N(x_i, \Theta)} (y_i - N(x_i, \Theta)) + \tau \sum_{y_i \geq N(x_i, \Theta)} (y_i - N(x_i, \Theta)) \right],$$
$$(4)$$

where $N(\cdot, \cdot)$ is a neural network with weights Θ and $0 < \tau < 1$ is the desired quantile. In the neural network quantile regression, the loss, described in Eq. 4 is optimized directly using standard stochastic gradient descent based on deep learning optimizers. In additional to the sources mentioned above, a nice and friendly illustration, along with a Python implementation using Keras can be found in [1].

An interesting observation regarding Eq. 4 is that, similar to the linear case, it creates a manifold that passes above the desired quantile of the training data points, such that the sum of l_1 distances between the data points and the manifold is minimized. The next section discusses the case where the manifold still has to lie between the data points in the desired way (quantile-wise), but instead of minimizing the sum of absolute differences it will minimize a different loss function.

3 Optimization of General Constrained Loss

Given a regression loss function of a neural network, and a number (or percentile) of samples, the suggested method optimizes the neural net to minimize the loss function such that only a specified fraction of samples will be above the predicted regression value of the neural network. Formally, given n samples, $x_i \in \mathbb{R}^d$, $i = 1, \ldots, n$ with their corresponding values, $y_i \in \mathbb{R}$ and a number $m \leq n$, the algorithm finds weights Θ in order to optimize a loss function $\mathcal{L}$:

$$\text{minimize} \quad \mathcal{L}(N(X, \Theta); Y) \tag{5}$$

$$\text{such that:} \quad \text{count}_i \left(\hat{y}_i \geq y_i \right) = m$$

where $N(X; \Theta)$ is the output of the neural network with parameters Θ given input data X. The predicted value is denoted by $\hat{y}$, i.e. $\hat{y} \triangleq N(x_i; \Theta)$. The *count* function returns the amount of times the condition inside holds and can be defined via the indicator function, i.e.

$$\text{card}_i \left(a_i > b_i \right) = \sum_i \mathbb{1}_{a_i > b_i}$$

One of the challenges Eq. 5 holds is dealing with the count function, which has no gradients and cannot be optimized directly using standard gradient methods. An example that can be given as a special case of Eq. 5 is to minimize the mean-squared-error (MSE) over n samples, such that the error of 10% (for example) of the predicted values will be above the real values:

$$\text{minimize} \quad \sum_{i=1}^{n} (N(x_i; \Theta) - y_i)^2$$

$$\text{such that:} \quad \text{count}_i \left(N(x_i; \Theta) \geq y_i \right) = 0.1n$$

In practice, some tolerance is allowed (as a parameter) for the accuracy of the constraint, so Eq. 5 can be modified to

$$\text{minimize} \quad \mathcal{L}(N(X; \Theta), Y) \tag{6}$$

$$\text{such that:} \quad |\text{count}_i \left(\hat{y}_i \geq y_i \right) - m| \leq \delta$$

where δ is the given tolerance for the accuracy of the count constraint.

3.1 Description of the Algorithm

The algorithm consists of optimizing Eq. 5 using alternations. The alternations can be viewed as non-linear and non-orthogonal projection operators. The first type of alternation moves from the current weights Θ to the closest set of weights $\hat{\Theta}$ which is a local minimum of the loss function. This operator is denoted by $\mathcal{P}_M$.

Definition 1 Given a training data set $\mathbf{X}$, a neural net $N(\Theta, \mathbf{X})$ with weights Θ and a loss function $\mathcal{L}(\Theta, X; Y)$ with a set of local minima $\mathcal{M}$, then $\mathcal{P}_M\Theta$ returns weights that are the nearest local minimum:

$$\mathcal{P}_M\Theta = \underset{\mathcal{L}(N(\hat{\Theta},X);Y)\in\mathcal{M}}{\text{argmin}} \|\Theta - \hat{\Theta}\|_2 \tag{7}$$

Definition 2 Let C be the set of all possible weights of a loss function $\mathcal{L}(N(\Theta, X); Y)$, such that the predictions of the neural net, $\{\hat{y}_i\}_{i=1}^n$, will be above the real values $\{y_i\}_{i=1}^n$ for m points in the training data set, up to tolerance δ. Formally:

$$C = \left\{\Theta: \quad |\text{count}_i (N(\Theta, x_i) \geq y_i) - m| \leq \delta\right\} \tag{8}$$

Definition 3 Given a training data set $\mathbf{X}$, a neural net $N(\Theta, \mathbf{X})$ with weights Θ and a set of valid count-constraint points C (Definition 2), then $\mathcal{P}_C(\Theta)$ returns the closest weights in C:

$$\mathcal{P}_C(\Theta) = \underset{\hat{\Theta}\in C}{\text{argmin}} \|\Theta - \hat{\Theta}\|_2 \tag{9}$$

Remark 1 Note that $\mathcal{P}_C$ does not depend on the loss function $\mathcal{L}$

Both $\mathcal{P}_C$ and $\mathcal{P}_M$ are implemented using stochastic gradient optimizers. The implementation of $\mathcal{P}_M$ is a standard neural network optimization. $\mathcal{P}_C$ is implemented by drifting iteratively from the current point Θ to a valid point $\mathcal{P}_C\Theta \in C$, such that if $\text{card}_i(\hat{y}_i > y_i)$ is too large, Θ is moved either against the direction of the gradient of $N(\hat{\Theta}, \mathbf{X})$ to reduce the count value or towards the direction of the gradient to increase the count function, if the count value is too small.

In practice, implementation of the above operators is done such that they return the nearest minimum is impossible in general, since it depends on the data, the architecture of the network and the loss function, which is typically a high-dimensional non-convex manifold. However, since the operators are implemented using stochastic gradient descent (or other optimizers), it is likely to assume that the weights returned by the operators are close (probably among the closest) to the point the operator started from, since the optimizer shifts from its starting points in small steps until the condition is satisfied.

Optimizing the loss function subject to a count constraint, can be done by the following alternating scheme, which alternates between Eqs. 10 and 11:

Algorithm 1 Satisfy count constraint, implementation of $\mathcal{P}_C$ operator

---

Require: $N(\Theta; X)$—neural network, Θ—current network weights, $Y = \{y_1, \ldots, y_n\} \in \mathbb{R}$—labels, $X = \{x_1, \ldots, x_n\} \in \mathbb{R}^d$—Input data, m—Number of samples to satisfy count constraint, δ—Tolerance for the count error, μ—Learning rate, MaxIter—Maximal number of iterations.

Ensure: $\hat{\Theta}$—optimized network weights

1: $i \leftarrow 0$
2: $\hat{Y} \leftarrow N(\Theta, X)$ # Compute predicted labels
3: $\hat{m} \leftarrow \text{card}_i(\hat{y}_i > y_i)$
4: **while** $(|\hat{m} - m| > \delta)$ AND $(i < \text{MaxIter})$ **do**
5:    **if** $\hat{m} > m$ **then**   # Not enough samples passed, increase value
6:       $L \leftarrow \frac{1}{n}\sum_{i=1}^{n} \hat{y}_i$
7:    **else**
8:       $L \leftarrow -\frac{1}{n}\sum_{i=1}^{n} \hat{y}_i$
9:    $\Theta \leftarrow \Theta - \mu\nabla_\Theta L$ # Optimize over batch
10:   $i \leftarrow i + 1$
11: **return** Θ

$$\Theta_i^M \leftarrow \mathcal{P}_M \Theta_i^C \tag{10}$$

$$\Theta_{i+1}^C \leftarrow \mathcal{P}_C \Theta_i^M \tag{11}$$

where Θ_0^C is an arbitrary starting point (random initialization of the weights).

Proposition 1 *Let Θ_i^C and Θ_i^M ($i \geq 1$) be a set of points (weights) obtained by a consecutive application of the alternation scheme (Eqs. 10 and 11) then the sequence $\|\Theta_i^C - \Theta_i^M\|$ converges.*

Proof Since $i \geq 1$, then according to Eq. 11, $\Theta_i^C \in C$ (Def. 2). By the definition of $\mathcal{P}_M$, Θ_i^M is the closest local minima to Θ_i^C and by the definition of $\mathcal{P}_C$, Θ_{i+1}^C is the closest valid count-constraint point to Θ_i^M. Since $\Theta_i^C \in C$ and $\Theta_{i+1}^C \in C$ is the closest point to Θ_i^M it follows that:

$$\|\Theta_i^M - \Theta_{i+1}^C\| \leq \|\Theta_i^M - \Theta_i^C\|. \tag{12}$$

By the definition of $\mathcal{P}_M$, $\Theta_{i+1}^M \in M$ is the closest local minima to Θ_{i+1}^C. Since $\Theta_i^M \in M$ it follows that:

$$\|\Theta_{i+1}^C - \Theta_{i+1}^M\| \leq \|\Theta_i^M - \Theta_{i+1}^C\| \tag{13}$$

Combining Eqs. 12 and 13 gives

$$\|\Theta_{i+1}^M - \Theta_{i+1}^C\| \leq \|\Theta_i^M - \Theta_i^C\|.$$

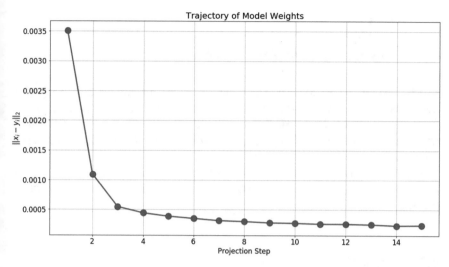

Fig. 1 The distance between the weights of a valid count-constraint point to the local minima followed by the application of $\mathcal{P}_C$ to it. Figure from [14] © 2021 IEEE

Since $\|\Theta_i^M - \Theta_i^C\|$ is monotonically decreasing and bounded it converges, which completes the proof. □

Proposition 1 states that the distance between a valid count-constraint point and a local minima point is monotonically decreasing and eventually converges. An interesting observation from the proposition is that it tells us where to look for the next minima/valid count-constraint point, which enables to decrease the step size of the stochastic gradient descent (SGD) proportionally to the distance between the two points. The proposition is illustrated in Fig. 1.

Additionally, the following observations infer directly from Proposition 1:

- Since the distance between a valid count-constraint point and a local minimum converges, it means (excluding pathological cases of points having *exactly* the same distance) that the algorithm iterates between one local minimum and one valid count-constraint point. Therefore, it converges to a specific local minimum/count-constraint point.
- The difference in the model's performance between those two points, depends on the distance and the Lipschitz constant of the neural network [7]. So if the distance is small (and the Lipschitz constant), then stopping in count-constraint point or in a local minimum should not make a big difference.

4 Results

4.1 A Toy Example: Motorcycle Data set

In this subsection, the algorithm was applied to the motorcycle data set [18] to minimize the MSE over several percentiles. The neural network used was a two layers fully connected network. The first hidden layer has 50 neurons with tanh as its activation function, following by a layer with 10 neurons and a ReLU activation function.

Figure 2 shows the results of optimizing the neural network over Eq. 6 for several quantiles—10%, 25%, 75%, 90% and MSE showing the applicability of the method.

4.2 A Real Use Case: Difficulty Adjustment in Mobile Games

In this subsection, we apply the method in this chapter to a real use case, where a more detailed description can be found in [14]. It was desired to design a difficulty level in a game. Players were divided into clusters, and it was desired to give each player a difficulty level such that a player will receive a difficulty level similar to what the player is usually playing and that the variance in the difficulty of each

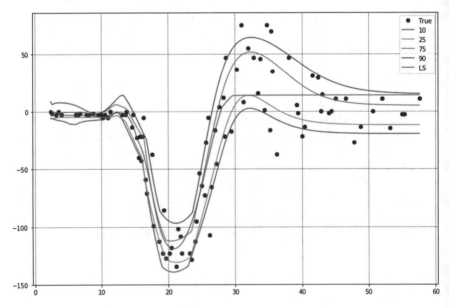

Fig. 2 A variety of curves that minimizes the MSE under different quantile constraints, and regular least squares minimization on the Motorcycle data set

cluster will be small, so similar players gets similar difficulty. In addition to that, a predetermined completion rate was defined, such that only a certain percentage of the players will be able to complete the level. For more details, the reader is referred to [14]. Mathematically, the loss function excluding the completion constraint is

$$\text{UX Loss}(\hat{\mathbf{D}}) = \text{var}(\hat{\mathbf{D}}) + \frac{\alpha}{M} \sum_{i=0}^{M} \left(d_i - \hat{d}_i \right)^2, \qquad (14)$$

where d_i denotes the actual difficulty of player i, $\hat{d}_i$ is the difficulty which we aim to find, $\hat{\mathbf{D}}$ denotes the set of required difficulties of all the players in the cluster of player i:

$$\hat{\mathbf{D}} = \{\hat{d}_0, \hat{d}_1, \ldots \hat{d}_M\},$$

where M is the size of the cluster and α is a parameter that controls the relative weight of the two parts of the loss function. In this experiment we used $\alpha = 1$. In addition, we had the constraint

$$|\text{count}_i \left(\hat{d}_i \geq d_i \right) - m| \leq \delta \qquad (15)$$

We performed an A/B test to verify the validity of our approach. The output was compared to our system with the difficulty levels set by a rule-based method currently used by game operators. The rule-based system is the result of several years of trial and error. It is a collection of *if-else* decisions applied to a variety of game parameters. It incorporates a great deal of knowledge about the game and generally provides satisfactory results.

As shown below, our approach outperformed the rule-based method. In addition to being superior in accuracy, our approach is automatic and saves time for game operators. Each change in the game mechanism requires manual adaptation of the rule-based system. The manual process is time consuming and prone to errors.

The test was carried out in an eight-day mini game (a feature inside the game) where the goal was to optimize the number of points each player had to obtain. About 800,000 players were in the control group and received rule-based difficulties, while about 200,000 players were in the test group receiving machine learning-based difficulties.

Table 1 compares the average completion rate achieved by our approach and the rule-based method with the target range defined by the product team. The result

Table 1 Comparison of the target completion rate with the result achieved by the rule based method and our approach

Target	Rule based	Our approach
8–10%	12.0%	8.7%

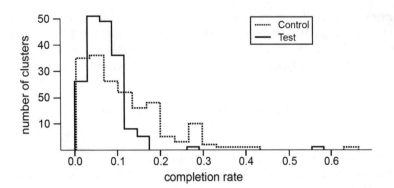

Fig. 3 A histogram of completion rates by clusters. The X-axis is the completion rate, and the Y-axis is the number of clusters that have the completion rate. The blue group is the control group, which is a rule-based method, and the orange group is our system. Figure based on [14] © 2021 IEEE

of the rule-based method is fine by the practical standards of the game, but our approach still outperforms it.

The difference between the methods is even more pronounced when we look at the distribution of the completion rates. This is where our approach really shines. Figure 3 shows the histogram of the completion rate by the clusters. Recall from [14] that the clusters are homogeneous groups of players computed by the K-Means algorithm. The variance in the completion rate of the control group is much higher than that of the test group.

There are 200 clusters. The number 200 was chosen since it created homogeneous clusters on the one hand and yet contained a relatively large number of players (around 1000) on the other hand. In the control group, 49 clusters had completion rates of more than 16%. In the test group, only 5 clusters had completion rates of more than 16%.

The implication is that, while the rule-based method achieves a satisfactory average completion rate, it falls short of reaching a sizable proportion of the population. The ability to control the completion rate of every subgroup of players is another advantage of our approach.

References

1. Abeywardana, S.: Deep quantile regression. https://towardsdatascience.com/deep-quantile-regression-c85481548b5a. Accessed 19 Sept 2021
2. Bottou, L.: Stochastic gradient descent tricks. In: Neural networks: Tricks of the trade, pp. 421–436. Springer, Berlin (2012)
3. Cannon, A.J.: Quantile regression neural networks: Implementation in r and application to precipitation downscaling. Comput. Geosci. **37**(9), 1277–1284 (2011)

4. Chiu, C.-H., Wen, T.-H., Chien, L.-C., Yu, H.-L.: A probabilistic spatial dengue fever risk assessment by a threshold-based-quantile regression method. PloS One **9**(10), e106334 (2014)
5. Elad, M.: Sparse and Redundant Representations: From Theory to Applications in Signal and Image Processing. Springer, Berlin (2010)
6. Evangelou, M., Adams, N.M.: An anomaly detection framework for cyber-security data. Comput. Secur. **97**, 101941 (2020)
7. Fazlyab, M., Robey, A., Hassani, H., Morari, M., Pappas, G.: Efficient and accurate estimation of Lipschitz constants for deep neural networks. In: Advances in Neural Information Processing Systems, pp. 11427–11438 (2019)
8. Gass, S.I.: Linear Programming: Methods and Applications. Courier Corporation (2003)
9. He, Y., Qin, Y., Wang, S., Wang, X., Wang, C.: Electricity consumption probability density forecasting method based on lasso-quantile regression neural network. Appl. Energy **233**, 565–575 (2019)
10. He, Y., Xu, Q., Wan, J., Yang, S.: Short-term power load probability density forecasting based on quantile regression neural network and triangle kernel function. Energy **114**, 498–512 (2016)
11. Koenker, R., Hallock, K.F.: Quantile regression. J. Econ. Perspect. **15**(4), 143–156 (2001)
12. Liu, D.C., Nocedal, J.: On the limited memory BFGS method for large scale optimization. Math. Program. **45**(1), 503–528 (1989)
13. Meinshausen, N., Ridgeway, G.: Quantile regression forests. J. Mach. Learn. Res. **7**(6) (2006)
14. Or, D.B., Kolomenkin, M., Shabat, G.: DL-DDA–Deep learning based dynamic difficulty adjustment with ux and gameplay constraints. In: IEEE Conference on Games (2021). https://ieee-cog.org/2021/assets/papers/paper_142.pdf
15. Pradeepkumar, D., Ravi, V.: Forecasting financial time series volatility using particle swarm optimization trained quantile regression neural network. Appl. Soft Comput. **58**, 35–52 (2017)
16. Rodrigues, F., Pereira, F.C.: Beyond expectation: deep joint mean and quantile regression for spatiotemporal problems. In: IEEE Transactions on Neural Networks and Learning Systems (2020)
17. Ruder, S.: An overview of gradient descent optimization algorithms (2016). arXiv preprint arXiv:1609.04747
18. Silverman, B.W.: Some aspects of the spline smoothing approach to non-parametric regression curve fitting. J. R. Stat. Soc. Series B (Methodological) **47**(1), 1–21 (1985)
19. Taylor, J.W.: A quantile regression neural network approach to estimating the conditional density of multiperiod returns. J. Forecasting **19**(4), 299–311 (2000)
20. Wang, H., Ruan, J., Zhou, B., Li, C., Wu, Q., Raza, M.Q., Cao, G.-Z.: Dynamic data injection attack detection of cyber physical power systems with uncertainties. IEEE Trans. Ind. Inform. **15**(10), 5505–5518 (2019)
21. Xu, Q., Deng, K., Jiang, C., Sun, F., Huang, X.: Composite quantile regression neural network with applications. Expert Syst. Appl. **76**, 129–139 (2017)

Model Fooling Threats Against Medical Imaging

Tuomo Sipola, Tero Kokkonen, and Mika Karjalainen

1 Introduction

The goal of the research is to examine the literature related to potential model fooling attacks against medical imaging, with digital pathology as the main interest. In the modern digitalised world, Artificial Intelligence (AI) based solutions are utilised extensively in everyday life. For example, paper [38] introduces an AI-based healthcare assistant. Heart functioning is analysed and predicted with neural networks by using electrocardiogram (ECG) data in the studies [40, 41] and similarly, electroencephalogram (EEG) data is analysed by AI for detecting brain tumors [33]. Syam and Marapareddy used deep neural networks for network intrusion detection, heart disease prediction and for skin cancer classification [52].

The usage of sub-disciplines of AI, Machine learning (ML) and Deep Learning (DL) based solutions is rapidly increasing in the medical imaging for prediction and decision making by itemizing and labeling disease patterns from image samples [25]. The large amounts of available information makes the medical domain very interesting for researchers so that new applications can be developed [45]. The tremendous development of medical imaging has produced advances in diagnostics and prediction of diseases [13, 3]. The benefit achieved by the DL in the analysis of modern medical big data is the capability for algorithmic realisation of the various

This chapter is an extended version of a paper published in the Second International Scientific Conference *"Digital Transformation, Cyber Security and Resilience"* (DIGILIENCE 2020) and published in the special conference issue of Information & Security: An International Journal [48].

T. Sipola (✉) · T. Kokkonen · M. Karjalainen
JAMK University of Applied Sciences, Jyväskylä, Finland
e-mail: tuomo.sipola@jamk.fi; tero.kokkonen@jamk.fi; mika.karjalainen@jamk.fi

associations and capability to combine learned lines or edges of low level to the higher-level shapes [21].

The vast development of machine learning has produced several modern examples of applying ML/DL for the medical imaging as computer-aided diagnosis (CAD) tools. Comprehensive review for ML in medicine is presented by authors of paper [39]. Hussein et al. studied lung and pancreatic tumor characterization with DL whereas Lu et al. utilised ensemble learning with data mining for predicting recurrent ovarian cancer. Among others, during this year, utilisation of ML/DL for medical image classification and detection is studied for example with brain tumors in [43, 49, 42] and breast cancer in [11, 44, 37]. It should also be noticed that developing AI for healthcare is a highly technical subject but in addition with usage of AI for healthcare there are ethical, legal and social challenges involved such as 'Data ownership, confidentiality and consent' or 'Medical moral and professional responsibility' [9].

Modern networked and digitalized cyber domain is an extremely complex entity that comprises unpredictable phenomena. A classical example of that complexity is a cyber attack against an electricity company, which may endanger the patient safety of the hospital. Finland's cyber security strategy [46] classifies healthcare as an area vulnerable to cyber security issues and states that these issues will be more important in the future. As known, there are several cyber attacks executed globally against healthcare infrastructure, and healthcare infrastructure is seen as valuable target for cyber attacks or an intrusion. The International Criminal Police Organization (INTERPOL) states that cyber attacks' target is shifting towards governments and critical health infrastructure during the ongoing COVID-19 pandemic [20].

As can be seen, ML/DL applications are widely applied in the medical imaging and simultaneously, the overall medical cyber domain is realised as a potential target for the cyber attacks. In this regard, our study focuses on the model fooling threats against medical imaging. During this study following threat categories were identified: (i) adversarial images, (ii) adversarial patches, (iii) one-pixel attacks, (iv) training process tampering and (v) generating fake data.

We investigated literature related to the possible cybersecurity threat vectors using a scoping review method. According to Munn et al. scoping review is a suitable method for the search for scientific gaps in the research area, or building the knowledge base or the synthesis of literature to confirm the research results [32]. In this paper, the point of scoping review is to seek support from previous research for the findings of this research, thus building a stronger knowledge base for the phenomenon. In the scoping review, we used Google Scholar and IEEE databases. Searches were performed by using the following search parameters: fooling neural networks, adversarial attack / adversarial example and medical imaging. Studies in English related to the medical domain were selected. Furthermore, studies with actual applications of the attacks were included. In addition, some essential methodology studies are mentioned.

This article is an extension of a short survey originally presented in the Second International Scientific Conference *"Digital Transformation, Cyber Security and Resilience"* (DIGILIENCE 2020) and published in the special conference issue of

Information & Security: An International Journal [48]. This research is expanded from the original as follows: we have identified more publications that are essential related to the topic and presented them in a new manner. In addition, we have restructured this paper to better reflect the contents of the identified research literature.

The paper is organised as follows: Fooling neural networks is introduced in Sect. 2. The specific categories of attacks are discussed in Sect. 3 and its subsections. The research is concluded with the found future research topics in Sect. 4.

2   Fooling Deep Neural Networks in Medical Imaging

Deep learning tries to combine simple concepts into a representation of the actual object. This is conducted by creating an artificial neural network of interconnected nodes [17]. The complex nature of these networks makes them susceptible to unexpected attacks, which force the network to output completely reverse results that are unlike the expected outcome. A reverse result in medical imaging could be harmful to the patient.

Adversarial attacks against deep learning image classifiers are plentiful. In a white-box attack, the attacker knows the internal workings of the classifiers. This is usually useful when using the neural network gradient as a way of finding adversarial examples. On the other hand, black-box attacks are performed against a system that has only its image input and classification result exposed to the attacker. The attack methods use optimization to find examples that produce the most diverging classification scores [56]. Computer vision is especially affected by these threats because deep neural networks are the most prominent method. Akhtar and Mian estimate that the Carlini & Wagner [8] and Universal perturbations [30] are the strongest methods. Both are white-box attacks, so they need the complete knowledge of the inner workings of the target classifier [2]. Furthermore, Afifi et al. demonstrate that simple color constancy errors can change the classification of a natural image [1].

Since many methods use a gradient as the guiding principle for the optimization, gradient masking and obfuscation could help to defend against these attacks. This would mislead the attacks or make the attack optimization very difficult to achieve. Another defence method is the use of robust optimization. Robust classifiers are less likely to behave in an unexpected manner, such as falling for an adversarial image. This could be achieved, e.g., with adversarial retraining. The third defence could be adversarial example detection before the input images are fed to the real classifier [56, 27]. Tizhoosh and Pantanowitz mention adversarial attacks as one of the challenges facing digital pathology. They raise the question whether minimal artifacts could reduce the reliability of neural network classifiers. This might be caused by the old problem of overfitting in artificial intelligence [54]. Akhtar and Mian propose three ways of defending against adversarial attacks. Firstly, modified training during learning or modified input during testing can be used. Secondly, they suggest modifying deep neural networks and their architecture. Thirdly, for unseen examples, an external model could be used to act as a network add-on [2]. The point of intervention and defence against these attacks is also a problem to be solved, which will probably need regulatory best practices since the problem resembles that of trying to counteract ever developing hacking attempts [14]. A recent survey by Apostolidis and Papakostas on adversarial attacks against medical image analysis discusses the robustness of deep neural networks. It identifies many image modalities that have been attacked: X-ray images, magnetic resonance imaging (MRI), computer tomography scans (CT), retinal images, histology and skin. In addition to the modalities, the survey lists attacks, their target models, detection methods and defences. The authors emphasize the need for robust models in automated medical imaging [4].

3   Attack Types

Based on the literature introduced in this study, Fig. 1 shows the most obvious attack vectors against medical imaging neural networks. The two proposed attack vectors are changing the training process to create a faulty AI model and modifying the input images, so that the classification fails even with a correctly working AI model.

There are several ways to attack against medical imaging. The main methods can be categorized as (i) adversarial images, (ii) adversarial patches, (iii) one-pixel attack, (iv) training process tampering and (v) generating fake data. Table 1 shows the identified attack methods and their use against medical imaging. The following subsections discuss each of these methods in more detail, introducing the methods themselves, and discussing their applications.

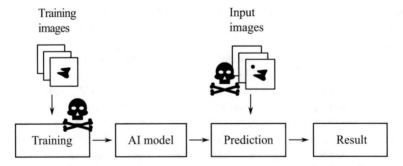

Fig. 1 The most prominent attack vectors described in literature. Tampering with training compromises the automated detection pipeline from the beginning. Modifying input images is perhaps the easier attack method and compromises the results of automated detection

Table 1 Adversarial methods against artificial neural networks, and their implementations in the medical domain. The *References* column shows general references about the methods, while the *Medical domain* column shows applications

Method	References	Medical domain
Adversarial images	[34, 31, 6, 28, 12, 19]	[35, 53, 15, 26]
Adversarial patches	[7]	[15]
One-pixel attack	[51, 50, 24, 55]	[36, 47, 23, 22]
Training tampering	[18, 57]	
Generating fake data		[29, 10, 5]

3.1   Adversarial Images

Adversarial images are images that are somehow changed by adding perturbation to create a misclassified image. As shown by Nguyen et al., it is possible to produce images that are unrecognizable to humans, but that are classified with 99.99% confidence by deep neural networks. Firstly, their adversarial examples include pictures that resemble noise generated by an evolutionary algorithm using direct encoding. Secondly, their other adversarial examples resemble wave patterns and lattices, which have been created by an evolutionary algorithm using indirect encoding. Their evolutionary optimization uses the classifying deep neural network as the fitness function, which makes the approach a black-box method [34].

Moossavi-Dezfooli et al. present the DeepFool algorithm that finds perturbations to deceive deep neural networks. They use a gradient descent algorithm to find those perturbations. The combination of an image and the perturbation is falsely classified as representing something that it does not [31]. Athalye et al. raise the question that viewpoint shifts, camera noise, and transformations can make adversarial examples less effective. They created a 3D-printed turtle that is classified as rifle from images taken of it in the physical world. The optimization process takes into account the expectation of transformation, which creates more robust adversarial examples [6].

Some other examples of adversarial images include those generated using adversarial noise [28], using a generative approach to fool black-box classifiers [12] and gradient shielding to identify sensitive regions where attacks could be executed [19].

Medical images have been used as targets for these kinds of adversarial images. Paschali et al. studied neural network performance under extreme inputs such as noise, outliers, and ambiguous data. They used fast gradient sign, DeepFool and saliency map attacks to create the adversarial images. They performed the attacks on skin lesion images and whole brain imaging [35]. Taghanaki et al. used three types of adversarial attacks: gradient-based, score-based and decision-based. These added perturbations to X-ray images producing images that look quite natural in some cases [53]. Finlayson et al. used projected gradient descent to create visually unnoticeable perturbations against fundoscopy, chest X-ray, and dermoscopy images [15].

Ma et al. created adversarial images in medical imaging domain using unnoticeable perturbations. They go on to claim that medical images can be more vulnerable than natural images in this context. Firstly, they suggest that medical images have larger high attention regions, which draw unnecessary attention from the neural network. Secondly, modern neural networks are designed for natural images, causing them to overparametrize for medical images. Furthermore, a simple adversarial image detector classifier is sufficient to protect the actual classifier from most of the attacks [26].

3.2 Adversarial Patches

Adversarial patches can be applied onto images to output any target class. These patches can be natural, meaning a cut-and-pasted part of an existing image, or generated using optimization, resulting in wild-looking but successful patches when applied. According to Brown et al., even small patches can shift the focus of the classifier to the patch and change the classification of the scene. Suitable patches are found with similar optimization as with adversarial images [7].

There have been examples of adversarial patches used against medical imaging. Finlayson et al. demonstrated that this method works against fundoscopy, chest X-ray, and dermoscopy images. Furthermore, they tested natural patches, patches built on the victim model and patches built on another independent model later used as attacks against the victim model [15].

3.3 One-pixel Attacks

One-pixel attack means that the alteration of color values of a single pixel will cause misclassification. Su et al. have shown that this extremely limited attack is successful against natural images. They use differential evolution optimization against the black-box classifier to find successful one-pixel examples [51]. Furthermore, they propose a variation of the attack with multiple objectives [50]. Gilmer et al. propose that small perturbations are adversarial against machine learning models because of the high-dimensional geometry of the data manifold [16].

Kügler et al. created simple problems about pose estimation of surgical tools in order to localize areas where one-pixel attacks were lucrative. They discovered that the vulnerable areas of the image are close to the decision boundary [24].

Vargas et al. propose propagation maps to illustrate how much the perturbations affect neural network layers. They discovered that complex neural networks let the single pixel propagate widely causing it to create unreasonable consequences to the classification result. Attacks against pixels located near the successful attacks are also quite effective [55].

There are not many examples of one-pixel attacks against real medical imaging data. Paul et al. attacked against the National Lung Screening Trial (NLST) dataset using a one-pixel attack. They also used fast gradient signed method (FGSM) attack, which was more successful. They applied an ensemble defence strategy to create more robust classifiers [36]. The concept of using one-pixel attacks against whole slide images was explored by Sipola and Kokkonen [47], and implemented by Korpihalkola et al. using an existing database of those images [23]. The attack was refined by optimizing the color so that the adversarial pixels would be less prominent to the human eye [22].

3.4 Training Process Tampering

A backdoored neural network has been trained with malicious training material that causes it to react in unexpected ways when given specific input. The act of infiltrating training data with malicious samples is called poisoning. Yang et al. used direct gradient method and auto-encoders to generate poisoned data for neural network training [57]. Gu et al. present this idea of including a hidden backdoor detector inside the classifier by using crafted training data. They demonstrate this threat using traffic signs, which causes the classifier to detect a stop sign as a speed limit sign [18].

3.5 Generating Fake Data

Not all applications of adversarial methods are malicious. Generative adversarial networks can also be used for synthesizing data samples [29]. Another application is to use generative adversarial methods to inpaint medical images that contain areas of missing data [5]. Another kind of proof of the power of adversarial images is that they can fool human experts. Chuquicusma et al. have shown that images produced by generative adversarial networks can fool radiologists [10]. Even if this is not an attack against a diagnosis tool, it shows the potential of generating fake data.

4 Conclusion

Machine learning based solutions are successfully used in healthcare, especially in the medical imaging for prediction and decision making in case of a potential tumor. Medical imaging and analysis methods are not safe from model fooling attacks. Suitable research exploits have been shown to successfully fool neural network models in this domain. The most prominent methods are (i) adversarial images, (ii) adversarial patches, (iii) one-pixel attacks, (iv) training process tampering and

(v) generating fake data. The first three (i)–(iii) main types of attacks against medical imaging are present in the scientific studies included in this review. In addition, generating fake data (v) for non-exploitative purposes was identified. Although it might seem that these attacks are quite elaborate, with a suitable target system and with a high value patient, an attacker could find it worthwhile to use an adversarial attack. Based on the conducted scoping review, future research could include a comprehensive systematic literature review of the phenomenon, especially for specific imaging modalities or attack methods. Further investigation needs to be focused on the deep neural network methods used in medical classifiers. The underlying causes and robustness of those networks are not yet apparent and the theoretical considerations still remain unresolved.

Acknowledgments This research is partially funded by The Regional Council of Central Finland/Council of Tampere Region and European Regional Development Fund as part of the Health Care Cyber Range (HCCR) project and The Cyber Security Network of Competence Centres for Europe (CyberSec4Europe) project of the Horizon 2020 SU-ICT-03-2018 program. The authors would like to thank Ms. Tuula Kotikoski for proofreading the manuscript.

References

1. Afifi, M., Brown, M.S.: What else can fool deep learning? Addressing color constancy errors on deep neural network performance. In: Proceedings of the IEEE International Conference on Computer Vision, pp. 243–252 (2019)
2. Akhtar, N., Mian, A.: Threat of adversarial attacks on deep learning in computer vision: a survey. IEEE Access **6**, 14410–14430 (2018). https://doi.org/10.1109/ACCESS.2018.2807385
3. Al-Sharify, Z.T., Al-Sharify, T.A., Al-Sharify, N.T., Naser, H.Y.: A critical review on medical imaging techniques (CT and PET scans) in the medical field. IOP Conf. Ser. Mater. Sci. Eng. **870**, 012043 (2020). https://doi.org/10.1088/1757-899x/870/1/012043
4. Apostolidis, K.D., Papakostas, G.A.: A survey on adversarial deep learning robustness in medical image analysis. Electronics **10**(17), 2132 (2021). https://doi.org/10.3390/electronics10172132
5. Armanious, K., Mecky, Y., Gatidis, S., Yang, B.: Adversarial inpainting of medical image modalities. In: ICASSP 2019 - 2019 IEEE International Conference on Acoustics, Speech and Signal Processing (ICASSP), pp. 3267–3271 (2019). https://doi.org/10.1109/ICASSP.2019.8682677
6. Athalye, A., Engstrom, L., Ilyas, A., Kwok, K.: Synthesizing robust adversarial examples. In: Proceedings of the 35th International Conference on Machine Learning, vol. 80, pp. 284–293. PMLR, Stockholm (2018)
7. Brown, T.B., Mané, D., Roy, A., Abadi, M., Gilmer, J.: Adversarial patch. arXiv preprint arXiv:1712.09665v2 (2018)
8. Carlini, N., Wagner, D.: Towards evaluating the robustness of neural networks. In: 2017 IEEE Symposium on Security and Privacy (SP), pp. 39–57 (2017). https://doi.org/10.1109/SP.2017.49
9. Carter, S.M., Rogers, W., Win, K.T., Frazer, H., Richards, B., Houssami, N.: The ethical, legal and social implications of using artificial intelligence systems in breast cancer care. Breast **49**, 25–32 (2020). https://doi.org/10.1016/j.breast.2019.10.001
10. Chuquicusma, M.J.M., Hussein, S., Burt, J., Bagci, U.: How to fool radiologists with generative adversarial networks? A visual turing test for lung cancer diagnosis. In: 2018 IEEE 15th

International Symposium on Biomedical Imaging (ISBI 2018), pp. 240–244 (2018). https://doi.org/10.1109/ISBI.2018.8363564

11. Cristovao, F., Cascianelli, S., Canakoglu, A., Carman, M., Nanni, L., Pinoli, P., Masseroli, M.: Investigating deep learning based breast cancer subtyping using pan-cancer and multi-omic data. IEEE/ACM Trans. Comput. Biol. Bioinform. 1–1 (2020). https://doi.org/10.1109/TCBB.2020.3042309

12. Deng, Y., Zhang, C., Wang, X.: A multi-objective examples generation approach to fool the deep neural networks in the black-box scenario. In: 2019 IEEE Fourth International Conference on Data Science in Cyberspace (DSC), pp. 92–99 (2019). https://doi.org/10.1109/DSC.2019.00022

13. Doi, K.: Computer-aided diagnosis in medical imaging: historical review, current status and future potential. Comput. Med. Imaging Graph. 31(4–5), 198–211 (2007)

14. Finlayson, S.G., Bowers, J.D., Ito, J., Zittrain, J.L., Beam, A.L., Kohane, I.S.: Adversarial attacks on medical machine learning. Science 363(6433), 1287–1289 (2019)

15. Finlayson, S.G., Chung, H.W., Kohane, I.S., Beam, A.L.: Adversarial attacks against medical deep learning systems. arXiv preprint arXiv:1804.05296v3 (2019)

16. Gilmer, J., Metz, L., Faghri, F., Schoenholz, S.S., Raghu, M., Wattenberg, M., Goodfellow, I., Brain, G.: The relationship between high-dimensional geometry and adversarial examples. arXiv preprint arXiv:1801.02774 (2018)

17. Goodfellow, I., Bengio, Y., Courville, A.: Deep Learning. MIT Press, Cambridge (2016). http://www.deeplearningbook.org

18. Gu, T., Liu, K., Dolan-Gavitt, B., Garg, S.: BadNets: Evaluating Backdooring Attacks on Deep Neural Networks. IEEE Access 7, 47230–47244 (2019). https://doi.org/10.1109/ACCESS.2019.2909068

19. Gu, Z., Hu, W., Zhang, C., Lu, H., Yin, L., Wang, L.: Gradient shielding: towards understanding vulnerability of deep neural networks. IEEE Trans. Netw. Sci. Eng. 1–1 (2020). https://doi.org/10.1109/TNSE.2020.2996738

20. INTERPOL, The International Criminal Police Organization: INTERPOL report shows alarming rate of cyberattacks during COVID-19 (2020). https://www.interpol.int/en/News-and-Events/News/2020/INTERPOL-report-shows-alarming-rate-of-cyberattacks-during-COVID-19. Accessed 4 Dec 2020

21. Ker, J., Wang, L., Rao, J., Lim, T.: Deep learning applications in medical image analysis. IEEE Access 6, 9375–9389 (2018). https://doi.org/10.1109/ACCESS.2017.2788044

22. Korpihalkola, J., Sipola, T., Kokkonen, T.: Color-optimized one-pixel attack against digital pathology images. In: Balandin, S., Koucheryavy, Y., Tyutina, T. (eds.) 2021 29th Conference of Open Innovations Association (FRUCT), vol. 29, pp. 206–213. IEEE (2021). https://doi.org/10.23919/FRUCT52173.2021.9435562

23. Korpihalkola, J., Sipola, T., Puuska, S., Kokkonen, T.: One-pixel attack deceives computer-assisted diagnosis of cancer. In: Proceedings of the 4th International Conference on Signal Processing and Machine Learning (SPML 2021), August 18–20, 2021, Beijing, China. ACM, New York (2021). https://doi.org/10.1145/3483207.3483224

24. Kügler, D., Distergoft, A., Kuijper, A., Mukhopadhyay, A.: Exploring adversarial examples. In: Stoyanov, D., Taylor, Z., Kia, S.M., Oguz, I., Reyes, M., Martel, A., Maier-Hein, L., Marquand, A.F., Duchesnay, E., Löfstedt, T., Landman, B., Cardoso, M.J., Silva, C.A., Pereira, S., Meier, R. (eds.) Understanding and Interpreting Machine Learning in Medical Image Computing Applications. Lecture Notes in Computer Science, vol. 11038, pp. 70–78. Springer International Publishing, Cham (2018). https://doi.org/10.1007/978-3-030-02628-8_8

25. Latif, J., Xiao, C., Imran, A., Tu, S.: Medical imaging using machine learning and deep learning algorithms: a review. In: 2019 2nd International Conference on Computing, Mathematics and Engineering Technologies (iCoMET), pp. 1–5 (2019). https://doi.org/10.1109/ICOMET.2019.8673502

26. Ma, X., Niu, Y., Gu, L., Wang, Y., Zhao, Y., Bailey, J., Lu, F.: Understanding adversarial attacks on deep learning based medical image analysis systems. Pattern Recogn. 110, 107332 (2020). https://doi.org/10.1016/j.patcog.2020.107332

27. Madry, A., Makelov, A., Schmidt, L., Tsipras, D., Vladu, A.: Towards Deep Learning Models Resistant to Adversarial Attacks. arXiv preprint arXiv:1706.06083v4 arXiv:1706.06083 (2019)
28. Mihajlović, M., Popović, N.: Fooling a neural network with common adversarial noise. In: 2018 19th IEEE Mediterranean Electrotechnical Conference (MELECON), pp. 293–296 (2018). https://doi.org/10.1109/MELCON.2018.8379110
29. Mikołajczyk, A., Grochowski, M.: Data augmentation for improving deep learning in image classification problem. In: 2018 International Interdisciplinary Ph.D Workshop (IIPhDW), pp. 117–122 (2018). https://doi.org/10.1109/IIPHDW.2018.8388338
30. Moosavi-Dezfooli, S., Fawzi, A., Fawzi, O., Frossard, P.: Universal adversarial perturbations. In: 2017 IEEE Conference on Computer Vision and Pattern Recognition (CVPR), pp. 86–94. IEEE Computer Society, Los Alamitos (2017). https://doi.org/10.1109/CVPR.2017.17
31. Moosavi-Dezfooli, S., Fawzi, A., Frossard, P.: Deepfool: a simple and accurate method to fool deep neural networks. In: 2016 IEEE Conference on Computer Vision and Pattern Recognition (CVPR), pp. 2574–2582 (2016). https://doi.org/10.1109/CVPR.2016.282
32. Munn, Z., Peters, M.D.J., Stern, C., Tufanaru, C., McArthur, A., Aromataris, E.: Systematic review or scoping review? guidance for authors when choosing between a systematic or scoping review approach. BMC Med. Res. Methodol. **18**, 143 (2018). https://doi.org/10.1186/s12874-018-0611-x
33. Murugesan, M., Sukanesh, R.: Automated Detection of Brain Tumor in EEG Signals Using Artificial Neural Networks. In: 2009 International Conference on Advances in Computing, Control, and Telecommunication Technologies, pp. 284–288 (2009). https://doi.org/10.1109/ACT.2009.77
34. Nguyen, A., Yosinski, J., Clune, J.: Deep neural networks are easily fooled: high confidence predictions for unrecognizable images. In: 2015 IEEE Conference on Computer Vision and Pattern Recognition (CVPR), pp. 427–436 (2015). https://doi.org/10.1109/CVPR.2015.7298640
35. Paschali, M., Conjeti, S., Navarro, F., Navab, N.: Generalizability vs. robustness: adversarial examples for medical imaging. arXiv preprint arXiv:1804.00504 (2018)
36. Paul, R., Schabath, M., Gillies, R., Hall, L., Goldgof, D.: Mitigating adversarial attacks on medical image understanding systems. In: 2020 IEEE 17th International Symposium on Biomedical Imaging (ISBI), pp. 1517–1521 (2020). https://doi.org/10.1109/ISBI45749.2020.9098740
37. Poonguzhali, N., Dharani, V., Nivedha, R., Ruby, L.S.: Prediction of breast cancer using electronic health record. In: 2020 International Conference on System, Computation, Automation and Networking (ICSCAN), pp. 1–6 (2020). https://doi.org/10.1109/ICSCAN49426.2020.9262398
38. Rai, S., Raut, A., Savaliya, A., Shankarmani, R.: Darwin: Convolutional neural network based intelligent health assistant. In: 2018 Second International Conference on Electronics, Communication and Aerospace Technology (ICECA), pp. 1367–1371 (2018). https://doi.org/10.1109/ICECA.2018.8474861
39. Rajkomar, A., Dean, J., Kohane, I.: Machine learning in medicine. N. Engl. J. Med. **380**(14), 1347–1358 (2019). https://doi.org/10.1056/NEJMra1814259
40. Rastgar-Jazi, M., Fernando, X.: Detection of heart abnormalities via artificial neural network: an application of self learning algorithms. In: 2017 IEEE Canada International Humanitarian Technology Conference (IHTC), pp. 66–69 (2017). https://doi.org/10.1109/IHTC.2017.8058202
41. Ravish, D.K., Shanthi, K.J., Shenoy, N.R., Nisargh, S.: Heart function monitoring, prediction and prevention of heart attacks: using artificial neural networks. In: 2014 International Conference on Contemporary Computing and Informatics (IC3I), pp. 1–6 (2014). https://doi.org/10.1109/IC3I.2014.7019580
42. Razzaq, S., Mubeen, N., Kiran, U., Asghar, M.A., Fawad, F.: Brain tumor detection from mri images using bag of features and deep neural network. In: 2020 International Symposium on Recent Advances in Electrical Engineering Computer Sciences (RAEE CS), vol. 5, pp. 1–6 (2020). https://doi.org/10.1109/RAEECS50817.2020.9265768

43. Ruiz, L., Martín, A., Urbanos, G., Villanueva, M., Sancho, J., Rosa, G., Villa, M., Chavarrías, M., Pérez, Á., Juarez, E., Lagares, A., Sanz, C.: Multiclass brain tumor classification using hyperspectral imaging and supervised machine learning. In: 2020 XXXV Conference on Design of Circuits and Integrated Systems (DCIS), pp. 1–6 (2020). https://doi.org/10.1109/DCIS51330.2020.9268650

44. Salama, W.M., Elbagoury, A.M., Aly, M.H.: Novel breast cancer classification framework based on deep learning. IET Image Process.**14**(13), 3254–3259 (2020). https://doi.org/10.1049/iet-ipr.2020.0122

45. Sasubilli, S.M., Kumar, A., Dutt, V.: Machine learning implementation on medical domain to identify disease insights using TMS. In: 2020 International Conference on Advances in Computing and Communication Engineering (ICACCE), pp. 1–4 (2020). https://doi.org/10.1109/ICACCE49060.2020.9154960

46. Secretariat of the Security Committee: Finland's Cyber security Strategy, Government Resolution 3.10.2019 (2019). https://turvallisuuskomitea.fi/wp-content/uploads/2019/10/Kyberturvallisuusstrategia_A4_ENG_WEB_031019.pdf

47. Sipola, T., Kokkonen, T.: One-pixel attacks against medical imaging: a conceptual framework. In: Rocha, Á., Adeli, H., Dzemyda, G., Moreira, F., Ramalho Correia A. (eds.) Trends and Applications in Information Systems and Technologies. WorldCIST 2021. Advances in Intelligent Systems and Computing, vol. 1365, pp. 197–203. Springer, Cham (2021). https://doi.org/10.1007/978-3-030-72657-7_19

48. Sipola, T., Puuska, S., Kokkonen, T.: Model fooling attacks against medical imaging: a short survey. Inf. Secur. Int. J. **46**(2), 215–224 (2020). https://doi.org/10.11610/isij.4615

49. Someswararao, C., Shankar, R.S., Appaji, S.V., Gupta, V.: Brain tumor detection model from mr images using convolutional neural network. In: 2020 International Conference on System, Computation, Automation and Networking (ICSCAN), pp. 1–4 (2020). https://doi.org/10.1109/ICSCAN49426.2020.9262373

50. Su, J., Vargas, D.V., Sakurai, K.: Attacking convolutional neural network using differential evolution. IPSJ Trans. Comput. Vis. Appl. **11**(1), 1–16 (2019)

51. Su, J., Vargas, D.V., Sakurai, K.: One pixel attack for fooling deep neural networks. IEEE Trans. Evol. Comput. **23**(5), 828–841 (2019). https://doi.org/10.1109/TEVC.2019.2890858

52. Syam, R., Marapareddy, R.: Application of deep neural networks in the field of information security and healthcare. In: 2019 SoutheastCon, pp. 1–5 (2019). https://doi.org/10.1109/SoutheastCon42311.2019.9020553

53. Taghanaki, S.A., Das, A., Hamarneh, G.: Vulnerability Analysis of Chest X-Ray Image Classification Against Adversarial Attacks. In: Stoyanov, D., Taylor, Z., Kia, S.M., Oguz, I., Reyes, M., Martel, A., Maier-Hein, L., Marquand, A.F., Duchesnay, E., Löfstedt, T., Landman, B., Cardoso, M.J., Silva, C.A., Pereira, S., Meier, R. (eds.) Understanding and Interpreting Machine Learning in Medical Image Computing Applications, pp. 87–94. Springer International Publishing, Cham (2018). https://doi.org/10.1007/978-3-030-02628-8_10

54. Tizhoosh, H.R., Pantanowitz, L.: Artificial intelligence and digital pathology: challenges and opportunities. J. Pathol. Inform. **9** (2018)

55. Vargas, D.V., Su, J.: Understanding the one-pixel attack: propagation maps and locality analysis. arXiv preprint arXiv:1902.02947 (2019)

56. Xu, H., Ma, Y., Liu, H.C., Deb, D., Liu, H., Tang, J.L., Jain, A.K.: Adversarial attacks and defenses in images, graphs and text: a review. Int. J. Autom. Comput. **17**(2), 151–178 (2020). https://doi.org/10.1007/s11633-019-1211-x

57. Yang, C., Wu, Q., Li, H., Chen, Y.: Generative poisoning attack method against neural networks. arXiv preprint arXiv:1703.01340 (2017)

Printed in the United States
by Baker & Taylor Publisher Services